주한미군지위협정(SOFA)

서명 및 발효 21

_____

주한미군지위협정(SOFA)

서명 및 발효 21

| 머리말

　미국은 오래전부터 우리나라 외교에 있어서 가장 긴밀하고 실질적인 우호·협력관계를 맺어 온 나라다. 6·25전쟁 정전 협정이 체결된 후 북한의 재침을 막기 위한 대책으로서 1953년 11월 한미 상호방위조약이 체결되었다. 이는 미군이 한국에 주둔하는 법적 근거였고, 그렇게 주둔하게 된 미군의 시설, 구역, 사업, 용역, 출입국, 통관과 관세, 재판권 등 포괄적인 법적 지위를 규정하는 것이 바로 주한미군지위협정(SOFA)이다. 그러나 이와 관련한 협상은 계속된 난항을 겪으며 한미 상호방위조약이 체결로부터 10년이 훌쩍 넘은 1967년이 돼서야 정식 발효에 이를 수 있었다. 그럼에도 당시 미군 범죄에 대한 한국의 재판권은 심한 제약을 받았으며, 1980년대 후반 민주화 운동과 함께 미군 범죄 문제가 사회적 이슈로 떠오르자 협정을 개정해야 한다는 목소리가 커지게 되었다. 이에 1991년 2월 주한미군지위협정 1차 개정이 진행되었고, 이후에도 여러 사건이 발생하며 2001년 4월 2차 개정이 진행되어 현재에 이르고 있다.

　본 총서는 외교부에서 작성하여 최근 공개한 주한미군지위협정(SOFA) 관련 자료를 담고 있다. 1953년 한미 상호방위조약 체결 이후부터 1967년 발효가 이뤄지기까지의 자료와 더불어, 이후 한미 합동위원회을 비롯해 민·형사재판권, 시설, 노무, 교통 등 각 분과위원회의 회의록과 운영 자료, 한국인 고용인 문제와 관련한 자료, 기타 관련 분쟁 자료 등을 포함해 총 42권으로 구성되었다. 전체 분량은 약 2만 2천여 쪽에 이른다.

2024년 3월

한국학술정보(주)

| 일러두기

· 본 총서에 실린 자료는 2022년 4월과 2023년 4월에 각각 공개한 외교문서 4,827권, 76만 여 쪽 가운데 일부를 발췌한 것이다.

· 각 권의 제목과 순서는 공개된 원본을 최대한 반영하였으나, 주제에 따라 일부는 적절히 변경하였다.

· 원본 자료는 A4 판형에 맞게 축소하거나 원본 비율을 유지한 채 A4 페이지 안에 삽입 하였다. 또한 현재 시점에선 공개되지 않아 '공란'이란 표기만 있는 페이지 역시 그대로 실었다.

· 외교부가 공개한 문서 각 권의 첫 페이지에는 '정리 보존 문서 목록'이란 이름으로 기록물 종류, 일자, 명칭, 간단한 내용 등의 정보가 수록되어 있으며, 이를 기준으로 0001번부터 번호가 매겨져 있다. 이는 삭제하지 않고 총서에 그대로 수록하였다.

· 보고서 내용에 관한 더 자세한 정보가 필요하다면, 외교부가 온라인상에 제공하는 『대한 민국 외교사료요약집』 1991년과 1992년 자료를 참조할 수 있다.

| 차례

정/리/보/존/문/서/목/록

기록물종류	문서-일반공문서철	등록번호	949 9622	등록일자	2006-07-27
분류번호	741.12	국가코드	US	주제	
문서철명	한.미국 간의 상호방위조약 제4조에 의한 시설과 구역 및 한국에서의 미국군대의 지위에 관한 협정 (SOFA) 전59권. 1966.7.9 서울에서 서명 : 1967.2.9 발효 (조약 232호) *원본				
생산과	미주과/조약과	생산년도	1952 - 1967	보존기간	영구
담당과(그룹)	조약	조약		서가번호	--
참조분류					
권차명	V.51 실무교섭회의 합의의사록. 제38-68차, 1964				
내용목차	* 일지 : 1953.8.7 　　이승만 대통령-Dulles 미국 국무장관 공동성명 　　　　　　　- 상호방위조약 발효 후 군대지위협정 교섭 약속 1954.12.2 　　정부, 주한 UN군의 관세업무협정 체결 제의 1955.1월, 5월　미국, 제의 거절 1955.4.28 　　정부, 군대지위협정 제의 (한국측 초안 제시) 1957.9.10 　　Hurter 미국 국무차관 방한 시 각서 수교 (한국측 제의 수락 요구) 1957.11.13, 26　정부, 개별 협정의 단계적 체결 제의 1958.9.18 　　Dawling 주한미국대사, 형사재판관할권 협정 제외 조건으로 행정협정 체결 의사 전달 1960.3.10 　　정부, 토지, 시설협정의 우선적 체결 강력 요구 1961.4.10 　　장면 국무총리-McConaughy 주한미국대사 공동성명으로 교섭 개시 합의 1961.4.15, 4.25　제1, 2차 한.미국 교섭회의 (서울) 1962.3.12 　　정부, 교섭 재개 촉구 공한 송부 1962.5.14 　　Burger 주한미국대사, 최규하 장관 면담 시 형사재판관할권 문제 제기 않는 조건으로 교섭 재개 통고 1962.9.6 　　한.미국 간 공동성명 발표 (9월 중 교섭 재개 합의) 1962.9.20~　제1-81차 실무 교섭회의 (서울) 　　1965.6.7 1966.7.8 　　제82차 실무 교섭회의 (서울) 1966.7.9 　　서명 1967.2.9 　　발효 (조약 232호)				

마/이/크/로/필/름/사/항

촬영연도	*롤 번호	화일 번호	후레임 번호	보관함 번호
2006-11-24	I-06-0072	04	1-386	

0001

<u>JOINT SUMMARY RECORD OF THE 38TH SESSION</u>

1. Time and Place: 3:30 - 4:30 P.M. January 9, 1964
   at the Foreign Ministry's Conference
   Room

2. Attendants:

ROK Side:

Mr. Chang, Sang Moon	Director European and American Affairs Bureau Ministry of Foreign Affairs
Mr. Shin Kwan Sup	Director Bureau of Customs Duty Ministry of Finance
Mr. Koo, Choong Whay	Chief, American Section Ministry of Foreign Affairs
Mr. Choo, Moon Ki	Chief, Legal Affairs Section Ministry of Justice
Col. Kim, Won Kil	Chief, Military Affairs Section Ministry of National Defence
Mr. Oh, Jae Hee	Chief, Treaty Section Ministry of Foreign Affairs
Mr. Kang, Suk Jae (Rapporteur and Interpreter)	2nd Secretary Ministry of Foreign Affairs
Mr. Lee, Chung Bin	3rd Secretary Ministry of Foreign Affairs
Mr. Lee, Keun Pal	3rd Secretary Ministry of Foreign Affairs

U.S. Side:

Mr. Philip C. Habib	Counselor for Political Affairs American Embassy
Col. Howard Smigelow	Deputy Chief of Staff 8th U.S. Army
Col. L.J. Fuller	Staff Judge Advocate United Nations Command
Capt. R.M. Brownlie	Assistant Chief of Staff USN/K
Capt. John Wayne	Assistant Chief of Staff USN/K

0002

Mr. Benjamin A. Fleck (Rapporteur and Press Officer)	First Secretary American Embassy
Mr. James Sartorius	2nd Secretary American Embassy
Mr. Robert A. Lewis	2nd Secretary and Consul American Embassy
Mr. Robert A. Kinney	J-5 8th U.S. Army
Maj. Robert D. Peckham	Staff Officer, JAG 8th U.S. Army
Mr. Kenneth Campen	Interpreter

1. Mr. Habib opened the meeting by stating that the U.S. side was about to lose one of its original members, Captain Brownlie, who was being transferred out of Korea on completion of his assignment here. Mr. Habib stated that Captain Brownlie had made many significant contributions to the progress of the negotiations and it was with a great deal of regret that the U.S. negotiators regarded his departure. Mr. Habib then introduced Captain John Wayne, Captain Brownlie's successor as Assistant Chief of Staff, J-5, United Nations Command, and also his successor on the U.S. SOFA negotiating team.

2. Mr. Chang expressed great regret at the departure of Captain Brownlie and welcomed Captain Wayne. Remarking that there was no ROK Navy representative on the Korean negotiating team, Mr. Chang predicted that Captain Wayne would make notable contributions to the negotiations.

3. Mr. Chang then remarked that this meeting was the first of the new year. He said the Korean negotiators began 1964 with renewed determination to achieve early completion of the negotiations. He pointed out that the negotiations had been in progress for one year and three months and that when they had begun it had been

0003

stated that entry into force of the SOFA would await the restoration of civilian government in the Republic of Korea. He stated that civilian government had now been restored and that the Korean negotiators wished to speed up the pace of the negotiations. He urged early tabling of drafts of the articles dealing with criminal jurisdiction and labor and suggested that negotiating meetings be held as often as possible, perhaps once a week instead of once every two weeks.

4. Mr. Habib replied that the U.S. negotiators shared the desire of their Korean counterparts to negotiate the Agreement as quickly as possible. He pointed out that the negotiations concerned exceedingly complicated matters to be covered by a complex Agreement which had to be negotiated line by line and sentence by sentence. He said the U.S. negotiators intended to table the remaining articles as soon as possible and had so informed Washington. They were also prepared to increase the frequency of meetings to four per month, provided progress continues to be made in the negotiations.

5. Mr. Habib went on to refer to the increased public attention being given to the negotiations. He said he wished to emphasize the view of the U.S. negotiators that the negotiations should not be conducted in the public press. To date, both sides have been able to maintain a united front with regard to press releases and public discussion of the negotiations. The U.S. side would like to see this united front maintained. The U.S. negotiators realize that the Prime Minister and the Foreign Minister from time to time are obliged to discuss with journalists

0004

the progress of the negotiations. The U.S. negotiators can have no objection to this. However, the U.S. negotiators do request that conscious and deliberate efforts continue to be made to avoid the appearance in the press of discussion of the substance of the negotiations. He pointed out that when such articles do appear, they are usually ill-informed. He expressed the hope that the Korean negotiators would discuss the problem in advance with the U.S. negotiators whenever they anticipated the need for discussion of the negotiations, which are classified, with the press, arising out of interpellations in the National Assembly or for other reasons.

6. Mr. Chang replied that he assumed Mr. Habib had been referring to recent articles appearing in the press. He said he felt that Mr. Habib's remarks were partially justified. He pointed out that questions had been posed concerning the SOFA negotiations during the recent press conferences held by the Prime Minister and the Foreign Minister. In those circumstances, he continued, the questions have to be answered and it did not appear that prior discussion with the U.S. negotiators was either feasible or justifiable.

7. Mr. Habib replied that the Prime Minister and Foreign Minister of course should answer questions concerning the progress of the negotiations. What he had been referring to were newspaper articles which included discussion of the content of the negotiations. He reminded the Korean negotiators that the negotiations are classified and that it is not customary diplomatic

0005

practice to reveal details of classified matters under discussion. He said the U.S. negotiators had full confidence in the judgement of the Korean negotiators and that he had raised the question only because it was likely to become more of a problem for the Korean negotiators from now on.

Non-Appropriated Fund Organizations

8. Turning to the Non-Appropriated Fund Organizations article, Mr. Habib recalled that at the previous meeting the Korean negotiators had objected to the inclusion in the U.S. draft of paragraph 2 the phrase "at rates no less favorable than those imposed on other purchasers". The Korean negotiators had indicated that the ROK Government has no intention of imposing discriminatory taxes on non-appropriated fund organizations. Taking this into account, and in order to meet the objections of the Korean negotiators to the original language, the U.S. side wished to propose the following text for paragraph 2, in place of the original U.S. draft:

> "2. No Korean tax shall be imposed on sales of merchandise or services by such organizations, except as provided in paragraph 1(b) of this article. Purchases within the Republic of Korea of merchandise and supplies by such organizations shall be subject to the Korean taxes to which other purchasers of such merchandise and supplies are subject unless otherwise agreed between the two Governments."

In tabling this proposed language, Mr. Habib said the U.S. negotiators wished the record to clearly show that the ROK Government will levy taxes on purchases by the non-appropriated fund organizations at rates no less favorable than those imposed on other purchasers.

0006

9. Mr. Chang replied that the Korean negotiators had made clear time after time that the ROK Government has no intention of imposing taxes at less favorable rates on purchases made by the non-appropriated fund organizations and therefore they had no objection to stating this in the record of negotiations. However, since the present system of taxation does not provide for the possibility of discriminatory rates, under what circumstances could such discriminatory rates be imposed? The Korean negotiators could foresee no such circumstances.

10. Mr. Habib replied that the U.S. side had met the request previously made by the Korean negotiators, by eliminating the phrase to which they had objected. Agreement had been reached on an understanding to be placed in the negotiating record. The Korean side had stated the intention of the ROK Government; the U.S. side had agreed to the Korean position. The proposed new language would ensure that any change in the Korean tax laws would not result in discriminatory taxes against the non-appropriated fund organizations.

11. Mr. Chang replied that the Korean negotiators appreciated the willingness of the U.S. negotiators to delete the phrase in question. However, the meaning of the new language was not yet clear. Was the U.S. side thinking of a situation in which taxes would be imposed on purchases by the military exchanges while other purchasers were not taxed?

12. Mr. Habib replied that this was a possibility; another would be a situation in which two or more tax rates existed. In either case, the military exchanges would

한·미국 간의 상호방위조약 제4조에 의한 시설과 구역 및 한국에서의 미국군대의 지위에 관한 협정(SOFA)
전59권. 1966.7.9 서울에서 서명 : 1967.2.9 발효(조약 232호) (V.51 실무교섭회의 합의의사록, 제38-68차, 1964) 13

be discriminated against. He reiterated that the U.S.
negotiators had met the objections of the Korean
negotiators. What difference of opinion regarding this
paragraph remained?

13. Mr. Chang said the Korean negotiators believed
the reference to "other purchasers" was unnecessary.
He suggested that discussion of this point be resumed
at the next meeting.

14. Mr. Habib said the U.S. negotiators could not
agree to deletion of the reference to other purchasers
but would be willing to discuss this point further at
the next meeting. In reply to Mr. Chang's query whether
"other purchasers" referred to foreign diplomats, Mr. Habib
replied that it did not. Pointing out that diplomats
are exempted from paying taxes under customary international practice, he said their status was totally
irrelevant to the point at issue. The language of the
paragraph states that purchases by the non-appropriated
fund organizations "shall be subject" to Korean taxes,
not "shall be exempt from" Korean taxes. Mr. Chang said
the Korean negotiators would make their position clear
at the next meeting.

15. Turning to paragraph 4, Mr. Habib recalled
that at the previous meeting, the Korean negotiators
had proposed the substitution of the word "through"
for the word "after" immediately preceding the word
"consultation". He said the U.S. negotiators agreed to
this change. In so doing, they were agreeing that
the Joint Committee was the channel through which the
required information was to be passed to the Korean tax
authorities. He also pointed out that in agreeing to
this change, it was the understanding of the U.S.

0008

negotiators that the U.S. armed forces would not be required to provide information to the Korean tax authorities which is not relevant to tax administration or which is detrimental to the security interests of the United States Government. The implementation of this understanding would be left to the Joint Committee.

16. Mr. Chang replied that the Korean negotiators appreciated the agreement of the U.S. negotiators to the change in language. In this connection, the Korean negotiators wished the record to show that the information referred to in paragraph 4 included customs information and that the information required would be provided by the U.S. armed forces on a timely basis and without delay.

17. Mr. Habib replied that the Joint Committee could be expected to work expeditiously and without delay. He pointed out that customs matters were dealt with in a separate article. Previous discussion of the customs article had shown the relationship between that article and the non-appropriated fund organizations article.

18. Mr. Chang replied that there seemed to be some difference of opinion regarding the scope of the information to be provided under paragraph 4. He suggested that this question be discussed further at the next meeting. Mr. Habib agreed and asked for the views of the Korean negotiators regarding the proposed Agreed Minute which had been tabled by the U.S. negotiators at the previous meeting to replace paragraph 5 of the U.S. draft.

19. Mr. Chang replied that the Korean negotiators had carefully studied the proposed Agreed Minute. They

0009

had concluded that if this language were agreed to, all Americans in the Republic of Korea except businessmen and missionaries would be covered by the Agreed Minute. In the view of the Korean negotiators, this language would provide coverage for people who should not be covered by the SOFA. He referred particularly to USOM contractors, who would be covered under category (c) and diplomats and UN personnel, who would be covered under category (f). He pointed out that the privileges of the USOM contractors are covered under other agreements with the ROK Government. With regard to the diplomats, and other aliens, the ROK Government is making efforts to suit the convenience of such persons, through improving the Foreigners' Commissary and in other ways. Because of continuing discussions with various ministries of the ROK Government, the Korean negotiators wished to reserve their position regarding this point. With regard to category (d), Mr. Chang noted that provision was made for the use of non-appropriated fund organization facilities by "organizations" in addition to such use by their personnel. He asked if there were any circumstance under which use by organizations rather than by persons was possible.

20. Mr. Habib replied that this was indeed possible, since the USO and the Red Cross, as organizations, purchased equipment for the use of the troops visiting their facilities. The use of the word "organizations" in category (d), therefore, was accurate and necessary.

21. Regarding category (f), Mr. Habib reminded the negotiators that he had referred at the last meeting to mutual problems with regard to the persons to be

0010

included under this category. Under the terms of the proposed language, if the ROK Government does not wish diplomats and UN personnel to be granted the use of non-appropriated fund organization facilities, they will not be granted such use. Also, if the armed forces decide that they do not wish to grant the use of such facilities to these persons, they will not do so, even if the ROK Government should be willing. The language thus provides a framework for the granting of such facilities to such persons only if mutually agreed upon by the ROK Government and the U.S. armed forces.

22. With regard to contractors, Mr. Habib continued, the U.S. negotiators were not trying to establish any new privileges. The persons who would be covered by category (c) now generally enjoy these privileges under the terms of their present contracts. This language is merely an attempt to regularize the current procedures. If such privileges were granted in the individual contracts, the armed forces still would not have the right to grant the use of their facilities if specific permission to do so is not included in the SOFA.

23. Mr. Chang stated that the Korean negotiators would reserve detailed comment for a later meeting. However, they would prefer to list in the Agreed Minute all the types of persons who would be granted the use of non-appropriated fund organization facilities.

24. Mr. Habib replied that the U.S. negotiators would consider this proposal. However, the adoption of Mr. Chang's suggestion would undoubtedly create great problems for the ROK Ministry of Foreign Affairs. There

0011

would be a constant stream of visitors to the Foreign
Ministry, complaining at having been left off the list.
The retention of category (f) in the Agreed Minute would
avoid many of these problems and would give both the
armed forces and the ROK authorities greater flexibility
in dealing with this extremely delicate problem, which
involved United Nations agencies among other possibilities.

25. In taking up consideration of the Customs Article,
Mr. Habib stated that the U.S. negotiators wished to
table an additional Agreed Minute, in order to make this
article consistent with the Non-Appropriated Fund
Organizations Article. While paragraph 2 of the Customs
Article permits duty-free importation of goods, the
language is inconsistent with the language of the Non-
Appropriated Fund Organizations Article, as now proposed.
Therefore, the U.S. negotiators proposed the following
additional Agreed Minute:

> "7. It is understood that the duty free
> treatment provided in paragraph 2 shall apply to
> materials, supplies, and equipment imported for sale
> through commissaries and non-appropriated fund
> organizations, under such regulations as the United
> States armed forces may promulgate, to those individuals
> and organizations referred to in Article _____ and
> its Agreed Minute."

26. Mr. Habib added that there was also need to
modify the language of Agreed Minute #1, since the Non-
Appropriated Fund Organizations Article, as proposed,
included more persons than just members of the armed forces,
the civilian component, and their dependents. Therefore,
the U.S. negotiators proposed the deletion from Agreed
Minute #1 of the phrase "the members of the United States
armed forces, the civilian component, and their dependents"

0012

and the insertion in its place of the phrase "persons
authorized by Article _____ and its Agreed Minute."

27. Mr. Habib recalled that at the previous meeting,
the Korean negotiators had proposed the deletion from
paragraph 5(c) of the phrase "including their authorized
procurement agencies and their non-appropriated fund
organizations provided for in Article _____", on the
grounds that this phrase was also included in Agreed
Minute #3 and there was no need for repetition. Mr.
Habib stated the U.S. negotiators agreed to the deletion
of this phrase from paragraph 5(c).

28. With regard to the proposed Agreed Minute tabled
by the U.S. negotiators and the change proposed by them
in Agreed Minute #1, Mr. Chang said the Korean negotiators
fully agreed with the necessity for consistency within
the SOFA. He pointed out, however, that agreement had not
yet been reached on what persons were to be covered by
the provisions of the Non-Appropriated Fund Organizations
Article. The Korean negotiators agreed to the deletion
of the phrase in question from paragraph 5(c), with the
understanding that final agreement had not yet been reached
with regard to the text of Agreed Minute #3. Mr. Habib
agreed.

29. Turning to paragraph 5(b), Mr. Chang stated
the understanding of the Korean negotiators that both
sides had agreed at previous meetings to the right of
the ROKG authorities to inspect parcels. The U.S. negotiators had proposed that this subparagraph read as follows:

0013

"Official documents under official seal and First Class mail in United States military postal channels under official postal seal". The U.S. negotiators had explained that parcels can be included in First Class mail but are kept separate from letter mail. They had also pointed out that the rates for sending parcels by First Class mail are very high and therefore most parcels are sent by parcel post rather than as First Class mail. He said the Korean authorities wished to inspect the parcels which are sent as First Class mail. What was being suggested was not a postal inspection but a customs inspection. The Korean negotiators, therefore, suggested that paragraph 5(b) read as follows:

> "5(b). Official documents under official seal and First Class letter mail in United States military postal channels under official postal seal."

30. Mr. Habib stated that the U.S. negotiators would consider the Korean proposal.

31. Turning to paragraph 5(c), Mr. Chang stated that in the past and currently goods imported for the Non-Appropriated Fund Organizations have been the subject of illegal transactions in the black market, to the great detriment of the Korean economy. The ROK Government has been trying to prevent such abuses, without much success. Therefore, the Korean negotiators wish to retain, in this paragraph, the right of customs inspection of such goods. If the U.S. negotiators did not find this acceptable, Mr. Chang stated that the Korean negotiators had some alternative suggestions to make.

32. Mr. Habib replied that the Korean negotiators were confusing the administrative and police function with the purpose of this article. The provisions of this

0014

article do not affect punitive and preventive measures to be taken under the provisions of other articles of the SOFA and/or other agreements. The right of customs inspection has no bearing or relevancy on the disposal of these goods. Such goods constitute military cargo, as the U.S. negotiators have repeatedly pointed out. Stating that no purpose would be served in repeating the already oft-repeated U.S. position, Mr. Habib asked the Korean negotiators to present their alternative proposals.

33. Mr. Ku stated that the U.S. negotiators had previously explained that persons guilty of illegally disposing of these goods would be dealt with under the provisions of the Respect for Local Law Article, the Criminal Jurisdiction Article, and the regulations of the U.S. armed forces. Paragraph #6 provides that these goods shall not be disposed of to persons not entitled to import such goods free of duty. He said this provision was too general. The provisions of the Respect for Local Law Article also were quite general. The Korean negotiators did not foresee that the Criminal Jurisdiction Article would contain detailed provisions on this matter. Therefore, methods of preventing such illegal transactions should be provided for in some other way. The right to inspect such goods on their entry into the Republic of Korea must be provided for.

34. Mr. Habib replied that Mr. Ku had not mentioned paragraphs 8 and 9 of this article, which were also relevant. Mr. Habib said the SOFA will establish the principle that

0015

there should not be abuses. The implementation of that
principle will be left to the Joint Committee. The U.S.
negotiators anticipated that both sides would provide
cooperation of the highest order to provide for the maximum
effective prevention of abuses. He asked if the Korean
negotiators had any specific suggestions to make.

35. Mr. Ku replied that the Korean negotiators
had explained why the ROKG authorities wished to have
the right of inspection. In order to solve this problem,
the Korean negotiators wished to table the following
proposed additional Agreed Minute:

> "4. The Korean authorities may request from
> the United States military authorities whatever
> information they deem necessary pertaining to all
> cargo consigned to the non-appropriated fund
> organizations and the United States military
> authorities shall promptly provide such information
> in the manner as is specified by the Korean authorities."

Inasmuch as Agreed Minute #3 refers to military cargo,
Mr. Ku explained, the Korean authorities wished to propose
the above Agreed Minute as Agreed Minute #4.

36. Mr. Habib said the U.S. negotiators would
consider the Korean proposal.

37. The next meeting was scheduled for January 17
at 2:00 p.m.

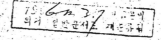

0016

JOINT SUMMARY RECORD OF THE 39TH SESSION

1. Time and Place: 2:00-3:15 P.M. January 17, 1964
                     at the Foreign Ministry's Conference
                     Room

2. Attendants:

   ROK Side:

   Mr. Chang, Sang Moon   Director
                             European and American Affairs
                             Bureau
                             Ministry of Foreign Affairs

   Mr. Shin, Kwan Sup   Director
                             Bureau of Customs Duty
                             Ministry of Finance

   Mr. Koo, Choong Whay   Chief, American Section
                             Ministry of Foreign Affairs

   Mr. Choo, Moon Ki   Chief, Legal Affairs Section
                             Ministry of Justice

   Mr. Oh, Jae Hee   Chief, Treaty Section
                             Ministry of Foreign Affairs

   Mr. Kang, Suk Jae   2nd Secretary
   (Rapporteur and   Ministry of Foreign Affairs
    Interpreter)

   Mr. Lee, Chung Bin   3rd Secretary
                             Ministry of Foreign Affairs

   Mr. Lee, Keun Pal   3rd Secretary
                             Ministry of Foreign Affairs

   U.S. Side:

   Mr. Philip C. Habib   Counselor for Political Affairs
                             American Embassy

   Col. Howard Smigelow   Deputy Chief of Staff
                             8th U.S. Army

   Col. L.J. Fuller   Staff Judge Advocate
                             United Nations Command

   Capt. John Wayne   Assistant Chief of Staff
                             USN/K

   Mr. Benjamin A. Fleck   First Secretary
   (Rapporteur and   American Embassy
    Press Officer)

0017

Mr. James Sartorius	2nd Secretary American Embassy
Mr. Robert A. Lewis	2nd Secretary and Consul American Embassy
Mr. Robert A. Kinney	J-5 8th U.S. Army
Maj. Robert D. Peckham	Staff Officer, JAG 8th U.S. Army
Mr. Kenneth Campen	Interpreter

1. Mr. Chang opened the 39th meeting by asking whether the U.S. negotiators had any further comment to make on paragraph 5(b) of the Customs Article.

2. Mr. Habib replied that, before responding to Mr. Chang's question, he wished to review the course of previous discussion of this sub-paragraph. At previous meetings, the Korean negotiators had indicated that what they were seeking was a deterrent to the illegal use of the military postal channels. They had expressed primary interest in the right to inspect parcels coming into Korea through those channels. The U.S. negotiators, for their part, had expressed concern over the possibility that inspection might cause delays in the delivery of the mail, which would result in a lowering of the morale of the troops.

3. Mr. Habib said he wished to remind the Korean negotiators that at the 37th negotiating meeting on December 27, the U.S. negotiators had offered to agree to the principle of the right of the Korean authorities to inspect non-first class mail, provided the Korean negotiators would agree to four understandings. Those understandings were as follows:

0018

a. Examination of parcels in the MPO mails in the ROK by ROK customs inspectors will be conducted so as not to damage the contents of the parcels inspected or delay delivery of the mail;

b. Such examinations will be conducted in U.S. MPO installations at designated points of mail distribution and in the presence of U.S. officials;

c. No parcel in the MPO mails will be removed from U.S. postal channels except as mutually agreed;

d. It is understood that the right of inspection will be exercised on a "spot check" basis so as not to unduly delay delivery or increase the administrative burden of the postal authorities.

4. Mr. Habib stated that the understandings which he had just read from the record of the 37th meeting had grown out of assurances given by the ROK negotiators in prior discussions of this subject. With those understandings, he continued, the U.S. negotiators were now prepared to agree to the principle of the right of the Korean authorities to inspect parcel mail, regardless of class. The Korean negotiators had indicated that their interest was in inspecting parcels coming into Korea through the MPO mails. The Korean negotiators could be assured of the full cooperation of the U.S. armed forces in implementing whatever provision was finally agreed upon. If the Korean negotiators agreed to the four understandings which he had just read, the U.S. negotiators wished to propose the following revised language for this subparagraph:

"(b) Official documents under official seal and First Class mail in the United States military postal channels obviously not containing merchandise;"

5. Mr. Habib pointed out that the proposed revised language would grant the right to inspect parcels in all classes of mail, including First Class and Air Parcel Post. He said the language suggested by the Korean negotiators ("First Class letter mail") was not satisfactory

0019

because it would not cover two special types of parcels which the U.S. negotiators believed should be exempted from inspection. The first of these consists of tapes containing recordings of personal messages which the troops send to, and receive from, their families in the United States. The second consists of photographic film being returned after having been sent to the United States for processing. Both types of parcels are individually and clearly marked. They do not contain merchandise and have only personal value. The U.S. negotiators equate them with letter mail.

6. Summing up the position of the U.S. negotiators with regard to paragraph 5(b), Mr. Habib stated that the revised language just tabled by the U.S. side would meet the needs of the Korean negotiators and would be acceptable to the U.S. negotiators, provided the Korean side accepted the four understandings which he had read from the record of the 37th meeting. He said the U.S. armed forces would extend all possible cooperation in the implementation of this provision.

7. In reply, Mr. Chang expressed the appreciation of the Korean negotiators that the U.S. side had obviously taken their previous proposal under consideration. He said that the Korean negotiators had been requesting the right to inspect parcels and that this right had been agreed upon in principle. He said the understandings read by Mr. Habib were fully understood by the Korean side and no further comment regarding them was necessary. Of course, it was agreed that delivery of the mail should not be unduly delayed but there might be delays which were

0020

unavoidable. He said the Korean side would present its views at the next meeting on the new language proposed by the U.S. negotiators. He asked whether the packages containing tape recordings and films were included in First Class letter mail. Also, the Korean negotiators wondered who would interpret the meaning of the word "obviously" in the implementation of the proposed new language.

8. With regard to Mr. Chang's remarks concerning unavoidable delays, Mr. Habib stated that what was really at issue was the definition of the word "unduly". He said it means that there will be no delay which is not warranted by the rights being exercised by the inspectors. He said on-the-spot decisions would be required and that if the U.S. armed forces believed that undue delays were occurring, the matter would be raised by the U.S. authorities in the Joint Committee. However, the U.S. negotiators looked forward to mutual cooperative efforts to ensure that no undue delays would occur. In response to Mr. Chang's question concerning packages containing tape recordings and films, Mr. Habib replied that such packages were included in Air Mail or First Class letter mail pouches, if postage was paid for such handling.

9. Mr. Chang stated that the Korean negotiators would give their views on the U.S. proposals at the next meeting. He then asked whether the U.S. side wished to comment on the proposal made at the previous meeting by the Korean negotiators to adopt a new Agreed Minute #4 in connection with paragraph 5(c). Mr. Habib replied that the U.S. negotiators had no comment to make on that proposal at that time.

한·미국 간의 상호방위조약 제4조에 의한 시설과 구역 및 한국에서의 미국군대의 지위에 관한 협정(SOFA)
전59권. 1966.7.9 서울에서 서명 : 1967.2.9 발효(조약 232호) (V.51 실무교섭회의 합의의사록, 제38-68차, 1964)

10. Mr. Chang stated that there were some remaining major points still unresolved in this article but suggested that the negotiators move on to the next item on the agenda. Mr. Habib said the U.S. negotiators would like to hear at the next meeting the views of the Korean negotiators regarding paragraph 3(b). Mr. Chang agreed.

11. Mr. Habib referred to the proposed change in Agreed Minute #1 and the proposed new Agreed Minute #7 which the U.S. negotiators had tabled at the last meeting. Mr. Chang replied that the Korean negotiators had studied the U.S. proposals but were not yet prepared to comment on them. He said the Korean side did not believe that the only reason for proposing them was to insure consistency between the Customs Article and the Non-Appropriated Fund Organizations Article. He referred to the mention in the proposed Agreed Minute #7 of commissaries, which were not mentioned elsewhere in the customs article or the non-appropriated fund organizations article.

12. Mr. Habib replied that he did not understand the first point which Mr. Chang appeared to be trying to make. In point of fact, the commissaries operated by the U.S. armed forces are appropriated fund activities and not non-appropriated fund activities. Therefore, mention has to be made of them in this article in order to make the text fully consistent with the administrative facts.

13. Mr. Chang asked what categories of personnel utilize the commissaries. Mr. Habib replied that at present personnel of the Embassy and USOM, as well as

of UNCURK and some of the other personnel who would fall under category (f) of the proposed Agreed Minute to the non-appropriated fund organizations article used the commissaries. He pointed out, however, that military personnel without resident dependents were not permitted to use these facilities. In addition, there were also other controls on their use, such as a limitation on the amount of supplies that can be purchased in a month.

14. Mr. Chang then asked whether, with the exception of military personnel lacking resident dependents, the persons permitted to use the commissaries were identical with the persons permitted to use the non-appropriated fund organizations. Mr. Habib replied that they were not identical. Colonel Fuller pointed out that the negotiators were not so much concerned with the question of who is entitled to use the commissaries at present but with the question of who will be authorized to use such facilities by the Status of Forces Agreement. He added that this proposed Agreed Minute had been designed to make the conditions of use of the commissaries consistent with those pertaining to the non-appropriated fund organizations.

15. Mr. Chang stated that the tone of the proposed Agreed Minute #7 implied that non-appropriated fund organization users could automatically use the commissaries. Mr. Habib stated that it would not be automatic. The U.S. armed forces have to be willing to permit such use and the ROK Government would have to agree with respect to persons falling under category (f).

16. Mr. Chang said that the proposed Agreed Minute #7 would permit the U.S. armed forces to extend commissary

0023

한·미국 간의 상호방위조약 제4조에 의한 시설과 구역 및 한국에서의 미국군대의 지위에 관한 협정(SOFA)
전59권. 1966.7.9 서울에서 서명 : 1967.2.9 발효(조약 232호) (V.51 실무교섭회의 합의의사록, 제38-68차, 1964)　　29

privileges to the users of non-appropriated fund organizations. Mr. Habib confirmed Mr. Chang's interpretation.
Mr. Chang stated that this was of concern to the ROK
negotiators. He asked whether the categories of persons
who might be authorized to use the commissaries were
identical with the categories listed in the proposed Agreed
Minute to the non-appropriated fund organizations article.
Mr. Habib replied that the decision as to who could use
the commissaries was based upon the regulations of the
U.S. armed forces.

17. Mr. Chang stated that the Korean negotiators
would like to have more specific information about who
would be permitted to use the commissaries and the non-
appropriated fund organizations under the provisions of
the U.S. proposals. He said the Korean negotiators
would present their views regarding the proposed Agreed
Minute #7 at the next meeting.

Utilities and Services

18. Turning to the article on utilities and services,
Mr. Chang reported that a subcommittee of negotiators
from both sides had met and discussed this article. On
the basis of that discussion, the Korean negotiators
wished to table a proposed revision of the article. In
tabling the revision, he pointed out that the Korean
negotiators had deleted from paragraph 3 the term
"however produced". As the Korean negotiators had
previously pointed out, this phrase had no meaning for
them. Mr. Chang said the Korean negotiators understood
from the remarks of the U.S. negotiators at the previous
meetings that the qualifying phrase refers only to the

0024

method and process of production. Therefore, the Korean negotiators did not understand why it should be included in the text when other qualifying phrases as to time (season), location and producers, such as "by whomever produced" were not included. In the proposed new Agreed Minute #1, he added, the Korean negotiators had included the term "changes determined by the Korean authorities", since both sides had previously agreed that the Korean authorities would make the final decision on changes in utilities rates or priorities.

19. Mr. Habib said that the U.S. negotiators would take the Korean proposed revision under consideration and comment thereon at a later meeting.

Military Post Offices

20. Turning to the Military Post Offices Article, Mr. Chang stated that the only point still unresolved was the inclusion of the phrase "and their dependents" in the U.S. draft of the Agreed Minute. He said this created difficulties for the ROK negotiators. There was no such provision in the Status of Forces Agreement with Japan; did dependents have the use of military post offices in Japan?

21. Mr. Habib replied that the phrase was included for the sake of clarity. Dependents did have the use of military post offices in Japan; in fact, this was true throughout the world. Although it was not mentioned in the SOFA with Japan, it was spelled out in other Status of Forces Agreements.

22. Mr. Chang noted that agreement had already been reached to convert paragraph 2 into an Agreed Minute.

한·미국 간의 상호방위조약 제4조에 의한 시설과 구역 및 한국에서의 미국군대의 지위에 관한 협정(SOFA)
전59권. 1966.7.9 서울에서 서명 : 1967.2.9 발효(조약 232호) (V.51 실무교섭회의 합의의사록, 제38-68차, 1964)   31

Mr. Habib confirmed this. Mr. Chang then stated that the
ROK negotiators would consider the explanation given
by the U.S. negotiators and would present their views
at the next meeting.

23. The next meeting was scheduled for January 24
at 2:00 p.m.

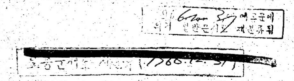

0026

JOINT SUMMARY RECORD OF THE 40TH SESSION

1. Time and Place: 2:00-4:00 P.M. January 24, 1964
   at the Foreign Ministry's Conference
   Room

2. Attendants:

   ROK Side:

미주과	앙고재	원일	담	당	과	승	국	정	보	범	차	차	관	장	관

Mr. Chang, Sang Moon — Director
European and American Affairs
Bureau
Ministry of Foreign Affairs

Mr. Koo, Choong Whay — Chief, American Section
Ministry of Foreign Affairs

Mr. Choo, Moon Ki — Chief, Legal Affairs Section
Ministry of Justice

Col. Kim, Won Kil — Chief, Military Affairs Section
Ministry of National Defense

Mr. Oh, Jae Hee — Chief, Treaty Section
Ministry of Foreign Affairs

Mr. Kang, Suk Jae — 2nd Secretary
(Rapporteur and Ministry of Foreign Affairs
Interpreter)

Mr. Lee, Chung Bin — 3rd Secretary
Ministry of Foreign Affairs

Mr. Lee, Keun Pal — 3rd Secretary
Ministry of Foreign Affairs

Mr. Lee, Jae Sup — Bureau of Customs Duty
Ministry of Finance

U.S. Side:

Col. Howard Smigelow — Deputy Chief of Staff
8th U.S. Army

Col. L.J. Fuller — Staff Judge Advocate
United Nations Command

Capt. John Wayne — Assistant Chief of Staff
USN/K

Mr. Benjamin A. Fleck — First Secretary
(Rapporteur and American Embassy
Press Officer)

Mr. James Sartorius — 2nd Secretary
American Embassy

0027

한·미국 간의 상호방위조약 제4조에 의한 시설과 구역 및 한국에서의 미국군대의 지위에 관한 협정(SOFA)
전59권. 1966.7.9 서울에서 서명 : 1967.2.9 발효(조약 232호) (V.51 실무교섭회의 합의의사록, 제38-68차, 1964)

33

Mr. Robert A. Lewis	2nd Secretary and Consul American Embassy
Mr. Robert A. Kinney	J-5 8th U.S. Army
Maj. Robert D. Peckham	Staff Officer, JAG 8th U.S. Army
Mr. Kenneth Campen	Interpreter

1. Brig. General G. G. O'Connor, Deputy Chief of Staff, Eighth United States Army, served as Chief Negotiator for the U.S. Government, in the absence of Mr. Habib. Mr. Chang introduced Mr. Lee Jae Sup, who was substituting for Mr. Sin Kwan-sop.

Military Post Offices

2. Mr. Chang, the ROK Chief Negotiator, stated that the ROK side had considered the explanation of the US side for the reasons the phrase "and their dependents" was included in the US draft of the Agreed Minute and that the US draft of the Agreed Minute was acceptable to the ROK side. However, in accepting the US draft of the MPO Article, the ROK Government negotiators desired to have the joint summary record clearly show the understanding that such acceptance does not prejudice the ROK Government position with regard to the inclusion of the phrase "and their dependents" referred to in other articles of the agreement, including those dealing with Customs and Invited Contractors. Mr. Chang emphasized that the acceptance by the Korean negotiators of the phrase, despite the fact that the dependants of U.S. Government personnel are not specifically provided with MPO privileges in the U.S.-Japan Status of Forces Agreement, constitutes a major concession on their part and expressed their hope that the U.S. negotiators would favorably consider the position of the Korean side on relevant matters, namely, paragraph 5(b) of the Customs Article

0028

which deals with the exemption of customs inspection
of mail. General O'Connor stated that neither side,
in agreeing on the MPO Article, automatically committed
itself in any way on related subjects in other articles.
On this basis, it was agreed that the US draft of the
MPO Article, including both the article and Agreed Minute,
was accepted by both sides.

Customs

3. General O'Connor referred to the new U.S. draft
of para. 5(b), tabled on January 17, which exempted
from ROK customs inspection US official documents under
official seal and First Class mail "obviously not
containing merchandies." He indicated that the proposal
takes into consideration the expressed ROK desire for the
right to inspect all categories of parcels in MPO channels
in Korea, and asked if the ROK negotiators found the
proposal acceptable. Mr. Chang replied that the ROK
side had considered the proposed new para. 5(b) and had
found it unacceptable. Mr. Chang stated that the phrase
"First Class mail obviously not containing merchandise"
would not only impair the exercise of the right of
inspection by the Korean authorities but also could be
a source of much dispute. Mr. Chang emphasized that it
had been agreed in principle that the ROK side was to
have the right to inspect all parcels entering Korea
through MPO channels. Therefore, the Korean negotiators
felt that the authority to determine whether certain
parcels contain merchandise or not should rest solely
with the Korean customs inspectors engaging in the
inspection, rather than the U.S. side, and that the
packages ostensibly not containing merchandise should be

0029

subject to the inspection for verification. Therefore, the proposed para. 5(b) tabled by the ROK negotiators on January 9, which would exempt from customs inspection "official documents' under official seal and First Class *letter* mail in United States military channels," should be accepted. However, he stated that the ROK side would be prepared to waive customs inspection of the two special type of goods mentioned by the US side at the January 17 meeting, namely, recorded tapes and photographic films which are of personal value and are individually and clearly so marked.

4. General O'Connor indicated that the US side had previously expressed objection to this para. 5(b) tabled by the Korean negotiators and had proposed a suitable substitute. The US side does not yet understand fully why the ROK side finds the US draft of para. 5(b) of January 17 unacceptable. Mr. Chang reiterated that if the US side accepted the ROK-proposed para. 5(b), the right of customs examination would be waived for such special types of articles as personal recorded tapes and films in MPO mail. The ROK side agreed that such a mutual understanding should be included in the Joint Agreed Summary. Mr. Chang stated that by so doing the Korean negotiators met the U.S. demand and, therefore, would see no difficulties on the part of the U.S. side in accepting the Korean proposal. General O'Connor indicated the US side would take the ROK proposal and statements under consideration and would reply at the next meeting.

5. General O'Connor noted that the ROK negotiators had not as yet given a specific response to the four understandings regarding ROKG customs inspection of MPO

0030

parcels, as read into the joint Agreed Summary by the US side on December 27, 1963, and January 17, 1964. Mr. Chang discussed the four points and indicated general concurrence in them, except for two proposed changes.

6. In the second understanding he desired deletion of the words "at designated points of mail distribution and". Mr. Chang indicated that if the designated points of inspection were too many, it would be beyond the capacity of the ROK Government to administer and that the ROK Government has grave concern in this regard. The ROK Government desires that the number of inspection sites be as few as possible, for inspection at designated points of mail distribution would be an extremely heavy burden on the ROK customs administration. Mr. Chang again proposed deletion of the phrase and suggested that the two sides should let arrangements regarding mail inspection sites be worked out by the Joint Committee. General O'Connor stated that as explained at a previous negotiating session (Agreed Summary, 35th meeting, November 14, 1963, para. 4 and 5), it is not practical to have customs inspection of MPO parcels at ports of entry, such as Inchon and Kimpo. MPO parcel mail arrives in Korea in large sealed metal containers, which are each sent, unopened, directly to one of the 17 main military post offices which are located in various parts of the ROK. These facts have been clearly explained, in pointing out why any inspections would impose a heavy administrative burden on the MPO system unless they were conducted at points of mail distribution. General O'Connor agreed that the Joint Committee, considering all relevant factors, could designate appropriate points of parcel inspection and, therefore,

0031

deletion of the phrase in ~~es~~ the second understanding, as proposed by the ROK side, would be agreeable.

7. Mr. Chang indicated that the second point of difference was in the fourth understanding, in which the ROK Government felt that the right of inspection would be on a "sample check" basis, rather than a "spot check" basis. Mr. Chang indicated that the Korean Government intends to send customs inspectors at all mutually agreed upon inspection site, and to examine parcels on the basis of sampling checks, so as to impose no great administrative burden or delay the mail. He asked whether the U.S. negotiators understood the words "spot check" in the same sense as the Korean side understood them. General O'Connor emphasized that any attempt to inspect all the parcel mail would certainly result in considerable delay of the mail. The terms "spot check" or "sample check" appear to have somewhat similar meanings, and it was mutually agreed that inspections should be at sites decided through the Joint Committee, and implemented so as not to delay the mail. Mr. Chang indicated that the ROK Government, in agreeing to sample checking at specified sites, does not prejudice its right in principle to inspect all parcels. General O'Connor replied the US Government conceded to the ROK the right to inspect all APO parcels, but agreed with the ROKG that actual inspections would be as indicated by the foregoing US-ROK agreed understandings.

8. Regarding para. 5(a), General O'Connor explained that the US draft of this paragraph stipulates that members of the United States armed forces shall not be subject to ROK customs examination when entering or leaving the Republic of Korea under military orders. He explained how,

0032

with the personnel rotation system in effect in Korea, the ROK desire to substitute the word "units" for "members" would subject almost all United States armed forces personnel to ROK customs examinations when entering or leaving Korea. General O'Connor asked if this is what the ROK side wanted. Mr. Chang replied that the ROK negotiators proposed the use of the word "units" rather than the US-proposed word "members" because they did desire all individuals in the U.S. armed forces to be subject to Korean customs inspection when entering and leaving Korea. Mr. Chang stated that in view of past abuses, the ROKG felt that all members of the U.S. armed forces entering and leaving Korea, except those which may move as "units," should be subject to ROK customs examinations. General O'Connor indicated that the United States was not asking for anything new in para. 5 (a), and that it has been the practice for both Japanese and ROK custom authorities to waive customs examinations for members of the US armed forces in Japan and Korea respectively. He pointed out that this exemption from customs inspection was to be applied only to members of the US armed forces, and not to the civilian component or to American dependents. Mr. Chang said that it was conceivable that there are many types of troop movements such as movements as units on order or as an individual or group solely for leave purpose or for official purposes. He stated that the Korean customs authorities are concerned with the inspection of individual members entering or leaving Korea solely for leave purposes. The ROK Government, therefore, desired to have the right of customs inspection for individual members rather than units. He indicated that even though the ROK Government might not actually subject all members of the US armed forces entering and leaving Korea to customs examination it wanted the SOFA to give it the 0033 right to do so. It was agreed to continue discussion of this subject at a subsequent meeting.

9. Regarding para. 5(c) and Agreed Minute No.3, Mr. Chang indicated he wanted to explain the reasons why the ROK negotiators did not want the term "military cargo" to include cargo for non-appropriated funds organizations. Mr. Chang emphasized that the present economic situations in Japan and Korea were much different, and that the illegal disposal in the past of goods brought into Korea duty-free through non-appropriated funds channels adversely effected the growth of certain segments of the Korean economy. Mr. Chang emphasized that the impact upon the Korean economy that might be effected by illegal disposal of NAF imports would be much greater than that on the Japanese economy, and that the ROK Government, therefore, could not agree to the same arrangements as were in effect in Japan. He stated that since Korean industries have already suffered much from the abuses of NAF goods, the ROK Government must have the right of custom inspection of NAF imports.

10. Mr. Chang asked if the term "military cargo" in the US-Japan SOFA covered goods for non-appropriated funds organizations, and how the inspection of such goods is accomplished in Japan. General O'Connor replied by reading para 3 of the customs Article which states US-Japan SOFA that the term "military cargo" does refer to goods imported for NAF organizations. He indicated that Japanese customs does not inspect such imports, and that the US authorities furnish the Japanese authorities with information on such imports from Government bills of lading, as indicated in the US-Japan SOFA. General O'Connor indicated that a similar procedure could be

0034

established in the ROK and on that basis he tabled the following proposed sentence, to be added to the US draft of Agreed Minute No.3:

"Pertinent information on cargo consigned to non-appropriated fund organizations will be furnished authorities of the Republic of Korea upon request through the Joint Committee."

11. General O'Connor stated that the US side would cooperate in supplying pertinent information to ROK authorities. The Joint Committee machinery could be used to screen requests and appropriate information, not involving the security of United States forces, would be furnished to ROK authorities. Mr. Chang indicated the ROK negotiators would take this proposed addition to Agreed Minute No.3 under consideration.

12. Mr. Chang requested additional information about US Government bills of lading relating to NAF goods, including whether all such goods were imported into Korea on government bills of lading. He also asked about any formal agreements relating to the subject of NAF goods being designated as "military cargo." General O'Connor indicated military shipping is usually on government bills of lading, and thus NAF fund imports usually would be on U.S. Government bills of lading. Regarding the questions on agreements and procedures related to NAF imports, General O'Connor stated the subject would be investigated further and the US side would report its findings at the next negotiating session.

13. Mr. Chang thanked the US side for its explanations and for the copies of the US Army Regulations regarding commissaries, which had been supplied to them. The ROK

0035

한·미국 간의 상호방위조약 제4조에 의한 시설과 구역 및 한국에서의 미국군대의 지위에 관한 협정(SOFA)
전59권. 1966.7.9 서울에서 서명 : 1967.2.9 발효(조약 232호) (V.51 실무교섭회의 합의의사록, 제38-68차, 1964)   41

negotiators are studying these materials and would explain the ROK position on the US draft of Agreed Minute No.7 at the next meeting. In response to questions, General O'Connor explained that all personnel who had commissary privileges also have NAF privileges. However, many persons have NAF privileges and not commissary privileges/ In general, unless USFK personnel maintain a household in Korea, they do not have commissary privileges. The basis on which USFK personnel are eligible for commissary privileges, therefore, is related to whether they have dependents and a household in Korea. Of course, relatively few of the total USFK personnel qualify for commissary privileges under this criteria.

14. Mr. Chang thanked General O'Connor for his explanations and indicated he would be ready to reply for the ROK Government on the commissary question at the next meeting.

15. Mr. Chang indicated that the ROK negotiators had studied the revised US draft of Agreed Minute No.1, and that it was acceptable to the ROK Government.

16. Mr. Chang stated that the ROK side was also willing to accept the US draft of para 3(b), thus demonstrating ROK cooperation in order to complete the SOFA negotiations as soon as possible. Mr. Chang asked that the U.S. negotiators reconsider the Korean position with regard to those points still unresolved in the Customs Article and reciprocate with the same spirit of cooperation. General O'Connor noted the US-ROK agreement on Agreed Minute No.1 and para 3(b), and expressed the hope that steady progress on the negotiations could continue to be realized through a spirit of mutual cooperation.

0036

17. Mr. Chang noted that agreement had now been reached on all provisions of the Customs Article, except para 5(a), 5(b) and 5(c), and Agreed Minutes 2, 3 and 7.

18. Mr. Chang stated that the ROK negotiators would prefer that the phrase relating to "other purchasers" in para 2 be deleted, but the US side had continuously insisted on such phraseology. The ROK side, believing the phrase of little significance, would be willing to accept the US draft of para 2, with the understanding that "other purchasers" referred to in the NAF organizations article should not be construed as being either applicable to or relevant to other purchasers such as certain foreign organizations or persons whom the Korean Government may in the future exempt from payment of certain taxes under specific arrangements with them. Mr. Chang explained that although the ROK negotiators do not perceive any necessity for the phraseology at present, in the future the ROK Government might desire to exempt from taxation some foreign agency which would come to Korea to help the economy. Although this was a hypothetical example, in such an event, the US might request similar exemption for NAF organizations in accordance with the phrase "unless otherwise agreed between the two governments." It was for this reason that the ROK side proposed that para 2 be accepted with the foregoing understanding. General O'Connor replied that the US side would take the ROK statements under consideration, and would discuss the subject again at the next meeting.

19. It was agreed to defer discussion of the only other two points still at issue in the Non-Appropriated Funds Article, in para 4 and the Agreed Minute, until the next meeting.

20. The next meeting was scheduled for Thursday, February 6, 1964, at 2:00 PM.

JOINT SUMMARY RECORD OF THE 41ST SESSION

1. Time and Place: 2:00-4:00 P.M. February 6, 1964
                    at the Foreign Ministry's Conference
                    Room

2. Attendants:

ROK Side:

Mr. Chang, Sang Moon   Director
                              European and American Affairs
                              Bureau

Mr. Shin, Kwan Sup   Director
                              Bureau of Customs
                              Ministry of Finance

Mr. Koo, Chong Whay   Chief, American Section
                              Ministry of Foreign Affairs

Mr. Choo, Moon Ki   Chief, Legal Affairs Section
                              Ministry of Justice

Col. Kim, Won Kil   Chief, Military Affairs Section
                              Ministry of National Defense

Mr. Oh, Jae Hee   Chief, Treaty Section
                              Ministry of Foreign Affairs

Mr. Kang, Suk Jae   2nd Secretary
(Rapporteur and   Ministry of Foreign Affairs
 Interpreter)

Mr. Chung, Woo Yeun   3rd Secretary
                              Ministry of Foreign Affairs

Mr. Lee, Chung Bin   3rd Secretary
                              Ministry of Foreign Affairs

Mr. Lee, Keun Pal   3rd Secretary
                              Ministry of Foreign Affairs

U.S. Side:

Mr. Philip C. Habib   Counselor
                              American Embassy

Col. Howard Smigelow   Deputy Chief of Staff
                              8th U.S. Army

Col. L.J. Fuller   Staff Judge Advocate
                              United Nations Command

Capt. John Wayne   Assistant Chief of Staff
                              USN/K

0038

Mr. Benjamin A. Fleck (Rapporteur and Press Officer)	First Secretary American Embassy
Mr. James Sartorius	2nd Secretary American Embassy
Mr. Robert A. Lewis	2nd Secretary and Consul American Embassy
Mr. Robert A. Kinney	J-5 8th U.S. Army
Maj. Robert D. Peckham	Staff Officer, JAG 8th U.S. Army
Mr. Kenneth Campen	Interpreter

1. Mr. Chang opened the meeting by welcoming Mr. Habib back to the negotiating table following the latter's visit to Washington on consultation. Mr. Chang expressed the hope that as a result of Mr. Habib's consultation in Washington, the negotiations would now move rapidly to a successful conclusion.

2. Mr. Chang then introduced Mr. Chung Wu-yong, who was attending the meeting in place of Mr. Cho Kwang-che.

3. Mr. Habib stated that the Korean negotiators had previously asked when the U.S. negotiators would table the U.S. drafts of the articles dealing with labor and criminal jurisdiction. As they were aware, the U.S. negotiators were prepared to table the draft of the Labor Procurement Article at this meeting. Based on his conversations in Washington, he predicted that the draft of the Criminal Jurisdiction Article would also be available for tabling very soon.

4. Mr. Chang replied that the Korean negotiators welcomed Mr. Habib's statement regarding the Criminal Jurisdiction Article and hoped that it would be tabled within two or three weeks.

0039

Customs

5. Taking up the Customs Article, Mr. Chang stated
that the Korean position with regard to the points still
at issue had been fully explained. With regard to
paragraph 5(b), the Korean negotiators, in order to meet
the concern of the U.S. negotiators, had stated the
willingness of the ROK Government to waive customs
inspection of photographic films and recorded tapes.
At the same time, the Korean negotiators had stated that
the latest version of paragraph 5(b) proposed by the
U.S. negotiators was unacceptable to the Korean negotiators.
He asked whether the U.S. negotiators wished to make any
further comment regarding this subparagraph.

6. Mr. Habib replied by referring to the four
understandings which the U.S. negotiators had twice read
into the Joint Agreed Summary. He said the U.S. negotiators
were prepared to agree to the latest version of paragraph
5(b) proposed by the Korean negotiators, provided the
Korean negotiators accepted those understandings, which
had been designed to forestall any delay in the delivery
of mail. Mr. Chang, at the previous meeting, had suggested
two minor changes in these understandings. The U.S. negotiators did not take exception to those changes. The purpose
of reading the understandings into the record was to
indicate to the Joint Committee the intentions of the
negotiators. The Joint Committee would implement the
provisions of this subparagraph. Referring to previous
references to "spot checks" and "sampling checks", Mr.
Habib stated that there was no need to debate the meaning
of the two terms, so long as both sides were talking
about the same process. The U.S. negotiators appreciated

0040

the concern of the Korean negotiators over having the
right of inspection, which the Korean negotiators had
previously discussed largely in terms of its effect as
a deterrent to abuses. The U.S. negotiators, therefore,
were willing to accept the latest Korean draft, provided
the Korean negotiators agreed to the four understandings,
thereby leaving the implementation of the subparagraph
to the Joint Committee with guidance as to the intent of
the negotiators.

7. Mr. Chang welcomed the statement of the Chief
U.S. negotiator accepting the Korean draft. He stated
that at the previous meeting the Korean negotiators had
stated their views with regard to the four understandings
concerning the paragraph 5(b) and these views had been
incorporated in the Joint Agreed Summary record of the
40th meeting. The Korean negotiators had also indicated
that although the ROK authorities had no intention of
inspecting every parcel in the MPO mail, their right to
inspect all MPO parcels should not be prejudiced. He
indicated concurrence of the Korean negotiators that
the understandings written into the Joint Summary Record
would serve as a guiding principle for the Joint Committee.
However, he stated the Korean side took it that the U.S.
negotiators agreed to the Korean draft of paragraph 5(b)
in the light of the statements made by the Korean side
regarding the four understandings at the previous meeting.

8. Mr. Habib replied in the affirmative. He said
the subparagraph gave the Korean authorities the right
to inspect parcels and left implementation to the Joint
Committee, which would take into account as guidance the

0041

discussion of this subject by the negotiators, as recorded
in the Joint Agreed Summary.

9. Full agreement was reached on the following text
of paragraph 5(b):

"5(b). Official documents under official seal
and First Class letter mail in United States military
postal channels under official postal seal."

10. Turning to paragraph 5(a), Mr. Habib noted that
there was still a difference of view regarding the use
of the word "units" or the word "members". He pointed
out that the U.S. draft, in using the word "members",
provides that dependents and members of the civilian
component shall be subject to customs inspection. He
noted that at the previous meeting the Korean negotiators
had raised the subject of "past abuses". He said the U.S.
negotiators were not aware of any past abuses and asked
the Korean negotiators to explain their remark.

11. Mr. Chang replied that the Korean negotiators
would be prepared to make evidence of such abuses available
to the U.S. negotiators outside of the formal negotiations.
Mr. Habib stated that he was not talking about postal
abuses but was referring to specifically to Mr. Chang's
statement at the previous meeting that in view of past
abuses, the ROK Government believed that all members
of the U.S. armed forces should be subject to ROKG customs
inspection, except those moving as members of units.

12. Mr. Habib said the U.S. negotiators would be
interested in a clarification of Mr. Chang's remark.
He said that the provision desired by the Korean negotiators
was not a normal provision in status of forces agreements
and the U.S. negotiators did not see the necessity for it.

0042

He said that the use of the word "members" in the U.S.
draft was based on the actual manner in which the personnel
of the U.S. armed forces enter and leave Korea. It was
intended, therefore, to be an accurate reflection of
current practices. He remarked that there appeared to be
a basic inconsistency in the position of the Korean
negotiators. If they were willing to forego inspection
for troops arriving as members of units, why were they
not also willing to forego inspection of troops arriving as
individuals? The U.S. negotiators had no objection to
the inspection of non-members of the armed forces. This
subparagraph applied to troops arriving under orders,
and assigned to units already in place.

13. Mr. Chang replied that the Korean negotiators
were aware of the circumstances under which the members
of the U.S. armed forces arrived in Korea. What the
Korean negotiators were seeking was the right to inspect
U.S. military personnel entering or leaving Korea for
purposes other than official business. Accordingly, the
Korean negotiators wished to amend the language of the
subparagraph to read as follows:

"5(a). Members of the United States armed forces
under orders entering or leaving the Republic of Korea
for official duty purposes but not for leave or
recreational purposes."

14. Mr. Habib replied that this proposal introduced
a new element into the discussion of this subparagraph.
The U.S. negotiators would study this proposal and give
their views at the next meeting.

15. Turning to paragraph 5(c), Mr. Chang recalled
that at the previous meeting, the Korean negotiators had
queried the U.S. negotiators about procedures in Japan
with regard to military cargo and cargo shipped to non-
appropriated fund organizations.

0043

16. Mr. Habib replied that other status of forces agreements have been written on the standard basic premise that all cargo shipped to the U.S. armed forces, including that shipped to non-appropriated fund organizations, is "military cargo". The Korean negotiators had also inquired concerning documentation of cargo. All military cargo, including cargo shipped to non-appropriated fund organizations, is shipped on government bills of lading or similar shipping documents. At the 40th meeting on January 24, the U.S. negotiators had indicated that the U.S. armed forces are prepared to cooperate with the Korean authorities by providing information concerning cargoes and had tabled a proposed additional sentence to Agreed Minute #3 which would provided for the furnishing of such information, upon the request of the Korean authorities, through the Joint Committee. The U.S. negotiators believed that this proposed language would fully satisfy the needs of the Korean authorities.

17. Mr. Chang stated that, according to the explanation given by the U.S. negotiators, goods shipped to non-appropriated fund organizations in Japan are included in the category of military cargo. However, the Korean negotiators understood that under the provisions of the U.S.-Japan Agreement cargo not shipped on government bills of lading was not considered to be military cargo.

18. Mr. Habib replied that this was an incorrect interpretation of the situation. He explained that the U.S. Government no longer uses bills of lading for all military cargo. The important factor is the consignment of the goods. In other words, if the cargo is consigned to the U.S. armed forces it is considered to be military

0044

cargo. Equally important was the fact that the U.S. negotiators had proposed a provision which would provide information to the ROK authorities concerning the consignment of such cargoes.

19. Mr. Chang stated that the U.S. negotiators had previously stated that in actual practice the Japanese authorities waive customs examination of non-appropriated fund organization cargoes. However, a literal reading of the U.S.-Japan SOFA indicated that the Japanese authorities have the authority to make such examinations.

20. Mr. Habib replied that the negotiators were not engaged in negotiating the SOFA with Japan. He said the Korean negotiators had asked for information concerning the types of cargo being imported into Korea by the U.S. armed forces. In order to meet this request, the U.S. negotiators had proposed the additional sentence to Agreed Minute #3. He said the article should be drafted so as to reflect the existing situation with respect to cargo shipments. He asked if what the Korean negotiators were really saying was that they wanted the SOFA to grant the Korean authorities the right of customs inspection and the right to levy customs duties on military cargoes. He said the U.S. negotiators were not prepared to agree to any such provisions.

21. Mr. Chang stated that the Korean negotiators wanted the SOFA to give to the Korean authorities the right to conduct customs inspection of goods shipped to non-appropriated fund organizations. He said the Korean negotiators were confused by the statements of the U.S. negotiators regarding the implementation of the SOFA with Japan. The Korean negotiators believed that the SOFA

0045

with Japan did not include non-appropriated fund organization goods in the category of military cargo. The U.S. negotiators had said that such goods were shipped on bills of lading and then, later, had spoken of "similar documents". Were they or were they not shipped on bills of lading? What were the similar documents which had been mentioned. The U.S. negotiators had an obligation to tell the Korean negotiators how the SOFA with Japan is implemented.

22. Mr. Habib denied any such obligation. However, he said the U.S. negotiators were not indisposed to answer any specific questions which the Korean negotiators might wish to ask. He did not know whether or not it would be possible to obtain statistics on the amount or types of cargo shipped to U.S. armed forces in Korea on bills of lading but the U.S. negotiators would be glad to attempt to obtain such information of the Korean negotiators were really interested in it. He pointed out that a bill of lading is a specific type of document; there are also other types of shipping documents. With regard to the inspection of goods consigned to non-appropriated fund organizations, Mr. Habib informed the Korean negotiators that according to a supervisor currently employed by the U.S. armed forces in Korea, who had worked in Japan for eleven years as a cargo supervisor, cargoes consigned to non-appropriated fund organizations there were never inspected by Japanese customs authorities.

23. Mr. Chang replied that the Korean negotiators did not believe it necessary to verify the fact that such goods are not inspected by Japanese customs authorities. The Korean negotiators did believe, however, that the SOFA with Japan gives the Japanese authorities the right to make such inspections and this was one of main reasons

0046

why the Korean side was concerned with the U.S.-Japan Agreement and asked the U.S. side to clarify its provisions. Mr. Habib replied that the U.S. negotiators do not agree with this interpretation of the SOFA with Japan.

24. Mr. Chang stated that the Korean negotiators had also noted that in paragraph 2 of the Customs Article in the SOFA with Japan, non-appropriated fund organizations are spelled out as a separate entity from the U.S. armed forces but in the related Agreed Minute there is no mention of them. In other words, the Agreed Minute refers only to cargo shipped to the armed forces on U.S. Government bills of lading but does not refer to cargo shipped to the non-appropriated fund organizations. There is no consistency between the text and the related Agreed Minute as far as the NAF organizations goods are concerned. There is ambiguity, therefore, in the SOFA with Japan and the Korean negotiators would appreciate clarification by the U.S. negotiators. For example, what arrangements have been made with the Japanese authorities to exempt cargoes shipped to non-appropriated fund organizations from customs inspection?

25. Mr. Habib replied that the text of the U.S.-Korea Agreement which was under negotiation is not ambiguous. It makes no distinction between the U.S. armed forces and the non-appropriated fund organizations, which are an integral part of the armed forces. If the Korean negotiators find ambiguity in this draft, the U.S. negotiators are prepared to discuss the question. The U.S. negotiators believed that ambiguities in other status of forces agreements, if any existed, should not be carried over into this agreement. He stated that the

한·미국 간의 상호방위조약 제4조에 의한 시설과 구역 및 한국에서의 미국군대의 지위에 관한 협정(SOFA) 전59권. 1966.7.9 서울에서 서명 : 1967.2.9 발효(조약 232호) (V.51 실무교섭회의 합의의사록, 제38-68차, 1964)

Korean negotiators were engaging in fruitless discussion and wasting time. He proposed that further discussion of this subparagraph be postponed until the Korean negotiators could find the time to read the U.S. draft.

26. Mr. Chang replied that the Korean negotiators agreed that there was no ambiguity in the U.S. draft because an improvement had been made over the text of the SOFA with Japan.

27. Mr. Habib replied that the improvement lay in the fact that the U.S. draft reflects actual current shipping practices. The definition of military cargo in this draft leaves no room for ambiguity.

28. Mr. Chang said that he would summarize the discussion as indicating that under the provisions of the SOFA with Japan, the Japanese authorities retain the right to conduct customs inspections of goods consigned to non-appropriated fund organizations, whereas the U.S. negotiators were demanding that the Korean negotiators give up this right. He suggested that further discussion of this subparagraph be postponed. He said the Korean negotiators would submit specific questions in writing concerning current practices in Japan.

29. Mr. Habib summarized the discussion by stating that the U.S. draft provides that all military cargoes will be exempt from customs inspection but that the U.S. armed forces will provide information regarding these cargoes, upon the request of the Korean authorities.

30. Turning to the proposed Agreed Minute #7, Mr. Chang referred to the inclusion of the word "commissaries", which had been discussed at previous meetings. He said the U.S. negotiators had indicated this Agreed Minute

0048

was necessary in order to make this article consistent with the article dealing with non-appropriated fund organizations. He said the Korean negotiators would like to suggest, in place of this Agreed Minute, the insertion of the word "commissaries" in paragraph 2 of this article. Agreement could be reached later on the persons who would be granted the use of the commissaries.

31. Mr. Habib pointed out that the granting of privileges is provided for in another article, not in this article. Furthermore, commissaries are already included in the language of paragraph 2. Insertion of the word "commissaries" there would not eliminate the need for the Agreed Minute. There really was no difference of opinion between the two sides regarding the need for this Agreed Minute and there was no need to delay agreement on it until after agreement was reached on the Non-Appropriated Fund Organizations Article.

32. Mr. Chang stated that the word "commissaries" should be inserted after the phrase "their procurement agencies" in paragraph 2. He suggested that further discussion of this point be deferred until a later meeting.

Non-Appropriated Fund Organizations

33. Mr. Chang recalled that at the previous meeting, the Korean negotiators had agreed to the new paragraph 2 proposed by the U.S. negotiators for the Non-Appropriated Fund Organizations Article, with the understanding that the phrase "other purchasers" should not be construed as being applicable or relevant to other purchasers such as foreign organizations or persons whom the ROK Government in the future might exempt from certain taxes under specific arrangements with them. Mr. Habib said the U.S. negotiators

0049

agreed to that understanding and that full agreement, therefore, had been reached on paragraph 2.

34. Mr. Chang stated that the Korean negotiators accepted paragraph 4 of the U.S. draft, as revised. He said the Korean negotiators required more time for the study of the Agreed Minute proposed by the U.S. negotiators and therefore proposed that further discussion be deferred until a later meeting.

Invited Contractors

35. Mr. Chang stated that the Invited Contractors Article had been discussed at previous meetings and that there were still unresolved differences between the two drafts. In order to speed up the negotiations, the Korean negotiators wished to suggest an alternative proposal. Under the terms of this proposal, the persons covered by the provisions of this article would be divided into two groups. The first group would be comprised of contractors, including corporations organized under the laws of the United States, and employees ordinarily resident in the United States. The second group would comprise third country national employees. Both the third country nationals and the dependents of contractors and the employees ordinarily resident in the U.S. in the first category would enjoy MPC, non-appropriated fund organization, and APO privileges.

36. Mr. Habib stated that the proposal made by the Korean negotiators had opened up a new line of negotiation which would have to be considered. He said the U.S. negotiators would study this proposal and give their views at a later meeting. Mr. Chang suggested that this matter be discussed informally but Mr. Habib replied that the

0050

U.S. negotiators preferred to discuss it in the formal negotiating sessions.

Labor Procurement

37. Mr. Habib indicated that the U.S. side was prepared to table a draft of the Labor Procurement Article. Mr. Chang replied that the Korean side was not prepared to table its draft and suggested that the drafts be exchanged the next day. It was agreed that the Secretaries of the two negotiating teams should exchange the drafts of this article as soon as the Korean was ready.

38. The next meeting was scheduled for February 14 at 2:00 p.m.

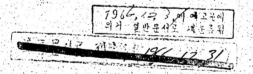

0051

JOINT SUMMARY RECORD OF THE 42nd SESSION

1. Time and Place: 2:00-4:40 P.M. February 14, 1964
   at the Foreign Ministry's Conference
   Room

2. Attendants:

ROK Side:

Mr. Chang, Sang Moon	Director European and American Affairs Bureau
Mr. Yoon, Doo Sik	Director Prosecutor's Bureau Ministry of Justice
Mr. Shin, Kang Sup	Director Employment Security Bureau Office of Labor Affairs
Mr. Koo, Chong Whay	Chief, American Section Ministry of Foreign Affairs
Mr. Choo, Moon Ki	Chief, Legal Affairs Section Ministry of Justice
Col. Kim, Won Kil	Chief, Military Affairs Section Ministry of National Defense
Mr. Oh, Jae Hee	Chief, Treaty Section Ministry of Foreign Affairs
Mr. Chung, Tai Kyun	Chief, Prosecutor's Section Ministry of Justice
Mr. Kang, Suk Jae (Rapporteur and Interpreter)	2nd Secretary Ministry of Foreign Affairs
Mr. Chung, Woo Young	3rd Secretary Ministry of Foreign Affairs
Mr. Lee, Chung Bin	3rd Secretary Ministry of Foreign Affairs
Mr. Lee, Keun Pal	3rd Secretary Ministry of Foreign Affairs

U.S. Side:

Mr. Philip C. Habib	Counselor American Embassy
Col. Howard Smigelow	Deputy Chief of Staff 8th U.S. Army
Col. L.J. Fuller	Staff Judge Advocate United Nations Command

0052

Col. Kenneth C. Crawford	Staff Judge Advocate's Office 8th U.S. Army
Capt. John Jayne	Assistant Chief of Staff USN/K
Mr. Benjamin A. Fleck (Rapporteur and Press Officer)	First Secretary American Embassy
Mr. James Sartorius	2nd Secretary American Embassy
Mr. Robert A. Lewis	2nd Secretary and Consul American Embassy
Mr. Robert A. Kinney	J-5 8th U.S. Army
Maj. Robert D. Peckham	Staff Officer, JAG 8th U.S. Army
Mr. O. C. Reed	Director Office of Civil Personnel 8th U.S. Army
Mr. Kenneth Campen	Interpreter
Mr. Jurio Hernandez	Labor Adviser 8th U.S. Army

1. Mr. Chang opened the meeting by introducing:
Mr. Shin Kang-sup, Director of the Employment Security
Bureau, Office of Labor Affairs, who was attending the
meeting in lieu of Mr. Shin Kwan-sop; Mr. Yoon Doo-sik,
Director, Prosecutor's Bureau, Ministry of Justice; and
Mr. Chung Tai-kyun, Chief of the Prosecutor's Section,
Ministry of Justice. Messrs. Shin and Yoon were attending
as negotiators and Mr. Chung as an observer.

2. Mr. Habib welcomed these gentlemen to the
negotiations and then introduced Colonel Kenneth C. Crawford,
of the Staff Judge Advocate's Office, Eighth United States
Army. Mr. Habib announced that Colonel Crawford was
joining the U.S. negotiating team and would eventually
serve as a replacement for Colonel Fuller, who would
be attending a few more meetings before his expected
transfer from Korea. Mr. Habib then introduced Mr. O.C.
Reed, Director of the EUSA Office of Civilian Personnel

0055

한·미국 간의 상호방위조약 제4조에 의한 시설과 구역 및 한국에서의 미국군대의 지위에 관한 협정(SOFA)
전59권. 1966.7.9 서울에서 서명 : 1967.2.9 발효(조약 232호) (V.51 실무교섭회의 합의의사록, 제38-68차, 1964)

59

and Mr. Julio Hernandez, Labor Adviser, who would attend those negotiating meetings at which the Labor Procurement Article would be discussed and advise the U.S. negotiators as necessary.

3. Mr. Chang welcomed Colonel Crawford, Mr. Reed, and Mr. Hernandez and expressed regret at the news of Colonel Fuller's imminent departure. Referring to the many contributions which Colonel Fuller had made to the negotiations, Mr. Chang said the Korean negotiators would be sorry to see him go.

Facilities and Areas

4. Turning to Facilities and Areas Article "C", Mr. Habib noted that the negotiators had been discussing the general subject of facilities and areas in separate articles as tabled by the U.S. negotiators. In this fashion, agreement had been reached on major portions of the subject. With regard to Article "C", only minor differences remained between the U.S. and Korean drafts. The Korean negotiators had previously made certain proposals regarding this article. The U.S. negotiators wished to respond to those proposals. At the same time, they wished to expedite agreement on all of the facilities and areas provisions and to eliminate instances of overlapping in the several articles dealing with this general subject. It was in this spirit that the U.S. negotiators wished to respond to the following proposals made previously by the Korean negotiators: (a) convert paragraph 14 of the Korean draft into a new paragraph 2 of the U.S. draft, deleting the words "supply or any other materials"; (b) convert the existing paragraph 2 of the U.S. draft into an Agreed Minute.

0054

5. Mr. Habib said the U.S. negotiators were prepared to agree to these Korean proposals but also wished to reach agreement on the article as a whole. He pointed out that the final sentence of paragraph 13 of the Korean draft referred to the subject of compensation. It was the view of the U.S. negotiators that this subject should be dealt with in only one article and since Article "D" dealt with that subject, it would be logical to concentrate discussion of compensation in Article "D", omitting it from Article "C". He reminded the negotiators that the general Korean position was in favor of compensation while the U.S. position was opposed to the payment of any compensation. Rather than debate this general question in discussion dealing with Article "C", the U.S. negotiators proposed deletion of the final sentence of paragraph 13 of the Korean draft, with no prejudice to the overall Korean on U.S. position on compensation.

6. Mr. Habib pointed out that full agreement on this article would be achieved if the Korean negotiators accepted the deletion of the final sentence of paragraph 13. With Articles "A" and "B" already agreed to, if agreement were reached on Article "C", the only remaining point at issue with regard to facilities and areas would be the question of compensation. The U.S. negotiators proposed that Article "D", which dealt with this subject, be placed on the agenda for discussion at an early meeting.

7. Mr. Chang stated that before giving an answer to the U.S. proposal, the Korean negotiators wished to point out that full agreement had not yet been reached on the text of paragraph 2 of the U.S. draft. Mr. Habib replied that at the 31st negotiating meeting on September 20, 1963, the Korean negotiators had proposed the conversion of the existing paragraph 2 of the U.S. draft

into an Agreed Minute. He pointed out that if the U.S. understanding that this proposal indicated agreement with the text was incorrect, the negotiators would have to begin negotiating this paragraph all over again.

8. Mr. Chang replied that the Korean proposal had been to delete paragraph 2 from the U.S. draft or convert it into an Agreed Minute. He said the Korean negotiators still had some question regarding the substance of this paragraph. While they had agreed to the deletion of the words "supply or any other materials" from paragraph 14 of the Korean draft, they had done so only in anticipation that agreement could be reached on the text of paragraph 2 of the U.S. draft. The Korean negotiators welcomed the agreement of the U.S. negotiators to substitute paragraph 14 for paragraph 2 of the U.S. draft. However, they still believed that private property extremely demolished should be compensated for. They had no objection to discussing the subject of compensation with reference to Article "D" but they believed that any such discussion should include the question of property extremely demolished.

9. Mr. Habib replied that the Korean negotiators certainly had the right to raise that question and the U.S. negotiators would expect them to do so. He reiterated the U.S. position against the payment of compensation and recalled that the Korean position favored such payment.

10. Mr. Chang replied that the Korean negotiators regretted to hear that the U.S. negotiators were not prepared to agree to the payment of compensation. He characterized Mr. Habib's statement as a unilateral declaration which would act as a deterrent to the

0056

negotiations. He said that unless the U.S. negotiators were prepared to discuss the subject and give due consideration to the Korean position, the Korean negotiators were not prepared to agree to the deletion of the final sentence of paragraph 13 of the Korean draft.

11. Mr. Chang asked whether the term "removable facilities" in paragraph 2 of the U.S. draft included facilities constructed as part of the military aid given to the ROK armed forces by the U.S. Government. Mr. Habib replied that such inclusion would be unreasonable and that the title to all facilities constructed as part of the military aid program was transferred to the ROK armed forces.

12. In response to Mr. Chang's previous remark regarding the U.S. position on compensation, Mr. Habib said that the U.S. negotiators had not indicated unwillingness to discuss the issue. They had merely suggested that such discussion be concentrated under one article (Article "D") in order to permit full agreement on Article "C". The U.S. negotiators had discussed the issue of compensation in the past and would continue to do so. He had stated that the U.S. Government was unwilling to pay compensation. The U.S. negotiators were prepared to discuss the reasons underlying this position, as well as the innumerable precedents which supported it. The U.S. negotiators had proposed deletion of the final sentence of paragraph 13 of the Korean draft, indicating that such deletion would in no way prejudice the Korean position in support of compensation or the U.S. position in opposition to it.

13. Mr. Chang thanked Mr. Habib for his clarification
of the matter of removable facilities. He noted that
there had been no change in the position of either side
regarding the payment of compensation. He also noted that
disagreement over the final sentence of paragraph 13
of the Korean draft was all that stood in the way of full
agreement on Article "C". He said the Korean negotiators
would give further consideration to this matter and give
their views at a subsequent meeting.

14. Mr. Ku remarked that there was still a question
with regard to removable facilities, and the loss or
damage which might occur to materials left behind by the
U.S. armed forces in facilities returned to the Republic
of Korea. If all such materials were evacuated by the
U.S. armed forces, there would be no problem. However,
if they were not all removed, the Korean negotiators
would like to ensure that the ROK Government would not
be held responsible for loss or damage to those left
behind.

15. Mr. Habib replied that there was nothing in the
text of the Agreement which said that the ROK Government
would be liable for such loss or damage. The Joint
Committee would supervise the transfer of such facilities
and there was no need for the negotiators to involve
themselves in this question. Property introduced into
Korea under the Military Assistance Program was governed
by separate agreements which will continue in effect after
the SOFA goes into effect. He pointed out that there is
no provision in the SOFA which dealt with MAP property,
which had been transferred to the Republic of Korea.

16. Mr. Chang said that the Korean negotiators would discuss the question of MAP property with the ministries concerned and would then discuss the question further at a subsequent negotiating meeting. Mr. Habib replied that this question had no relevance to the SOFA negotiations.

Invited Contractors

17. Turning to the article on Invited Contractors, Mr. Habib recalled that at the previous meeting, the Korean negotiators had made a general proposal which seemed to the U.S. negotiators to suggest the possibility of making a distinction between U.S. contractors and their employees and other contractors and their employees. The U.S. negotiators would like to have an explanation in greater detail of the privileges which these groups would enjoy under the terms of the Korean proposal. Noting that the U.S. draft provided certain privileges under paragraphs 3, 5, 6, 7 and 8 (not yet tabled), he asked how the Korean negotiators proposed to deal with third country nationals. Specifically, what did the Korean negotiators have in mind with regard to taxes, customs, foreign exchange, driving permits, license, and similar privileges, with regard to third country nationals and dependents? He noted that the U.S. armed forces are currently engaged in a program to replace gradually all third country nationals with Koreans, as soon as a sufficient number of trained Koreans is available.

18. Mr. Chang replied that at the last meeting the Korean negotiators had made a new proposal with a view

한·미국 간의 상호방위조약 제4조에 의한 시설과 구역 및 한국에서의 미국군대의 지위에 관한 협정(SOFA)
전59권. 1966.7.9 서울에서 서명 : 1967.2.9 발효(조약 232호) (V.51 실무교섭회의 합의의사록, 제38-68차, 1964)

to arriving at a mutually agreeable text of this article. They had presented briefly the framework of this proposal and had suggested an informal meeting for further discussion. Since the U.S. negotiators had rejected an informal meeting, the Korean negotiators had revised their original draft of the article and wished to table a new draft at this time. He said that Mr. Chung would explain the main features of the new draft.

19. Mr. Chung summarized the main features of the revised Korean draft of the article in the following terms. It would permit persons, including corporations organized under the laws of the United States, to employ third country nationals, who would be given the use of non-appropriated fund organizations, military post offices, and military payment certificates, under the terms of Agreed Minute #1. It would also extend those privileges to dependents, including the dependents of third country nationals, under the terms of Agreed Minute #2. Mr. Chung noted that the revised draft omitted the provisions of paragraph 3(i) of the U.S. draft, pertaining to driving permits and registration of vehicles, since the Korean negotiators believed that invited contractors should be subject to Korean laws and regulations in regard to these matters. He also noted that the revised draft did not provide for an exemption from payment of taxes arising out of the use and ownership of private vehicles. Nor did it include the provisions of the Agreed Minute of the U.S. draft. Finally, the Korean revision deletes the provisions of paragraph 3(j) of the U.S. draft, which would provide exemption from the laws and regulations of Korea with respect to terms and conditions of

0060

employment. Mr. Chung pointed out that the Korean draft of the Labor Procurement Article provides that the terms and conditions of employment in so far as they apply to Korean persons should be those laid down by Korean legislation.

20. Mr. Habib thanked Mr. Chung for his explanation of the revised Korean draft. He said the U.S. negotiators would study it and comment at a subsequent meeting.

Criminal Jurisdiction

21. The negotiators then exchanged drafts of the Article dealing with criminal jurisdiction. Mr. Chang stated that, in his capacity as Chief Negotiator for the Korean side, he wished to express great satisfaction that these drafts had finally been tabled. The Korean negotiators looked forward to a mutually satisfactory agreement on this subject, based on mutual cooperation by both negotiating teams. Mr. Habib replied that the U.S. negotiators had indicated in December that they hoped to be able to table the U.S. draft at about this time and were glad that their prediction had proved accurate. The U.S. negotiators looked forward to quiet, systematic, and fruitful discussion of this subject.

Labor Procurement

22. Turning to the article on labor procurement, Mr. Habib said that it would be helpful to both sides to have a presentation of general views on this subject. He then asked Colonel Fuller to present the views of the U.S. negotiators.

23. Colonel Fuller stated that it is the intention of the U.S. armed forces to continue to act as a good and

enlightened local employer and in general to conform
to Korean practices, customs, and Korean labor laws,
consistent with the ROK-US defense mission. The U.S.
armed forces intended to permit their employees to join
voluntarily unions or employee groups and to have the
same right to strike as employees in comparable positions
of employment with the armed forces of the ROK. Stating
that as the U.S. draft reflected current Labor practice,
and the result of fifteen years of U.S. employment
practice, Colonel Fuller suggested that the U.S. draft
serve as the basis for negotiation. He asked whether
the Korean negotiators had any questions regarding the
content of the U.S. draft.

24. Mr. Chang replied that before asking question,
he would like to sum up the basic differences between
the two drafts, as the Korean negotiators saw them.
The three fundamental differences were as follows:

The basic principle embodied in the Korean draft
is to uphold and protect the rights of the Korean workers,
as stipulated under the provisions of the applicable
Korean laws. Therefore, the Korean draft provides that
(a) local labor requirements of the U.S. armed forces
"shall be satisfied with the assistance of the Korean
authorities". (b) The Korean draft provides that the
conditions of employment and work shall be laid down by
ROK legislation, whereas the U.S. draft provides only for
"general conformity" with Korean labor legislation,
customs and practices. He remarked that there was, in
this respect, a wide gap between the two drafts. (c)
The Korean draft included detailed and fundamental
provisions in order to cope with problems arising from

possible dismissal of a worker by the U.S. armed forces
for security reasons. Inasmuch as there are these substantial differences between the two drafts, the Korean
negotiators believed that it would be more useful and
more fruitful to use the Korean draft as the basis for
negotiation.

25. Mr. Chang stated that the identification, in
the U.S. draft, of Korean Service Corps members as employees
of the ROK Government posed a difficult problem to the
Korean negotiators. They wondered what the basis of this
statement in the U.S. draft was, since they had been
unable to find any evidence that would support it.

26. Colonel Fuller asked Mr. Chang to repeat the
three basic differences which the Korean negotiators
had found in their study of the two drafts. Mr. Chang
summarized the three differences as follows:

    (a) The U.S. draft provides for direct hire,
whereas the Korean draft provides that local labor
requirements shall be satisfied with the assistance
of the ROK Government;

    (b) The U.S. draft provides only for "general
conformity" with Korean laws and regulations,
whereas the Korean draft provides that working
conditions shall be those prescribed by ROK
legislation;

    (c) The Korean draft provides detailed provisions
covering the discharge of employees for security
reasons, whereas the U.S. draft is silent on this
subject.

27. Colonel Fuller asked what the phrase "with
the assistance of the Korean authorities" in the Korean
draft meant. Mr. Chang replied that according to
current practice, the U.S. armed forces with certain
exceptions, hire their Korean employees directly.

0063

However, the Korean negotiators believed that in order to make the most effective and efficient use of Korean labor, all hiring should be done in coordination with the appropriate Korean agencies.

28. In response to Colonel Fuller's inquiry as to the nature of such agencies, Mr. Chang stated that there are currently in operation many employment offices and that in the future, many specialized employment offices will be established. In response to further questioning, Mr. Chang stated that the only agency referred to by the Korean draft was that which operates employment offices, which serves only as a labor recruiting service. As Mr. Chang had indicated that this service was currently used to some extent by the U.S. armed forces, Colonel Fuller asked how present practice would be changed under the provisions of the Korean draft. Mr. Chang said that in future it was planned to have all employment for the U.S. armed forces handled by this agency.

29. In reply to a series of questions by Colonel Fuller, Mr. Chang stated that it was the Korean intention to have this agency handle only recruiting for the U.S. armed forces and that the agency would not hire or fire, promote, demote, discipline, or assign such employees. When asked how the agency would assist in recruiting, Mr. Chang said that if there were a requirement for 1 person, the agency would send 3 or 4 eligible persons to the armed forces. The armed forces would then make the final selection.

30. In reply to questions by Colonel Fuller regarding the cost of such an employment service, Mr. Chang stated

0064

that the Korean draft provides that the U.S. armed
forces shall reimburse the ROK Government. He said
such reimbursement would only be for advertisement fees,
travel expenses, and other costs incurred directly in
the recruitment of labor for the U.S. armed forces.
Inasmuch as the employment agency was run by the ROK
Government, there would be no charge to the U.S. armed
forces to cover the expenses of salaries, materials,
and supplies.

31. In reply to further questioning by Colonel Fuller,
Mr. Chang stated that there are currently about 40
branches of the employment agency scattered throughout
the country, with one or two in every city having a
population of 50,000 or over. The ROK Government obtains
laborers for its public works and construction projects
from this agency. However, government officials are
recruited through the Ministry of Government Administration.

32. Mr. Chang pointed out, in reply to a question,
that the Korean draft would permit the U.S. armed forces
to hire employees only with the assistance of ROK
Government authorities, and the U.S. forces would not be
permitted to recruit employees from other sources.
Colonel Fuller then asked why the Korean negotiators
were offering the U.S. armed forces assistance which the
armed forces had not asked for and did not need but
would be obliged to pay for. Mr. Chang replied that
reimbursement was being asked only for legitimate expenses
incurred by the employment agency. He said the details
could be worked out by the Joint Committee.

한·미국 간의 상호방위조약 제4조에 의한 시설과 구역 및 한국에서의 미국군대의 지위에 관한 협정(SOFA)
전59권. 1966.7.9 서울에서 서명 : 1967.2.9 발효(조약 232호) (V.51 실무교섭회의 합의의사록, 제38-68차, 1964)

33. Colonel Fuller replied that the U.S. armed forces had not found any need for the type of assistance that was being offered. He pointed out that currently the armed forces were hiring employees from lists of persons who had previously lost their jobs with the armed forces as a result of reductions in force. The armed forces would no longer be able to rehire such people if they were forced to hire only those persons sent to them by a Korean employment agency.

34. Mr. Chang replied that he understood Colonel Fuller's remark. However, it was based on past experience and procedures. The Korean negotiators' position was that all future requirements of the U.S. armed forces were to be met with ROKG assistance. Since there currently existed in the ROK a surplus of labor, employees might have to accept employment under unfavorable conditions unless the situation were regularized by ROK Government supervision. To the ROK Government, it was important to see that Korean labor legislation was enforced. The U.S. negotiators had indicated that implementation of the provisions of the Korean draft would cause difficulties for the U.S. armed forces. If the U.S. negotiators would point out the difficulties and problems, the Korean negotiators would be glad to consider them and discuss the matter further at a subsequent meeting.

35. Colonel Fuller asked if all other employers in Korea were required to use the government employment service. If the U.S. armed forces were the only employer required to obtain all its employees from this service, how was that "regularizing" the situation?

36. Mr. Chang replied that the ROK Government met
its requirements through the use of the employment
service and the Ministry of Government Administration.
However, private employers were not compelled to use
the employment service in all areas of the country.

37. Colonel Fuller pointed out that no matter how
small the cost, use of this employment service by the
U.S. armed forces would cause some increase over the
present cost of hiring employees. Currently, the U.S.
armed forces were under compulsion to reduce costs, yet
the Korean proposal would cause in increase in their
labor costs.

38. In answer to Mr. Chang's earlier question
concerning the Korean Service Corps, Colonel Fuller
stated that since 1950 these persons had been secured
and hired for the U.S. armed forces by the ROK government, currently by the Ministry of Health and Social
Affairs and the U.S. armed forces have consistently
considered them to be ROK Government employees and not
U.S. Government employees.

39. Mr. Chang commented that Colonel Fuller had
indicated that one of the difficulties in implementing
the Korean proposals would be increased cost to the U.S.
armed forces. However, the Korean negotiators believed
that the reimbursement costs would be only nominal and
should cause the U.S. armed forces little concern.
The Korean negotiators could assure the U.S. negotiators
that these costs would not impose unreasonable difficulties on the U.S. armed forces.

한·미국 간의 상호방위조약 제4조에 의한 시설과 구역 및 한국에서의 미국군대의 지위에 관한 협정(SOFA)
전59권. 1966.7.9 서울에서 서명 : 1967.2.9 발효(조약 232호) (V.51 실무교섭회의 합의의사록, 제38-68차, 1964)

40. Regarding the Korean Service Corps, Mr. Chang said that the Korean negotiators had been unable to find anything in the relevant materials that would indicate any clear agreement on the status of KSC employees. They wondered, therefore, under what circumstances such an agreement had been reached. The KSC employees were paid by the U.S. armed forces and were not ROK Government employees. The ROK Government merely recruited them for the U.S. armed forces.

41. At this point, the meeting was adjourned. The next meeting was scheduled for February 20 at 2:00 p.m.

1966. 12. 31

1966. 12. 31에 예고문에 의거 일반문서로 재분류됨

0068

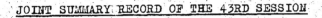
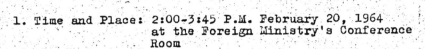

JOINT SUMMARY RECORD OF THE 43RD SESSION

1. Time and Place: 2:00-3:45 P.M. February 20, 1964
   at the Foreign Ministry's Conference
   Room

2. Attendants:

ROK Side:

Mr. Chang, Sang Moon	Director European and American Affairs Bureau
Mr. Koo, Chong Whay	Chief, American Section Ministry of Foreign Affairs
Mr. Lee, Chai Sup	Staff Officer Customs Bureau Ministry of Finance
Mr. Ham, Chung Ho	Prosecutor Ministry of Justice
Col. Kim, Won Kil	Chief, Ministry Affairs Section Ministry of National Defense
Mr. Oh, Jae Hee	Chief, Treaty Section Ministry of Foreign Affairs
Mr. Kang, Suk Jae (Rapporteur and Interpreter)	2nd Secretary Ministry of Foreign Affairs
Mr. Chung, Woo Young	3rd Secretary Ministry of Foreign Affairs
Mr. Lee, Chung Bin	3rd Secretary Ministry of Foreign Affairs
Mr. Lee, Keun Pal	3rd Secretary Ministry of Foreign Affairs
Mr. Kim, Nai Sung	Staff Officer Europe Section Ministry of Foreign Affairs

U.S. Side:

Mr. Philip C. Habib	Counselor American Embassy
Brig. Gen. G. G. O'Connor	Deputy Chief of Staff 8th U.S. Army
Col. Howard Smigelow	Deputy Chief of Staff 8th U.S. Army

0069

Col. L. J. Fuller	Staff Judge Advocate United Nations Command
Col. Kenneth C. Crawford	Staff Judge Advocates Office 8th U.S. Army
Capt. John Wayne	Assistant Chief of Staff USN/K
Mr. Benjamin A. Fleck (Rapporteur and Press Officer)	First Secretary American Embassy
Mr. James Sartorius	2nd Secretary American Embassy
Mr. Robert A. Lewis	2nd Secretary and Consul American Embassy
Mr. Robert A. Kinney	J-5 8th U.S. Army
Maj. Robert D. Peckham	Staff Officer, JAG 8th U.S. Army
Mr. O. C. Reed	Director Office of Civil Personnel 8th U.S. Army
Mr. Kenneth Campen	Interpreter
Mr. Jurio Hernandez	Labor Adviser 8th U.S. Army

1. Mr. Chang opened the meeting by introducing
Mr. Yi Chae-sup of the Ministry of Finance, substituting
for Mr. Sin Kwan-sup; Mr. Ham Chung-ho of the Ministry
of Justice; Mr. Kim Nai-sung of the Foreign Ministry;
and Mr. Chung U-young, who would serve from now on as
interpreter for the Korean negotiators. Mr. Habib welcomed
these gentlemen to the negotiating table.

Invited Contractors

2. Taking up the Invited Contractors Article,
Mr. Habib remarked that the U.S. negotiators had considered
carefully the various proposals previously made by the
Korean negotiators. Before making counter-proposals, he
said he wished to emphasize certain aspects of the way in
which the U.S. armed forces fulfill their mission. The
complicated organizational framework of the U.S. armed

0070

forces, which is sometimes confusing to a non-member of those forces, is a fact of life worldwide. Invited contractors are a very important part of that framework and are not just ordinary businessmen, as the Korean negotiators have claimed. These contractors are in Korea solely for the purpose of carrying out certain specific functions for the armed forces. They are a part of the overall military organization. Their role and functions are much the same as the role and functions of the civilian component. The services, privileges, and immunities which they enjoy are no different from those enjoyed by any other army of the military establishment. For these reasons, the revised draft proposed by the Korean negotiators does not meet the needs of the situation.

3. At the same time, Mr. Habib continued, certain aspects of the U.S. draft had presented difficulties for the Korean negotiators. He recalled discussion of this article at the 22nd negotiating meeting and read the following paragraphs from the Agreed Joint Summary of that meeting:

> "9. Mr. Hwang reiterated the view of the Korean side that inasmuch as the SOFA would be an agreement between the United States Government and the ROK Government, this article should cover only United States corporations and residents of the United States. Although quite willing to extend the suggested privileges and immunities to such corporations and residents, the ROK Government would find it difficult to extend the same treatment to third-country nationals. He said if the U.S. side would agree to the ROK position, the Korean side was prepared to consider favorably the inclusion of dependents or residents of the United States under the provisions of this article.

> "10. .... Mr. Hwang remarked that the ROK draft was similar to the provisions of the SOFA with Japan, which made no mention of third-country nationals. He said if the U.S. side would accept the Korean side's language regarding this point, the Korean side would accept the U.S. side's language regarding dependents and 'other armed forces in Korea under the Unified Command'..."

0071

4. Mr. Habib stated that he had read the above paragraphs into the record of this discussion for a special purpose. The U.S. negotiators had taken into account the Korean position as explained by Mr. Hwang and had tried to develop language which would meet it and still be in accord with the practical realities of the situation. The U.S. negotiators recognized that third-country nationals caused difficulties for the Korean negotiators. Therefore, the U.S. negotiators wished to propose some changes in the U.S. draft.

5. The first proposed change, Mr. Habib continued, was to insert in paragraph 1 following the word "employees" the words "who are ordinarily resident in the United States". He pointed out that this additional clause pertained only to "employees" and not to "persons, including corporations". This additional language would bar third-country national employees from the provisions of the SOFA, with the exception of those covered by a proposed Agreed Minute #2, which Mr. Habib thereupon tabled.

6. Mr. Habib pointed out that the proposed Agreed Minute #2 provided that any third-country national in the employment of the U.S. armed forces in Korea on the effective date of the Agreement will continue to enjoy whatever privileges he has enjoyed prior to that date, so long as he continues in the job which he holds on that date. Mr. Habib stated that this proposal took into account the concern of the Korean negotiators and at the same time was intended to serve as a transitional mechanism. The U.S. armed forces, he pointed out, have already begun a program of replacing third-country

0072

nationals with trained Koreans. This program will grandually
so replace all of the third-country nationals but it would
not be equitable to try to do this all at once.

7. Mr. Habib then tabled paragraph 8 of the Invited
Contractors Article, saying that this paragraph had been
held in abeyance until after the tabling of the draft
of the Criminal Jurisdiction Article. He stated that this
paragraph was self-explanatory.

8. Mr. Habib remarked that each side has now tabled
drafts of all of the substantive articles of the Agreement.
This constituted a milestone in the negotiations in which
all could take satisfaction. He said the articles dealing
with ratification and duration of the Agreement could be
discussed after agreement had been reached on the substantive articles.

9. Mr. Chang thanked Mr. Habib for his explanation
of the revisions proposed by the U.S. negotiators. He
remarked that there was a big difference between these
proposed changes and the revised draft which the Korean
negotiators had tabled. He said the Korean negotiators
would take the U.S. proposals under consideration and
would comment on them at a subsequent meeting.

10. Mr. Chang said he wished to comment on the
revised draft proposed by the Korean negotiators, who
believed that the status of invited contractors was
different from the status of civilian employees and
dependents. He stated it was not correct to believe that
the Korean negotiators had considered them as just ordinary
aliens. The Korean negotiators understood the contributions
made by the contractors and the importance of their work
worldwide. Therefore, the ROK Government was prepared

0073

to give them some privileges not ordinarily accorded
aliens. Mr. Chang said that the Korean negotiators would
study the record to see whether their present position
was different from the position previously taken by them,
as the U.S. negotiators had alleged. He said the fundamental
objective of the Korean negotiators in proposing a revised
draft had been to try to present language which took into
account the concern of the U.S. negotiators. The Korean
negotiators believed their revised draft constituted
a great concession on their part.

11. Regarding the proposals just made by the U.S.
negotiators, Mr. Chang said the Korean negotiators would
like to ask a few questions. Mr. Habib had indicated that
the proposed additional clause in paragraph 1 would modify
only "employees". Did this mean that corporations could
be third-country national corporations, under the terms
of the U.S. draft as revised? Mr. Habib replied that
this was a correct interpretation. He pointed out that
there might be occasions when it would be necessary for
the U.S. armed forces to invite a contractor from a third
country to come to Korea to do a special job. However,
the employees of such a contractor would have to be
ordinarily resident in the United States in order to be
covered by the provisions of this article.

12. Mr. Chang said the Korean negotiators welcomed
Mr. Habib's explanation of the intention of the U.S.
armed forces to replace third-country nationals. Mr. Habib
reiterated that this program was already under way.
Mr. Chang then asked if it was the intention of the U.S.

0074

armed forces to introduce additional third-country
nationals after the SOFA went into effect, and if so,
what privileges did the U.S. armed forces intend them
to have? Mr. Habib replied that there was no intention
to bring in any third-country nationals after the Agreement
went into force, but if any were brought in, they would
have no privileges under the terms of the U.S. draft article.

Security Measures

13. Turning to the article dealing with security
measures, Mr. Habib recalled that each side had tabled
a draft and explained its position on what the U.S.
negotiators considered to be minor, non-substantive
differences between the two drafts. The Korean negotiators
had then urged that further discussion of this article be
post-poned until after the Invited Contractors Article had
been tabled and discussed. The latter article had now
been discussed and the U.S. negotiators presumed that the
Korean negotiators now wished to make their views known
regarding the Security Measures Article.

14. Mr. Chang replied that the position of the Korean
negotiators regarding this article had not changed. He
suggested that since discussion of the Invited Contractors
Article had not yet been completed, discussion of the
Security Measures Article be postponed.

15. Mr. Habib stated that the U.S. negotiators had
no objection to such a postponement. However, they believed
this to be an article expressing general intent. No matter
what final wording was ultimately agreed upon for the
Invited Contractors Article, it would have no effect on the

한·미국 간의 상호방위조약 제4조에 의한 시설과 구역 및 한국에서의 미국군대의 지위에 관한 협정(SOFA)
전59권. 1966.7.9 서울에서 서명 : 1967.2.9 발효(조약 232호) (V.51 실무교섭회의 합의의사록, 제38-68차, 1964)

wording of this article. In making additions to the
language of the SOFA with Japan, the U.S. negotiators
were attempting to improve upon the latter agreement.
Invited contractors should be mentioned specifically
in this article because of the provision in the Invited
Contractors Article which stated that specific provisions
of the SOFA would not apply to the contractors unless
the pertinent articles specifically mentioned them.
The U.S. negotiators believed this article to be non-
controversial, since it calls for cooperation and the
taking of necessary measures. There is no substantive
difference between the positions of the two sides and
the U.S. negotiators would like to reach agreement and
get this article out of the way.

16. Mr. Chang replied that the reference in the
first sentence of this article to contractors and employees
should be deleted. He said that the security of such
persons would be fully protected by existing Korean laws
and regulations. He further stated that the Korean
negotiators could not accept the phrase "of the persons
referred to in this paragraph, and their property" in
the second sentence of the U.S. draft. He said the ROK
Government was prepared to seek legislation if needed,
for protection of property belonging to the U.S. Government but not of property belonging to private individuals.

17. In response to Mr. Habib's question whether the
ROK Government was prepared to protect only official property,
Mr. Chang replied in the affirmative, adding that existing
Korean laws and regulations provided adequate protection
for private property. Mr. Habib stated that the U.S.
negotiators understood the Korean position and would take
it under consideration.

0076

18. Mr. Chang stated that the Korean negotiators found the reference to the Criminal Jurisdiction Article in Paragraph 8 of the U.S. draft of the Invited Contractors Article, which the U.S. negotiators had just tabled, to be unacceptable. Similarly, ithey found the reference to the Criminal Jurisdiction Article in the last sentence of the U.S. draft of the Security Measures Article to be also unacceptable.

19. Mr. Habib explained that this reference was necessary in order to remove any possibility of this article infringing upon the Criminal Jurisdiction Article, particularly with regard to inter se offenses. He said that if this reference were not included, the ROK Government, under the terms of the Security Measures Article, might have a claim to jurisdiction over a member of the U.S. armed forces who had committed an offense involving destruction of the equipment or property of the U.S. Government. He pointed out that it was necessary to make the text of this article consistent with the text of the Criminal Jurisdiction Article and that this would be accomplished by the inclusion of the phrase in question, regardless of the final agreed text of the Criminal Jurisdiction Article.

20. Mr. Chang stated that the Korean negotiators had not fully understood the import of the phrase but they still believed that it should be deleted from the article. Mr. Habib urged the Korean negotiators to study the question from a legal standpoint. He pointed out that the phrase modifies the entire sentence, not just the immediately following clause. He suggested that each side consider

한·미국 간의 상호방위조약 제4조에 의한 시설과 구역 및 한국에서의 미국군대의 지위에 관한 협정(SOFA)
전59권. 1966.7.9 서울에서 서명 : 1967.2.9 발효(조약 232호) (V.51 실무교섭회의 합의의사록, 제38-68차, 1964)

the other's position and be ready to discuss this article
again at a subsequent meeting.

    21. At this point it was agreed to adjourn the
meeting. The next meeting was scheduled for February
28 at 2:00 p.m.

0078

JOINT SUMMARY RECORD OF THE 44TH SESSION

1. Time and Place: 2:00-4:00 P.M. February 28, 1964
                   at the Foreign Ministry's Conference
                   Room

2. Attendants:

ROK Side:

Mr. Chang, Sang Moon	Director European and American Affairs Bureau
Mr. Yoon, Doo Sik	Director Prosecutor's Bureau Ministry of Justice
Mr. Chung, Tai Kyun	Chief Prosecutor's Section Prosecutor's Bureau Ministry of Justice
Mr. Lee, Myung Hi	Prosecutor Prosecutor's Bureau Ministry of Justice
Mr. Koo, Choong Whay	Chief, American Section Ministry of Foreign Affairs
Mr. Lee, Chai Sup	Staff Officer Customs Bureau Ministry of Finance
Col. Kim, Won Kil	Chief, Ministry Affairs Section Ministry of National Defense
Mr. Oh, Jae Hee	Chief, Treaty Section Ministry of Foreign Affairs
Mr. Kang, Suk Jae (Rapporteur and Interpreter)	2nd Secretary Ministry of Foreign Affairs
Mr. Chung, Woo Young	3rd Secretary Ministry of Foreign Affairs
Mr. Lee, Chung Bin	3rd Secretary Ministry of Foreign Affairs
Mr. Lee, Keun Pal	3rd Secretary Ministry of Foreign Affairs
Mr. Kim, Nai Sung	Staff Officer Europe Section Ministry of Foreign Affairs

0079

한·미국 간의 상호방위조약 제4조에 의한 시설과 구역 및 한국에서의 미국군대의 지위에 관한 협정(SOFA)
전59권. 1966.7.9 서울에서 서명 : 1967.2.9 발효(조약 232호) (V.51 실무교섭회의 합의의사록, 제38-68차, 1964)

85

U.S. Side:

Mr. Philip C. Habib	Counselor American Embassy
Brig. Gen. G.G. O'Connor	Deputy Chief of Staff 8th U.S. Army
Brig. Gen. L.J. Fuller	Staff Judge Advocate United Nations Command
Col. Howard Smigelow	Deputy Chief of Staff 8th U.S. Army
Col. Kenneth C. Crawford	Staff Judge Advocates Office 8th U.S. Army
Capt. John Wayne	Assistant Chief of Staff USN/K
Mr. Benjamin A. Fleck (Rapporteur and Press Officer)	First Secretary American Embassy
Mr. James Sartorius	2nd Secretary American Embassy
Mr. Robert A. Lewis	2nd Secretary and Consul American Embassy
Mr. Robert A. Kinney	J-5 8th U.S. Army
Mr. Robert D. Peckham	Staff Officer, JAG 8th U.S. Army
Mr. Kenneth Campen	Interpreter

1. Mr. Chang opened the meeting by extending the congratulations of the Korean negotiators to Brig. General Fuller, who had been promoted that very morning. Mr. Chang then introduced the following gentlemen: Mr. YUN Tu-sik, Director of the Prosecutor's Bureau, Ministry of Justice; Mr. CHUNG Tai-kyun, Chief of the Prosecutor's Section, Ministry of Justice; and Mr. YI Myung-hi, Prosecutor, from the same office. Mr. Habib welcomed these gentlemen to the negotiations.

Criminal Jurisdiction

2. Taking up the Criminal Jurisdiction Article, Mr. Chang stated that he wished to make some introductory remarks. He then made the following statement:

0080

We do not think it is necessary to emphasize the
importance our people attach to the article dealing
with criminal jurisdiction of the prospective Status of
Forces Agreement now under negotiation between the two
parties. However, I would like to reiterate that the
successful and speedy conclusion of our present negotiations entirely depends upon how soon we can come to
an agreement on this Article.

We have studied most carefully the draft tabled
by the U.S. negotiators at the 42nd meeting. To our
great disappointment, however, the Korean negotiators
have found that fundamental differences are wide between
the two sides' drafts on the subject matter.

Aside from various differences of major or minor
nature, we believe that there is a fundamental
difference in the approach of both sides. While the
Korean side is trying to replace the Taejon Agreement,
concluded "in view of prevailing conditions of warfare",
with a new one based on the spirit of mutual respect and
under totally different conditions, it seems that the
basic position of your side is to modify the already
existing agreement.

We noted with grave concern that the U.S. negotiators
have incorporated in their draft article a totally
irrelevant concept of geographical limitation in the
application of our rights to exercise jurisdiction over
the Korean territory. Under the provisions of the U.S.
draft, the authorities of the Republic of Korea is
precluded from exercising its jurisdiction in certain
areas of Korean territory under the term of "combat

0081

한·미국 간의 상호방위조약 제4조에 의한 시설과 구역 및 한국에서의 미국군대의 지위에 관한 협정(SOFA)
전59권. 1966.7.9 서울에서 서명 : 1967.2.9 발효(조약 232호) (V.51 실무교섭회의 합의의사록, 제38-68차, 1964)

87

zone". The concept of the combat zone may be useful for military operational purposes during war time but we believe this concept should have no room for consideration in negotiating this "criminal jurisdiction". Moreover, the extent of the so called "combat zone" you have suggested covers most of the area and zone where most of United States armed forces are currently stationed. According to our statistics and records, major offenses and accidents were committed or happened in that zone in the past. Without jurisdiction over that part of Korea, the agreement would have very little meaning to us.

Furthermore, your draft requests the Korean authorities to waive in cases where there are concurrent rights, except under special circumstances in the specific case, in recognition of the primary responsibility of the U.S. military authorities for maintaining good order and discipline among the members of the United States armed forces, civilian component and their dependents.

Your draft also requests us to give sympathetic consideration even in the exercise of exclusive jurisdiction in recognition of the effectiveness of administrative and disciplinary sanctions to be exercised by the U.S. Authorities. However, we believe that the right of exclusive jurisdiction of a State should not be waived in favour of administrative or disciplinary sanctions of the military authorities of another State.

We also noted your side's intention to have primary right to exercise jurisdiction over the members of the U.S. armed forces with respect to offenses which, if committed by the members of the armed forces of Korea, would be tried by court-martial. We do not know whether or not the U.S. negotiators before proposing

0082

this have studied the existing Korean Military Law.
According to the said law, as far as the members of
the Korean armed forces and civilian components are
concerned, the court-martial has exclusive right to
exercise jurisdiction with respect to all offenses no
matter whether they are committed on or off duty and
however minor they are in nature. Without waiting
further explanation, it becomes quite clear that the
U.S. side is demanding exclusive jurisdiction over all
members of the U.S. armed forces regardless of the
nature and place of the offenses committed.

As all of us know well, the problem of determining
the scope of jurisdiction constitutes the backbone
of the entire Article and consequently the agreement
as a whole. The imposition of such conditions as
indicated in your draft would be quite contrary to our bona
fide intentions of negotiating this Status of Forces
Agreement. Now, at this point, let us make assumption that
we come to an agreement on the basis of your draft,
what would be left for us then? We really wonder what
sort of jurisdiction we are supposed to exercise, and
over whom? It would have been simpler for your side
only to provide for over what cases the Korean authorities could exercise their jurisdiction, instead of
enumerating so many conditions under which our right
to exercise jurisdiction is limited, in practice, to
a degree of non-existence.

Your draft also requests that the U.S. military
authorities should have primary right in the custody
of an accused member of the United States armed forces

0083

or civilian component or of a dependent even if he is in the hands of the Republic of Korea. It further provides that the Korean authorities should give sympathetic consideration to the request of the U.S. authorities asking for turn-over of offenders who are serving a sentence of confinement imposed by a Korean court. The acceptance of this request would mean almost total waiver of our remaining token right.

What I mentioned above are but a few of the examples which make our two positions fundamentally and substantially different. As a whole, we are under a impression that the contents of your draft article are not much different from those of the Taejon Agreement, as far as the substance of the matter is concerned. We do hope that this is certainly not the desire of the U.S. negotiators. We want your side to understand that the people of Korea have been anxious for more than a decade to see the conclusion of the Status of Forces Agreement. Unfortunately, your draft does not meet the desire of the Korean people. The Korean negotiators, therefore, find it difficult to accept the draft tabled by the United States negotiators as a basis of our further discussions.

In view of the above explanation, we sincerely hope that your side would reconsider your position on the subject of criminal jurisdiction or accept our draft as a basis for conducting the negotiation. We will now table our draft Agreed Minutes.

3. Mr. Habib stated that he wished to make a few general remarks in reply to those made by Mr. Chang.

0084

He said the U.S. negotiators had not expected that the
Korean negotiators would accept the U.S. draft. Nor
did the U.S. negotiators accept the Korean draft. The
drafts had been exchanged in order to provide a basis for
negotiation. The purpose of each draft was to set forward
as clearly as possible the views of each side on the
subject of criminal jurisdiction.

4. Mr. Habib said the purpose of the U.S. negotiators
could be stated very simply. With regard to the judicial
rights of the individual, the U.S. negotiators are bound
by Congressional, moral, ethical, and personal desires
to insure that the U.S. military and civilian personnel
in the Republic of Korea pursuant to the terms of the
Mutual Security Treaty receive judicial treatment according to standards acceptable to the United States. He
said the U.S. negotiators believe that this purpose can
be achieved through the adoption of provisions consonant
with the large body of precedents which has been developed.
If both sides are responsive to the Korean desires and
the U.S. needs, the U.S. negotiators believe that a
criminal jurisdiction article can be negotiated successfully.

5. Mr. Habib said the U.S. negotiators would like to
call to the attention of the Korean negotiators the
fact that the article which was about to be negotiated
would be something quite unique among status of forces
agreements. He pointed out that it would cover a very
considerable number of U.S. troops. The only similar situation was that in the Federal Republic of Germany, where
the United States also has large numbers of troops.

0085

Additional important factors in the situation in the
Republic of Korea, which do not exist anywhere else in
the world, include the facts that U.S. forces are in tacti-
cal, combat positions under a condition of armistice,
and in fulfillment of special international obligations.
This is a unique situation. It cannot be equated with
the situation anywhere else in the world.

6. The Korean negotiators, Mr. Habib continued,
appear to have a tendency to want to equate the situation
in the Republic of Korea with the situation in Japan.
The draft of this article tabled by the Korean negotiators
reflects that tendency. In Japan, the United States has
only a few thousand support troops in special compounds.
Furthermore, the Status of Forces Agreement with Japan
was negotiated more than ten years ago. In the actual
application of that agreement, procedures have developed
which differ from the actual text of the agreement.
The Korean negotiators tended to follow blindly the text
of the agreement, while ignoring the practice.

7. Mr. Habib pointed out that a more suitable
precedent than the SOFA with Japan would be the SOFA
with the Federal Republic of Germany, or the SOFA with
the West Indies, or perhaps the Australian or Netherlands
Agreements, which are modifications of the NATO Agreement.
He urged that the negotiators not attempt to pattern the
ROK SOFA after one which is completely alien to the
conditions existing in the Republic of Korea.

8. Mr.Habib said that the U.S. negotiators did not
intend to reply immediately to the opening statement by

0086

the Korean negotiators, in view of the fact that the
Agreed Minutes of the Korean draft had just been tabled.
The U.S. negotiators would study carefully the remarks
made by the Korean chief negotiator and would be prepared
to discuss the various elements of the article in a
logical fashion at a subsequent meeting. There should
be no question in the minds of any of the negotiators that
both sides are trying to reach agreement on a text which
will meet the needs of both sides. The opening remarks
of the Korean chief negotiator appeared to indicate that
the Korean negotiators believed the intention of the U.S.
negotiators to be invidious. This was not the case.
The U.S. negotiators must see to it that the article
provides that measure of judicial right to U.S. personnel
to which they are entitled. How to accomplish this
was a task that challenged the ingenuity of both sides.
However, it could not be accomplished by taking the SOFA
with Japan and adding three or four additional restrictions.
Such a course would not be acceptable to the U.S. negotiators.

9. Mr. Habib asked the Korean negotiators to keep
in mind the purpose of the U.S. negotiators. He reminded
them that both drafts were subject to negotiation. The
U.S. negotiators would study the Korean draft and present
their sincere response at a subsequent meeting. Mr. Chang
agreed that both sides should give further consideration
to the subject and be prepared to discuss the article
again at the next meeting.

Publicity Regarding the Negotiations

10. Mr. Habib stated that before leaving the Criminal
Jurisdiction Article, he wished to call the attention

0087

한·미국 간의 상호방위조약 제4조에 의한 시설과 구역 및 한국에서의 미국군대의 지위에 관한 협정(SOFA)
전59권. 1966.7.9 서울에서 서명 : 1967.2.9 발효(조약 232호) (V.51 실무교섭회의 합의의사록, 제38-68차, 1964)

93

of the Korean negotiators to an article appearing in
that day's press (Chosun Ilbo and Taehan Ilbo) which was
attributed to officials of the Foreign Ministry and
which made invidious references to the U.S. draft of
this article. The U.S. negotiators wished to suggest
that Foreign Ministry officials not state their negotiating
positions in the press and, above all, not state the
negotiating positions of the U.S. negotiators. He reminded
the Korean negotiators that at the outset of the negotiations, it had been agreed that the negotiations would
not be discussed in detail with the press by either side.
The U.S. negotiators, in accordance with that agreement,
had declined to discuss the substance of the negotiations
with reporters. However, the reporters had indicated to
Mr. Habib that Foreign Office officials did not share this
view.

11. Mr. Habib stated that the U.S. negotiators would
not agree to negotiate in the press. If any further
articles of the type he had cited appeared in the press,
the U.S. negotiators would suspend the negotiations and
take the matter up with high officials of the ROK
Government. Continued appearance in the press of articles
of this sort could only create trouble, since they were
based on no facts or a very poor interpretation of the
facts. If the Korean negotiators wished to arouse the emo-
tions of the Korean people, for completely unwarranted
reasons, this would be the way to do it. But the U.S.
negotiators would not be parties to such a course of action.
The U.S. negotiators were determined to negotiate a Status
of Forces Agreement but they would not negotiate it
in the public press. The U.S. negotiators would continue

008

to refuse to discuss details of the negotiations with newsmen. They asked the Korean negotiators to adopt a similar stance.

12. Mr. Chang replied that the U.S. negotiators misunderstood the situation. They had implied that the Korean negotiators were conducting a press campaign. In the Republic of Korea, as in the United States, there is freedom of the press. When reporters write speculative articles concerning the negotiations, they cite Foreign Ministry officials as their sources. There was nothing which the Korean negotiators could do to stop such a practice. The Korean negotiators did abide by the agreement made at the beginning of the negotiations and did not carry out any press campaign to influence the course of the negotiations. However, the people of the Republic of Korea have an interest in these negotiations second only to their interest in the normalization negotiations with Japan. Consequently, the Korean press, unavoidably, would tend to produce a considerable number of articles and comentaries on the negotiations, factual or speculative. The Korean negotiators found the remark made by the U.S. negotiators to suspend negotiations to be quite regrettable.

13. Mr. Habib replied that the U.S. negotiators believed that discussion in the press of what occurs during the negotiating meetings is equally regrettable. The U.S. negotiators believed that the least the Korean negotiators could do would be to have the newspapers publish retractions of speculative stories. He said he wished to discuss this matter further with the Korean negotiators outside of the negotiating sessions.

한·미국 간의 상호방위조약 제4조에 의한 시설과 구역 및 한국에서의 미국군대의 지위에 관한 협정(SOFA)
전59권. 1966.7.9 서울에서 서명 : 1967.2.9 발효(조약 232호) (V.51 실무교섭회의 합의의사록, 제38-68차, 1964) 95

Utilities and Services

14. Turning to the article dealing with utilities and services, Mr. Habib stated that the Korean negotiators had made valuable suggestions for revising this article. The U.S. side was prepared to agree in principle to almost all of these suggestions.

15. In paragraph 3(a), Mr. Habib stated, the U.S. negotiators agreed to the deletion of the phrase "however produced", with the understanding that the negotiating record should clearly show that no discrimination based on type or manner of production of utilities or services will occur.

16. Mr. Habib stated that the U.S. negotiators accepted the proposal of the Korean negotiators that paragraph 4 of the U.S. draft be deleted from this article and be made a separate article.

17. With regard to Agreed Minute #2 of the revised Korean draft, the U.S. negotiators accepted the Korean text, including the phrase "unless otherwise agreed by the two governments", but stipulated that the negotiating record show that the U.S. Government has no current intention of agreeing otherwise.

18. Mr. Habib then tabled revised drafts of Agreed Minutes #1 and #3, which the U.S. negotiators believed to be consistent with the views on the Korean negotiators. The U.S. negotiators suggested that the Korean negotiators study these revisions and give their views at the next meeting.

19. The revision of Agreed Minute #1 tabled by the U.S. negotiators reads as follows:

0090

"It is understood that any changes determined
by the Korean authorities in priorities, conditions,
and rates or tariffs, applicable to the United
States armed forces shall be the subject of consultation in the Joint Committee prior to their
effective date."

20. The revision of Agreed Minute #3 tabled by the
U.S. negotiators reads as follows:

"In an emergency the Republic of Korea
agrees to take appropriate measures to assure provision of utilities and services necessary to meet
the needs of the United States armed forces."

21. Mr. Chang stated that the Korean negotiators
accepted the deletion of the phrase "however produced"
with the understanding which Mr. Habib had mentioned.
They also agreed to the placing of paragraph 4 elsewhere
in the Agreement as a separate article. They understood
the position of the U.S. negotiators with regard to
Agreed Minute #2 and wished to state for the record
that the ROK Government also had no immediate plans for
agreeing otherwise. Mr. Chung stated that there appeared
to be no difference in substance between the drafts of
Agreed Minutes #1 and #3 tabled by the two sides.
However, the Korean negotiators would study the U.S.
revisions and give their views at a later meeting.

22. At this point, it was agreed to hold the next
meeting on March 6 at 2:00 p.m. and the meeting was
adjourned.

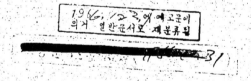

0091

<u>JOINT SUMMARY RECORD OF THE 45TH SESSION</u>

1. Time and Place: 2:00-4:10 P.M. March 6, 1964
                    at the Foreign Ministry's Conference
                    Room (No. 1)

2. Attendants:

ROK Side:

Mr. Chang, Sang Moon	Director European and American Affairs Bureau
Mr. Yoon, Doo Sik	Director Prosecutor's Bureau Ministry of Justice
Mr. Shin Kang Sup	Director Employment Security Bureau Office of Labor Affairs
Mr. Koo, Choong Whay	Chief, American Section Ministry of Foreign Affairs
Mr. Chung, Tai Kyun	Chief Prosecutor's Section Prosecutor's Bureau Ministry of Justice
Col. Kim, Won Kil	Chief, Military Affairs Section Ministry of National Defense
Mr. Oh, Jae Hee	Chief, Treaty Section Ministry of Foreign Affairs
Mr. Chung, Woo Young (Rapporteur and Interpreter)	3rd Secretary Ministry of Foreign Affairs
Mr. Lee, Chung Bin	3rd Secretary Ministry of Foreign Affairs
Mr. Lee, Keun Pal	3rd Secretary Ministry of Foreign Affairs
Mr. Kim, Nai Sung	Staff Officer Europe Section Ministry of Foreign Affairs

U.S. Side:

Mr. Philip C. Habib	Counselor American Embassy
Brig. Gen. G.G. O'Connor	Deputy Chief of Staff 8th U.S. Army

0092

Brig. Gen. L.J. Fuller	Staff Judge Advocate United Nations Command
Col. Howard Smigelow	Deputy Chief of Staff 8th U.S. Army
Col. Kenneth C. Crawford	Staff Judge Advocates Office 8th U.S. Army
Mr. Benjamin A. Fleck (Rapporteur and Press Officer)	First Secretary American Embassy
Mr. James Sartorius	2nd Secretary American Embassy
Mr. Robert A. Kinney	J-5 8th U.S. Army
Mr. Robert D. Peckham	Staff Officer, JAG 8th U.S. Army
Mr. Kenneth Campen	Interpreter
Mr. D.C. Reed	Director Office of Civil Personnel 8th U.S. Army

Utilities and Services

1. Mr. Chang opened the meeting by recalling that at the previous meeting, agreement had been reached on the text of the utilities and services provisions and Agreed Minute #2. He said the Korean negotiators were prepared to agree to the revised Agreed Minute #1 tabled at the previous meeting by the U.S. negotiators. The Korean negotiators did so with two understandings to be recorded in the negotiating record. The first understanding was that consultation in the Joint Committee, which will provide an opportunity for the U.S. authorities to make known their views concerning proposed changes, will in no way prejudice the right of the ROK authorities to make the final decision regarding such changes. The second understanding was that there might be rare occasions on which the ROK authorities would not be able to provide advance consultation. One such occasion might occur, for instance, if the National Assembly should pass a law on December 31 providing for rate 93

changes to go into effect on January 1. Mr. Chang
stated that this would be an extreme case and the
Korean negotiators did not anticipate its occurrence.

2. Mr. Chang stated that the Korean negotiators
were also prepared to agree to the revised Agreed
Minute #3 tabled at the previous meeting by the U.S.
negotiators, with the understanding that the measures
to be taken by the ROK authorities would be such measures
as were determined to be appropriate by the ROK and U.S.
authorities through consultation.

3. Mr. Habib replied that the U.S. negotiators
agreed to the first understanding stated by the Korean
negotiators with regard to Agreed Minute #1. The
second understanding did not appear to pose any great
problems. The U.S. negotiators assumed that if there
were pending in the National Assembly a bill dealing
with rate changes, the provisions of the bill would be
known and discussed in the Joint Committee prior to the
bill's passage. The U.S. negotiators accepted both
understandings, since the Joint Committee would be
capable of handling the situations to which they
pertained. The U.S. negotiators also agreed to the
understanding stated by the Korean negotiators with
regard Agreed Minute #3.

4. Full agreement was thereupon reached on the
text of the provisions dealing with utilities and services.

Accounting Procedures

5. The negotiators confirmed the agreement reached
at the previous meeting to make paragraph 4 of the U.S.
draft of the utilities and services provisions into a
separate article in the Status of Forces Agreement.

0094

Labor Procurement

6. Turning to discussion of the Labor Procurement Article, Brig. Gen. Fuller stated that the U.S. negotiators wished to make a general comment. In 1945, he pointed out, both Japan and Germany were conquered enemy countries. U.S. forces occupied those countries in a military occupation. As a defeated enemy, the Japanese Government, in so far as it was allowed to govern, did so only as an agent of the Supreme Commander of the Allied Powers. As for labor, the Japanese Government was simply called upon to provide it wherever the Supreme Commander required it. It was provided free, without any cost to the United States. In both Japan and Germany the wages of this labor were paid by the Japanese or German governments, without any reimbursement by the United States. These wages were part of the occupation costs paid by a defeated enemy. This was the origin of the system of indirect hire which the U.S. armed forces use today in Japan. As both Japan and Germany went through successive stages and were converted from enemies to allies, the nature of the U.S. military presence changed from that of military occupiers to that of visiting forces and the occupation costs came to be shared, with the United States Government taking over the payment of some of them, including labor costs. But the system of indirect hire, which still exists in Japan, in which the Japanese Government obtains the labor force for the U.S. armed forces, is a carryover from the military occupation of a defeated enemy country. The U.S. armed forces do not have any such arrangement with any of the other free countries

0095

in the Pacific area. In China, the Philippines,
Australia, Okinawa, Vietnam, Thailand, and Korea, the
U.S. armed forces hire labor directly in the free
labor market. It is not impressed by the local government for the U.S. armed forces in any of these countries.
Such an arrangement would not be proper, for it would
be typical of a military occupation. The U.S. armed
forces are in Korea not as military occupiers but at
the invitation of the ROK Government and in response
to the call of the United Nations. The relationship
between the ROK Government and the U.S. armed forces
is that of host and guest. They are free and equal
allies in a common cause. The employment of labor by
the U.S. armed forces in Korea has been that typical
of a free employer on the one hand and a free labor
force on the other. The U.S. armed forces have tried
to be a good employer in conformity with Korean labor
laws and practice. They will continue to be such.
But it would be grossly improper and a very backward
step after 19 years of free labor practice for the
SOFA negotiators now to adopt the Japanese labor
article based on an impressed labor system imposed upon
a defeated enemy.

7. Gen. Fuller explained that it was for the
foregoing reasons that the U.S. draft of the Labor
Procurement Article is worded as it is and is not based
on the Japanese article. During the previous discussion
of this article, the Korean negotiators had raised
certain objections to the U.S. draft. In consequence,
the U.S. negotiators wished to propose certain changes
in the U.S. draft which they believed would meet the

0096

desires of the Korean negotiators. These changes
are taken not from the Japanese article but instead
are designed to make the U.S. draft more fully representative of the stated preferences of the Korean negotiators.

8. In paragraph 1(b), Gen. Fuller continued, the
U.S. negotiators offered to delete the phrase "who is
an employee of the Government of Korea", as had been
suggested by the Korean Negotiators.

9. In paragraph 2, the U.S. negotiators proposed
the addition of the words "and upon request by the
employer, with the assistance of the authorities of the
Republic of Korea". This also was based upon a suggestion
by the Korean negotiators. Gen. Fuller pointed out
that while this language was not exactly that suggested
by the Korean negotiators, it was absolutely as far as
the U.S. negotiators could go in that direction. The
U.S. armed forces simply can not be bound to obtain no
employees at all except through ROK governmental agencies.
In an agreement designed to create a status for the
U.S. armed forces somewhat better than that of tourists
and businessmen, the U.S. armed forces cannot accept a
limitation on employing a labor force which is more
restrictive than those placed upon businessmen operating
in the Republic of Korea, whether Korean or third-
country nationals. Gen. Fuller pointed out that the
revised language proposed by the U.S. negotiators was
very similar to that in the labor article of the recently
negotiated SOFA with Australia. Australia is an important
ally of the United States and is a first-class power
in the Pacific area. The U.S. negotiators asked the
Korean negotiators to give weight to these facts in
their consideration of this proposal.

0097

10. From paragraph 3 of the U.S. draft, Gen. Fuller continued, the U.S. negotiators offered to delete the words "provided however, that an employer may terminate employment whenever the continuation of such employment would materially impair the accomplishment of the mission of the United States armed forces" and to place them instead in the Agreed Minutes as the second sentence of Agreed Minute #2, where they would then read: "Moreover, the United States Government may terminate employment whenever the continuation of such employment would materially impair the accomplishment of the mission of the United States armed forces". Gen. Fuller remarked that this proposal was designed to meet an objection previously made by the Korean negotiators.

11. As their fourth proposal, Gen. Fuller continued, the U.S. negotiators offered to add a new Agreed Minute to read as follows:

"3. It is understood that the Government of the Republic of Korea shall be reimbursed for direct costs incurred in providing assistance requested pursuant to paragraph 2."

This proposal was being made in response to a suggestion made by the Korean negotiators during previous discussion of this article.

12. Finally, Gen. Fuller stated, the U.S. negotiators had been authorized to state that the principle of withholding by the U.S. armed forces of employee contributions to social security and of income tax payments is acceptable to the United States Government. The U.S. authorities believed that an obligation to withhold such contributions and payments is included in the commitment in the U.S. draft to establish labor practices "in general conformity" with Korean labor laws, customs, and practices. However, should the Korean negotiators desire to include in the article

0098

a specific reference to this obligation to withhold taxes, the U.S. negotiators believed that suitable language could be worked out.

13. Gen. Fuller stated that the U.S. negotiators would like to make one additional comment concerning the language in paragraph 3 of the U.S. draft, which calls for general conformity with Korean labor laws, customs, and practices. The United States fully recognizes the sovereignty of the Republic of Korea. At the same time, it should be remembered that the United States is also a sovereign nation and that under accepted principles of international law, it is not proper for one sovereign government to hail another sovereign government into its courts as a defendant or before its administrative tribunals as a respondent. It is precisely for this reason that the U.S. armed forces cannot now or at any time in the future agree to comply with any law which requires the Government of the United States to appear when summoned before a court or board. This is not done in Japan or Germany. In those states, the judicial or administrative actions brought by employees or their representatives are defended or responded to by the governments of Japan and Germany, not by the United States Government. The U.S. armed forces are most willing to be helped and advised by the competent ministries of the ROK Government in the settlement of any labor dispute but the U.S. negotiators cannot agree that the United States Government give up a right inherent in every sovereign state not to be brought against its will before the tribunals of another sovereign state.

0099

The position of the United States Government on this point cannot change, either in Korea or anywhere else in the world. It is a universal principle of international law.

14. Gen. Fuller reiterated that the five proposals just made by the U.S. negotiators had been made out of a desire to be responsive to the legitimate requirements of the Korean negotiators. The proposals do not fully meet the Korean position, as expressed in the previous discussion of this article, but they are as far as the U.S. negotiators can go toward meeting the Korean position. He asked the Korean negotiators to give full consideration to these proposals and state their views at the next meeting.

15. Mr. Chang thanked Gen. Fuller for his explanation of the U.S. proposals and stated that the Korean negotiators would comment on them at the next meeting.

Criminal Jurisdiction

16. Turning to the Criminal Jurisdiction Article, Mr. Habib stated that the U.S. negotiators had carefully examined the statement made by Mr. Chang at the previous meeting, in presenting the comments of the Korean negotiators on the U.S. draft of this article. The U.S. negotiators would respond to the six points made by Mr. Chang and would discuss a number of points which he had not mentioned. Before doing so, however, Mr. Habib said the U.S. negotiators would like to make a general statement.

17. Mr. Habib said Mr. Chang had stated that, in general, it appeared to be the U.S. intention to retain jurisdiction over members of the U.S. armed forces in

0100

Korea, to the maximum extent possible. This is indeed
the U.S. intention, for the reason spelled out in full
in the Agreed Minutes of the U.S. draft. The reason
is that it is the primary responsibility of any military
commander to maintain good order and discipline among
his troops and associated personnel. To do so, he must
have jurisdiction over them. In all of its status of
forces agreements, the U.S. Government attempts to preserve
maximum control by a commander over his troops and
associated personnel. This is done in two ways: first,
by providing in the agreement a legal basis for the
exercise of jurisdiction by the military commander and
second, by providing in Agreed Minutes or in other less
formal arrangements for the waiver to the United States
by the host country of a maximum number of cases in which
the host country has jurisdiction. This is the world-
wide practice of the U.S. Government. It is reflected
in the U.S. draft.

18. Referring to the six points which Mr. Chang
had discussed in his statement, Mr. Habib recalled
that Mr. Chang had questioned the U.S. proposal to designate a combat zone in which the military commander
could have exclusive jurisdiction. This proposal is
designed to take into account the military purpose of
the presence of the U.S. armed forces in Korea and to
take into account the unique conditions which exist
here. Korea is the only area in the world in which
it is proposed to bring under a status of forces agreement U.S. combat troops deployed in battle position
against an active enemy. It is essential in such a
combat area that the combat troops be instantly.

0101

responsive to the will of their military commander.
Their situation is not at all the same as that of
administrative troops living in rear areas in England,
France, Italy, and Japan. In those countries, U.S.
troops live in and among the civilian population and
carry on their duties much as any civilian would do.
By contrast, the troops in the forward areas in Korea
live in their battle positions with their weapons ready
to fight off an aggressor. It is not appropriate
that they should be hailed away from these positions
upon complaint made in some distant court. They are
totally amenable to a rigid code of military justice
and any criminal act of theirs does not go unpunished.
The U.S. commanders must retain their power to punish
these troops and under U.S. law they are well able to
do so.

19. Mr. Habib stated that if the Korean negotiators
had some question about the geographical extent of such
a combat zone, as had been indicated by Mr. Chang at the
previous meeting, the U.S. negotiators were quite
willing to discuss what its proper boundaries should be.
While the Korean negotiators had referred to certain major
offenses which had occurred in this zone, there have also
occurred numerous incursions from North Korea. These
have been met by the armed action of both U.S. and ROK
forces. At this point, the U.S. negotiators displayed
a map of the area, on which were delineated the Demili-
tarized Zone, the Civilian Control Line, and the proposed
boundary of the combat zone. Pinpointed on the map
were the sites of North Korean incursions which had
occurred since October, 1962. Mr. Habib pointed out
that the map did not take into account the almost
nightly disturbances in the DMZ.

0102

20. Mr. Habib then referred to the second point
regarding which Mr. Chang had expressed concern: the
U.S. proposal for waiver of cases where there are
concurrent rights of jurisdiction. Mr. Habib pointed
out that this is a standard provision in most of the
U.S. status of forces agreements. He cited particularly
the Netherlands and Greek bilateral agreements with
the United States in the NATO area; the West Indies
agreement in the western hemisphere; the new German
agreement, which applies to the situation which is the
closest approach to the combat conditions existing in
Korea; and the 12 years of practice under the Japanese
agreement in the Pacific area. He then provided to
the Korean negotiators a copy of <u>Department of Defense
Statistics on the Exercise of Criminal Jurisdiction by
Foreign Tribunals over United States Personnel, 1
December 1961 - 30 November 1962</u>, an annual publication
which shows the percentages of waiver in all countries
where U.S. forces are stationed. This book shows that
during the latest year for which published reports are
available, of all cases in which the host government
had the primary right to exercise jurisdiction about
60% were waived to the United States. In Japan over
90% of such cases were waived to the United States.
Mr. Habib remarked that these figures have been fairly
constant over the entire 12-year experience of the U.S.
armed forces with status of forces agreements. There
appears to be nothing objectionable to the host governments in waiving jurisdiction granted to them under
these agreements.

21. The third point to which Mr. Chang had objected, continued Mr. Habib, was the Agreed Minute proposed by the U.S. negotiators which asked the ROK Government to give sympathetic consideration to the waiver of cases in which the Agreement would give the Korean authorities exclusive jurisdiction. In many cases of offenses committed by members of the civilian component and dependents, an administrative or disciplinary sanction may be appropriate instead of a criminal penalty. In such a case, both the ROK Government and the U.S. Government may be willing to forego a criminal penalty. The U.S. proposal states merely that the ROK Government will give sympathetic consideration to such a proposal. It does not seem reasonable to the U.S. negotiators that the Korean negotiators would object to such a humanitarian statement, which does not commit the ROK Government to any action in a particular case but merely states that it will give sympathetic consideration. The ultimate decision in any such case is left totally to the discretion of the ROK Government.

22. Mr. Habib then referred to the objection of the Korean negotiators to the U.S. proposal that if an offense committed by a member of the ROK armed forces would have been tried by court-martial, then such an offense committed by a member of the U.S. armed forces would also be subject to trial by court-martial, convened under the authority of a U.S. military commander. If a ROK soldier is to be tried for an offense by a court-martial under ROK law, then a U.S. soldier committing the same offense should be tried by a court-martial

0104

under U.S. law. This seems fair and reasonable to the U.S. negotiators. Asking why it did not seem fair and reasonable to the Korean negotiators, Mr. Habib pointed out that if the Korean negotiators insisted that a U.S. soldier committing such an offense should be tried by a Korean civil court, they would be making a special provision outside of present Korean law to handle such a case and they would be disregarding the military status of the offender, a status which ROK law does recognize for ROK soldiers.

23. Mr. Habib noted that the Korean negotiators had also raised the question of pre-trial custody. The U.S. negotiators had proposed that such custody be retained by the U.S. armed forces. They had made this proposal partly because an examination of the ROK pre-trial detention facilities had indicated that they are not satisfactory places for an American soldier, civilian employee, or dependent to be confined while awaiting trial and partly because of the many cases reported in Korean newspapers in which persons awaiting trial in Korean courts have been subjected to torture and compulsion to incriminate themselves. The U.S. armed forces do not intend to subject their personnel to such pre-trial treatment. The U.S. armed forces will undertake to guarantee that accused persons will be held in Korea if they are to be tried in Korean courts and will not be allowed to escape ROK jurisdiction. With such an undertaking on the part of the U.S. armed forces, there should be no need for the Korean negotiators to insist upon pre-trial custody in ROK facilities.

Mr. Habib pointed out that the U.S. proposal would
provide economic benefits to the ROK Government since
it would avoid making it necessary for the ROK authorities to make any special provisions for detention of
U.S. personnel awaiting trial. He also noted that the
U.S. armed forces in Germany retain full pre-trial
custody in all cases.

24. Mr. Habib recalled that Mr. Chang had also
questioned the U.S. proposal that the ROK Government
give sympathetic consideration to a request from the
U.S. authorities that an offender serve his post-trial
sentence in a U.S. prison rather than in a Korean
prison. He pointed out that this proposal had been
made first not by the U.S. negotiators but by Foreign
Ministry officials during a conference with Embassy
officers in 1961. This proposal also would be economic-
ally beneficial to the ROK Government.

25. Having thus discussed the six points raised
by the Korean negotiators in Mr. Chang's statement of
February 28, Mr. Habib said he would like to discuss
several points not mentioned in that statement. A
major point of difference between the two drafts is the
manner in which they deal with the "performance of duty
certificate". While the U.S. draft makes it clear that
the issuance of this certificate by U.S. military authorities is conclusive, the Korean draft provides that
the final determination of the validity of such a
certificate would be made not by the U.S. authorities,
nor even by a Korean court, but instead would be made
administratively by a local prosecutor. The U.S.
position expresses world-wide practice in status of forces
agreements since their beginning in 1952. There is no
precedent anywhere for the Korean proposal. In the

0106

case of NATO, the negotiating record makes it clear that
it was the understanding of the negotiators that the
question of the performance of duty could be determined
only by the authorities of the visiting forces. This
has been the universal practice in NATO ever since.
In only one case did a NATO government question a duty
certificate. In the Martin case in France, the Court
of Cassation, the highest court in France, decided for
all time that such a certificate was final and could
not be questioned by the French Government. In many
agreements, the finality of the duty certificate is
spelled out; in those cases where it is not spelled out,
it has been accepted in practice. This is entirely
reasonable, as no one other than a military commander
is competent to determine whether one of his soldiers is
or is not performing an assigned duty.

26. A further difference between the two drafts,
Mr. Habib continued, is that in many critical paragraphs
the Korean text omits the word "dependent" and limits
the coverage of this article to members of the armed
forces and the civilian component. The United States
Government is certainly as much concerned about the
treatment of dependents as about the treatment of
members of the armed forces and civilian employees.
The U.S. negotiators must insist, therefore, that
dependents be covered in the SOFA with the ROK Government in the same way that they are covered in the
agreements with Japan and all the NATO governments.
If the Korean negotiators were concerned about the
effect of the U.S. Supreme Court decisions in 1960
regarding military jurisdiction over civilians, Mr.
Habib stated, the U.S. negotiators would like to point

0107

out that: (a) the U.S. armed forces have as much
jurisdiction over dependents as they do over the
civilian component, which has been included in the
Korean draft; and (b) all of the status of forces
agreements concluded since the 1960 decisions have
included the word "dependent", just as the earlier ones
did.

27. Mr. Habib then noted that the Korean draft
omits any reference to the outbreak of hostilities,
which is covered by paragraph 11 of the U.S. draft.
In the event of a reopening of hostilities and any
penetration of the ROK by Communist forces, the full
strength of the U.S. armed forces will be needed to fight
them off. U.S. personnel cannot be left to be overrun
in ROK prisons or be absent from their duties while
defending themselves in civilian courts. The U.S.
military justice system will deal adequately with any
wrongdoing.

28. Mr. Habib also noted that the Korean draft
makes no provision for the disposition of cases which
may have arisen prior to the coming into effect of
the SOFA. This is covered by paragraph 12 of the U.S.
draft, which is based exactly on the corresponding
paragraph of the SOFA with Japan. The U.S. negotiators
do not believe the Korean negotiators can have any
serious objection to it.

29. Mr. Habib stated that during disorders of the
sort which would justify the imposition of martial law,
the U.S. armed forces could not allow their personnel
to be tried by the summary procedures of ROK military
courts. The U.S. draft provides against such an eventuality;
the Korean draft does not.

0108

30. The U.S. draft, Mr. Habib pointed out, lists trial safeguards which have been shown to be necessary as a result of a study of Korean criminal procedure, laws, and practices. These safeguards relate to public trial, confidential access to counsel, a right to examine the evidence and to be present when it is received, and many other points.

31. Mr. Habib then referred to the U.S. Agreed Minute regarding the provision of assistance in providing witnesses in each other's courts. He stated that this is a fair and equal Minute, with reciprocal provisions. The corresponding Agreed Minute in the Korean draft is entirely one-sided, has no equivalent in any other status of forces agreement, and is not acceptable to the U.S. negotiators. Among its other objectionable features, it is so broad as to permit U.S. officials to be called into Korean courts to testify on their conduct of their duties and on the official business of the United States Government. This is contrary to international practice and is not called for in any other SOFA. It is not acceptable to the U.S. negotiators.

32. Mr. Habib stated that the Korean draft is unduly restrictive on the military police powers of the U.S. armed forces and would prevent U.S. military police from being able to control such allied forces as the Thai and Turk contingents. This limitation is not desirable either for the U.S. armed forces or for the ROK Government.

33. Mr. Habib stated that a number of other differences exist between the two drafts but that some

0109

of them are related to the major differences already
discussed; when the major differences have been resolved,
the minor ones may be more easily reconciled. Mr. Habib
indicated that the U.S. negotiators had now responded
to the statement made at the previous meeting by the
Korean negotiators. In addition, he had made some
preliminary comments on points which had not been
mentioned by the Korean negotiators. The U.S. negotiators,
in giving their views on the key elements of this article,
had suggested that some of the differences between the
two drafts were not as great as the Korean negotiators
might have thought. They had referred to precedents
in other status of forces agreements and in actual
practice under those agreements, so that the present
negotiations might benefit from those precedents.
The U.S. negotiators had also pointed out the uniqueness
of the conditions under which the U.S. armed forces
operated in Korea and the effect of this uniqueness
on the provisions of this article. In discussing this
article, the U.S. negotiators had identified those
facts in the situation which create problems for them
and for the U.S. armed forces. If they had been
critical, they hoped that the Korean negotiators would
take the criticism in the spirit in which it had been
given. The U.S. negotiators believed that a basis
had now been laid for negotiation of this article.
They were prepared to listen to any comments which the
Korean negotiators might wish to make.

34. Mr. Chang replied that at the previous meeting,
the Korean negotiators had not attempted to mention
all of the differences between the two drafts because

0110

they had wished to concentrate on the most important
points. They now wished to make some further remarks,
including some indirect comments on the remarks just
made by Mr. Habib.

35. Mr. Chang stated that the Korean negotiators
had noticed that the U.S. draft used the term "civil
authorities of the Republic of Korea" rather than
"authorities of the Republic of Korea." This appeared
to imply that members of the U.S. armed forces would be
subject to Korean civilian courts but nor to Korean
military courts. However, under Korean law, even
civilians are subject to court-martial for specific
offenses under special circumstances. Nevertheless,
the Korean Supreme Court has final appellate jurisdiction over courts-martial, thereby guaranteeing to every
defendant his basic human rights to the maximum extent.

36. Mr. Chang noted that the Korean draft uses the
term "military authorities of the United States" whereas
the U.S. draft uses the term "authorities of the United
States". The Korean negotiators hoped that this did not
imply that the U.S. negotiators were thinking in terms
of some U.S. authority other than U.S. military authorities
having jurisdiction in the Republic of Korea. If that
is the case, the Korean negotiators found no difficulty
for the U.S. side to accept the Korean draft.

37. Referring to the concept of the combat zone,
Mr. Chang recalled that at the last meeting the Korean
negotiators had objected to this apparent intention on
the part of the U.S. negotiators to restrict the
jurisdiction of the ROK authorities over a portion of

0111

ROK territory. Korean nationals ought to be equally
treated before the law and constitutions. Consequently,
the Korean negotiators were not in a position to differentiate the benefits of law, protection and means of
redress on the basis of difference in locality. In this
respect also, the concept of combat zone would hardly
be compatible with the spirit of the ROK Constitution.

38. With regard to the question of duty certificates,
Mr. Chang said the Korean negotiators had defined specific
procedures in the Korean draft in order to prevent this
matter from becoming a controversial issue in the future
in actual application. They had tried to avoid ambiguity
by defining the exact meaning of "duty offenses".

39. Mr. Chang stated that the position of the Korean
negotiators with regard to dependents had been made
clear during discussion of other articles. They
believed that, in application of judicial rights also,
a clear distinction should be made between dependents
and members of the armed forces and the civilian
component who are performing military missions.
They believed that dependents should be excluded from
the application of this article.

40. Regarding exclusive jurisdiction, Mr. Chang
stated that both drafts give to the ROK Government the
right to exercise exclusive jurisdiction with respect
to offenses punishable by Korean law but not by U.S.
law. In such cases, the Korean negotiators believe
the right of the ROK Government to exercise jurisdiction
is inalienable and not subject to waiver.

0112

41. Mr. Chang noted also that the U.S. draft
provides for a general waiver of the primary right
to exercise jurisdiction. He said such a provision
is not consonant with the principle of mutual recognition by each government of the primary right of
jurisdiction of the other which was specifically set
forth in both texts. With regard to precedents in
other status of forces agreements regarding waiver,
Mr. Chang indicated that the Korean authorities
were prepared to waive in as many cases as in the
precedents refered to by the U.S. negotiator, but
believed that this Agreement should contain the same
language and expressions as other status of forces
agreements.

42. Mr. Chang stated that the Korean negotiators
would respond more specifically at the next meeting to
the statement made at today's meeting by the U.S.
negotiators. Mr. Habib suggested that the next meeting
be devoted to answering questions regarding the two
drafts. It was agreed to hold the next meeting on March
13 at 2:00 p.m. The meeting was then adjourned.

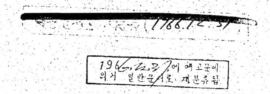

한·미국 간의 상호방위조약 제4조에 의한 시설과 구역 및 한국에서의 미국군대의 지위에 관한 협정(SOFA)
전59권. 1966.7.9 서울에서 서명 : 1967.2.9 발효(조약 232호) (V.51 실무교섭회의 합의의사록, 제38-68차, 1964)

JOINT SUMMARY RECORD OF THE 46TH SESSION

1. Time and Place: 2:00-4:10 P.M. March 13, 1964
   at the Foreign Ministry's Conference
   Room (No.1)

2. Attendants:

ROK Side:

Mr. Chang, Sang Moon	Director European and American Affairs Bureau
Mr. Yoon, Doo Sik	Director Prosecutor's Bureau Ministry of Justice
Mr. Shin, Kwan Sup	Director Customs Bureau Ministry of Finance
Mr. Koo, Choong Whay	Chief, American Section Ministry of Foreign Affairs
Mr. Chung, Tai Kyun	Chief Prosecutor's Section Prosecutor's Bureau Ministry of Justice
Col. Kim, Won Kil	Chief, Military Affairs Section Ministry of National Defense
Mr. Oh, Jae Hee	Chief, Treaty Section Ministry of Foreign Affairs
Mr. Chung, Woo Young (Rapporteur and Interpreter)	3rd Secretary Ministry of Foreign Affairs
Mr. Lee, Keun Pal	3rd Secretary Ministry of Foreign Affairs
Mr. Kim, Nai Sung	Staff Officer Europe Section Ministry of Foreign Affairs

U.S. Side:

Mr. Philip C. Habib	Counselor American Embassy
Brig. Gen. G.G. O'Connor	Deputy Chief of Staff 8th U.S. Army
Brig. Gen. L.J. Fuller	Staff Judge Advocate United Nations Command

0114

Col. Howard Smigelow	Deputy Chief of Staff 8th U.S. Army
Col. Kenneth C. Crawford *Assistant chief of staff* *USN/K*	Staff Judge Advocates Office 8th U.S. Army
Mr. Benjamin A. Fleck (Rapporteur and Press Officer)	First Secretary American Embassy
Mr. James Sartorius	2nd Secretary American Embassy
X Mr. Edward Hurwitz *Robert D. Peckham* *staff officer JAG* *8th U.S. Army*	2nd Secretary American Embassy
Mr. Robert A. Kinney	J-5 8th U.S. Army *Interpreter*
Mr. Kenneth Campen	

Accounting Procedures

1. Mr. Chang opened the meeting by referring to the decision reached previously to make paragraph 4 of the U.S. draft of Article "D" a separate article in the Agreement. He said the Korean negotiators were prepared to agree to the text of the paragraph as tabled by the U.S. negotiators, with the understanding that existing arrangements for the use of utilities and services and payment therefor by the U.S. armed forces will continue in effect unless otherwise agreed by the two governments, which was previously confirmed by general Fuller at the 35th session.

2. Mr. Habib replied that the U.S. negotiators confirmed that understanding and believed that it was implicit in the language of Agreed Minute #2 to the Utilities and Services provisions. He noted that the negotiators had now reached full agreement on the Accounting Procedures Article.

Local Procurement

3. Turning to the article on local procurement, Mr. Chang stated that Mr. Sin would present the views of the Korean negotiators. Mr. Sin stated that the

0115

Korean negotiators accepted the U.S. draft of paragraph 3 and Agreed Minute #3, with the provision that the U.S. negotiators agree to a new Agreed Minute #4 to read as follows:

> "4. Regarding paragraph 3, it is understood that 'materials, supplies, equipment and services procured for official purposes' refers to direct procurement by the United States armed forces or their authorized procurement agencies from Korean suppliers. 'Materials, supplies, equipment and services procured for ultimate use' refers to procurement by contractors of the United States armed forces from Korean suppliers of items to be incorporated into or necessary for the production of the end product of their contracts with the United States Armed Forces."

4. In response to queries concerning his statement that the Korean negotiators accepted the text of Agreed Minute #3, Mr. Sin indicated that in subparagraph (b) the Korean negotiators wished to substitute the term "authorized representative of the United States armed forces" for the term "authorized agent of the United States armed forces."

5. He also stated that the agreement of the Korean negotiators to paragraph 3 was conditioned upon (a) U.S. acceptance of an understanding that the U.S. will be given exemption only in the last stages of procurement unless it is agreed in the Joint Committee that the tax for which exemption is sought may be identified specifically and forms a significant part of the purchase price of the item, and (b) agreement by the U.S. negotiators to the insertion of the words "in advance" following the words "appropriate certification" in the first sentence of paragraph 3 of the U.S. draft. Further, the Korean agreement to the inclusion of the traffic tax in the list of exemptions was conditioned

0116

upon the explanation given by the U.S. negotiators
at the 26th negotiating meeting that this exemption
would apply only to bulk purchases of transportation
by the U.S. armed forces and not to purchases by
individual travellers. Mr. Habib replied that the
U.S. negotiators would take these proposed understandings
under consideration.

6. Mr. Sin stated that the Korean negotiators
would accept the text of Agreed Minute #2, provided the
phrase "appropriate persons" was changed to "appropriate
representatives". He said if the U.S. negotiators
accepted the Korean proposals, full agreement on this
article would be achieved.

7. Mr. Habib replied that the U.S. negotiators
would study the Korean proposals and respond to them
as soon as possible.

Security Measures

8. Turning to the Security Measures Article,
Mr. Chang stated that there were three points at issue,
namely, (a) should invited contractors be covered by
the provisions of this article?; (b) should language
be included in this article to make it consistent with
the Criminal Jurisdiction Article?; and (c) should
individual persons and their property be covered by
the provisions of this article? He said the Korean
negotiators were prepared to make concessions with
regard to the first two points. They would agree to
the inclusion in the Korean draft respectively of the
phrase "the persons who are present in the Republic
of Korea pursuant to Article ____ "between the words
'the civilian component' and 'their dependents' and

0117

한·미국 간의 상호방위조약 제4조에 의한 시설과 구역 및 한국에서의 미국군대의 지위에 관한 협정(SOFA)
전59권. 1966.7.9 서울에서 서명 : 1967.2.9 발효(조약 232호) (V.51 실무교섭회의 합의의사록, 제38-68차, 1964) 123

the phrase "consistent with Article___,",before the
words "for the punishment of offenders" if the U.S.
negotiators would agree to delete the phrase "of the
persons referred to in this paragraph, and their
property". Mr. Habib replied that the U.S. negotiators
would study this proposal and respond at a subsequent
meeting.

Labor Procurement

9. Turning to the Labor Procurement Article,
Mr. Chang stated that he would discuss, paragraph by
paragraph, the modifications proposed by the U.S. negotiators at the previous meeting. The Korean negotiators
had no objection to the deletion of the phrase "who is
an employee of the Government of Korea" from paragraph
1(b). However, the Korean negotiators saw no reason why
the members of the Korean Service Corps should be exempted
from the application of this article. They are ordinary
laborers and their exclusion from the provisions of
this article would be incompatible with the Korean
laws and regulations of Labour and the spirit of the
Constitution of the Republic of Korea. Article 29,
paragraph 1 of the constitution states that workers
shall have the right of independent association, collective
bargaining and collective action for the purpose of
improving their working conditions.

10. The U.S. negotiators had explained that the
direct hire system in Japan was left over from an earlier
period of military occupation, Mr. Chang continued.
Although the situation in the Republic of Korea was
not one of military occupation, the Korean authorities
were seeking to avoid a situation in which surplus

0118

Korean labor could be hired under adverse conditions.
Therefore, the Korean negotiators proposed the following
alteration in paragraph 2 of the Korean draft of this
article. In the first sentence after the word "satisfied",
add the words "to the maximum extent practicable".
Following the first sentence, a new sentence should be
inserted, to read as follows:

"In case the United States military authorities
exercise direct recruitment and employment of
laborers, they shall provide the Government of the
Republic of Korea with the relevant information
required for labor administration."

11. Mr. Chang stated that the Korean negotiators
had been pleased by the statement of the U.S. negotiators
that the United States Government accepted the principle
of withholding taxes and social security contributions.
However, this was provided for in paragraph 2 of the
Korean draft. If the U.S. negotiators found the
language in this draft to be unacceptable, the Korean
negotiators were prepared to consider any alternative
language which the U.S. negotiators might wish to propose.

12. Mr. Chang recalled that the U.S. negotiators
had proposed transferring the final clause of paragraph
3 of the U.S. draft to be added to Agreed Minute #2.
Inasmuch as this would not change the meaning of the
provision in any way, the Korean negotiators did not
find the proposal acceptable. Mr. Habib stated that in
that case, the U.S. negotiators withdrew the proposal.

13. Mr. Chang then referred to the previous discussion
by the U.S. negotiators of the meaning of "general
conformity" with Korean labor laws, customs, and practices.
He said the Korean negotiators wished to have labor

0119

disputes settled in accordance with the existing
Korean laws and regulations. The U.S. negotiators,
however, appeared to be trying to create new regulations.
They had said that it was not proper for one sovereign
power to hail another sovereign power into its courts.
The Korean negotiators proposed that this entire
question be discussed in an informal meeting away
from the negotiating table.

14. Mr. Habib replied that the U.S. negotiators
were not prepared to discuss important matters of
principle such as this outside of the formal negotiations.
They wanted the record to show clearly that the United
States Government will not submit itself to Korean
courts, arbitration panels, or similar bodies. This
was a logical position, taken in accordance with
international law.

15. Regarding "general conformity", Mr. Habib said
that the United States armed forces intended to continue
to act as a good employer and to conform voluntarily
to Korean laws and practices to the same extent as other
Korean employers. However, the U.S. armed forces
could not promise to conform precisely because of the
unforeseeable nature of certain personnel and management
decisions which had to be made from time to time. An
example would be the necessity of terminating exployment
for security reasons. Questions of security could
vitally affect the accomplishment by the U.S. armed
forces of their mission in Korea, a mission which they
had to accomplish under unique conditions. The U.S.
armed forces were not prepared to submit cases involving

0120

security to ROK arbitration panels or courts. If the Korean authorities had any doubts or questions as to the manner in which the U.S. armed forces were conforming with Korean laws and regulations, they could always raise those questions in the Joint Committee.

16. Brig. General Fuller commented that agreement with the Korean position would prevent the U.S. armed forces from discharging employees for security reasons. In effect, the Korean negotiators were proposing that the U.S. armed forces be prevented from taking action which would prevent the impairment of the accomplishment of their mission in Korea.

17. Mr. Chang replied that the Korean negotiators had proposed an informal discussion for the purpose of asking questions and hearing explanations by the U.S. negotiators on the matters which had just been discussed. If the U.S. negotiators did not wish to hold an informal discussion, the Korean negotiators withdrew their proposal. With regard to the question of security cases, the U.S. negotiators misunderstood the Korean position. Mr. Chang pointed out that the Korean draft of this article fully covers the question of dismissals for security reasons.

18. In response to a question by General Fuller, Mr. Chang stated that the Korean negotiators objected to the phrase "would materially impair" in paragraph 3 of the U.S. draft. He said that interpretation of this phrase might well be controversial. There was no way of gauging the extent to which the U.S. armed forces might go in using this provision. It could be used as

an excuse for any type of firing, including a reduction in force. Under the terms of the Korean draft, the U.S. armed forces could terminate employment for security reasons.

19. General Fuller stated that it was necessary for the U.S. armed forces to have the authority to terminate employment which would materially affect the accomplishment of their mission, inasmuch as their mission was the only reason for their presence in the Republic of Korea.

20. General Fuller asked the Korean negotiators to explain what they meant by "relevant information required for labor administration". Mr. Chang replied that the reference was to the number of employees hired, the places of employment, the job classification of their positions, and similar information.

21. General Fuller commented that one reason why the U.S. armed forces have not made fuller use in the past of the ROK labor offices is that these offices have been able to provide only common labor, whereas the bulk of the requirements of the U.S. armed forces are for skilled and semi-skilled laborers, such as typists, clerks, plumbers, engineers, etc.

22. Mr. Chang stated that the Korean negotiators were puzzled by one comment made at the previous meeting by the U.S. negotiators. General Fuller had said that in Japan and Germany, the U.S. Government was not made the respondent in labor disputes which were taken to court. The Korean negotiators had noticed that the

0122

language of the SOFA with Iceland was similar to the language of the Korean draft. Did this mean that the U.S. Government did go to court in Iceland?

23. General Fuller replied that in Iceland, as elsewhere, the U.S. Government did not act as respondent. He said the host government, as the employer, defended the cases in court. In Iceland, the Icelandic Government is the employer and the SOFA does not call for the United States Government to act as the defendant in such cases. General Fuller pointed out that this procedure is not that which is being proposed by the U.S. negotiators. He said the U.S. negotiators would draft a statement answering the questions of the Korean negotiators, which pertained to the Korean draft.

Criminal Jurisdiction

24. Turning to the Criminal Jurisdiction Article, Mr. Habib stated that the U.S. negotiators wished to respond to the statement made at the previous meeting by the Korean negotiators and to ask some questions regarding the Korean position.

25. Mr. Habib recalled that the Korean negotiators had objected to that provision of the U.S. draft which would exempt U.S. personnel from the jurisdiction of ROK military courts during time of martial law. He pointed out that in no other status of forces agreement has the U.S. Government agreed to give the host government such jurisdiction. It should not surprize the Korean negotiators, therefore, that the U.S. negotiators have no intention to agree to any such provision in the SOFA with the Republic of Korea. Although the Korean draft is silent on this point, the Korean negotiators had pointed out that U.S. personnel would be subject

0123

to Korean military courts unless the Agreement contains a provision such as that which is included in the U.S. draft. Therefore, the U.S. negotiators would like to hear the Korean negotiators state again their position on this point.

26. With regard to the official duty certificate, Mr. Habib recalled that the Korean negotiators had indicated that their reason for providing the procedures contained in paragraph 3(a)(ii) of their draft and for including a definition of official duty in the Agreed Minutes of their draft was to avoid disputes over the interpretation of "official duty". Far from avoiding disputes, the Korean provisions would foster disputes. In keeping with worldwide precedents, the U.S. negotiators believe that duty is best defined by those who assign the duty. In actual fact, the definition suggested by the Korean negotiators was illogical and contrary to reality.

27. As an example, Mr. Habib asked the Korean negotiators to consider the case of artillery firing practice on a firing range. Korean nationals wander onto the range while the firing is in progress and are hit. Under the Korean definition, firing of the shells which hit the Koreans would not be considered in line of duty, since wounding civilians is not a "normal function" of artillery practice firing. This definition is palpably unacceptable to the U.S. negotiators. Mr. Habib reminded the Korean negotiators that this article deals with criminal jurisdiction, not civil liability, which is provided for elsewhere in the

0124

Agreement. If the Korean negotiators were concerned
that U.S. officers might abuse their trust in executing
duty certificates, the U.S. negotiators could assure the
Korean negotiators that the execution of the duty
certificates would be done in a responsible manner
by responsible officers. This is the procedure followed
elsewhere; there is no reason to establish an entirely
new precedent which is inconsistent with normal world-
wide practice. The U.S. negotiators, therefore, could
not agree to the Korean draft.

28. Regarding pre-trial custody, Mr. Habib asked
why the Korean authorities desired it when the U.S.
armed forces were prepared to obligate themselves to
produce defendants on request and to prevent them from
escaping Korean jurisdiction. He pointed out that in
actual practice, the Japanese authorities have shown
no desire for pre-trial custody.

29. Regarding post-trial custody, Mr. Habib
reiterated that the U.S. authorities had previously
received from the ROK Government a suggestion that the
U.S. authorities might take post-trial custody of
defendants convicted under ROK jurisdiction. The U.S.
negotiators had thought that they were responding to
this suggestion. The U.S. draft would not obligate
the Korean authorities in any way but would merely call
on them to entertain a request for post-trial custody.
Unless this provision were included in the Agreement,
the U.S. authorities would not have the right to take
post-trial custody, even if the Korean authorities
wanted them to do so.

30. With regard to dependents, Mr. Habib stated that the Korean negotiators apparently did not agree with the coverage given by the U.S. draft. He pointed out that the number of dependents who would be covered by the SOFA would be relatively small, since most of the military dependents in Korea were MAAG dependents who would not be covered by the SOFA. The Korean negotiators should consider the fact that dependents are covered by this article in every other status of forces agreement.

31. Mr. Habib commented that the provision of the U.S. draft which permitted waiver of exclusive jurisdiction by the ROK Government had been included as an attempt to assist the Korean authorities. It was thought desirable to provide for some procedure which would permit the ROK authorities to avoid the holding of a trial in cases over which they might not wish to exercise jurisdiction. In such cases, the U.S. authorities would take appropriate administrative action against the offenders.

32. Mr. Habib said the waiver of concurrent jurisdiction was another matter. Under other status of forces agreements, the rate of waiver had proved to be very high. The U.S. negotiators would like to hear the Korean negotiators state their position on this question, as well as on the other points which Mr. Habib had just discussed.

33. Mr. Chang stated that with regard to the questions of U.S. personnel being subject to ROK military courts and the coverage of dependents, the

Korean negotiators had already stated that they found
it difficult to accept the U.S. position in principle
because of conflict with the ROK Constitution. However,
the Korean negotiators were not adamant on these questions
and there was room for further negotiation.

34. In response to a question by Mr. Habib as to
what provision on the Constitution was relevant, Mr. Chang
stated that the U.S. proposals on these two subjects
were not in keeping with the spirit of the ROK constitution. Mr. Habib replied that the SOFA was being
negotiated in connection with existing Korean laws,
not just with regard to spirit.

35. Mr. Chang asked whether the U.S. negotiators
had any further comments to make regarding the Korean
position. Mr. Habib replied that the Korean negotiators
had expressed some concern over the fact that the U.S.
draft used the term "authorities of the United States"
rather than "military authorities of the United States".
He said this was a matter of internal concern for
the United States and should not worry the Koreans.
The language had been made broad enough to provide
for any possible exercise of jurisdiction by U.S.
authorities.

36. Mr. Habib referred to the Korean comments
regarding the U.S. proposal for the recognition of a
combat zone. The Korean negotiators had said that the
ROKG could not sacrifice the right of a citizen of the
Republic of Korea to seek redress in Korean courts simply
because he llived in a certain geographical area.
Mr. Habib reminded the Korean negotiators that when a
U.S. soldier is prosecuted in a court of the Republic

of Korea, the citizen who has been injured by the soldier obtains no redress. The punishment is by the sovereign, the Republic of Korea, and is punishment for a violation of the sovereign's laws. The criminal jurisdiction article of the SOFA, therefore, grants no Korean citizen the right of redress. He must seek redress in the civil courts, not the criminal courts. The existence of a combat zone in which the U.S. authorities would exercise exclusive jurisdiction would not mean that U.S. personnel would not be amenable to civil jurisdiction within that area. The liability of a U.S. soldier to an individual ROK citizen for a wrong committed against the latter is not within the purview of the criminal jurisdiction article but falls elsewhere in the Agreement.

37. Finally, Mr. Habib referred to the Korean proposal that U.S. soldiers should be subject to trial by ROK civilian courts, even though they were accused of committing offenses for which Korean soldiers were tried by Korean courts-martial. He said the U.S. negotiators could not understand why the Korean negotiators could not agree that if a Korean soldier is tried by a Korean court-martial, a U.S. soldier should be tried by a U.S. court-martial for the same type of offense.

38. Mr. Chang stated that the Korean negotiators would respond at the next meeting to the views expressed by the U.S. negotiators at this meeting. It was agreed to hold the next meeting on March 20 at 2:00 p.m.

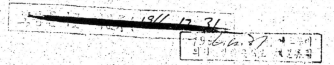

1. Time and Place: 3:00-5:00 P.M. March 20, 1964
   at the Foreign Ministry's Conference
   Room (No.1)

2. Attendants:

   ROK Side:

   Mr. Chang, Sang Moon — Director
   European and American Affairs
   Bureau

   Mr. Yoon, Doo Sik — Director
   Prosecutor's Bureau
   Ministry of Justice

   Mr. Koo, Choong Whay — Chief, American Section
   Ministry of Foreign Affairs

   Mr. Chung, Tai Kyun — Chief
   Prosecutor's Section
   Prosecutor's Bureau
   Ministry of Justice

   Col. Kim, Won Kil — Chief, Military Affairs Section
   Ministry of National Defense

   Mr. Kang Suk Jae — 2nd Secretary
   Ministry of Foreign Affairs

   Mr. Lee, Chung Bin — 3rd Secretary
   Ministry of Foreign Affairs

   Mr. Chung, Woo Young — 3rd Secretary
   (Rapporteur and — Ministry of Foreign Affairs
   Interpreter)

   Mr. Lee, Keun Pal — 3rd Secretary
   Ministry of Foreign Affairs

   Mr. Kim, Nai Sung — Staff Officer
   Europe Section
   Ministry of Foreign Affairs

   U.S. Side:

   Mr. Philip C. Habib — Counselor
   American Embassy

   Brig. Gen. G.G. O'Connor — Deputy Chief of Staff
   8th U.S. Army

   Brig. Gen. L.J. Fuller — Staff Judge Advocate
   United Nations Command

0129

Col. Howard Smigelow	Deputy Chief of Staff 8th U.S. Army
Col. Kenneth C. Crawford	Staff Judge Advocates Office 8th U.S. Army
Capt. John Wayne	Assistant Chief of Staff USN/K
Mr. Benjamin A. Fleck (Rapporteur and Press Officer)	First Secretary American Embassy
Mr. James Sartorius	2nd Secretary American Embassy
Maj. Robert D. Peckham	Staff Officer JAG 8th U.S. Army
Mr. Robert A. Kinney	J-5 8th U.S. Army
Mr. Kenneth Campen	Interpreter

Criminal Jurisdiction

1. In opening the meeting, Mr. Chang said that he would like to respond to the questions and statements made by the chief U.S. negotiator at the previous meetings.

2. With regard to the phrase "authorities of the Republic of Korea", Mr. Chang said the Korean negotiators do not want to limit Korean authority to the civil side. As he had mentioned at the previous meeting, a member of the American forces, their civilian component, or one of their dependents may have to be subject to trial by the Korean military tribunals in cases where ordinary Korean civilians would be triable by the Korean military courts. The Korean Constitution, in Article 106, states that in cases of espionage on military affairs, offenses against sentinels and sentry-posts, distribution of harmful food to armed forces, and offenses against prisoners of war, civilians and soldiers alike would be subject to the military tribunal in accordance with provisions of law. If the Korean negotiators accepted

0130

the U.S. version of "civil authorities of the Republic
of Korea", the Korean authorities would have to initiate
criminal proceedings against such offenses only in a
civil court. It is the understanding of the Korean
negotiators that espionage or violation of any law
relating to official secrets of the state may be tried
by the civil court. However, they believe that offenses
involving espionage on military affairs should be
dealt with by the military court rather than the civil
court for security reasons.

3. As for the problem of trying American servicemen
by Korean military courts under Martial Law, the U.S.
negotiators had stated that the U.S. armed forces could
not allow their personnel to be tried by the summary
procedures of ROK military courts. The existing code of
criminal procedures applicable in the case of civil
courts is also applied at military courts even under
martial law. The Korean negotiators understand that the
concern of the U.S. negotiators, indicated by the
reference to summary procedures, may be over the composition of the Korean military tribunal, which the Korean
negotiators believe to be more or less universal. If
that understanding is correct, Mr. Chang continued, the
Korean negotiators would further like to know what are
the other elements of concern to the U.S. negotiators,
as expressed in their reference to summary procedures.

4. Regarding the official duty certificate, the
Korean negotiators do not challenge the contention of
the U.S. negotiators that the local commander may well
determine whether one of his soldiers is or is not on duty.

0131

However, determination of whether an offense arising
out of an act or omission committed on duty has a
genuine link with the performance of official duty
should not be made by a field commander but by a judicial
officer who has the sole authority to take up criminal
cases under Korean laws. The example given by the U.S.
negotiators of artillery firing practice on a firing
range is irrelevant to the criminal case under discussion
and not to the point. The Korean negotiators would like
to give an example, said Mr. Chang, which would justify
their concern on this point. Suppose a soldier was ordered
to proceed from Seoul to Suwon on official business.
He had to park his car on the street somewhere along
the Yongdongpo main street and unfortunately became involved
in a quarrel with a Korean and committed assault and
battery or serious injury. Even though this example sounds
like a hypothetical case, we cannot rule out the possibility
of such unfortunate cases occurring. What the Korean
negotiators contend in such a case is that a local
commander may well certify that the offense was committed
during the hours of the soldier's duty, but he is not
empowered to determine whether the offense arose out of
an act or omission directly related to the official
order he issued.

5. Further, Mr. Chang said, the U.S. draft has not
attempted to formulate any concise explanation of when
an offense does arise out of an act or omission done
in the performance of official duty. This is why the
Korean negotiators had prepared in their draft the

0132

exact meaning of "official duty". If the U.S. negotiators don't like some of the wording in the Korean draft, the Korean negotiators would propose to modify it in line with a circular of the United States Army, Far East, which was published in January, 1956. The Korean negotiators believe that the U.S. authorities could have no objection to accepting the Korean proposal, because such definition of "official duty" is their own interpretation.

6. With regard to dependents, Mr. Chang continued, the status of the dependents is substantially different from that of the members of the U.S. armed forces and civilian component. Dependents of members of the U.S. armed forces in Korea are not in the same position as members of the forces and the civilian component. Moreover, they are not subject to the same strict discipline as are members of the armed forces. However, as the Korean negotiators had indicated at the last meeting, they are not trying to be inflexible in their approach to this problem.

7. With regard to the problem of waiving exclusive jurisdiction by the Korean Government, Mr. Chang continued, the U.S. side had stated that its request for sympathetic consideration was nothing but a humanitarian statement. However, the Korean negotiators feel that the problem under discussion is something more than a humanitarian affair. In brief, inasmuch as the right of exclusive jurisdiction is inalienable, the Korean authorities do not desire to obligate themselves to the extent that they have to give sympathetic consideration to the request for waiver. Furthermore, the U.S. side had stated that the provision as indicated in the U.S. draft is an attempt

0133

to assist the Korean authorities. The U.S. negotiators
are offering the Korean authorities assistance for which
the latter do not ask.

8. With respect to waiver of concurrent jurisdiction,
Mr. Chang continued, the Korean negotiators are well
aware that the rate of waiver in other countries had
proved to be very high. As he had mentioned before, the
Korean authorities are prepared to waive in as many
cases as in the precedents referred to by the U.S.
negotiators. However, the Korean negotiators are unable
to understand why the provision in this agreement should
be differently worded than similar provisions in other
agreements. The U.S. negotiators had said further that the
provision as stated in the U.S. draft is a standard
provision in most Status of Forces Agreements, but so far
as the Korean negotiators know, there is no such provision
in any of the existing Status of Forces Agreements,
particularly the last paragraph of the U.S. draft,
barring the host country and its nationals from instituting criminal proceedings in case the Joint Committee
fails to come to an agreement on the question of waiver.

9. The U.S. negotiators insist, continued Mr. Chang,
that if an offense committed by a member of the ROK
armed forces would have been tried by court-martial,
then such an offense committed by a member of the United
States armed forces would also be subject to trial by
American court-martial. The Korean negotiators recalled
that at previous meetings, the U.S. negotiators time
and again had pointed out that the Korean draft should be
discussed in line with precedents in other SOFA's.
Since the Korean negotiators believe that most of the

0134

receiving countries in the precedents have military law and military courts, the Korean negotiators expected to find provisions similar to those the U.S. negotiators have proposed in this regard. Therefore, they wished to ask the U.S. negotiators in what Status of Forces Agreement and with what country they have made identical provisions. Mr. Chang stated that the Korean negotiators are really at a loss to find the real intention of the U.S. negotiators in proposing this provision. Unless the U.S. negotiators withdrew this proposition, the Korean authorities would have to give up entirely their right to exercise criminal jurisdiction over members of the U.S. military forces.

10. With regard to the term "authorities of the United States", Mr. Chang continued, the U.S. negotiators had stated that the language had been made broad enough to provide for any possible exercise of jurisdiction by U.S. authorities. He said the Korean negotiators would like to emphasize that the subject and matters of discussion throughout this SOFA negotiation is the military status of the U.S. armed forces but not any other U.S. authority in Korea. It is utterly inconceivable that any United States authority other than the U.S. military authorities would have jurisdiction in Korea. Moreover, the Korean negotiators could not find any similar provision in any other SOFA. In this respect, they would appreciate an explanation of any possible difficulty envisaged by the U.S. negotiators in case the word "military" is inserted.

0135

11. Regarding so-called "combat zone", as the
Korean negotiators repeatedly had made clear, criminal
jurisdiction and the military operation are totally
different concepts, which cannot be confounded. The
imposition of a geographical limitation on the exercise
of jurisdiction is incompatible with the sovereign judicial
right to be exercised throughout the territory of the
Republic of Korea and is not acceptable to the Korean
negotiators. They hope the difficulties indicated by
the U.S. negotiators with regard to the so-called "combat
zone" may be dealt with and solved by an agreeable and
effective exercise of waiver of the right of jurisdiction.

12. Regarding trial safeguards, Mr. Chang continued,
the U.S. negotiators had said that as a result of study
of Korean criminal procedures, laws and practices, it
was necessary to list trial safeguards. However, the
Korean negotiators found the provisions provided in the
U.S. draft article are more or less the same as those
provided in the Korean Constitution and the Code of
Criminal Procedures. That is the reason why the Korean
negotiators had not enumerated such provisions in their
draft. If the U.S. negotiators desire to insert these
provisions in the SOFA, in principle, the Korean negotiators
have no objection to it.

13. Mr. Habib reminded the Korean negotiators that
the question of pre-trial custody was also a matter of
concern to the U.S. negotiators. Noting that Mr. Chang
had not discussed this question in his just-concluded
remarks, Mr. Habib asked for a statement of the Korean
position regarding pre-trial custody. Mr. Chang replied
that pre-trial custody was closely connected with the
question of post-trial custody. The Korean negotiators

0136

wished to withhold comment on both subjects until a later meeting.

14. Regarding Korean military courts, Mr. Habib inquired whether it was not the case that Article 106 of the ROK Constitution stated that military tribunals "may", not "must", exercise jurisdiction over civilians during periods of martial law. Mr. Chang acknowledged this to be the case. In effect, Mr. Habib continued, it would not be a violation of the Constitution if that right of jurisdiction were not exercised. The people who drafted the Constitution had recognized that the exercise of jurisdiction over criminal cases by military tribunals was not necessarily the best way of handling those cases. The U.S. negotiators, Mr. Habib said, did not believe that the Korean negotiators were seriously concerned with Korean military jurisdiction over Americans. They would reserve further comment on this point until later discussion of specific sections of this article.

15. Mr. Habib pointed out that the U.S. negotiators had not claimed that the provision in the U.S. draft providing for waiver of concurrent jurisdiction was a standard provision in all status of forces agreements. What he had said previously was that the reference to waiver in the text of both the U.S. and Korean drafts of this article was standard language. The Agreed Minutes, of course, were another matter. The language in the U.S. draft of the Agreed Minutes was not the standard language.

16. Mr. Habib stated that Mr. Chang had made two statements indicating willingness on the part of the Korean negotiators to consider the U.S. point of view.

The first of these was Mr. Chang's statement that the enumeration of trial safeguards was consistent with ROK law and that if the U.S. negotiators wished to include such an enumeration in this article, the Korean negotiators would not object in principle. The second was Mr. Chang's statement that the Korean negotiators were not inflexible on the subject of dependents. Mr. Habib said the U.S. negotiators would defer discussion on these points until the Korean position had been somewhat refined.

17. In other respects, Mr. Habib continued, there appeared to be no recognition on the part of the Korean negotiators of other problems existing with regard to this article or of the explanations given by the U.S. negotiators. In particular, the Korean negotiator's discussion of the duty certificate was difficult to accept. He pointed out that there was a profound difference between the example given by the U.S. negotiators and that given by the Korean negotiators. In the Korean negotiators' example, the offense was clearly not an on-duty offense. But in the example given by the U.S. negotiators, an on-duty offense would be construed as an off-duty offense, according to the definition of off-duty offenses which the Korean negotiators wished to include in the Agreement. Mr. Habib again pointed out that in no status of forces agreement is there any such definition, the reason being that only the commander who assigns the duty is able to determine whether or not an offense was committed in the line of that duty. In some status of forces agreements, there is provision for a review system. Where such a system has been used, the finding has always been that only the commander is competent to determine what constitutes duty.

0138

18. Pointing out that there was a great similarity in the two drafts, Mr. Habib suggested that the negotiators, having exchanged views in general terms, now proceed with a paragraph by paragraph discussion of the drafts in order to identify the specific differences existing in the texts.

19. Mr. Chang agreed but said that before proceeding to paragraph by paragraph discussion, the Korean negotiators wished to make a few further comments. With regard to enumeration of trial safeguards, they agredd to the idea of an enumeration but they did not necessarily accept the entire enumeration in the U.S. draft. With regard to the subject of dependents as a whole, the U.S. negotiators could accept the statement of the Korean negotiators at face value but detailed discussion should be deferred until a later meeting. With regard to the duty certificate question, the U.S. negotiators should not have any difficulty in accepting the definition published in the January, 1956 circular of the U.S. Army, Far East, either as part of the text or as an understanding in the negotiating record.

20. The negotiators then began paragraph by paragraph discussion and in paragraph l(a) noted that the Korean draft contained the word "military" in front of the word "authorities" while the U.S. draft contained the phrase "and their dependents" and referred to "all" criminal and disciplinary jurisdiction.

21. Mr. Habib stated that if the Korean negotiators were unwilling to include the phrase "and their dependents" in this subparagraph, their position was not very flexible. He pointed out that if dependents were to be subject to U.S. jurisdiction, they would have to be mentioned in this subparagraph.

한·미국 간의 상호방위조약 제4조에 의한 시설과 구역 및 한국에서의 미국군대의 지위에 관한 협정(SOFA) 전59권. 1966.7.9 서울에서 서명 : 1967.2.9 발효(조약 232호) (V.51 실무교섭회의 합의의사록, 제38-68차, 1964)

22. Mr. Chang replied that inclusion or exclusion of the word "all" was not an important matter and could be discussed later. On the other hand, the question of whether to refer to "authorities" or "military authorities" was a very important question which was not just simply a matter of wording but a question which affects the judicial rights of the Korean people as a whole. With regard to dependents, the Korean negotiators believed that measures could be worked out to include them in this article without specifically referring to them in this subparagraph. He pointed out that the U.S. negotiators had not made any definite explanation as to how far the U.S. military courts have jurisdiction over dependents. The Korean negotiators wished to know what the U.S. authorities would do regarding those persons over whom the armed forces would have no jurisdiction.

23. Mr. Habib replied that the U.S. armed forces would have disciplinary jurisdiction over such persons. It was also possible that in future, jurisdiction will be provided that does not exist at present. In wartime, the armed forces would have jurisdiction over dependents under the provisions of the "hostilities" paragraph in the U.S. draft. In this connection, Mr. Habib urged the Korean negotiators to study carefully the provisions of paragraph 2(b), which provides that the Republic of Korea will have exclusive jurisdiction over offenses not punishable by U.S. law.

24. In reply to Mr. Chang's query whether paragraph 2(b) included or excluded disciplinary action, Mr. Habib stated that an offense could be handled either by criminal jurisdiction or by disciplinary jurisdiction. If the

0140

offense were not punishable by U.S. law, and was punishable
by ROK law, paragraph 2(b) provides that the ROK authorities
could exercise jurisdiction, if they decided to do so.
It gives them the right to exercise jurisdiction but they
do not have to do so if they do not wish to.

25. In response to a further query by Mr. Chang
whether the U.S. authorities would take disciplinary
action or turn the defendant over to the Korean authorities,
in the case of an offense punishable by Korean law but not
by U.S. law, Mr. Habib stated that paragraph 2(b) would
give the ROK Government the right to exercise jurisdiction.
As an example, Mr. Habib asked the Korean negotiators to
consider the case of a dependent who commits murder. He
is not punishable by U.S. law but is punishable by Korean
law. Therefore, the ROK authorities would have jurisdiction.
However, there might be cases in which the Korean authorities would not wish to exercise their jurisdiction.
In those cases, they could waive their jurisdiction, either
concurrent or exclusive, according to the provisions of
the U.S. draft.

26. In paragraph 1(b), Mr. Habib identified the
key difference as being the use of "civil authorities"
in the U.S. draft, compared with "authorities" in the
Korean draft. Also, the U.S. draft states that the
Korean authorities "shall have the right to exercise
jurisdiction" whereas the Korean draft says they "shall
have jurisdiction". This is not a substantial point,
Mr. Habib said, but the language of the U.S. draft is
similar to the language of paragraph 1(a) in both drafts.

27. Pointing out that the Korean negotiators had
previously said that all Korean soldiers are tried by

0141

courts-martial, Mr. Habib asked if the language of the
Korean draft meant that all U.S. soldiers would be tried
by Korean courts-martial. Mr. Chang replied that all
members of the ROK armed forces are subject to trial by
court-martial. However, the "authorities" referred to
in the Korean draft could be either civilian or military.
Mr. Habib asked why all members of the ROK armed forces
are subject to trial by court-martial. Could it have
any connection with the fact that they are serving in
a combat zone? Mr. Chang said he would answer that
question at a subsequent meeting.

28. Mr. Chang also suggested deferring discussion
of "shall have the right to exercise jurisdiction" versus
"shall have jurisdiction" until a subsequent meeting.
The Korean negotiators believed the difference in language
could be easily reconciled.

29. Turning to paragraph 2, Mr. Habib pointed out
that the use of the term "military authorities" in the
Korean draft and the inclusion of the phrase "and their
dependents" in the U.S. draft had already been discussed.
Subparagraphs (b) and (c) were identical in both drafts.

30. In paragraph 3(a), Mr. Habib noted the same
differences in language regarding the use of the term
"military authorities" and the phrase "and their dependents"
in the Korean and U.S. drafts, respectively. Subparagraph (a)
(i) in both drafts was identical. In subparagraph (a) (ii)
of the Korean draft appeared the definition of on-duty
offenses which the Korean negotiators had just indicated
need not necessarily be included in the text of the
Agreement.

0142

31. Mr. Chang stated that if agreement could be reached by the negotiators on the definition contained in the U.S. Army Far East circular which he had mentioned, it need not be included in the text. Mr. Habib replied that the U.S. negotiators would not agree on a definition of duty. There is no such definition in any status of forces agreement. By definition, duty is what the commander calls duty. This is a universally accepted principle.

32. Mr. Chang replied that if the U.S. negotiators would accept the second and third sentences of subparagraph (a) (ii) of the Korean draft, the Korean negotiators would be willing to delete the first sentence, which constituted the definition of duty. Mr. Habib replied that this proposal was unacceptable to the U.S. negotiators. He said the U.S. negotiators were prepared to discuss how the commanding officer could responsibly fulfill his function of defining duty but they were unable to agree to any proposal which would vest that function in some person not connected with the duty.

33. Mr. Chang stated that the Korean negotiators were not insisting that agreement on the definition of duty contained in the U.S. Army Far East circular be included in the text of the article or even in an Agreed Minute. If the negotiators could just reach agreement on that definition, there would be no problem in solving this question.

34. At this point, the negotiators broke off substantive discussion to spend the last few minutes of the meeting in bidding farewell to General Fuller and to Mr. Kang, each of whom was attending his last negotiating session prior to departure on another assignment.

0143

35. The next meeting was scheduled for March 27, at 2:00 p.m.

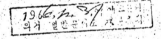

0144

JOINT SUMMARY RECORD OF THE 48TH SESSION

1. Time and Place: 3:30-5:00 P.M. April 3, 1964
   at the Foreign Ministry's Conference
   Room (No.1)

2. Attendants:

   ROK Side:

   Mr. Chang, Sang Moon   Director
                                 European and American Affairs
                                 Bureau

   Mr. Yoon, Doo Sik   Director
                                 Prosecutor's Bureau
                                 Ministry of Justice

   Mr. Shin Kwan Sup   Director
                                 Customs Bureau
                                 Ministry of Finance

   Mr. Koo, Choong Whay   Chief, American Section
                                 Ministry of Foreign Affairs

   Mr. Chung, Tai Kyun   Chief
                                 Prosecutor's Section
                                 Prosecutor's Bureau
                                 Ministry of Justice

   Col. Kim, Won Kil   Chief, Military Affairs Section
                                 Ministry of National Defense

   Mr. Lee, Chung Bin   3rd Secretary
                                 Ministry of Foreign Affairs

   Mr. Chung, Woo Young   3rd Secretary
   (Rapporteur and   Ministry of Foreign Affairs
   Interpreter)

   Mr. Lee, Keun Pal   3rd Secretary
                                 Ministry of Foreign Affairs

   Mr. Kim, Nai Sung   Staff Officer
                                 Europe Section
                                 Ministry of Foreign Affairs

   U.S. Side:

   Mr. Philip C. Habib   Counselor
                                 American Embassy

   Brig. Gen. G.G. O'Connor   Deputy Chief of Staff
                                 8th U.S. Army

   Col. Howard Smigelow   Deputy Chief of Staff
                                 8th U.S. Army

0145

Col. Kenneth C. Crawford	Staff Judge Advocates Office 8th U.S. Army
Capt. John Wayne	Assistant Chief of Staff USN/K
Mr. Benjamin A. Fleck (Rapporteur and Press Officer)	First Secretary American Embassy
Mr. Robert A. Lewis	2nd Secretary American Embassy
Maj. Robert D. Peckham	Staff Officer JAG 8th U.S. Army
Mr. Robert A. Kinney	J-5 8th U.S. Army
Mr. Kenneth Campen	Interpreter
Mr. Ogden C. Reed	Civilian Personnel Director 8th U.S. Army

Labor Procurement

1. General O'Connor opened the meeting by referring to the information sheet on the Korean Service Corps which had been passed to the Korean negotiators prior to the meeting. He stated that Lt. Colonel Mulkey was present to answer any questions which the Korean negotiators might wish to ask concerning the KSC. He pointed out that one of the unique features of the KSC is its mobility. Because of the necessity for moving components of the KSC from place to place as the situation requires, members are paid more than ordinary laborers of the same category. The KSC, General O'Connor continued, is a para-military organization, which has its own distinctive uniform, operates its own messes, and is commanded by military officers. Therefore, its personnel do not logically fit under the category of "employee" as defined in the U.S. draft of the Labor Procurement Article.

2. Mr. Chang thanked the U.S. negotiators for the information which they had furnished concerning the KSC.

0146

He remarked that the Korean negotiators had been unable,
however, to identify or find any traces of the agreement
between the United Nations Command and the Government
of the Republic of Korea, referred to in information
sheet provided by the U.S. side.

3. Lt. Colonel Mulkey stated that the signed
documents were on file with the Staff Judge Advocate.
He pointed out that, among other provisions, the agreement
stipulated that not more than 7,000 persons were to be
enrolled in the KSC at any one time. General O'Connor
stated that the U.S. negotiators would furnish a copy
of the pertinent documents to the Korean negotiators.

4. Mr. Chang stated that the records available
to the Korean negotiators showed that on March 8, 1955,
at the 8th session of the 24th National Assembly, it was
agreed that recruitment to the KSC should be suspended.
Mr. Chang added that the records showed that from
September, 1955, KSC members were supplied from the
free labor market. Mr. Chang pointed out that this
matter had already been discussed at three or four negotiating meetings and that a few more such discussions appeared to be necessary even after the agreements cited by
the U.S. negotiators have been produced. The Korean
negotiators suggested, therefore, that mention of the
KSC be deleted from the Status of Forces Agreement and
the entire question of the Korean Service Corps be taken
up as a separate matter of discussion outside of the
framework of the status of forces negotiations.

5. Mr. Habib replied that the U.S. negotiators would
study this proposal carefully to see whether it was feasible.

한·미국 간의 상호방위조약 제4조에 의한 시설과 구역 및 한국에서의 미국군대의 지위에 관한 협정(SOFA)
전59권. 1966.7.9 서울에서 서명 : 1967.2.9 발효(조약 232호) (V.51 실무교섭회의 합의의사록, 제38-68차, 1964) 153

6. Mr. Chang went on to say that the Korean
negotiators were not concerned about the benefits or
amenities made available to KSC members. What they
were concerned about was that the conditions under which
KSC members are recruited should conform to the Korean
labor laws. Mr. Habib pointed out that under the
existing arrangements, the KSC members are recruited for
the U.S. armed forces by the Korean authorities. The
conditions under which they were recruited were, therefore,
the responsibility of the Korean authorities. He
asked whether the Korean negotiators believed that KSC
members should have the right to strike. Mr. Chang
replied in the affirmative. Mr. Habib pointed out that
KSC members are under military discipline and that the
Korean officers under whom they serve would probably
take a very dim view of giving them the right to strike.
Mr. Habib commented that it appeared that the Korean
negotiators wished to modify the nature of the KSC or
even eliminate it entirely. Mr. Chang stated that there
was no intention on the part of the Korean negotiators
to eliminate the KSC, and indicated that the Korean
Government would continue to provide the KSC labors upon
request by the U.S. armed forces. He emphasised that
the Korean negotiators believed that the KSC labors,
while they are supplied for employment by U.S. military
forces, are entitled to all the priveleges and rights
provided in the Korean labor laws.

7. General O'Connor remarked that in response to
questions asked by the Korean negotiators at the 46th
meeting on March 13, the U.S. negotiators had passed
to the Korean negotiators a fact sheet regarding the
provisions in certain other status of forces agreements

0148

for legal representation by the host government of the
U.S. armed forces in their capacity as employer.

8. Mr. Chang thanked the U.S. negotiators for the
information which had been provided but indicated that
the Korean negotiators wished to ask some questions.
First, the second paragraph of the fact sheet referred
to countries where a system of indirect hire is in
effect. Does this mean that in those countries where direct
hire is in effect, the U.S. Government would be a party
to legal suits under the provisions of the Labor Procurement Article? Major Peckham replied that General Fuller
had already answered that question at an earlier meeting.
Major Peckham said he wished to reiterate the position
of the U.S. Government. That position, an accepted
principle of international law, is that the U.S. Government consents to be sued only in its own courts and not
in the courts of any other nation.

9. General O'Connor pointed out that paragraph 3
of the U.S. draft states that the conditions of employment,
compensation, and the labor-management practices
established by the U.S. armed forces for their employees
shall be in general conformity with the labor laws, customs
and practices of the Republic of Korea. The U.S. armed
forces in Korea have as their objective to be a good
employer. In achieving that objective, they aim to provide
favorable conditions for their Korean personnel to help
develop employee skills and to utilize the Korean
employees as effectively as possible in support of
joint U.S.-ROK security objectives. He said that

0149

Mr. Reed, Director of the Office of Civilian Personnel, was present at the meeting in order to discuss the direct hire personnel system operated by the U.S. armed forces for their Korean work force. General O'Connor remarked that the U.S. negotiators believed that the wage and labor practices to be discussed by Mr. Reed are in general conformity with ROK labor laws and compare favorably with the practices of other employers of Korean personnel.

10. Mr. Reed then read the statement attached to this Agreed Summary as Appendix I.

11. General O'Connor stated that the purpose of Mr. Reed's explanation had been to demonstrate to the Korean negotiators that the U.S. armed forces, as an employer, act in general conformity with Korean laws and practices, as stated in paragraph 3 of the U.S. draft. The U.S. negotiators believed their draft should be satisfactory to both sides, while the Korean draft, based as it was on the Japanese system of indirect hire, was not applicable to the situation in Korea.

12. Mr. Chang stated that Mr. Reed's presentation had been very informative and enlightening. The Korean negotiators did not dispute the fact that the present treatment of Korean employees by the U.S. armed forces is fair and meets the standards of the Korean labor laws. However, the Korean negotiators had to insist that Korean employees should not be treated under the provisions of any other law than Korean law. To apply the provisions of some other country's laws to Korean employees would be an infringement of the sovereignty of the Republic of Korea. This was particularly the case with regard to the matters covered under Sections 5 and 6 of Mr. Reed's statement.

0150

13. Mr. Habib replied that the negotiators were
not negotiating the labor practices mentioned by Mr. Reed.
They were negotiating paragraph 3 of this article.
The U.S. draft of this paragraph stated that the Korean
employees of the U.S. armed forces would be treated
"in general conformity with the labor laws, customs and
practices of the Republic of Korea". Obviously, at any
time the Korean authorities believed that the practices
of the U.S. armed forces were not in conformity with Korean
laws and practices, the Korean authorities could raise the
question in the Joint Committee. In the process of negotiation, each side will have exercised its sovereignty in
agreeing to the provisions of this article. It was
the impression of the U.S. negotiators that the ROK Labor
Office was quite satisfied with the labor practices of the
U.S. armed forces. Mr. Reed confirmed this statement
by Mr. Habib. In fact, said Mr. Reed, the ROK Labor
Office had been particularly satisfied during the past
year. Mr. Habib remarked that it was obvious that the
U.S. armed forces must respect, and have been respecting,
the desire of the Korean authorities to protect the
interests of the Korean employees of the U.S. armed forces.
Paragraph 3 of the U.S. draft will allow the Korean
authorities to take issue with any apparent disparity at
any time, in keeping with the process of constant consultation in the Joint Committee.

14. Mr. Chang stated that as a matter of principle,
any specific aspect of administration in a sovereign state
should be regulated by the laws of that state and not by
the laws of another state. Since the U.S. negotiators had
indicated that the labor practices of the U.S. armed
forces would conform to Korean labor laws, why could the

0151

U.S. negotiators not accept the Korean draft of this
paragraph? The Korean negotiators did not understand
the insistence of the U.S. negotiators on including
the phrase "general conformity".

15. General O'Connor stated that the Korean draft was
addressed to an entirely different type of labor system
than the one that was currently in effect in Korea.
He suggested that informal discussion of this article
might facilitate agreement. He also asked whether the
Korean negotiators wished to state any views concerning
paragraphs 4, 5 and 6 of the U.S. draft, which had no
equivalents in the Korean draft. Mr. Chang stated that
the views of the Korean negotiators regarding those paragraphs
would depend upon the wording ultimately agreed upon
for paragraph 3.

Invited Contractors

16. Turning to the Invited Contractors Article,
Mr. Chang stated that the Korean negotiators had not
changed their intention to limit the application of
this article, insofar as corporations are concerned, to
corporations organized under the laws of the United
States. The Korean negotiators were still prepared, as had
been stated by the Korean Chief Negotiator at the 22nd
meeting, to consider favorably the inclusion of dependents
if the U.S. negotiators were willing to agree to this
limitation on corporations. If the U.S. negotiators would
so agree, the Korean negotiators were prepared to agree
to the following:

0152

a. In paragraph 1, insertion of the words "and the dependents of such persons" following the words "United States";

b. Acceptance of Agreed Minute #2 of the U.S. draft and withdrawal of Agredd Minutes #1 and #2 of the Korean draft;

c. Modification of paragraph 8 of the Korean draft to read as follows: "The Korean authorities shall have the primary right to exercise jurisdiction over the contractors, their employees, and the dependents of such persons referred to in paragraph 1 ... "

d. Acceptance of Agreed Minute #1 of the U.S. draft, in order further to accommodate the desires of the U.S. negotiators.

Mr. Chang stated that in accepting Agreed Minute #2 of the U.S. draft, the Korean negotiators had taken note of the statement by the U.S. negotiators that the U.S. armed forces are gradually replacing third-country contractor employees with Korean nationals and have no intention to bring in any additional third-country nationals after the Agreement comes into force.

17. Mr. Habib remarked that it appeared that the negotiators had come a long way toward agreement on this article. He said the U.S. negotiators would study the Korean proposals and give their views at a later meeting.

18. Mr. Habib noted that the Korean negotiators had not referred to paragraph 3. Recalling that agreement had been reached on the subparagraphs of paragraph 3 from (a) through (h), he wondered why the Korean negotiators

0153

wished to omit subparagraph (i), dealing with driving
permits and vehicle registration. Believing that the
Korean position might be the result of lack of sufficient
details concerning the types and numbers of vehicles
used by the invited contractors, the U.S. negotiators
were prepared to supply that information. Mr. Habib
thereupon passed to the Korean negotiators a table
containing this information. This table is attached to
this Joint Summary as Appendix II. Mr. Habib asked
whether the concern of the Korean negotiators was
centered upon vehicles owned by the employees of the
contractors.

19. Mr. Chang replied that the Korean negotiators
were concerned about vehicles owned by both the employees
and the contractors. Mr. Habib then pointed out that
employee-owned vehicles numbered only 20 out of a total
of 720. He also pointed out that 85% of all the vehicles
used by the contractors were owned by the U.S. Government,
with only 15% owned by the contractors. In reply to
Mr. Chang's question regarding the difference between
government-owned and contractor-owned vehicles, Mr. Habib
replied that there were certain special types of vehicles
required by the contractors for certain kinds of work.
These vehicles were not normally available in Korea
from armed forces sources and therefore were brought in
by the contractors themselves. Mr. Chang thanked Mr.
Habib for the tabulation, which he said would be helpful.
Mr. Chang indicated it was not the ROK Government's
intention to tax U.S. government-owned vehicles, and
that the ROK side would examine the tabulation of invited
contractors vehicles and present the ROK views later.

0154

Security Measures

20. Turning to the Security Measures Article, Mr. Habib noted that the U.S. negotiators had informally discussed with the Korean negotiators certain proposed alternative language which would remove from the text of this article the specific reference to legislation. The U.S. negotiators did not believe that a commitment to legislation was necessary in the article but they did want the negotiating record to show that "such actions" would include legislation, when appropriate; for example, to ensure the security of U.S. Government property.

21. Mr. Chang stated that the alternative langugage suggested by the U.S. negotiators was not acceptable. He suggested certain changes in language which would make the alternative language read as follows:

> "The Republic of Korea will take such actions as it deems necessary, with the cooperation of the United States where appropriate, to ensure the adequate security and protection of the United States Armed Forces, the members thereof, the civilian component, the persons present in the Republic of Korea pursuant to Article ____, their dependents and their property, and the installations, equipment, property, records and official information of the United States, and, as consistent with Article ____, for the punishment of offenders under the applicable laws of the Republic of Korea."

22. Mr. Habib said the U.S. negotiators would study the Korean proposal. However, the language which they had proposed did not appear to impose any obligation on the Republic of Korea to take adequate measures to ensure the security of the U.S. armed forces.

23. It was agreed to hold the next meeting on April 10 at 2:00 p.m.

0155

JOINT SUMMARY RECORD OF THE 49TH SESSION

1. Time and Place: 2:00 - 4:00 P.M. April 10, 1964
   at the Foreign Ministry's Conference
   Room (No.1)

2. Attendants:

ROK Side:

Mr. Chang, Sang Moon	Director European and American Affairs Bureau
Mr. Yoon, Doo Sik	Director Prosecutor's Bureau Ministry of Justice
Mr. Koo, Choong Whay	Chief, American Section Ministry of Foreign Affairs
Mr. Chung, Tai Kyun	Chief Prosecutor's Section Prosecutor's Bureau Ministry of Justice
Col. Kim, Won Kil	Chief, Military Affairs Section Ministry of National Defense
Mr. Lee, Keun Pal (Rapporteur and Interpreter)	3rd Secretary Ministry of Foreign Affairs
Mr. Ahn, Yun Ki	3rd Secretary Ministry of Foreign Affairs
Mr. Lee, Kae Chul	3rd Secretary Ministry of Foreign Affairs
Mr. Park, Won Chul	3rd Secretary Ministry of Foreign Affairs
Mr. Kim, Nai Sung	Staff Officer Europe Section Ministry of Foreign Affairs

U.S. Side:

Mr. Philip C. Habib	Counselor American Embassy
Brig. Gen. G.G. O'Connor	Deputy Chief of Staff 8th U.S. Army
Col. Howard Smigelow	Deputy Chief of Staff 8th U.S. Army

0156

Col. Kenneth C. Crawford	Staff Judge Advocates Office 8th U.S. Army
Capt. John Wayne	Assistant Chief of Staff USN/K
Mr. Benjamin A. Fleck (Rapporteur and Press Officer)	First Secretary American Embassy
Mr. Robert A. Lewis	2nd Secretary American Embassy
Maj. Robert D. Peckham	Staff Officer JAG 8th U.S. Army
Mr. Robert A. Kinney	J-5 8th U.S. Army
Mr. Kenneth Campan	Interpreter

1. Mr. Chang opened the meeting by introducing the following new faces of the Korean negotiating team: Mr. Ahn Yun-ki, Mr. Lee Kae-chul, and Mr. Park Won-chul, all of the Foreign Ministry. Mr. Chang also announced that during the absence of Mr. Chung Woo Young at a training course, the interpreter for the Korean negotiators would be Mr. Lee Keun-pal. Mr. Habib welcomed the new Korean negotiators on behalf of the U.S. negotiators.

Invited Contractors

2. Discussion was begun on the Invited Contractors Article with a series of questions by the Korean negotiators with regard to the tabulation of contractor-used vehicles which the U.S. negotiators had tabled at the previous meeting. These questions elicited the following information from the U.S. negotiators. The vehicles listed in the tabulation as being "contractor-owned" are owned by the legal entity which has signed the contract with the U.S. armed forces. This legal entity is usually a corporation,

0157

although in one or two cases the legal entity may be
an individual contractor. Those vehicles which are
not owned by a legal entity are entered in the
"privately-owned column. The important criterion in
this regard is whether the vehicle is used in the
performance of the contract. Contractor-owned vehicles
are registered in the name of the legal entity; privately-
owned vehicles are registered in the name of the individual
owner. Ownership can be verified by examination of
the ownership certificate, registration certificate,
or insurance papers.

3. Mr. Habib stated that the questions being raised
by the Korean negotiators were matters of administration
and that there would be procedures worked out so that
the Joint Committee could readily obtain such information,
should it so desire. The U.S. negotiators wondered
why the Korean negotiators appeared to be so intent on
distinguishing between contractor-owned and privately-
owned vehicles. What did the Korean negotiators wish
to propose regarding this subject?

4. Mr. Chang replied that the Korean negotiators
wished to know how to distinguish privately-owned
vehicles from the others because they intended to make
the privately-owned vehicles subject to the same Korean
laws and regulations as those owned by ordinary aliens, while
according certain privileges only to the vehicles which
were used by the contractors in the performance of their
contracts.

5. Mr. Habib replied that the U.S. negotiators
were prepared to listen to the proposal of the Korean

0158

negotiators. However, the U.S. negotiators wished to make clear that the owners of these privately-owned vehicles were not ordinary aliens. For the purposes of the Agreement, a contractor is in Korea solely to perform a contract for the U.S. armed forces. He can not, therefore, be considered to be in the same category as the ordinary foreign resident.

6. Mr. Chang replied that the Korean negotiators had already agreed to accord those privileges enumerated in Paragraph 3, except subparagraph (i) to the invited contractors as well as to members of the U.S. armed forces and the civilian component; they were not, therefore, equating the contractors with ordinary aliens. However, the taxes and fees connected with registration and licensing of vehicles were local assessments and a distinction should be made, therefore, between privately-owned vehicles and others. The privately-owned vehicles should be subject to the same fees and regulations as those owned by ordinary aliens.

7. Mr. Habib said the U.S. negotiators understood the Korean position. The Korean negotiators, however, should take into account the fact that 90% of the contracts are on a cost plus fixed fee basis. This means that if a contractor purchases a vehicle for use in fulfilling the contract, the U.S. Government bears the cost. Consequently, contractors are not permitted to have more vehicles than are necessary.

Criminal Jurisdiction

8. Turning to the Criminal Jurisdiction Article, Mr. Habib recalled that at the last previous meeting

0159

devoted to this article, discussion had not been
completed on paragraph 3. He suggested, therefore,
that discussion be resumed with subparagraph (a)(ii),
which dealt with the question of duty offenses. During
the previous discussinn, the Korean negotiators had
stated that they would not insist that the definition
of duty, as contained in the circular published by the
U.S. Army, Far East in January, 1956, be included in
the text of the Agreement or in the Agreed Minutes.
The Korean chief negotiator had stated that if agreement could be reached on that definition, there would be
no problem in solving this matter. The U.S. negotiators
had considered the Korean suggestion that the definition
might be included in the negotiating record. They
believed that this might offer a sound and satisfactory
way of handling the problem. Therefore, if the Korean
negotiators would accept the Agreed Minute #2 in the
U.S. draft re paragraph 3(a), the U.S. negotiators
agreed that the following definition could be placed
in the negotiating record as the basis on which duty
certificates would be issued:

> "The term 'official duty' as used in Article___
> and the Agreed Minutes is not meant to include all
> acts by members of the Armed Forces and the
> civilian component during periods when they are on
> duty, but is meant to apply only to acts which
> are required to be done as functions of those
> duties which the individuals are performing.
> Thus, a substantial departure from the acts a
> person is required to perform in a particular
> duty usually will indicate an act outside of his
> 'official duty'".

Mr. Habib called the attention of the Korean negotiators
to the fact that the above definition was based on the
full text of the definition which had appeared in the
Army circular which they had cited, and not on the
partial text suggested by the Korean negotiators.

0160

9. Mr. Chang stated that the Korean negotiators would examine the U.S. proposal and give their views at a later meeting. He suggested that the negotiators resume their paragraph by paragraph consideration of this article.

10. Mr. Habib agreed to continue paragraph by paragraph discussion but stated that the U.S. negotiators would like to deviate from the exact sequence of the paragraphs in order to clarify the thinking of each side on specific points at issue. In order to enable the U.S. negotiators to expedite consideration of certain key issues, therefore, he wished to refer to paragraph 9 and its related Agreed Minutes. At the 47th negotiating meeting, the Korean negotiators had stated that they accepted the principle of enumerating trial safeguards in the Agreement but that they did not necessarily agree with the actual enumeration in the U.S. draft. The U.S. negotiators would like to know what specific portions of that enumeration were objectionable to the Korean negotiators.

11. Mr. Chang replied that there was no serious difference of opinion with regard to the text of paragraph 9. However, the enumeration in the related Agreed Minute caused the Korean negotiators some difficulties, which they would clarify in the near future. They wished to know whether the enumeration in the Agreed Minute could be converted into an understanding in the negotiating record.

12. Mr. Habib replied that this matter was of fundamental importance, so far as the United States

한·미국 간의 상호방위조약 제4조에 의한 시설과 구역 및 한국에서의 미국군대의 지위에 관한 협정(SOFA)
전59권. 1966.7.9 서울에서 서명 : 1967.2.9 발효(조약 232호) (V.51 실무교섭회의 합의의사록, 제38-68차, 1964) 167

Government was concerned. Trial safeguards lie at the heart of the question of jurisdiction. This matter was of such great concern to the U.S. authorities, including the Congress, that the U.S. negotiators must insist that the enumeration of trial safeguards be retained in the text of the Agreement and the Agreed Minutes, rather than placed in the negotiating record.

13. Mr. Chang stated that the Korean negotiators would make their specific views on this matter known at a later meeting. Briefly expressed, they were of the opinion that the enumeration in the Agreed Minute overlapped that contained in paragraph 9, which was extensive, and that the enumeration in the Agreed Minute could therefore be incorporated into the negotiating record.

14. The negotiators then resumed paragraph by paragraph examination of the texts, beginning with paragraph 3(b). The use of the term "military authorities of the United States" in the Korean draft, as compared with "authorities of the United States" in the U.S. draft was found to occur in paragraphs 4, 5(a), 5(b), 6(a), 6(b), 7(a) and 7(b). It was agreed that when the question of usage was finally decided, the same usage would be used in all of these paragraphs.

15. Subparagraphs (b) and (c) of paragraph 3 were found to be identical. In paragraph 4, it was noted that the word "armed" had been omitted from the phrase "armed forces" in the Korean draft. Mr. Habib pointed out that the term "armed forces" is used throughout the Agreement and should be considered, therefore, to be the standard usage.

0162

16. In paragraph 5(a), Mr. Habib pointed out that the U.S. draft uses the language "have custody" while the Korean draft uses "exercise jurisdiction". This difference arises out of the differing provisions in the two drafts with regard to custody. When the question of language relating to custody is settled, agreement on the language of paragraph 5(a) will be almost automatic.

17. Mr. Habib noted that paragraph 5(b) of the Korean draft omitted the word "promptly". The U.S. negotiators believed that it was important that there should be prompt notification of arrest. Mr. Chang stated that the Korean negotiators believed this to be a reciprocal matter and that if the U.S. military authorities promptly notified the ROK authorities, as provided for in paragraph 5(c) of the Korean draft, the ROK authorities would reciprocate.

18. Mr. Habib replied that paragraph 5(c) of the Korean draft had no counterpart in the U.S. draft. Nor did it have any precedents in the NATO Agreement or the Agreement with Japan, the reason being that it imposes on the U.S. military forces an onerous requirement which serves no fundamental purpose. The absence of such a provision has created no problems in the countries mentioned but its inclusion in this Agreement would undoubtedly create problems. Why did the Korean negotiators wish to include it? Mr. Chang replied that he would give the Korean views on this question at a subsequent meeting.

0163

19. Mr. Habib pointed out that the U.S. draft of paragraph 5(c) used the phrase "a dependent" instead of the phrase "their dependents" which appeared in the Korean draft. The U.S. negotiators considered "a dependent" to be standard usage and preferable. Mr. Chung said the Korean negotiators accepted usage of the phrase "a dependent".

20. With regard to paragraph 5(c) of the U.S. draft and its counterpart, 5(d) of the Korean draft, Mr. Habib stated that in these provisions the question of custody arises. Whereas, the U.S. language provides procedure for retention of custody by the U.S. authorities, the Korean language is a considerable revision of the similar paragraphs in the NATO and Japanese Agreements and provides for a handing over to Korean custody upon the issuance of a warrant. Mr. Habib added that the U.S. negotiators do not believe that retention of custody by the U.S. authorities will interfere with the course of justice. On the contrary, they believe that such a provision has much to commend it. This is a matter of major, substantial interest to the U.S. Government. The U.S. authorities have reservations about existing Korean facilities for both pre-trial and post-trial custody. He noted that the proposal for post-trial custody, contained in the last sentence of the U.S. draft of paragraph 5(c), was a response to indications given by earlier Korean negotiators that they would prefer that post-trial custody not be a Korean responsibility and that they would welcome a provision such as this one. The U.S. negotiators believed that

0164

neither pre-trial nor post-trial custody by the
U.S. authorities would interfere with the judicial
proceedings. Furthermore, they saw many advantages
to the proposal.

21. Mr. Chang asked whether the phrase in the U.S.
draft "pending completion of all judicial proceedings"
was intended to include all the proceedings of the
trial or trials up to final sentencing. If that were
the case, the phrase "until custody is requested by
the authorities of the Republic of Korea " would have
no meaning at all. Mr. Habib replied that the phrase
meant until all appellate proceedings have been completed.

22. It was noted that paragraph 6(a) and (b)
and paragraph 7(a) were identical except for the aforementioned inclusion of the word "military" from before
the word "authorities" in the Korean draft.

23. In paragraph 7(b), Mr. Habib noted that there were
two additional sentences in the U.S. draft, relating back
to paragraph 5(c). If agreement were reached on post-
trial custody, he explained, these two sentences would
be essential, since without them the U.S. authorities
could not carry out post-trial custody. He also pointed
out that these provisions did not indicate any intention
on the part of the U.S. authorities to avoid just
punishment of convicted offenders.

24. It was noted that the two drafts of paragraph 8
were identical, except for the inclusion of "military"
and the omission of "armed" in the Korean draft and the
addition in the U.S. draft of the words "his sentence
has been remitted or suspended, or he". In this connection,
Mr. Chang requested an explanation of the terms

0165

suspension, remission, and pardon, which was provided by Colonel Crawford.

25. It was noted that the two drafts of paragraph 9 were identical, except for some minor changes of wording in subparagraphs (e) and (f) of the Korean draft.

26. It was noted that the two drafts of paragraph 10(a) were identical. Mr. Habib noted that paragraph 10 (b) of the Korean draft would not give the U.S. armed forces the authority to maintain discipline and order among other elements of the United Nations Command, such as the Thai and Turk contingents. Noting that the situation in this regard in Korea was perhaps unique, Mr. Habib pointed out that the U.S. draft was also not satisfactory. However, the U.S. draft did provide additional authority to the U.S. military police to ensure the security of members of the U.S. armed forces outside of their facilities and areas. He said the U.S. negotiators would consider this matter and submit suggested changes at a later date.

27. Mr. Habib pointed out that there was no counterpart in the Korean draft to paragraph 11 in the U.S. draft. Mr. Chang replied that the Korean negotiators had not yet decided whether to agree to the inclusion of this paragraph in the Criminal Jurisdiction Article or to make it a separate article. When they reached a decision, they would table their proposed draft.

28. Mr. Habib pointed out that there also was no counterpart in the Korean draft for paragraph 12

0166

of the U.S. draft. He said that provisions such as those in paragraph 12 were normal in such agreements. Mr. Chang replied that the Korean negotiators agreed in principle with the provisions of paragraph 12.

29. Mr. Chang asked if it would be possible for the U.S. negotiators to provide the Korean negotiators with the texts of the arrangements, agreements, and practices referred to in the preamble to the Agreed Minutes in the U.S. draft. Mr. Habib replied that there was no precise and complete text which applied to current arrangements or practices. It was agreed that the Korean negotiators should meet informally with Colonel Crawford for an explanation of existing arrangements and practices.

30. It was decided to leave paragraph by paragraph discussion of the Agreed Minutes until the next meeting, which was scheduled for April 17 at 2:00 p.m.

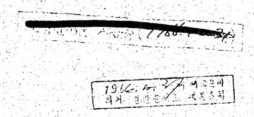

한·미국 간의 상호방위조약 제4조에 의한 시설과 구역 및 한국에서의 미국군대의 지위에 관한 협정(SOFA) 전59권. 1966.7.9 서울에서 서명 : 1967.2.9 발효(조약 232호) (V.51 실무교섭회의 합의의사록, 제38-68차, 1964)

JOINT SUMMARY RECORD OF THE 50TH SESSION

1. Time and Place: 3:00 - 4:45 P.M. April 23, 1964
                   at the Foreign Ministry's Conference
                   Room (No.1)

2. Attendants:

ROK Side:

Mr. Chang, Sang Moon   Director
                              European and American Affairs
                              Bureau

Mr. Koo, Choong Whay   Chief, American Section
                              Ministry of Foreign Affairs

Mr. Oh, Jae Hee   Chief, Treaty Section
                              Ministry of Foreign Affairs

Mr. Chung, Tai Kyun   Chief
                              Prosecutor's Section
                              Prosecutor's Bureau
                              Ministry of Justice

Mr. Lee, Myung Hi   Prosecutor
                              Prosecutor's Bureau
                              Ministry of Justice

Maj. Lee, Kye Hoon   Military Affairs Section
                              Ministry of National Defense

Mr. Lee, Keun Pal   3rd Secretary
(Rapporteur and   Ministry of Foreign Affairs
 Interpreter)

Mr. Lee, Kae Chul   3rd Secretary
                              Ministry of Foreign Affairs

Mr. Park, Won Chul   3rd Secretary
                              Ministry of Foreign Affairs

Mr. Kim, Nai Sung   Staff Officer
                              Europe Section
                              Ministry of Foreign Affairs

U.S. Side:

Mr. Philip C. Habib   Counselor
                              American Embassy

Brig. Gen. G.G. O'Connor   Deputy Chief of Staff
                              8th U.S. Army

Col. Howard Smigelow   Deputy Chief of Staff
                              8th U.S. Army

0168

r

Col. Kenneth C. Crawford	Staff Judge Advocates Office 8th U.S. Army
Capt. John Wayne	Assistant Chief of Staff USN/K
Mr. Benjamin A. Fleck (Rapporteur and Press Officer)	First Secretary American Embassy
Mr. Robert A. Lewis	2nd Secretary American Embassy
Mr. James Sartorius	2nd Secretary American Embassy
Maj. Robert D. Peckham	Staff Officer JAG 8th U.S. Army
Mr. Robert A. Kinney	J-5 8th U.S. Army
Mr. Kenneth Campen	Interpreter

1. Mr. Chang opened the meeting by introducing
Major YI Kae-hun, who was sitting in for Colonel Kim Won-kil.

2. Taking up the Criminal Jurisdiction Article,
Mr. Chang stated that the Korean side was ready to respond
to the remarks made by the United States negotiators
at the previous meeting concerning trial safeguards.
Mr. Chang then made the following statement:

a. The provision of Agreed Minute #1 re Paragraph
9 of the Korean draft guarantees to all persons on
trial in Korean courts not only those rights enumerated
in paragraph 9 of the main text tabled by the United
States negotiators, but also such other rights as are provided
under the Constitution and laws of the Republic of Korea.
Therefore, the Korean negotiators, with the view to
eliminating unnecessary and duplicate enumeration, propose
the deletion of the following trial safeguards and rights
enumerated in the U.S. agreed minutes: the first sentence
of the Agreed Minute re Paragraph 9(a), the latter part
of the second paragraph/the Agreed Minute re Paragraph

0169

9(b), the Agreed Minute re Paragraph 9(c) and (d), the
Agreed Minute re Paragraph 9(f), the first paragraph of the
Agreed Minute re Paragraph 9, the additional rights
enumerated in subparagraphs (b), (c), (d), (g), (h), (j)
and the remaining paragraphs of the Agreed Minute re
Paragraph 9, except the third and fourth paragraphs.

      b. The following provisions are either objectionable
or questionable from the view point of relevant laws and
regulations currently in effect and our views and
counter-proposals on these provisions were presented.

      (1) <u>Re paragraph 9(a)</u>

      With respect to a military tribunal
provided in the second sentence of the Agreed Minute
re Paragraph 9(a), the Korean negotiators would like
to withhold their views until such time as the matter
would be taken up in connection with the text of Paragraph
2 at a subsequent meeting.

      (2) <u>Re paragraph 9(b)</u>

      The Korean negotiators propose to delete
the sentence with respect to the right to be informed a
reasonable time prior to trial of the nature of the evidence
that is to be used against the accused since there is
no counterpart provision in the Korean code of criminal
procedures and it is contrary to the spirit of the
existing Law. However, in accordance with the provisions
of articles 291, 292, 293, 296 and 307 of the Korean
Code of Criminal Procedure, during the proceedings of
a trial, the nature of the evidence is informed to the
accused.

      (3) <u>Re paragraph 9(e)</u>

      If the United States negotiators delete
the word "confidentially" from the draft, the Korean

0170

negotiators will have no objection to the right to legal representation. The present Korean system requires placing the accused under surveillance of the competent officer during the interview. However, such presence of an officer shall not in any way interfere with the right of a counsel to communicate freely with the accused.

(4) Re paragraph 9(g)

1) The Korean negotiators guarantee that a representative of the Government, a counsel, an interpreter, and the accused himself are all given the right to be present at all of the judicial proceedings. Therefore, it is entirely within the scope of discretion on the part of such a representative whether or not to exercise the already granted right. The Korean negotiators deem it extremely unfair that the absence of a representative of his own accord nullifies the statements of the accused, whereas the absence of a representative and the admissibility of statements as valid evidence are different matters. The Korean negotiators, therefore, propose to delete the sentence "and no statement of the accused taken in the absence of such a representative shall be admissible as evidence in support of the guilt of the accused."

2) The second Agreed Minute re Paragraph 9 of the Korean draft regarding a public trial should be included as an additional sentence in the Agreed Minute re Paragraph 9(g) of the U.S. draft so that the provision of that Agreed Minute may not prejudice the provisions of article 105 of the Constitution and article 53 of the Court Organization Law. While these provisions guarantee that trials and decisions of the courts shall be open

한·미국 간의 상호방위조약 제4조에 의한 시설과 구역 및 한국에서의 미국군대의 지위에 관한 협정(SOFA) 전59권. 1966.7.9 서울에서 서명 : 1967.2.9 발효(조약 232호) (V.51 실무교섭회의 합의의사록, 제38-68차, 1964) 177

0171

to the public, they also provide that trials may be
closed to the public by a court decision when there is a
possibility that open trials may disturb the public safety
and order or be harmful to decent customs.

(5) Additional right (a)

The Korean negotiators are prepared to
accept the U.S. draft with the understanding that U.S.
side would bear the expenses incurred in accordance
with the provision of Article 56-2 of the Korean Code
of Criminal Procedure.

(6) Additional right (e)

The Korean negotiators propose the deletinn
of the subparagraph with respect to the right thet the
accused shall not be subject to a heavier penalty than
the one that was applicable at the time the alleged
criminal offense was committed. The Korean negotiators
have no objection to it; however, regarding the latter
part of subparagraph (e), it would be contrary to the
spirit of the judicial appeal system, if a prosecutor,
defender of public interests, were not permitted to appeal
to a higher court when he considers the amount of
punishment or the judgement of facts are not proper.
Consequently, a heavier penalty may be imposed by a
higher court when appeal of a prosecutor is granted.
Therefore, the Korean negotiators propose the U.S.
draft be replaced by the following:

"shall not be subject to a heavier penalty
than the one that was applicable at the time the alleged
criminal offense was committed or was adjudged by the
court of the first instance as the original sentence when
an appeal of a case is made by or on behalf of the
accused."

0172

(7) <u>Additional right (f)</u>

The Korean negotiators wish to hear clarification of the meaning of the phraseology "requirement of proof."

(8) <u>Additional right (i)</u>

The Korean negotiators interpret the U.S. draft as implying merely that U.S. offenders should not be subject to punishment other than the decision of a judicial court. If the interpretation is correct, and concurred in the by U.S. side, the Korean side may further consider the U.S. draft.

(9) <u>Additional right (k)</u>

With respect to the provision of sub-paragraph (k), the Korean negotiators propose the following alternative draft:

"shall be entitled to request the postponement of his presence at a trial if he is physically or mentally unfit to stand trial and participate in his defense;"

The U.S. version does not preclude a possibility of abuses of such right as provided in U.S. draft by the accused. Furthermore, the Korean negotiators deem it proper for the court to give consideration to the request of the accused and approve the postponement of trial. The above proposal is also compatible with the provision of article 306 of the Korean Code of Criminal Procedure regarding the suspension of procedure of public trial on the basis of mental or physical unfitness.

(10) 1) Regarding the right provided in the third paragraph of the Agreed Minute re Paragraph 9, the Korean negotiators propose the deletion of the word "improper" from the U.S. draft to avoid the ambiguity of the meaning of the word.

0173

2) With respect to the right provided
in the fourth paragraph of the Agreed Minute re Paragraph
9, the Korean negotiators propose the deletion of the
provision for the reason explained in the clause of
additional right (e). Article 361 and 383 of the Korean
Code of Criminal Procedure enumerate reasons of appeal
to an appellate or the Supreme Court respectively.

3. Mr. Habib thanked the Korean negotiators for
their detailed presentation of their views on this subject.
He said the U.S. negotiators would study Mr. Chang's
remarks carefully before making a point-by-point response.
However, they would like to clarify and reach agreement on
certain basic principles underlying the matter of trial
safeguards. The Korean negotiators had just stated the
position that rights enumerated in the Constitution of the
Republic of Korea need not be enumerated in the Status of
Forces Agreement. The United States negotiators were of
the opinion that if certain rights are enumerated in the
ROK Constitution, there is no question but that they should
also be enumerated in the SOFA. This should not be
considered unnecessary duplication. The first principle,
therefore, on which the U.S. negotiators sought agreement
was the principle that a trial safeguard or other right can
be included in the SOFA, regardless of whether it is or is
not stated in the ROK Constitution. The U.S. negotiators
believed that the Korean negotiators were willing to
agree to this principle.

4. Mr. Habib pointed out that the question of
including in the SOFA rights which were not included
in the body of ROK law or mentioned in the ROK Constitution
was a separate matter. The grant of jurisdiction by the
U.S. Government does not imply that the U.S. Government

0174

is prepared to allow its people to be subject to trial
procedures contrary to U.S. law, custom or practice.
The U.S. negotiators presumed that this was a subject
for negotiation and that the Korean negotiators were prepared to negotiate. He pointed out that if the negotiations
resulted in agreement on inclusion in the SOFA of safeguards
not found in the ROK penal code but deemed necessary for
the protection of members of the U.S. armed forces, the
ROK penal code could be adjusted to bring it into accord
with the SOFA. He reminded the negotiators that they
were not negotiating the treatment of Korean citizens.
They were negotiating the treatment of American servicemen
who were in Korea through no choice of their own under the
terms of a treaty of mutual security. As an example of
the type of question under discussion, Mr. Habib pointed
out that confessions obtained illegally or improperly
were admitted as evidence in trials in the Republic of
Korea but not in the United States.

     5. Summing up, Mr. Habib stated that the U.S.
negotiators sought agreement to the following two principles:

     a. Rights included in the ROK Constitution
can be included specifically in the Status of Forces
Agreement; and

     b. Rights not mentioned in the ROK Constitution
or included in Korean laws can be included in the Status
of Forces Agreement.

Mr. Habib emphasized that the U.S. negotiators were not
seeking any violation of the ROK Constitution but were attempting to negotiate a SOFA which would provide the safeguards
for members of the U.S. armed forces which the U.S.
Government considers essential. The negotiation of such

0175

an agreement is in consonance with both the ROK Constitution and the U.S. Constitution and with accepted principles of international law. The U.S. negotiators would like to hear the views of the Korean negotiators regarding these principles.

6. Mr. Chang replied that the Korean negotiators believed that the major trial safeguards were listed in paragraph 9 of the Criminal Jurisdiction Article. They believed that rights already guaranteed in Korean laws and the ROK Constitution should not be enumerated in an Agreed Minute in addition to being enumerated in the text of the article and they considered it unnecessary duplication. They also wished to point out that the Agreed Minute proposed by the U.S. negotiators contained provisions not found in other status of forces agreements. Since the U.S. negotiators had emphasized the importance which they attached to the first principle mentioned by Mr. Habib, the Korean negotiators would take it into consideration to work out a mutually acceptable solution.

7. With regard to the second principle stated by Mr. Habib, Mr. Chang said that inclusion of rights not mentioned in Korean law was subject to negotiation. Inasmuch as inclusion of such rights in the SOFA would necessitate amendment of the Korean laws, the Korean negotiators wished to minimize the number of exceptional Laws.

8. Mr. Habib expressed satisfaction with Mr. Chang's reply.

9. Mr. Chang said the Korean negotiators found the term "improper means" to be ambiguous since they believe the meaning of the term "improper means" was included in the meaning of the term "illegal means". How did it differ from "illegal means". Colonel Crawford replied that "illegal means" were means that were clearly again 0176

the law. "Improper means" referred to methods and procedures that were considered by a U.S. judge to be not up to an acceptable standard. He said that the two terms were synonymous for all practical purposes.

10. Mr. Habib stated that the negotiators had established two very helpful principles. The U.S. negotiators would study the statement made by Mr. Chang at the beginning of the meeting and would present their views at the next meeting. The U.S. negotiators had always assumed that whatever provisions were finally agreed to might require Korean legislation and that the ROK Government was prepared to seek such legislation.

11. It was then agreed to begin paragraph-by-paragraph discussion of the Agreed Minutes. Mr. Habib briefly reviewed the three Agreed Minutes re Paragraph 1(b), which have no counterparts in the Korean draft. The first of these would provide for the establishment of a "combat zone". This proposal and the Korean opposition to it constitute one of the fundamental differences in the two drafts.

12. Mr. Habib pointed out that the second Agreed Minute re Paragraph 1(b) would suspend the Criminal Jurisdiction Article during periods of martial law. He said that martial law would be relevant only to Korean citizens and that there was no reason to presume any requirement that the ROK Government should exercise martial law rights over U.S. personnel. Under the provisions of the ROK Constitution, the declaration of martial law is an extraordinary procedure.

0177

13. As a practical matter, Mr. Habib continued, the third Agreed Minute re Paragraph 1(b), which would prevent the application of the SOFA to offenses committed outside Korea, is relatively unimportant. However, it is techinically desirable because Korean law provides for the punishment of such offenses.

14. Mr. Chang replied that the Korean negotiators had already explained their opposition to the establishment of a combat zone. He asked how many duty and non-duty offenses had been committed during the past year in the area which the U.S. negotiators wished to designate as a combat zone. Mr. Habib said the U.S. negotiators would provide whatever data were available.

15. With regard to martial law, Mr. Chang pointed out that it was declared only in times of national emergency and that it applied to all persons resident in the Republic of Korea, not just to ROK citizens. With regard to offenses committed outside the Republic of Korea, Mr. Chang said that the third Agreed Minute proposed by the U.S. negotiators was incompatible with Article 5 of the ROK Criminal Code. Such a provision would prejudice the judicial rights of the ROK Government and would constitute a major infringement on ROK sovereignty. Therefore it was unacceptable. Mr. Chang stated that Article 5 provides for the punishment of aliens who violate, while outside ROK territory, ROK laws dealing with insurrection, aggression, the national flag, currency, securities, documents and seals. He pointed out that there was in other status of forces agreements no provision similar to the proposed third Agreed Minute. He said the Korean negotiators would present at a later meeting counter-proposals to the first and second Agreed Minutes re Paragraph1(b) proposed by the U.S. negotiators.

0178

16. Mr. Habib replied that it was clear that the U.S. negotiators have no intention of infringing on Korean sovereignty. He again explained that conclusion of the Status of Forces Agreement would be an act of Korean sovereignty, not an infringement on it.

17. Turning to the Agreed Minute re Paragraph 2, which also had no counterpart in the Korean draft, Mr. Habib stated that this Minute would provide for voluntary waiver of jurisdiction by the ROK Government in cases in which it enjoyed exclusive jurisdiction. He said the U.S. negotiators wished to emphasize the word voluntary in this connection. Unless this provision were included in the SOFA, the U.S. authorities would be unable to assume jurisdiction if the ROK authorities wished to waive.

18. Mr. Chang replied that the Korean negotiators had no difficulty in accepting the principle of voluntary waiver of exclusive jurisdiction. However, they believed that some arrangement could be worked out without spelling it out in an Agreed Minute. Mr. Habib replied that the U.S. negotiators would explore the legality of such an arrangement.

19. Mr. Habib pointed out that the U.S. and Korean drafts of the Agreed Minute re Paragraph 2(c) were identical in substance.

20. Mr. Habib stated that another basic difference in the two drafts lay in the Agreed Minute re Paragraph 3 proposed by the U.S. negotiators. He stated that the exercise of the waiver of jurisdiction has developed to a high degree in the countries where the United States has status of forces agreements. In Japan, for instance, over 90% of the cases are waived by the Japanese Government. The U.S. negotiators believe that the Korean authorities do not intend to try all cases and do intend to exercise

0179

the right of waiver. The U.S. Agreed Minute would provide that the ROK Government could seek a recall of waiver in those cases in which it wished to exercise jurisdiction. The presumption in the Korean draft is that in cases of particular importance to the ROK Government, it will not waive its jurisdiction. In the U.S. draft, the presumption is that in such cases, the ROK Government will recall its waiver. The ROK Government is interested in establishing its right to exercise jurisdiction; this would be spelled out in the text of the Article. The U.S. negotiators are interested in obtaining a maximum degree of waiver in order to maintain discipline and order among the U.S. armed forces.

21. Mr. Chang replied that the ROK authorities, as he had already indicated, were willing to waive in as many cases as other governments. The status of forces agreements with Japan and the NATO countries do not contain this provision; yet they waive jurisdiction in a high percentage of cases. There is no reason why the Korean authorities should not do the same. Furthermore, the Korean negotiators did not like this particular provision because it would not permit them to exercise the right of recall of waiver without going through the Joint Committee. The Korean negotiators would present a counter-proposal at the next meeting.

22. Turning to the Agreed Minutes re Paragraph 3(a), Mr. Habib stated that the first of these reflected the concern of the U.S. negotiators over the fact that the Korean draft of the Criminal Jurisdiction Article would provide that members of the U.S. armed forces would be subject to treatment different from that to which members of the ROK armed

0180

forces would be subject. Korean soldiers would be subject to trial by court martial for the same offenses for which U.S. soldiers would be subject to trial by Korean civil courts. He asked the Korean negotiators to consider the case of two friends, one an American soldier, the other a KATUSA soldier who were spending some off-duty time together and happened to get into a fight with some third party. The KATUSA soldier would be tried by court martial but the American would be haled before a Korean court, under the provisions of the Korean draft.

23. Regarding the second Agreed Minute re Paragraph 3 (a), Mr. Habib reminded the Korean negotiators that the U.S. negotiators had made a proposal at the last meeting to agree to insert the definition of official duty into the negotiating record, provided the Korean negotiators would accept the second Agreed Minute re Paragraph 3(a) in the U.S. draft. He asked for the comments of the Korean negotiators regarding this proposal.

24. Mr. Chang replied that the Korean negotiators believed that the definition of official duty should be considered to be a separate matter from that of the issuance of a duty certificate. They did not agree, therefore, to the proposal of the U.S. negotiators. However, they had no objection to inclusion in the summery record of the definition of official duty tabled by the U.S. negotiators at the previous meeting without refferring to the issuance of a duty certificate. They would present a counter-proposal at the next meeting.

25. Mr. Habib stated that in principle, the U.S. negotiators had no objection to the Agreed Minute re Paragraph 4 in the Korean draft, to which there was no

한·미국 간의 상호방위조약 제4조에 의한 시설과 구역 및 한국에서의 미국군대의 지위에 관한 협정(SOFA) 187
전59권. 1966.7.9 서울에서 서명 : 1967.2.9 발효(조약 232호) (V.51 실무교섭회의 합의의사록, 제38-68차, 1964)

counterpart in the U.S. draft. However, the word
"dependents" was missing. The U.S. negotiators would
comment further on this matter after consulting Washington.

26. Mr. Habib stated that the Agreed Minute re
Paragraph 5(b) in the Korean draft was related to the ques-
tion of pre-trial custody. From the point of view of the
U.S. negotiators, this Agreed Minute was not necessary.
However, when a decision was finally reached on pre-trial
custody, the fate of this Agreed Minute would be determined.

27. Turning to the Agreed Minutes re Paragraph 6,
Mr. Habib stated that the first Minute of the Korean draft
was much too broad in definition, for it would make officers
of the United States subject to account before Korean
courts for their conduct of the official business of the
United States and could require them to bring official
records of the United States into court in response to a
summons. He said such a provision was not found in any other
SOFA. The U.S. negotiators believed it to be an unreasonable
requirement. Also, the second Agreed Minute of the Korean
draft would place an obligation on witnesses somewhat similar
to extradition proceedings. The U.S. negotiators did
not believe that the Korean negotiators really intended
that the U.S. armed forces would be obligated to return a
serviceman from any place in the world if he were wanted
as a witness in the course of an investigation or trial in
Korea.

28. Mr. Habib pointed out that Agreed Minute #3 re
Paragraph 6 in the U.S. draft has a precedent in the SOFA
with the Federal Republic of Germany. The experience of
the U.S. armed forces has shown that occasionally an

official of either government may be summoned to testify and may be asked questions which affect the security of his government. The U.S. negotiators believe that the Korean negotiators would not want a Korean official to disclose such matters before a U.S. court-martial. Nor does the U.S. Government want its officials to be forced to disclose such matters before Korean courts.

29. Finally, Mr. Habib pointed out that while courts-martial in the United States have the authority to issue a summons, they cannot do so in Korea. Therefore, the U.S. negotiators, in the fifth paragraph of Agreed Minute #1 re Paragraph 6, were proposing language to make this possible through the offices of the ROK Government.

30. Mr. Chang requested an explanation of the term "military exigency" used in Agreed Minute #1 re Paragraph 6 of the U.S. draft.

31. Mr. Habib replied that the certificate provided for by the U.S. draft would state why a witness could not appear at the exact time for which he had been summoned and how long he would be unavailable. The U.S. armed forces would not be arbitrary in this matter and would not avail themselves of this provision in a capricious manner. Under the circumstances in which the U.S. armed forces were present in Korea, it was quite possible that his military duties would prevent a soldier from appearing as a witness at the exact time or on the precise day specified in a summons. He said that this provision was intended to apply to individual cases and did not carry any connotation of general emergency conditions.

32. Mr. Chang remarked that the U.S. draft of this Agreed Minute referred to both witnesses and defendants.

0183

Mr. Habib replied that the U.S. armed forces would be bound by this provision to produce the defendant as well as witnesses. Mr. Chang replied that the Korean negotiators would give their views regarding this Agreed Minute at the next meeting. At this point, the meeting was adjourned.

33. It was agreed to hold the next meeting on May 1 at 2:00 p.m.

0184

JOINT SUMMARY RECORD OF THE 51ST SESSION

1. Time and Place: 2:00 - 4:00 P.M. May 5, 1964 at
                   the Foreign Ministry's Conference
                   Room (No.1)

2. Attendants:

   ROK Side:

   Mr. Chang, Sang Moon   Director
                                 European and American Affairs
                                 Bureau

   Mr. Koo, Choong Whay   Chief, American Section
                                 Ministry of Foreign Affairs

   Mr. Oh, Jae Hee   Chief, Treaty Section
                                 Ministry of Foreign Affairs

   Mr. Choo, Moon Ki   Chief
                                 Legal Affairs Section
                                 Ministry of Justice

   Mr. Cho, Choong Hoon   Chief
                                 Customs Section
                                 Ministry of Finance

   Maj. Lee, Kye Hoon   Military Affairs Section
                                 Ministry of National Defense

   Mr. Chung, Woo Young   3rd Secretary
   (Rapporteur and   Ministry of Foreign Affairs
    Interpreter)

   Mr. Lee, Kae Chul   3rd Secretary
                                 Ministry of Foreign Affairs

   Mr. Whang, Young Chae   3rd Secretary
                                 Ministry of Foreign Affairs

   Mr. Park, Won Chul   3rd Secretary
                                 Ministry of Foreign Affairs

   U.S. Side:

   Mr. Philip C. Habib   Counselor
                                 American Embassy

   Brig. Gen. G.G. O'Connor   Deputy Chief of Staff
                                 8th U.S. Army

   Col. Howard Smigelow   Deputy Chief of Staff
                                 8th U.S. Army

0185

Col. Kenneth C. Crawford	Staff Judge Advocates Office 8th U.S. Army
Capt. John Wayne	Assistant Chief of Staff USN/K
Mr. Benjamin A. Fleck (Rapporteur and Press Officer)	First Secretary American Embassy
Mr. Robert A. Lewis	2nd Secretary American Embassy
Mr. James Sartorius	2nd Secretary American Embassy
Maj. Robert D. Peckham	Staff Officer JAG 8th U.S. Army
Mr. Robert A. Kinney	J-5 8th U.S. Army

1. Mr. Chang opened the meeting by introducing Mr. Cho, Choong Hoon, Chief of the Customs Section, Ministry of Finance, who was attending the meeting in place of Mr. Sin Kwan-sop; and Mr. Hwang, Young Chae of the America Section, Ministry of Foreign Affairs. Mr. Habib welcomed these gentlemen to the negotiations.

Local Procurement

2. Taking up the article on Local Procurement, Mr. Habib recalled that at the 46th negotiating meeting the Korean negotiators had made certain suggestions for revision of the U.S. draft. He said the U.S. negotiators were prepared to respond to those suggestions. The U.S. negotiators also wished to introduce some non-substantive changes in wording in paragraph 1 in order to make the language of that paragraph consistent with the wording of paragraphs 2 and 3 and with the new Agreed Minute #4 proposed by the Korean negotiators.

0186

3. Mr. Habib then tabled a revised paragraph 1, reading as follows:

"1. The United States may contract for any materials, supplies, equipment and services (including construction work) to be furnished or undertaken in the Republic of Korea for purposes of, or authorized by, this Agreement, without restriction as to choice of contractor, supplier or person who provides such services. Such materials, supplies, equipment and services may, upon agreement between the appropriate authorities of the two Governments, also be procured through the Government of the Republic of Korea."

4. With regard to the revisions proposed by the Korean negotiators, Mr. Habib stated that provided the Korean negotiators agreed to two understandings, the U.S. negotiators accepted the following changes in the U.S. draft:

a. Paragraph 3 - the words "in advance" to be added following the word "certification";

b. Agreed Minute #2 - the word "representatives" to be substituted for the word "persons";

c. Agreed Minute #3 - the word "representative" to be substituted for the word "agent";

d. Addition of the Agreed Minute #4 proposed by the Korean negotiators.

5. Mr. Habib recalled that at the 46th negotiating meeting, the Korean negotiators had indicated their agreement to Paragraph 3 of the U.S. draft was conditioned upon: (a) "U.S. acceptance of an understanding that the U.S. will be given exemption only in the last stages of procurement unless it is agreed in the Joint Committee that the tax for which exemption is sought may be identified specifically and forms a significant part of the purchase price of the item", and (b) agreement by the U.S. negotiators to the insertion of the words "in advance" following the words "appropriate certification" in the first sentence

0187

of Paragraph 3. Mr. Habib stated the U.S. negotiators agreed to these two conditions and to the other changes proposed by the Korean negotiators, provided the Korean negotiators would agree for the record that: (a) a tax for which exemption is sought will not be collected so long as it is under discussion in the Joint Committee, and (b) traffic tax exemptions will be continued on the basis of current practice, under which all U.S. armed forces personnel travelling on official Travel Requests obtain exemption.

6. Mr. Habib stated that the first understanding which he had mentioned was a logical corollary of the first condition stated by the Korean negotiators. With regard to the second understanding, he said the U.S. negotiators believed that the ROK Government had no intention to apply the traffic tax to bulk purchases of transportation for official travel. He said the term "bulk purchases" was a bit confusing. Actually, all official travel is performed on the basis of Travel Requests issued by the U.S. military authorities. The military authorities enter into annual contracts with the railroads and air lines for the purchase of transportation. The individual traveller who is travelling on official business presents a Travel Request to the ticket office and is issued a ticket which is charged to the annual contract. Mr. Habib stated that the U.S. negotiators were responding directly to the proposals made by the Korean negotiators and hoped that full agreement could now be reached on this article.

7. Mr. Chang expressed the gratitude of the Korean negotiators for the response made by the U.S. negotiators

to the Korean proposals. He stated that he foresaw no
difficulty in reaching agreement on the proposed revision
of Paragraph 1 and on the other changes, including the
understandings proposed by the U.S. negotiators. However,
the Korean negotiators would study the statements made
by the U.S. negotiators and reply at the next meeting.

Customs

8. Turning to the Customs Article, Mr. Cho recalled
that the question of "members" or "units" in Paragraph 5 (a)
was still unresolved. He asked if the U.S. negotiators
had any additional comments to make on this subject.
Mr. Habib replied that the U.S. negotiators had no further
comment to make at that time with regard to Paragraph 5(a).

9. Mr. Cho stated that the Korean negotiators
wished to make some further remarks with regard to Agreed
Minute #3 of the U.S. draft. As written, he said, the
Agreed Minute would exempt from customs inspection cargo
consigned to non-appropriated fund organizations as well
as cargo consigned to the U.S. armed forces. Whereas the
latter type of cargo consisted of goods under the control
of the U.S. armed forces, cargo consigned to the non-
appropriated fund organizations consisted of goods which
would be sold for profit in post exchanges operated by civilian managers.

10. Mr. Habib interrupted at this point to say that
to regard the post exchange as a business was to misconstrue
the function and purpose of the post exchange. An army is
not just guns and ammunition, he continued; it is all of
the goods which are necessary to keep the soldier adequately
equipped and trained, in good health, and to maintain his
morale. Furthermore, the post exchanges are under the
close and continous control of the armed forces.

11. Mr. Cho said that he did not mean to imply that the post exchanges were not controlled by the armed forces. However, in the past the Korean economy has been affected by the influx of PX goods. This is the very reason why the Korean negotiators wish to make clear distinction between purly military cargo and PX goods. For example, in May, 1961, a Seventh Division post exchange had imported 10,000 yards of men's suiting. Inasmuch as the average monthly consumption of suiting by the Seventh Division was 90 yards, 10,000 yards was clearly an unreasonable quantity. In a second example, the First Ordnance Battalion at Uijongbu had imported 65 pairs of women's shoes from Hong Kong. As a result of an investigation by U.S. authorities, however, these shoes had been returned to Hong Kong. Because of cases like those which he had just cited, Mr. Cho continued, the Korean negotiators could not agree to exempt unconditionally from customs inspection all goods imported by non-appropriated fund organizations. The Korean negotiators were not questioning the existence of the post exchanges but they were concerned that there should be adequate safeguards against abuses by individuals. They realized that certain measures in this regard were enumerated in this and other articles of the Agreement and that U.S. and Korean agencies were cooperating to curb illegal activities. Nevertheless, such activities have been uncovered in the past and the Korean negotiators were convinced that customs inspections by Korean inspectors would check such undesirable activities in the future.

12. Although the U.S. negotiators had expressed the

0190

fear that inspection might damage or delay the delivery
of goods, Mr. Cho went on, the Korean negotiators could
assure them that this would not be the case. If the
U.S. side would consent to give the Korean Customs the
right of inspection on goods consigned to non-appropriated
fund organization, the Korean negotiators were prepared
to discuss detailed measures which could be taken to insure
that there would be no damage or delay. The Korean
negotiators wished to point out that in Article 6 of the
Mutual Security Treaty with Japan and in Article 11 of
the SOFA with Japan, exemption from customs inspection
was granted only to those unaccompanied goods shipped on
a Government Bill of Lading. Goods accompanying units
were exempted on the presentation of a certificate signed
by the unit commander. It was quite clear to the Korean
negotiators that in the SOFA with Japan cargo consigned to
non-appropriated fund organizations was not considered to
be a part of military cargo. There was no reason why the
SOFA with the Republic of Korea should not have the same
provision. Moreover, the economic situation in the
Republic of Korea was different from that in Japan.
The illegal disposal of PX goods has adversely affected
the growth of certain elements of the Korean economy.
It has been the practice to inspect goods consigned to
the post exchanges through commercial channels from
other countries than the United States. Currently, Korean
customs officials were inspecting such goods, particularly
watches, cameras, radios, etc. Therefore, there should
be no difficulty in the future in having Korean customs officials inspect such goods. Military cargo is used solely
for military purposes but goods consigned to the non-
appropriated fund organizations are used for various

0191

purposes. Therefore, the proposal of the Korean negotiators would serve the purposes of the U,S. armed forces stationed in Korea.

13. Mr. Habib remarked that the U.S. negotiators had already commented on innumerable occasions in the past in great detail on the arguments put forward by Mr. Cho. Nevertheless, he would refute them once again. In the first place, the non-appropriated fund organizations were an integral part of the U.S. military establishment and were regulated by military regulations. In this respect, there was no difference between a gallon of gasoline imported for use in an army jeep and a candy bar imported for consumption by a soldier. In the second place, the function of this Agreed Minute is to define military cargo. It is not concerned with illegal activities, which are covered elsewhere in this article and in other articles of the Agreement. There is no connection between a definition of military cargo and the illegal disposal of goods. In the third place, the U.S. negotiators had already explained that a definition referring to a Government Bill of Lading is no longer feasible because Government Bills of Lading are no longer used for all shipments. The text of the SOFA with Japan is no longer applicable in practice and the Japanese authorities do not inspect.

14. Mr. Habib said the examples of violations cited by the Korean negotiators were irrelevant to the question of defining military cargo. In any case, most of the violations of this type known to the Korean authorities had been originally discoverdd by U.S. armed forces investigators, not Korean customs officials. Stating

0192

that the legitimate concern of the Korean authorities
was with the quantity of goods imported, not with the
fact of importation itself, Mr. Habib pointed out that
Agreed Minute #1 states explicitly that the importation
of goods by non-appropriated fund organizations "shall
be limited to the extent reasonably required for such use."

15. Mr. Habib then called the attention of the Korean
negotiators to the various provisions of the article designed
to deal with the prevention of abuses - Agreed Minute #4,
which calls for "every practicable measure" to ensure
that there will be no violation of Korean customs laws
and regulations; Agreed Minute #5, which authorizes
the Korean customs authorities to raise abuses or infringe-
ments with the appropriate authorities of the U.S. armed
forces; Paragraph 9, which provides that each side will
assist the other in conducting inquiries and collecting
evidence; Paragraph 6, which prohibits illegal disposal of
such goods; and Paragraph 8, which calls upon the U.S.
armed forces to take all necessary steps to prevent abuses.
Mr. Habib reiterated that all of these provisions regarding
the prevention of abuses have nothing to do with the
question of defining military cargo. The U.S. negotiators
expect that the Joint Committee will set up procedures to
carry out all of the provisions which he had just cited.
Furthermore, the U.S. negotiators had proposed, at the
40th negotiating meeting on January 24, 1964, that an
additional sentence be added to Agreed Minute #3,
providing that pertinent information concerning cargo
consigned to non-appropriated fund organizations would be
furnished to the Korean authorities on request. The

implementation of this provision would be up to the
Joint Committee.

16. Mr. Habib stated that the U.S. armed forces were
not in the business of black-marketing. Individuals,
both American and Korean, were responsible for the
existence of the black market. The U.S. authorities
were just as concerned over this problem as the Korean
authorities. There existed just as much opportunity for
the diversion of goods such as tires as for the diversion
of goods such as radios. The way to control diversions was
to achieve better policing and greater cooperation
between the law enforcement agencies of the two governments.

17. Mr. Cho replied that the Korean negotiators
were seeking to establish preventive measures rather
than improve investigative procedures after violations
have occurred. Although the actual implementation of
the SOFA with Japan might differ from the language of the
SOFA itself, still the definition in the SOFA with the
Republic of Korea should be equivalent to that in the SOFA
with Japan. Although the additional sentence proposed by the
U.S. negotiators for Agreed Minute #3 would provide that
information be furnished to the Joint Committee, there would
be no way to confirm that the importation of goods was being
restricted to a "reasonable quantity".

18. Mr. Habib replied that documentation of shipments
should be adequate verification. The Joint Committee
could decide what type of documentation would be required.
The U.S. armed forces were prepared to provide all
necessary information to live up to the provisions of the
Agreement. The whole purpose of this article and the

0194

Agreement as a whole was to give the Joint Committee a
framework in which to function. The text proposed
by the U.S. negotiators was sufficient to prevent illegal
activities.

19. Mr. Chang remarked that the objective of both
sides was the same but the methods proposed for achieving
that objective were different. The Korean negotiators
wanted to provide for customs inspection; the U.S.
negotiators did not. The Korean negotiators would study
the matter further.

20. Mr. Habib stated that the procedures proposed by
the U.S. negotiators were more efficient and less cumbersome
than those proposed by the Korean negotiators. He
reminded the Korean negotiators that the U.S. negotiators
were determined to uphold the principle that official
cargo should not be subject to customs inspection.

Claims

21. Turning to the Claims Article, Mr. Chu tabled
proposed Agreed Minutes which the U.S. negotiators
agreed to study and comment on at a later meeting.

22. It was agreed to hold the next meeting on May 12
at 2:00 p.m.

한·미국 간의 상호방위조약 제4조에 의한 시설과 구역 및 한국에서의 미국군대의 지위에 관한 협정(SOFA)
전59권. 1966.7.9 서울에서 서명 : 1967.2.9 발효(조약 232호) (V.51 실무교섭회의 합의의사록, 제38-68차, 1964)　201

0195

JOINT SUMMARY RECORD OF THE 52ND SESSION

3/3

1. Time and Place: 3:00 - 4:15 P.M. May 20, 1964 at
   the Foreign Ministry's Conference
   Room (No.1)

2. Attendants:

ROK Side:

Mr. Chang, Sang Moon	Director European and American Affairs Bureau
Mr. Koo, Choong Whay	Chief, American Section Ministry of Foreign Affairs
Mr. Oh, Jae Hee	Chief, Treaty Section Ministry of Foreign Affairs
Mr. Hur, Hyong Koo	Chief Prosecutors Section, Ministry of Justice
Mr. Cho, Choong Hoon	Chief Customs Section Ministry of Finance
Maj. Lee, Kye Hoon	Military Affairs Section Ministry of National Defense
Mr. Chung, Woo Young (Rapporteur and Interpreter)	3rd Secretary Ministry of Foreign Affairs
Mr. Lee, Kae Chul	3rd Secretary Ministry of Foreign Affairs
Mr. Lee, Keun Pal	3rd Secretary Ministry of Foreign Affairs
Mr. Park, Won Chul	3rd Secretary Ministry of Foreign Affairs

U.S. Side:

Mr. Philip C. Habib	Counselor American Embassy
Col. Howard Smigelow	Deputy Chief of Staff 8th U.S. Army
Capt. John Wayne	Assistant Chief of Staff USN/K
Col. Kenneth C. Crawford	Staff Judge Advocates Office 8th U.S. Army

0196

Mr. Benjamin A. Fleck (Rapporteur and Press Officer)	First Secretary American Embassy
Mr. Robert A. Kinney	J-5 8th U.S. Army
Lt. Col. Charles Wright	Staff Judge Advocate's Office Eighth United States Army
Maj. Robert D. Peckham	Staff Officer JAG 8th U.S. Army
Mr. James Sartorius	2nd Secretary American Embassy
Mr. Kenneth Campen	Interpreter

1. Mr. Chang opened the meeting by introducing a new member of the ROK negotiating team, Mr. Hur, Hyong Koo, Chief of the Prosecutors Section, Ministry of Justice. Mr. Habib responded by introducing Lt. Colonel Charles Wright, of the Staff Judge Advocate's Office, Eighth United States Army, who will be succeeding Major Peckham as a member of the U.S. negotiating team. Both gentlemen were warmly welcomed to the negotiations.

Criminal Jurisdiction

2. Taking up the Criminal Jurisdiction Article, Mr. Chang made the following statement:

Since the drafts on the subject of Criminal Jurisdiction were exchanged at the 42nd meeting, the positions of both sides have become quite clear through a number of meetings over three months. During the period, both sides have had considerable time to study each others' positions as well as their major concerns. We believe past sessions have been productive in this sense.

However, we still face a wide gap between the two positions and the Korean negotiators believe it is high time for both sides to endeavor to narrow down the differences which exist between the two drafts and readjust their positions based on the spirit of friendly understanding and mutual cooperation.

0197

On our part, we have carefully studied and reviewed the concerns and difficulties of the U.S. side as indicated through the meetings and have decided to make a voluntary concession in order to accommodate the U.S. side's desire as far as we can go. As you will notice, the new proposal which the Korean negotiators are going to table at today's meeting is indeed a great concession. We sincerely hope that the U.S. negotiators would give due consideration on our new proposals and would convey your views at a later meeting.

Now I would like to explain our new proposals item by item. First, in paragraph 1(a) of our draft, we offer to replace the phrase "the members of the United States armed forces and the civilian components" with a new phrase reading "all persons subject to the military law of the United States."

Our new proposal may not sound to you like a very new idea. However, by proposing this phrase, we are prepared to recognize the jurisdiction of U.S. military authorities in Korea over the dependents to the extent they are subject to U.S. military law. Whether the dependents are coverdd by the uniform code of military justice or not is an internal matter on your side.

With regard to "authorities of the United States" to exercise criminal jurisdiction in Korea, we have designated the U.S. military authorities as sole authorities to exercise criminal jurisdiction since it is inconceivable for us that authorities other than U.S. military authorities would exercise jurisdiction within the Republic of Korea.

The chief U.S. negotiator stated at the 46th session that this is a matter of internal concern for the U.S. and that the language had been made broad enough to provide

0198

for any possible exercise of jurisdiction by U.S. authority.
However, we are of the opinion that it is not the internal
concern solely for the U.S. We believe that the exercise
of Criminal Jurisdiction in Korea by the authorities of
the United States, whether they be military authorities
or other than military authorities, has to be mutually
agreed upon. We have serious concern over the statement
which implies the possibility of U.S. authorities in Korea
other than military authorities exercising judicial power
in Korea.

As for the authorities of the Republic of Korea
exercising criminal jurisdiction, we understand your
intention of limiting our authorities to the civil side
is motivated from apprehension that the U.S. military
personnel might be tried by Korean court-martial. We
are prepared to assure you that we would not exercise
jurisdiction over U.S. military personnel by military
tribunal under any circumstances. Accordingly we propose
to record this assurance in the joint minutes and we believe
you would accept our version. We are sure that our new
proposal will certainly meet your requirements.

Turning to the so-called "combat zone", basically,
our position of not recognizing the concept of combat zone
remains as before. We understand that the U.S. side's
primary objective to establish a combat zone is to ensure
combat readiness of the U.S. troops by having exclusive
criminal jurisdiction in that area. Our view is that a
workable arrangement in the custody clause and waiver
clause could be agreed upon to satisfy your concern without
resorting to the concept of a combat zone. Accordingly,

0199

we would suggest revision in our draft of the two respective clauses on the condition that the U.S. side will withdraw the concept of a combat zone.

With respect to the Agreed Minute re Paragraph 3(c) of our draft concerning the problem of waiver of primary right to exercise jurisdiction, we offer to add the following paragraph as the first paragraph "the authorities of the Republic of Korea will, upon the notification of individual cases falling under the waiver provided in Article ____ paragraph 3(c) from the military authorities of the United States, waive its primary right to exercise jurisdiction under Article ____ except where they determine that it is of particular importance that jurisdiction be exercised by the authorities of the Republic of Korea."

Further, we propose to add the words "In addition to the foregoing provisions" before the second paragraph which has been placed as the first paragraph in our original draft. We are also prepared to consider the U.S. paragraph which reads "To facilitate the expeditious disposal of offenses of minor importance, arrangements may be made between United States authorities and the competent authorities of the Republic of Korea to dispense with notification".

As you may notice in our proposal, we are greatly binding ourselves by this paragraph, because under this clause we have to waive most of the cases by simple notification from the U.S. side. Under this clause, our ground for retaining primary right despite the waiver **request** is extremely limited due to the key phrase "particular importance". We would like to recall that at the previous meeting your side stated that the U.S. intention is to obtain maximum waiver. We believe that our new proposal would effectively meet your requirements.

0200

As to the procedure for mutual waiver, we would prefer to settle the detailed arrangements through the Joint Committee. However, in accordance with the principle set forth above, we could conceive the following detailed procedures for future reference: "When the Korean authorities hold the view that by reason of special circumstances in a specific case, major interests of the Korean administration of justice make imperative the exercise of the Korean jurisdiction, They will notify the military authorities of the United States of that opinion within a reasonable period. In case an understanding cannot be reached in discussion between the both sides, the U.S. military authorities will seek agreement of the Joint Committee within fifteen days from the date of receipt of such notification. If the U.S. authorities do not reply within fifteen days, the request for waiver will be deemed to have recalled." We have mentioned the above procedures as an example. We would propose that the final procedures would be negotiated at the Joint Committee.

With respect to the provisions of paragraph 5(d) of the Korean draft regarding the pre-trial custody of the accused, we wish to propose the following revision and an additional paragraph 5(e):

"Paragraph 5(d) An accused member of the United States Armed Forces or civilian component over whom the Republic of Korea is to exercise jurisdiction will, if he is in the hands of the United States, be under the custody of the United States during all judicial proceedings and until custody is requested by the authorities of the Republic of Korea.

0201

"The military authorities of the United States may transfer custody to the Korean authorities at any time and shall give sympathetic consideration to any request for the transfer of custody which may be made by the Korean authorities in specific cases."

"Paragraph 5(e) In respect of offenses solely against the security of the Republic of Korea provided in Paragraph 2(c), custody shall remain with the authorities of the Republic of Korea."

In order to meet the desires of the U.S. negotiators to the maximum extent, we propose to provide some additional provisions to facilitate expeditious investigation and trial on the part of the authorities of the Republic of Korea.

With respect to the provisions regarding the custody in the hands of the Republic of Korea, we are assuring you that custody will be turned over to the hands of the United States unless there is any specific reason and if there arises any question as to the existence of adequate cause and necessity to retain such accused, it will be determined at the Joint Committee.

With respect to pre-trial custody of the security offenses, we would like to emphasize that the custody of such offender should rest with the authorities of the Republic of Korea since an offender of the security offenses against the Republic of Korea could disclose security information to others, while he is in the hands of the authorities other than Korea. Accordingly the Korean negotiators find no reason why the military authorities of the United States should take custody of such

0202

an offender.

The Korean negotiators would like to delete from the provision of paragraph 3(a)(ii) of the Korean draft the following language "provided that such act or omission is directly related to the duty. The question as to whether offenses were committed in the performance of official duty shall be decided by a competent district public prosecutor of the Republic of Korea. In case the offender's commanding officer finds otherwise, he may appeal from the prosecutor's decision to the Ministry of Justice within ten days from the receipt of the decision of the prosecutor, and the decision of the Minister of Justice shall be final." We propose the following alternative draft as Agreed Minute re Paragraph 3(a)(ii). If the U.S. negotiators accept the proposed alternative draft, the Korean negotiators would give favorable consideration to the U.S. proposal made at the previous meeting to record in the Joint Summary the definition of official duty modified after the FEAF version of 1956:

"Re Paragraph 3(a)(ii)

"Where a member of the United States armed forces or civilian component is charged with an offense, a certificate issued by a staff judge advocate on behalf of his commanding officer stating that the alleged offense, if committed by him, arose out of an act or omission done in the performance of official duty, shall be sufficient evidence of the fact for the purpose of determining primary jurisdiction, unless the contrary is proved.

한·미국 간의 상호방위조약 제4조에 의한 시설과 구역 및 한국에서의 미국군대의 지위에 관한 협정(SOFA) 전59권. 1966.7.9 서울에서 서명 : 1967.2.9 발효(조약 232호) (V.51 실무교섭회의 합의의사록, 제38-68차, 1964)

"If the chief prosecutor of the Republic of Korea considers that there is proof contrary to the certificate of official duty, he will refer the matter to the Joint Committee for decision.

"The above statements shall not be interpreted to prejudice in any way Article 308 of the Korean Code of Criminal Procedure."

The Korean negotiators believe the alternative draft would meet the desires expressed by the United States negotiators with respect to the issuance of a duty certificate for determining primary jurisdiction over offenses arising out of an act done in the performance of official duty.

However, the Korean negotiators, taking into account the highly legal affairs involved, deem it proper that a Staff Judge Advocate should exercise the right to make such determination on behalf of the commanding officer at divisional level.

With respect to the validity of a duty certificate, the Korean draft provides that a certificate shall be sufficient evidence of the fact for the purpose of determining primary jurisdiction, unless the contrary is proved, whereas the U.S. draft provides that it shall be conclusive. The Korean negotiators believe that the Korean authorities should be accorded the opportunity to express their views as to the validity of a certificate in the event they find evidence contrary to the certificate.

The Korean draft provides the Joint Committe as the reviewing system of disputes to work out a mutually acceptable solution.

Further, the Korean negotiators reserve to the court the power to make determination of fact by referring to Article 308 of the Korean Code of Criminal Procedure.

0204

With respect to the martial law clause, we have already mentioned our intention of giving assurance that the U.S. military personnel would not be subject to Korean courts-martial. As we understand your major interest in this clause is not to subject U.S. military personnel to our military tribunal which would be established under martial law, we believe that with this assurance your major requirement is satisfied and we hope your side would withdraw the provisions with regard to martial law.

3. At the conclusion of Mr. Chang's statement, Mr. Habib said he wished to ask a few questions. First, did Mr. Chang's final comment, regarding the desire of the Korean negotiators to eliminate the reference in the U.S. draft to martial law, relate only to military personnel? Mr. Chang replied that the U.S. military personnel to which he referred in his statement included members of the U.S. armed forces and civilian components.

4. Mr. Habib then referred to Mr. Chang's statement that members of the U.S. armed forces would not be subject to trial by ROK court-martial under any circumstances. He asked if he had correctly understood Mr. Chang to say that this assurance would be read into the Agreed Joint Summary and not placed in the Agreed Minutes. Mr. Chang replied that this was a correct interpretation of the Korean negotiators' proposal.

5. Mr. Habib asked whether the Korean negotiators' position regarding U.S. jurisdiction over dependents was limited to the provisions of Paragraph 1. Mr. Chang replied that it was not limited to Paragraph 1, but would apply to the relevant paragraphs. However, the rights and privileges of dependents to be covered by the rest of the

article should be dealt with through further negotiation.

6. Mr. Habib then stated that the U.S. negotiators believed that the Korean negotiators had presented some constructive proposals. The U.S. negotiators welcomed the spirit in which those proposals had been made. The U.S. negotiators would study the Korean proposals carefully and would consult with Washington in detail. They would then try to present an equally comprehensive exposition of the U.S. views.

7. Mr. Habib noted that Mr. Chang had not mentioned the question of trial safeguards. He asked if the Korean position on this question remained unchanged. Mr. Chang replied affirmatively.

8. Mr. Habib recalled that the negotiators had previously discussed the question of including in the SOFA specific reference to certain safeguards which were enumerated in the ROK Constitution. He said it was not clear whether the Korean negotiators agreed or disagreed that specific reference should be made in the SOFA to such safeguards. The U.S. negotiators assumed that if a safeguard were mentioned in the Constitution the Korean negotiators could not object to its inclusion in the SOFA.

9. In reply, Mr. Chang said he would reiterate the Korean position. He said the Korean negotiators could not object if the U.S. negotiators wished to include in the SOFA items which are enumerated in the ROK Constitution and laws. However, it was a matter of style. If such safeguards are enumerated in the SOFA, the enumeration would have to include all the items listed in the Constitution. The Korean negotiators had included some safeguards in their proposed text but the U.S. negotiators wanted to include additional items. The Korean negotiators would study

0206

this matter and respond at a later meeting.

10. Mr. Habib recalled that he had proposed two principle during the course of the 50th meeting, namely, that items included in the ROK Constitution could be included in the SOFA and that items not included in the ROK Constitution could be included in the SOFA. Once these two principles were established, he continued, negotiators could decide which items to include to make the SOFA more easily to both sides.

11. As an example of the U.S. negotiators' concern, Mr. Habib referred to the Agreed Minute re Paragraph 9(b) in the U.S. draft. He said that the ROK negotiators apparently agreed with the first paragraph of this Agreed Minute but had proposed deletion of the second paragraph, claiming that there is no counterpart in the Korean criminal procedures and that it is contrary to the spirit of the existing law. This paragraph guarantees the counsel of an accused the right to examine and copy the statements of witnesses prior to trial when these statements are contained in the file of the case. The Korean negotiators had argued that under the ROK code of criminal procedure, the accused is given the opportunity to know the nature of the evidence against him and that this would suffice. The U.S. negotiators, however, believed that the right sought for the accused in the second paragraph of this Agreed Minute was a common sense right which would not be incompatible with ROK law. Mr. Habib then quoted Article 275 of the ROK criminal code, which reads in part as follows: "(1) The court may, upon application, permit the prosecutor or the accused or his counsel to

한·미국 간의 상호방위조약 제4조에 의한 시설과 구역 및 한국에서의 미국군대의 지위에 관한 협정(SOFA)
전59권. 1966.7.9 서울에서 서명 : 1967.2.9 발효(조약 232호) (V.51 실무교섭회의 합의의사록, 제38-68차, 1964) 213

examine the accused or other witnesses and to inspect evidence before the date fixed for trial ...". He pointed out that the right sought by the U.S. negotiators for incorporation in the SOFA was comparable in spirit to this provision of the ROK code, although not worded exactly the same.

12. As another example of a safeguard deemed necessary by the U.S. negotiators, Mr. Habib referred to the proposed Agreed Minute Re Paragraph 9(e). The Korean negotiators had argued that the Korean legal system requires that the accused be kept under surveillance by a competent Korean officer during any interview held by the accused with his counsel. They had therefore argued in favor of deleting the word "confidentially" from the proposed Agreed Minute. The U.S. negotiators believed that if a counsel is to perform effectively, he must be able to have his client confide in him without fear of being overheard. This could be accomplished by having the interview between the accused and his counsel take place in a locked room with a Korean guard posted outside.

13. As a further example of the variance between the positions of the two sides regarding trial safeguards, Mr. Habib referred to the Korean proposal to incorporate the second Agreed Minute Re Paragraph 9 of the Korean draft into the Agreed Minute re Paragraph 9(g) of the U.S. draft. This was undoubtedly an effort by the Korean negotiators to retain in force the provisions of Article 109 of the ROK Constitution, which reads as follows: "Trials and decisions of the courts shall be open to the public; however, trials may be closed to the public by a court when there is a possibility that such trials

0208

may disturb the public safety and order or be harmful to decent customs." Mr. Habib pointed out that the provisions of the Agreed Minute re Paragraph 9(g) of the U.S. draft were not intended to apply to the general public in all circumstances but were intended only to ensure that a representative of the U.S. Government would be able to attend all the proceedings connected with a trial, including any *in camera* proceedings.

14. Summing up, Mr. Habib pointed out that differences exist in both law and procedure between the U.S. legal system and that of the Republic of Korea. In some cases, these differences can be met by interpretation of the Korean laws. In other cases, the Korean laws may have to be amended to make them compatible with the terms of the SOFA. Such amendment of local law has taken place in connection with almost every SOFA which has been negotiated.

15. Mr. Chang stated that the Korean negotiators were in general agreement with the explanation given by the U.S. negotiators of the latter's position with regard to trial safeguards. The Korean negotiators were ready to settle through negotiation those items not presently covered by the ROK Constitution and laws. However, it did not seem necessary to them to include in the SOFA items which are already included in the Constitution and laws.

16. Mr. Habib pointed out that basic principles should be clearly stated in the SOFA, inasmuch as laws can be changed. The negotiators should bear in mind the fact that the passage of *ex post facto* laws has been a feature of recent Korean history.

17. Mr. Chang said the Korean negotiators understood

0209

the concern of the U.S. negotiators. However, if
the laws were changed, the changes would be in the direction
of more protection of human rights rather than less.
Mr. Habib expressed the hope of the U.S. negotiators
that this would be true but their lack of conviction,
based on experience, that any changes in current
laws would necessarily be for the better.

18. It was agreed to hold the next meeting on
May 28 at 2:00 p.m.

<u>JOINT SUMMARY RECORD OF THE 53RD SESSION</u>

1. Time and Place: 2:00 - 4:15 P.M. May 28, 1964 at
   the Foreign Ministry's Conference
   Room (No.1)

2. Attendants:

ROK Side:

Mr. Chang, Sang Moon	Director European and American Affairs Bureau
Mr. Koo, Choong Whay	Chief, American Section Ministry of Foreign Affairs
Mr. Oh, Jae Hee	Chief, Treaty Section Ministry of Foreign Affairs
Mr. Cho, Choong Hoon	Chief Customs Section Ministry of Finance
Maj. Lee, Kye Hoon	Military Affairs Section Ministry of National Defense
Mr. Ahn, Yun Gi	3rd Secretary Ministry of Foreign Affairs
Mr. Lee, Kae Chul	3rd Secretary Ministry of Foreign Affairs
Mr. Lee, Keun Pal (Rapporteur and Interpreter)	3rd Secretary Ministry of Foreign Affairs
Mr. Park, Won Chul	3rd Secretary Ministry of Foreign Affairs
Mr. Hwang, Young Jae	3rd Secretary Ministry of Foreign Affairs

U.S. Side:

Mr. Philip C. Habib	Counselor American Embassy
Brig. Gen. G.G. O'Connor	Deputy Chief of Staff 8th U.S. Army
Col. Howard Smigelow	Deputy Chief of Staff 8th U.S. Army
Capt. John Wayne	Assistant Chief of Staff USN/K
Col. Kenneth C. Crawford	Staff Judge Advocates Office 8th U.S. Army

0211

Mr. Benjamin A. Fleck (Rapporteur and Press Officer)	First Secretary American Embassy
Mr. Robert A. Kinney	J-5 8th U.S. Army
Lt. Col. Charles Wright	Staff Judge Advocate's Office 8th U.S. Army
Mr. Robert A. Lewis	2nd Secretary American Embassy
Mr. Edward Hurwitz	2nd Secretary American Embassy

Local Procurement

1. Mr. Chang opened the meeting by stating that the revision of Paragraph 1 of the Local Procurement Article and the two understandings proposed by the U.S. negotiators at the 51st meeting were acceptable to the Korean negotiators, provided the U.S. negotiators would agree to include in the Agreed Joint Summary a statement to the effect that the inclusion of the word "services" in Paragraph 1 would not in any way affect the provisions of the Labor Procurement Article. Mr. Habib replied that this understanding was acceptable to the U.S. negotiators. Full agreement was thereupon reached on the Local Procurement Article.

Foreign Exchange Controls

2. Turning to the Foreign Exchange Controls Article, Mr. Chang said that the only remaining point of difference was to be found in the Agreed Minute. The U.S. draft used the term "highest rate" while the Korean draft used the term "basic rate." In order to resolve this difference, the Korean negotiators proposed that instead of either of the foregoing terms, the phraseology "buying rate of the foreign exchange bank" be used. He pointed out that since the adoption of the new conversion system, there is only one buying rate now applicable.

0212

3. Mr. Habib said that the U.S. negotiators would study the Korean proposal. However, their initial reaction was that the proposal did not meet their requirement. The proposition set forth in the U.S. draft of the Agreed Minute was very simple. It would provide that funds would be converted by the U.S. armed forces "in accordance with the Korean Foreign Exchange Control Law and regulations", and at the highest rate which is not unlawful. The Korean negotiators were suggesting that the present buying rate at the Bank of Korea is the highest buying rate which is not unlawful. The U.S. negotiators agreed that this was a fact at that moment. However, laws can be changed and adjustments in rates can be made unilaterally. The purpose of the U.S. draft was to provide in advance for any such changes or adjustments in the future, in order to avoid discriminatory rates. The Korean proposal does not take into account the long-term nature of the Status of Forces Agreement or the necessity to provide for changes in the law without changing the purpose of the Agreement. The reluctance of the Korean negotiators to agree to the establishment of this principle led the U.S. negotiators to suspect that there may be some intention on the part of the Korean authorities to alter the exchange rate in the future to the detriment of the U.S. armed forces. Naturally, the U.S. negotiators wished to preclude such alteration. If necessary, the U.S. negotiators would submit the Korean proposal to Washington, but the reply from Washington would certainly be identical with the position just expressed.

4. Mr. Chang replied that the language proposed by the Korean negotiators would meet the requirements of the U.S.

0213

authorities under the present exchange system and would
guarantee that there would be no discriminatory treatment
of the U.S. armed forces. If any changes in the exchange
rate should occur in the future, the Korean negotiators
hoped that both sides would negotiate a mutually acceptable
solution. If the U.S. negotiators insisted that the
language of this Agreed Minute should meet all foreseeable
contingencies, then the phrase "equitable rate" should
suffice. The language of the U.S. draft bore the connotation
that the official exchange rate is not a unitary rate. The
language was therefore unacceptable to the Korean negotiators.
Mr. Chang said they would consider this question further
and comment at the next meeting.

5. Mr. Habib replied that the U.S. negotiators fully
understood the present system. He pointed out that it is
not unusual in many countries for various exchange rates to
exist simultaneously. The U.S. negotiators were not
prepared to agree that if the rate is changed, the rate
charged to the U.S. armed forces would be subject to
negotiation. He pointed out that there is no Status of
Forces Agreement under the provisions of which the system
proposed by the U.S. negotiators is not the practice. The
Korean negotiators could not expect the U.S. negotiators to
agree to a loophole which might require the U.S. armed forces
to convert at an unfavorable rate. The unwillingness
of the Korean negotiators to agree to this principle made the
U.S. negotiators all the more certain that it was a required
principle.

6. Mr. Chang stated that the Korean negotiators did
not intend that the U.S. armed forces should be subject to
unfavorable treatment. They believed that the principles
expressed in both drafts are identical. The difficulty was
a purely technical one of finding suitable language. To
use the term "highest rate" implied that there was more

0214

than one official rate.

7. Mr. Habib pointed out that it was not a question of official or unofficial rates. There could be a legal rate which was higher than the "official" rate. In any case, the U.S. negotiators agreed to study this matter for further discussion at a later meeting.

Military Payment Certificates

8. Turning to the Military Payment Certificates Article, Mr. Chang stated that there were three points at issue. The first was the phrase in Paragraph 1(b) of the U.S. draft: "to the extent authorized by United States law". This language did not clarify how those persons not subject to U.S. military law would be arrested and punished if they abuse privileges relating to MPC. The Korean negotiators recalled that Colonel Solf had sought to clarify this point by stating that the U.S. armed forces could take administrative measures against such persons. The Korean negotiators were of the opinion that such administrative actions should not preclude the ROK authorities from punishing such offenders. In short, persons not subject to U.S. military law should be subject to trial and punishment in accordance with ROK law. Accordingly, the Korean negotiators proposed the insertion of the phrase "subject to the Military Law of the United States" after the word "dependent" in Para. 1(d) of the Korean draft. The Korean negotiators believed that the U.S. authorities could punish the member of the U.S. armed forces and civilian component without the phrase "to the extent authorized by the U.S. Law".

0215

Therefore, the Korean negotiators have reached the conclusion that the phrase "to the extent authorized by the U.S. Law" should be deleted from Para. 1(b) of the U.S. draft.

9. Secondly, Mr. Chang continued, there was disagreement over the phrase in Paragraph 1(d) of the Korean draft "after the date of coming into force of this agreement". The Korean negotiators now agreed to the deletion of this phrase.

10. Thirdly, there was disagreement over the Agreed Minutes tabled by each side. The Korean negotiators requested that the U.S. negotiators withdraw the U.S. Agreed Minute and agree to insertion of the Korean Agreed Minute in the Agreed Joint Summary.

11. With regard to the first point made by Mr. Chang, Mr. Habib replied that the recollection of the Korean negotiators was quite correct and that the U.S. negotiators had explained why the inclusion of the phrase "to the extent authorized by United States law" was necessary. The Korean negotiators were seeking to be reassured that inclusion of this phrase would in no way derogate from the jurisdictional authority of the ROK Government over persons not subject to U.S. law. He pointed out that jurisdictional authority is determined by the provisions of the Criminal Jurisdiction Article. There is nothing in either the U.S. draft or the Korean draft of the HPC article which would affect that authority.

12. Mr. Habib welcomed the agreement of the Korean negotiators to delete the phrase "after the date of coming into force of this agreement".

0216

13. With regard to the third point raised by Mr. Chang, Mr. Habib replied that the U.S. negotiators were willing to delete the U.S. Agreed Minute if the Korean negotiators would agree to delete the Korean Agreed Minute. The U.S. negotiators wished to remove from the SOFA the whole question of compensation for MPC's held by unauthorized persons. Furthermore, they could not agree to the inclusion of any language which might be construed as indicating an obligation on the part of the U.S. authorities to compensate illegal holders of MPC's.

14. Mr. Chang replied that the U.S. negotiators appeared to have misunderstood the proposal made by the Korean negotiators. The Korean negotiators had proposed deletion of the U.S. Agreed Minute and inclusion of the Korean Agreed Minute in the Agreed Joint Summary.

15. Mr. Habib stated that the U.S. negotiators had understood very well the Korean proposal. He said the U.S. negotiators could not object if the Korean negotiators proposed to include in the Agreed Joint Summary language indicating that the Korean authorities had no intention of abandoning their intention to raise the question of compensation for discussion at some future date. However, the U.S. negotiators could not agree to the inclusion of any language which would imply an obligation on the U.S. authorities to pay compensation. With that understanding, the U.S. negotiators were prepared to delete both Agreed Minutes. The U.S. negotiators would study the matter further to see whether some alternative wording might not be drafted for inclusion in the Agreed Joint Summary instead of the Korean Agreed Minute. Mr. Chang expressed the desire of the Korean negotiators that whatever alternative wording was developed would incorporate the spirit of the Korean

0217

Agreed Minute.

Customs

16. Turning to the Customs Article, Mr. Habib recalled
that full agreement had been reached on this article,
except for Paragraph 5(a) and Agreed Minutes 2,3 and 7.
He inquired whether the Korean negotiators were prepared to
accept Agreed Minute 3 of the U.S. draft, including the
proposed additional sentence.

17. Mr. Chang said the Korean negotiators wished to
ask a few questions concerning the proposed additional
sentence. First, was cargo consigned to the non-appropriated fund organizations clearly distinguishable from
other cargo in terms of packing or markings on them? Secondly,
were the U.S. authorities prepared to provide for NAFO cargo
packing lists as well as invoices and other documents which
the Korean customs authorities might deem necessary?

18. Mr. Habib replied that cargo consigned to non-
appropriated fund organizations is clearly distinguishable
from other cargo in terms of markings and documentation.
According to the terms of the U.S. draft, the Joint Committee
will provide information pertinent to such cargo on request.
He said the U.S. authorities fully intend to live up to the
obligations placed upon them by the provisions of this article.
There was no intent to conceal what is normally considered
to be pertinent information.

19. Mr. Chang then indicated that the Korean negotiators
desired that all pertinent information regarding NAFO
cargo should be provided automatically to the Korean customs
officials, without going through the Joint Committee. If the
Korean customs authorities detected something amiss, then
they would take the matter to the Joint Committee but they

0218

did not want to have to request the Joint Committee for
information every time a ship came into port. Therefore,
they wished to establish the principle in the SOFA that the
pertinent information, including invoices, packing lists,
and customs declarations would be provided routinely to the
Korean customs officials on an automatic basis by the U.S.
armed forces.

20. In reply to these arguments, Mr. Habib stated
that the U.S. negotiators were negotiating on the principle
that the Joint Committee would be responsible for administering
the Status of Forces Agreement. They were unwilling,
therefore, to include administrative details of the type
desired by the Korean negotiators in the Agreement itself.
What the Korean negotiators were proposing would prove to
be an administrative nightmare. There was nothing in the
U.S. draft which would prevent the establishment of a
system such as that proposed by the Korean negotiators.
However, it was the responsibility of the Joint Committee,
not the negotiators, to decide how the SOFA was to be administered. Therefore, the Joint Committee should decide what
constituted "pertinent" information and by what means that
information would be provided to the Korean authorities.

21. Mr. Chang said it was the responsibility of the
negotiators to decide on the principle whether the pertinent
information be provided to the Korean side on an automatic
basis or not. If the U.S. negotiators would agree to the
principle, the Korean negotiators were prepared to consider
the U.S. additional sentence in order to settle the argument
on Agreed Minute 3 of the U.S. draft.

0219

22. Mr. Habib asked if the Korean negotiators would be satisfied in case the U.S. negotiators assured the Korean side that pertinent information will be furnished to the Korean Authorities on an automatic basis upon request through the Joint Committee. Mr. Chang indicated the possibility of acceptance by the Korean negotiators of the assurance made by Mr. Habib provided that the U.S. side would eliminate the procedure of going through the Joint Committee.

23. At this point, it was agreed to adjourn the meeting. The next meeting was scheduled for June 5 at 3:00 p.m.

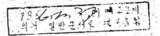

0220

JOINT SUMMARY RECORD OF THE 54TH SESSION

1. Time and Place: 3:00 - 4:15 P.M. June 9, 1964 at
   the Foreign Ministry's Conference
   Room (No.1)

2. Attendants:

ROK Side:

Mr. Chang, Sang Moon	Director European and American Affairs Bureau
Mr. Koo, Choong Whay	Chief, American Section Ministry of Foreign Affairs
Mr. Oh, Jae Hee	Chief, Treaty Section Ministry of Foreign Affairs
Mr. Cho, Choong Hoon	Chief Customs Section Ministry of Finance
Col. Kim, Won Kil	Chief Military Affairs Section Ministry of National Defense
Mr. Chung, Woo Young	3rd Secretary Ministry of Foreign Affairs
Mr. Ahn, Yun Gi	3rd Secretary Ministry of Foreign Affairs
Mr. Lee, Kae Chul	3rd Secretary Ministry of Foreign Affairs
Mr. Lee, Keun Pal (Rapporteur and Interpreter)	3rd Secretary Ministry of Foreign Affairs
Mr. Park, Won Chul	3rd Secretary Ministry of Foreign Affairs
Mr. Hwang, Young Jae	3rd Secretary Ministry of Foreign Affairs

U.S. Side:

Mr. Philip C. Habib	Counselor American Embassy
Brig. Gen. G.G. O'Connor	Deputy Chief of Staff 8th U.S. Army
Col. Howard Smigelow	Deputy Chief of Staff 8th U.S. Army
Col. Kenneth C. Crawford	Staff Judge Advocates Office 8th U.S. Army

0221

Mr. Frank R. La Macchia	First Secretary American Embassy
Mr. Benjamin A. Fleck (Rapporteur and Press Officer)	First Secretary American Embassy
Mr. Robert A. Kinney	J-5 8th U.S. Army
Lt. Col. Charles Wright	Staff Judge Advocate's Office 8th U.S. Army
Mr. Robert A. Lewis	2nd Secretary American Embassy
Mr. Edward Hurwitz	2nd Secretary American Embassy

1. Mr. Habib opened the meeting by introducing Mr. La Macchia, who was joining the U.S. negotiating team in place of Mr. Sartorius. Mr. Chang welcomed Mr. La Macchia on behalf of the Korean negotiators.

Military Payment Certificates Article

2. Taking up the first item on the agenda, the MPC Article, Mr. Chang asked if the U.S. negotiators had any comments to make. Mr. Habib replied that at the 53rd meeting, the Korean negotiators had suggested the inclusion in the Agreed Joint Summary of a statement referring to the desire of the ROK Government to obtain compensation for Military Payment Certificates in its possession. The U.S. negotiators understood that the Korean negotiators, in making that suggestion, were indicating their willingness to set aside the question of compensation from the Status of Forces Agreement by removing from the text of the Agreement any reference to the question. At the same time, the U.S. negotiators were compelled to make clear the position of the U.S. Government that it was under no obligation to pay

such compensation. Each side, therefore, was trying not to prejudice its position while recognizing that the SOFA was not the instrument by which a solution to this problem would ultimately be found.

3. In an attempt to meet the needs of both sides, Mr. Habib continued, the U.S. negotiators had formulated language which they proposed as an understanding to be placed in the Agreed Joint Summary. He thereupon tabled the following language:

"The ROK and U.S. negotiators agree that nothing in the Status of Forces Agreement in any way prevents the appropriate authorities of either the Republic of Korea or the United States from raising any appropriate matter at any time with each other. The U.S. negotiators recognize the desire of the ROK authorities to discuss the disposal of Military Payment Certificates under custody of the ROK Government. However, both the ROK and U.S. negotiators have agreed to remove from the SOFA text any reference to the question of compensation for Military Payment Certificates held by unauthorized persons. This agreement does not prejudice the position of either party in connection with discussion of this question through other channels."

4. Mr. Chang commented that the ROK negotiators believed this proposal to be a very constructive suggestion. They wished to know whether the term "any appropriate matter" was intended to include "the question of compensation for Military Payment Certificates held by unauthorized persons". Upon being assured by Mr. Habib that the former term was intended to include the latter, Mr. Chang stated that the Korean negotiators would consider this proposal and comment upon it at a later meeting.

5. Mr. Habib then referred to the proposal of the Korean negotiators to delete from Paragraph 1(b) of the U.S. draft the phrase "to the extent authorized by U.S. law" and to insert after the word "dependents" the phrase "subject to the Military Law of the United States." He

0223

commented that resolution of this point would have to
await agreement on the equivalent point in the Criminal
Jurisdiction Article. The U.S. negotiators, therefore,
would reserve comment on the Korean proposals until agreement had been reached on the relevant provisions of the
Criminal Jurisdiction Article.

Foreign Exchange Controls

6. Turning to the Foreign Exchange Controls Article,
Mr. Chang restated the position of the Korean negotiators
that the ROK Government had no intention whatsoever of
imposing discriminatory rates on the U.S. armed forces.
In an attempt to satisfy the needs of the U.S. negotiators,
the ROK negotiators had tabled at the last meeting a suggested
revision of the Agreed Minute which would provide that
funds would be convertible "at the buying rate of the
foreign exchange bank". This proposal had not been agreed
to by the U.S. negotiators. The Korean negotiators wished
to make clear the reasons for their inability to accept
the language proposed by the U.S. negotiators: "at the
highest rate ... which, at the time the conversion is made,
is not unlawful in the Republic of Korea." He explained
that under the present system there is a market rate which
is neither unlawful nor identical with the bank rate and
upon which the bank rate is based. It should be noted
that if the market rate should be higher than the bank
rate, then a literal interpretation of the U.S. language
would naturally lead to application of the market rate
rather than the bank rate, even though the Korean negotiators
believe the intention of the U.S. side is otherwise.
This was why the U.S. language is unacceptable to the
Korean negotiators.

0224

7. Mr. Habib replied that at the present time the bank rate may be the highest rate. However, it will not necessarily remain so indefinitely. Therefore, there is a possibility of discriminatory rates being charged at some future time. The Korean negotiators were trying to make the current system fit the problem, while the U.S. negotiators were trying to devise language to meet possible future problems. If a rate were "lawful", it must have been provided for in ROK laws and regulations. If it has been so provided for, the U.S. armed forces should be able to take advantage of it. So far, the Korean negotiators had not proposed language which would ensure that discrimination would not take place. If the Korean negotiators accepted the premise that no discriminatory rates would be imposed upon the U.S. armed forces, the U.S. negotiators knew of no simpler way of stating this premise than in the language which they had proposed.

8. Mr. Chang reiterated the assurances previously given by the ROK negotiators that the U.S. armed forces will not be discriminated against. He asked whether the armed forces would demand conversion at the market rate if the market rate became higher than the bank rate.

9. Mr. Habib replied that the U.S. negotiators would study this question. However, their preliminary answer was in the affirmative since the whole purpose of the present certificate system of exchange was to provide a floating and realistic exchange rate, based on market demand. After consultation and thorough study of this question, the U.S. negotiators would give their considered views at a later meeting.

한·미국 간의 상호방위조약 제4조에 의한 시설과 구역 및 한국에서의 미국군대의 지위에 관한 협정(SOFA)
전59권. 1966.7.9 서울에서 서명 : 1967.2.9 발효(조약 232호) (V.51 실무교섭회의 합의의사록, 제38-68차, 1964) 231

10. Mr. Chang thanked Mr. Habib for his reply and stated that the point raised by Mr. Habib was exactly the reason why the U.S. language was unacceptable. The ROK negotiators were not prepared to agree to conversion by the U.S. armed forces outside of the foreign exchange banks. In a further effort to resolve the differences over this question, the Korean negotiators wished to propose another formulation. They were prepared to accept the U.S. draft of the Agreed Minute, with the addition after the word "unlawful" of the phrase "and is applicable in transactions at foreign exchange banks", and also with the understanding that the phrase "highest rate" refers to the buying rate of the banks and not to the selling rate. This addition was made with a view to avoid any possible misunderstanding that "the highest rate" may refer to the market rate which is also not unlawful.

11. Mr. Habib stated that the U.S. negotiators would study this proposal and reply at a later meeting.

Customs

12. Turning to the Customs Article, Mr. Habib reviewed the discussion at the previous meeting of Agreed Minute #3. The Korean negotiators had proposed that the U.S. armed forces provide information regarding cargo consigned to non-appropriated fund organizations on an automatic basis. The U.S. negotiators were prepared to agree to this proposal, provided that it was made clear that the process of providing such information would be regulated and controlled through requests made to the Joint Committee. The Agreed Joint Summary could show that the negotiators agreed to the principle of automaticity and to the automatic provision

0226

of pertinent information through the Joint Committee.
This would then mean complete agreement on Agreed Minute #3.

13. Mr. Chang replied that the ROK negotiators understood the U.S. position. The ROK negotiators also agreed to the principle of automaticity but believed that it was necessary to have such agreement recorded in the Agreed Minute itself, rather than in the Agreed Joint Summary since the Korean negotiators were making a great concession from their original position and the additional sentence proposed by the U.S. negotiators was the counter-proposal to the Korean agreed minute regarding the information on NAFO goods. To that end, they proposed the following language as a substitution for the additional sentence previously proposed for Agreed Minute #3 by the U.S. negotiators:

"Pertinent information on all cargo consigned to non-appropriated fund organizations shall routinely be furnished to the Korean authorities and on specific cases, additional information shall be provided to the Korean authorities upon request through the Joint Committee. The extent of pertinent information shall be determined by the Joint Committee."

14. Mr. Habib pointed out that this proposal was considerably different from the proposal made by the Korean negotiators at the previous meeting. The U.S. negotiators had replied to the previous proposal. With regard to this latest proposed language, the U.S. negotiators wondered what was meant by the phrase "additional information"?

15. Mr. Chang replied that "pertinent information" referred to that information which would be supplied on a routine basis, while "additional information" referred to that information which would not be supplied on a routine basis.

한·미국 간의 상호방위조약 제4조에 의한 시설과 구역 및 한국에서의 미국군대의 지위에 관한 협정(SOFA)
전59권. 1966.7.9 서울에서 서명 : 1967.2.9 발효(조약 232호) (V.51 실무교섭회의 합의의사록, 제38-68차, 1964) 233

16. Mr. Habib stated that the English translation of the Korean proposal was defective. Perhaps more suitable wording could be worked out. The U.S. negotiators would study the proposal and reply at a later meeting.

17. At this point the meeting was adjourned. The next meeting was scheduled for June 19 at 3:00 p.m.

JOINT SUMMARY RECORD OF THE 55TH SESSION

1. Time and Place: 3:00 - 5:00 P.M. June 19, 1964 at
   the Foreign Ministry's Conference
   Room (No.1)

2. Attendants:

ROK Side:

Mr. Chang, Sang Moon — Director
European and American Affairs
Bureau

Mr. Koo, Choong Whay — Chief, American Section
Ministry of Foreign Affairs

Mr. Cho, Choong Hoon — Chief
Customs Section
Ministry of Finance

Maj. Lee, Kye Hoon — Military Affairs Section
Ministry of National Defense

Mr. Ahn, Yun Gi — 3rd Secretary
Ministry of Foreign Affairs

Mr. Lee, Kae Chul — 3rd Secretary
Ministry of Foreign Affairs

Mr. Lee, Keun Pal
(Rapporteur and
Interpreter) — 3rd Secretary
Ministry of Foreign Affairs

Mr. Park, Won Chul — 3rd Secretary
Ministry of Foreign Affairs

U.S. Side:

Mr. Philip C. Habib — Counselor
American Embassy

Brig. Gen. G.G. O'Connor — Deputy Chief of Staff
8th U.S. Army

Col. Howard Smigelow — Deputy Chief of Staff
8th U.S. Army

Capt. John Wayne — Assistant Chief of Staff
USN/K

Col. Kenneth C. Crawford — Staff Judge Advocates Office
8th U.S. Army

0229

Mr. Frank R. La Macchia	First Secretary American Embassy
Mr. Benjamin A. Fleck (Rapporteur and Press Officer)	First Secretary American Embassy
Mr. Robert A. Kinney	J-5 8th U.S. Army
Lt. Col. Charles Wright	Staff Judge Advocate's Office 8th U.S. Army
Mr. Robert A. Lewis	2nd Secretary American Embassy
Mr. Kenneth Campen	Interpreter

Security Measures

1. The meeting was begun with a discussion of the
Security Measures Article. Mr. Habib recalled that the
article was last discussed at the 48th negotiating meeting,
at which time the Korean negotiators had counter-proposed
certain language in response to a U.S. revision of the
article which had previously been discussed informally.
The Korean counter-proposal differed from the U.S. revision
in that the former would provide that "the Republic of Korea
will take such actions as it deems necessary" whereas the
latter would provide that "the Republic of Korea will take
such actions as may be necessary". The Korean negotiators
had indicated that their proposed language had a precedent
in the SOFA with the Federal Republic of Germany. The U.S.
negotiators wished to point out that while Article 29 of
the German SOFA uses the words "it deems", that article deals
with legislative measures only and does not include the basic
commitment to cooperate with the U.S. armed forces in
ensuring the security and protection of persons and property.
The broader commitment is contained in Paragraph 2(b) of
Article 3 of the German SOFA. The language of the latter

0229

0230

article is analogous to that of the revision proposed by
the U.S. negotiators. In some ways, Mr. Habib continued,
the language of the German SOFA is more restrictive than
that being proposed by the U.S. negotiators. For example,
Paragraph 2 of Article 3 of the German SOFA uses the
words "the cooperation provided for in paragraph 1 of this
article shall extend ..."

2. Mr. Habib stated that the problem in connection
with this article was one of principle. The Korean
negotiators wanted to give the ROK Government unilateral
responsibility for security measures rather than providing
for a cooperative effort by both sides. The purpose of this
article is to provide an explicit understanding that certain
security measures will be taken for the protection of the
American elements involved. Inasmuch as the ROK Government
was already taking such measures and was likely to continue
to do so, the Korean negotiators appeared to be creating
a problem where none existed. The U.S. negotiators suggested
that the Korean negotiators examine carefully Article 3
of the German SOFA as well as Article 29. These two articles
together set a clear precedent.

3. Mr. Chang replied that the wording of the German
SOFA appeared to be stricter than that proposed by the
Korean negotiators. The Korean negotiators did not think
it appropriate to adopt language which would provide for the
passage of legislation "to ensure the punishment of offenders".

4. Mr. Habib replied that there was no mention of
legislation in the revision proposed by the U.S. negotiators.
He also pointed out again that Article 29 of the German SOFA,
on which the Korean negotiators were apparently basing their
counter-proposal, was restricted specifically to legislation.

0231

He recalled that the U.S. negotiators had formulated
their proposed revision in response to earlier objections
by the Korean negotiators to the inclusion in the article
of any reference to legislation regarding the protection
of persons, dependents, and their property.

5. Mr. Chang asked if the phrase "such actions as may
be necessary" could be construed to include legislation.

6. In reply, Mr. Habib referred to the Agreed Joint
Summary of the 48th negotiating session, which revealed that
the U.S. negotiators had already answered this question
as follows: "The U.S. negotiators did not believe that a
commitment to legislation was necessary in the article but
they did want the negotiating record to show that 'such
actions' would include legislation, when appropriate; for
example, to ensure the security of U.S. Government property".

7. Mr. Chang stated that the revision proposed by
the U.S. negotiators included provision for legislation
covering persons and their property. This would place a
great obligation on the ROK Government. The Korean
negotiators believed the original draft was clearer because
it divided the actions to be taken by the ROK Government
into two distinguishable categories. The Korean negotiators,
therefore, proposed that the original drafts of this article
be used as the bases for further negotiation.

8. Mr. Habib asked whether the Korean negotiators were
proposing to return to the position which they had adopted
at the 46th negotiating meeting, at which they had made
certain proposals with regard to the original drafts. Mr.
Chang replied affirmatively. Mr. Habib then stated that
the U.S. negotiators were willing to return to the original
drafts for further negotiation. However, this brought the
negotiators back to the same old problem — the Korean

0232

negotiators were unwilling to agree to an assurance of
cooperative effort to ensure the protection of U.S. persons
and their property. Instead of a provision calling for
cooperation, the Korean negotiators were insisting on provision
for unilateral determination by the ROK Government of what
steps would be necessary.

9. Mr. Habib stated the U.S. negotiators were
prepared to agree to adoption of the original U.S. draft
of the article, with the deletion of the phrase "of the
persons referred to in this paragraph, and their property",
as proposed by the Korean negotiators, provided the Korean
negotiators would agree to the inclusion in the negotiating
record of the following understanding:

> "In cooperating with each other under this Article
> the two governments agree that each will take such
> measures as may be necessary to ensure the security
> and protection of the U.S. Armed Forces, the members
> thereof, the civilian component, the persons who
> are present in the Republic of Korea pursuant to the
> article dealing with Invited Contractors, their dependents
> and their property."

10. Mr. Chang asked if the phrase "such measures" in
the proposed understanding could be construed to include
legislation. Mr. Habib said that the phrase could include
legislation, if and when legislation was appropriate.
Mr. Chang stated that if that were the case, the language
was unacceptable to the Korean negotiators.

11. Mr. Habib stated that the U.S. negotiators had
come a long way toward meeting the position of the Korean
negotiators. However, the armed forces needed to have some
sense of security and also needed language in this article
which would give them recourse to the ROK Government.

12. Mr. Chang replied that existing ROK laws fully
protect the persons, dependents and their property.

0233

Therefore, the Korean negotiators thought it was not necessary to bind the ROK Government to seek legislation regarding the protection of invited contractors, dependents, and their property.

13. Mr. Habib commented that no other government with which a SOFA has been negotiated has balked at seeking legislation, if such legislation was necessary or appropriate. He urged the Korean negotiators to study the precedents.

14. Mr. Chang stated that the discussion had clarified the points of difference with regard to this article. The Korean negotiators could not accept the proposal made by the U.S. negotiators if that proposal included provision for legislation to ensure the protection of persons, dependents, and their property.

Military Payment Certificates

15. Turning to the article dealing with Military Payment Certificates, Mr. Chang stated that the Korean negotiators accepted the understanding proposed by the U.S. negotiators at the 54th meeting for inclusion in the Agreed Joint Summary (see paragraph 3, Agreed Joint Summary, 54th Negotiating Meeting). He noted that there still remained an unresolved question of language in Paragraph 1(b) of the article.

16. Mr. Habib recalled that at the 54th meeting the U.S. negotiators had indicated resolution of this question would depend upon agreement on the equivalent point in the Criminal Jurisdiction Article. When agreement was reached on the latter article, this point would be resolved. Therefore, the U.S. negotiators suggested that the Military Payment Certificates Article be set aside until agreement had been reached on the Criminal Jurisdiction Article. Mr. Chang agreed.

0234

<u>Customs</u>

17. Turning to the Customs Article, Mr. Habib recalled
that at the 54th meeting, the Korean negotiators had proposed
alternative language for Agreed Minute #3. The U.S.
negotiators had formulated alternative language which
was more precise but which included the provisions desired
by the Korean negotiators. He then tabled the following
revision of Agreed Minute #3:

> "The term 'military cargo' as used in paragraph 5(c)
> is not confined to arms and equipment but refers to
> all cargo consigned to the United States armed forces
> (including their authorized procurement agencies and
> their non-appropriated fund organizations provided
> for in Article ____). Pertinent information on cargo
> consigned to non-appropriated fund organizations will be
> furnished on a routine basis to authorities of the
> Republic of Korea. The extent of the pertinent
> information will be determined by the Joint Committee."

18. Mr. Chang stated that the Korean negotiators would
consider this proposal and comment on it at a later meeting.
Mr. Habib expressed the hope that the Korean negotiators
could at least agree in principle to this proposal, so
that negotiations could proceed with regard to other portions
of this article.

19. Mr. Chang replied that the proposal just tabled
by the U.S. negotiators did not include any reference to
the provision of additional information. He said the Korean
negotiators sought a system whereby certain information
would be provided on a routine basis and in specific cases,
in addition to the routine information, other information
which the Korean authorities may deem necessary should be
provided on request to the Joint Committee. The Joint
Committee, of course, would determine the extent of the
pertinent information to be provided.

0235

20. In reply, Mr. Habib referred to the Joint Committee Article, pointing out that under its provisions, the Korean authorities could apply to the Joint Committee at any time for whatever information they desired. There was no need, therefore, to include a redundant provision to this effect in the Agreed Minutes to the Customs Article. The Korean negotiators had asked for a provision for the delivery of information on an automatic basis to Korean authorities. The language proposed by the U.S. negotiators gave them such a provisions.

Foreign Exchange Controls

21. Turning to the Article dealing with Foreign Exchange Controls, Mr. Habib recalled that at the 54th meeting, the Korean negotiators had tabled proposed additional language to be included in the Agreed Minute. The U.S. negotiators could not agree to the Korean proposal, which did not meet the problem. Mr. Habib recalled that the Korean negotiators had suggested the possibility of the existence of a lawful exchange rate outside of the foreign exchange banks. He pointed out that the current ROK foreign exchange system provides for a floating exchange rate coupled with a market mechanism consisting of the exchange certificate system. The Korean negotiators seemed to assume that the U.S. armed forces would continue to purchase won only at the bank rate. If the bank rate were pegged at 255 won to the dollar and not permitted to float, the U.S. armed forces might be the victims of discrimination if they continued to buy at the bank rate. Traditionally, the ROK Government has operated on the basis of pegged rates. However, the new system provides the possibility of flexibility. If it operates as intended, the bank rate will be adjusted automatically

0236

to keep pace with the market rate. The foreign exchange banks, however, have the capability of adjusting the system. If the operation of the system is adjusted for other purposes, the U.S. armed forces are unwilling to pay the cost of such adjustment through the payment of discriminatory rates.

22. The language of the U.S. draft, Mr. Habib continued, requires no legislative changes by the ROK Government, nor does it impinge on the sovereign right of that government to change the operation of the foreign exchange system as it sees fit. The question of the operation of the present system will be discussed, of course, through channels other than those of the SOFA negotiations, since it is of great importance to other U.S. interests in Korea. The principle remains the same, however, insofar as the SOFA negotiations are concerned. That principle is that the U.S. armed forces intend to abide by Korean law 100% but do not intend to permit themselves to be subjected to discriminatory exchange rates.

23. Mr. Habib added that the U.S. armed forces did not wish, furthermore, to make it attractive to the ROK Government to establish discriminatory rates. He pointed out that discrimination against the U.S. armed forces would not be in the best interests of the ROK Government. Such action would force the U.S. armed forces to reconsider their policy of purchasing on the local market, would inhibit foreign exchange earnings from U.S. sources, and would foster the growth of black market activities, which both the U.S. authorities and the ROK authorities sought to avoid.

한·미국 간의 상호방위조약 제4조에 의한 시설과 구역 및 한국에서의 미국군대의 지위에 관한 협정(SOFA) 전59권. 1966.7.9 서울에서 서명 : 1967.2.9 발효(조약 232호) (V.51 실무교섭회의 합의의사록, 제38-68차, 1964) 243

24. Mr. Chang asked if he interpreted Mr. Habib's remarks correctly to the effect that if the market rate increased in value over the bank rate, the U.S. armed forces intended to purchase at the market rate.

25. Mr. Habib, in turn, asked Mr. Chang if it were not a fact that under the present system, if the difference between the market rate and the bank rate became more than 2%, the bank rate would be adjusted automatically? Mr. Chang replied in the affirmative.

26. Mr. Habib then stated that this 2% was in fact administrative leeway which permitted the banks to avoid a situation in which the bank rate would have to be adjusted each time the market rate rose or fell by a fraction of a point. To all intents and purposes, so long as the 2% provision was operative, there was little difference between the market rate and the bank rate. However, if the market rate were permitted to rise to 15% or 20% higher than the bank rate without any adjustment in the bank rate, why should the U.S. armed forces not be able to buy at the higher rate? Why would the ROK Government want to discriminate against them?

27. Mr. Chang stated that the reluctance of the U.S. negotiators to agree to the additional language proposed by the Korean negotiators implied that the U.S. armed forces were thinking of purchasing foreign exchange outside the foreign exchange banks. Mr. Habib replied that the U.S. armed forces would prefer not to purchase outside the foreign exchange banks. However, trading in foreign exchange certificates is legal under the present system. The language proposed by the Korean negotiators would open up the possibility of discriminatory rates. All the U.S. armed forces wanted

0238

was to be able to purchase at the highest rate which is not unlawful. They had no intention or desire to do anything other than abide by ROK laws.

28. It was agreed to hold the next meeting on June 26 at 3:00 p.m.

JOINT SUMMARY RECORD OF THE 56TH SESSION

1. Time and Place: 3:00 - 4:45 P.M. June 26, 1964 at
   the Foreign Ministry's Conference
   Room (No.1)

2. Attendants:

ROK Side:

Mr. Chang, Sang Moon	Director European and American Affairs Bureau
Mr. Koo, Choong Whay	Chief, America Section Ministry of Foreign Affairs
Mr. Cho, Choong Hoon	Chief Customs Section Ministry of Finance
Col. Kim, Won Kil	Chief Military Affairs Section Ministry of National Defense
Mr. Oh, Jae Hee	Chief, Treaty Section Ministry of Foreign Affairs
Mr. Ahn, Yun Gi	3rd Secretary Ministry of Foreign Affairs
Mr. Lee, Keun Pal (Rapporteur and Interpreter)	3rd Secretary Ministry of Foreign Affairs
Mr. Hwang, Young Jae	3rd Secretary Ministry of Foreign Affairs
Mr. Park, Won Chul	3rd Secretary Ministry of Foreign Affairs

U.S. Side:

Mr. Philip C. Habib	Counselor American Embassy
Brig. Gen. G.G. O'Connor	Deputy Chief of Staff 8th U.S. Army
Col. Howard Smigelow	Deputy Chief of Staff 8th U.S. Army
Capt. John Wayne	Assistant Chief of Staff USN/K
Col. Kenneth C. Crawford	Staff Judge Advocate 8th U.S. Army

0240

Mr. Frank R. La Macchia	First Secretary American Embassy
Mr. Benjamin A. Fleck (Rapporteur and Press Officer)	First Secretary American Embassy
Mr. Robert A. Kinney	J-5 8th U.S. Army
Lt. Col. Charles Wright	Staff Judge Advocate's Office 8th U.S. Army
Mr. Robert A. Lewis	2nd Secretary American Embassy
Mr. Kenneth Campen	Interpreter

Invited Contractors

1. Opening the meeting with the Invited Contractors Article, Mr. Habib recalled that at the 48th meeting, the Korean negotiators had indicated that if the U.S. negotiators would agree to the inclusion of the phrase "organized under the laws of the United States" after the word "corporations" in Paragraph 1 of the U.S. draft, the Korean negotiators would agree to the following:

> a. In Paragraph 1, insertion of the words "and the dependents of such persons" following the words "United States";

> b. Acceptance of Agreed Minute #2 of the U.S. draft and withdrawal of Agreed Minutes #1 and #2 of the Korean draft;

> c. Acceptance of Agreed Minute #1 of the U.S. draft.

2. Mr. Habib stated that the U.S. negotiators were now prepared to accept the Korean proposal. As a result, full agreement was now reached on Paragraph 1, which, as revised, reads as follows:

> "1. Persons, including corporations organized under the laws of the United States, their employees who are ordinarily resident in the United States, and the dependents of such persons, present in Korea solely for the purpose of executing contracts with the United States for the benefit of the United States armed forces or other armed forces in Korea under the Unified

0241

Command receiving logistical support from the
United States armed forces, who are designated by
the Government of the United States in accordance
with the provisions of paragraph 2 below, shall,
except as provided in this Article, be subject to
the laws and regulations of Korea."

3. Mr. Habib stated that the U.S. negotiators, in
order to retain a degree of flexibility regarding third-
country corporations, would like to obtain the agreement
of the Korean negotiators to the inclusion in the negotiating
record of the following understanding:

"If the U.S. authorities determine that there would
be significant advantage for U.S.-ROK mutual defense to
utilize one or more third-country corporations as USFK-
invited contractors, the authorities of the Government
of the Republic of Korea shall give sympathetic
consideration to a U.S. request to extend the benefits
of this agreement to such non-U.S. corporations."

Mr. Habib pointed out that a case might arise in which the
use of a third-country corporation would be to the mutual
advantage of the ROK and U.S. forces in carrying out their
mission of defending the Republic. Stating that the U.S.
negotiators had already waived any right to include third-
country corporations within the provisions of this article,
Mr. Habib said the proposed understanding would serve only
as guidance to the Joint Committee. He pointed out that it
would refer only to corporations and not to third-country
nationals.

4. Mr. Habib said the U.S. negotiators also wished to
confirm that references throughout the article (in paragraphs
2, 3, 4, 5 and 6) to "such persons" were references to
contractors, their employees, and their dependents, as
identified in paragraph 1.

5. Mr. Chang stated that the Korean negotiators
appreciated the acceptance by the U.S. negotiators of the
proposal made by the Korean negotiators at the 48th meeting.

0242

However, they understood that this acceptance was conditioned upon acceptance by the Korean negotiators of the understanding just proposed by the U.S. negotiators. They did not believe that the understanding would carry much weight if it were placed in the negotiating record. However, if there were indications that it would be to the mutual advantage of the two governments for defense of the Republic of Korea to engage a third-country corporation, the Korean authorities were prepared to give sympathetic consideration to such a request by the U.S. armed forces. Therefore, the Korean negotiators agreed to the understanding.

6. Mr. Habib stated that the understanding had not been proposed as a condition for acceptance of the previous Korean proposal. It was intended to serve as a guide to the Joint Committee and would show that the negotiators had considered this particular possibility.

7. Mr. Habib noted that the revised draft of the article tabled by the Korean negotiators on February 14, 1964 contained in Paragraph 2(a) the apparently inadvertent omission of the phrase "the United States for". He added that paragraph 6 of the Korean revised draft should be slightly revised to improve the style. The Korean negotiators stated, however, that inasmuch as they had already agreed to Paragraph 6 of the U.S. draft at the 32nd meeting, the text of that version of the paragraph should be considered to be the agreed text.

8. Mr. Chang asked for the U.S. position with regard to Agreed Minute #3 proposed by the Korean negotiators. Mr. Habib replied that the negotiators had already reached agreement in Paragraph 6 on the principle of exemption from

taxation. This is a principle which the U.S. negotiators believe should be applied and maintained. It was not proper to levy taxes on persons who normally would expect exemption and who, indeed, are granted exemption by the terms of Paragraph 6. Furthermore, the size of the taxes levied by the Korean authorities on privately-owned automobiles was unusually large.

9. Mr. Chang replied that Korean laws and regulations require privately-owned vehicles to be registered with the local authorities. Such registration in turn required the owners to pay the local fees and assessments. Even members of the armed forces should pay such local fees but the requirement on them to do so has been waived in view of their mission. The Korean negotiators believed that privately-owned vehicles of contractors and their employees and dependents should be required to pay these local fees and assessments. Mr. Chang stated that the local assessments are, in fact, payments for the use of roads and highways.

10. Mr. Habib pointed out that the vehicles under discussion actually remained in the country for only a relatively short period. When their owners departed, the vehicles were taken out of the country. If they were not taken out, they were sold and the relevant taxes were paid at the time of the sale. The U.S. negotiators believed that the ROK Government made a distinction between taxation and registration. The U.S. negotiators were not unprepared to consider the payment of registration fees on privately owned vehicles but they wished to maintain the principle of exemption from taxation.

11. Mr. Chang said the Korean negotiators understood the U.S. position. They believed that fees and taxes were closely

0244

related to the registration of vehicles. They would study the question and comment further at a later meeting.

12. Mr. Habib remarked that the U.S. negotiators were merely attempting to arrive at a position similar to that which existed in other countries. In other countries registration fees were collected but heavy taxes such as those imposed in the Republic of Korea were non-existent.

Security Measures

13. Each side indicated that its position with regard to the Security Measures Article had not changed. Neither side had any alternative proposals to suggest and it was agreed to give further study to the matter.

Customs

14. Turning to the Customs Article, Mr. Chang recalled that at the 55th meeting agreement had been reached in principle that pertinent information with regard to cargo consigned to non-appropriated fund organizations would be furnished to the Korean authorities on a routine basis. However, the Korean negotiators still desired that other information deemed necessary by the ROK Customs authorities in specific cases should be furnished on request through the Joint Committee. The Korean negotiators would accept the revised Agreed Minute #3 tabled by the U.S. negotiators at the 55th meeting if the U.S. negotiators would agree to the inclusion of the following two understandings in the negotiating record:

   a. Pertinent information to be provided on a routine basis shall include at least invoices and packing lists;

   b. In addition to the provisions of routine information, other information which the ROK authorities may

0245

deem necessary in specific cases shall promptly be
provided on request through the Joint Committee.

15. In reply, Mr. Habib stated that the original
proposal regarding pertinent information had been made by
the Korean negotiators, in a revised version of Agreed
Minute #3 tabled by them at the 54th meeting. In that
proposal, the Korean negotiators themselves had suggested
that the extent of the pertinent information was to be
decided by the Joint Committee. The U.S. negotiators had
agreed to that suggestion. In the view of the U.S.
negotiators, the provision of additional information upon
request to the Joint Committee is provided for in any article,
paragraph, or clause of this Agreement. Mr. Habib suggested
that the Korean negotiators reexamine the Joint Committee
Article and all of the other commitments to provide
information being made in this and other articles. Instead
of the two understandings proposed by the Korean negotiators,
the U.S. negotiators wished to propose the following
understanding, which was stated in the simplest possible
terms:

"With respect to Agreed Minute #3, in addition
to the information provided on a routine basis, other
pertinent information will be provided on request
through the Joint Committee."

16. Mr. Chang stated that the Korean negotiators believed
there should be a statement to the effect that the pertinent
information should include at least packing lists and
invoices.

17. Mr. Habib pointed out that a thorough discussion
of documentation had been held prior to the submission by
the Korean negotiators of their proposed revised Agreed
Minute #3. During that previous discussion, the Korean

negotiators had indicated that they recognized the function
of the Joint Committee. The U.S. negotiators had accepted
without question the principle of automaticity proposed
by the Korean negotiators. The U.S. negotiators, however,
were not prepared at this point to begin implementation of
the Agreement. That was the job of the Joint Committee.
The Korean negotiators had already agreed to let the Joint
Committee decide the extent of the pertinent information to
be provided. If it were spelled out in this article, it
might as well be spelled out in every article. The U.S.
negotiators believed that implementation of the Agreement
should be left to the Joint Committee.

18. Mr. Chang stated that the Korean negotiators
recognized that it was the function of the Joint Committee
to determine the extent of the pertinent information to be
furnished. However, packing lists and invoices are essential
elements of information regarding non-appropriated fund cargo.
U.S. objections to mentioning them specifically were of
concern to the Korean negotiators, lest the Joint Committee
might not agree to include them as components of the pertinent
information.

19. Mr. Habib pointed out that he had said nothing that
could be so construed. He pointed out that there might be
other kinds of documentation which would be better than
packing lists. Was it the intention of the Korean negotiators
that every sealed container entering the Republic of Korea
be opened in order to obtain the packing list? Such a
procedure would be administratively unsound and extremely
unwise from the point of view of security.

20. Mr. Chang stated that the Korean negotiators would
study the U.S. counter-proposal and comment at a later meeting.

21. The next meeting was scheduled for July 8 at 3:00 p.m.

JOINT SUMMARY RECORD OF THE 57TH SESSION

1. Time and Place: 3:00 - 4:00 P.M. July 8, 1964 at the Foreign Ministry's Conference Room (No.1)

2. Attendants:

ROK Side

Mr. Chang, Sang Hoon	Director European and American Affairs Bureau
Mr. Koo, Choong Whey	Chief, America Section Ministry of Foreign Affairs
Mr. Cho, Choong Hoon	Chief Customs Section Ministry of Finance
Mr. Hur, Hyong Koo	Chief Prosecutors Section Ministry of Justice
Col. Kim, Won Kil	Chief Military Affairs Section Ministry of National Defense
Maj. Lee, Kye Hoon	Military Affairs Section Ministry of National Defense
Mr. Ahn, Yun Gi	3rd Secretary Ministry of Foreign Affairs
Mr. Lee, Keun Pal (Rapporteur and Interpreter)	3rd Secretary Ministry of Foreign Affairs
Mr. Hwang, Young Jae	3rd Secretary Ministry of Foreign Affairs

U.S. Side:

Mr. Philip C. Habib	Counselor American Embassy
Brig. Gen. G.G. O'Connor	Deputy Chief of Staff 8th U.S. Army
Col. Howard Smigelow	Deputy Chief of Staff 8th U.S. Army
Capt. John Wayne	Assistant Chief of Staff USN/K
Col. Kenneth C. Crawford	Staff Judge Advocate 8th U.S. Army

0248

Mr. Benjamin A. Fleck (Rapporteur and Press Officer)	First Secretary American Embassy
Mr. Robert A. Kinney	J-5 8th U.S. Army
Lt. Col. Charles Wright	Staff Judge Advocate's Office 8th U.S. Army
Mr. Robert A. Lewis	2nd Secretary American Embassy
Mr. Edward Hurwitz	2nd Secretary American Embassy

Customs

1. Mr. Chang opened the meeting by referring to previous discussions of the Customs Article. He recalled that with regard to Agreed Minute #3, the negotiators had already agreed on language that would provide for the furnishing by the U.S. armed forces on a routine basis of pertinent information on cargo consigned to non-appropriated fund organizations. He recalled that at the 56th meeting the Korean negotiators had offered to accept the revision of Agreed Minute #3 tabled by the U.S. negotiators at the 55th meeting if the U.S. negotiators would agree to include two understandings in the negotiating record. In reply, the U.S. negotiators had counterproposed the following understanding:

> "With respect to Agreed Minute #3, in addition to the information provided on a routine basis, other pertinent information will be provided on request through the Joint Committee."

2. Mr. Chang stated that informal conversations had been held subsequent to the 56th meeting and had been fruitful, in the opinion of the Korean negotiators. The Korean negotiators were now prepared to agree to the revision of Agreed Minute #3 tabled by the U.S. negotiators, provided the U.S. negotiators would agree to include the following two understandings in the negotiating record:

0249

a. Pertinent information shall include cargo manifests and shipping documents;

b. In addition to information provided on a routine basis, other pertinent information will be provided on request through the Joint Committee. Mr. Chang noted that if the U.S. negotiators would agree to these understandings full agreement would be reached on Agreed Minute #3.

3. Mr. Habib replied that the U.S. negotiators agreed to the inclusion of the proposed understandings in the negotiated record and that full agreement had been reached on Agreed Minute #3.

4. Mr. Habib suggested that the negotiators clear up the remaining points of difference in this article. He recalled that at the 41st meeting, the Korean negotiators had tabled a proposed revision of Paragraph 5(a), with the purpose of distinguishing between members of the U.S. armed forces entering or leaving the Republic of Korea on orders and those travelling for recreational purposes. The U.S. negotiators agreed with the principle proposed by the Korean negotiators but wished to suggest alternative language which was simpler and more precise than that of the Korean revision. Mr. Habib then tabled the following language:

> "(a) Members of the United States armed forces under orders, other than leave orders, entering or leaving the Republic of Korea;"

5. Mr. Chang asked whether travel for rest and recreation ("R and R") was included in the term "leave orders". Upon being assured by Mr. Habib that this was the case, Mr. Chang stated that the Korean negotiators agreed to the revised wording proposed by the U.S. negotiators.

0250

6. Mr. Habib stated that the U.S. negotiators wished to clarify certain aspects of paragraph 5(b). In that subparagraph, the negotiators had agreed to exempt First Class letter mail under official postal seal from customs examination. During discussions of this subparagraph, the Korean negotiators had stated on several occasions that the Korean authorities had no interest in inspecting First Class letter mail. In view of those statements, and in view of the fact that there might be occasions when First Class letter mail might enter the ROK lacking the official postal seal, the U.S. negotiators would like the Korean negotiators to reaffirm their previous statements that the ROKG has no intention of inspecting First Class letter mail even when it is not under official postal seal. Mr. Habib pointed out that it was the intention of the U.S. authorities that such mail should always enter the ROK under official seal but that if this was not always the case, it would still be clearly identifiable as First Class mail.

7. Mr. Chang replied that even if First Class letter mail entering the ROK through military post offices was not under official postal seal, the ROKG would not inspect such mail, in accordance with the relevant ROK laws and regulations.

8. Mr. Habib said that the U.S. negotiators also wished to clarify the term "official documents". This term included documents and parcels bearing an official endorsement or addressed to a military organization. Mr. Chang asked whether the term included documents and parcels addressed to individuals in their official capacity. Mr. Habib explained that mail addressed to a military organization included that addressed either to the organization itself or to "The Commanding Officer" of the organization. Personal mail

0251

addressed to individual officers by name would not fall within this definition. Mr. Chang replied that the Korean negotiators agreed with this interpretation of the term "official documents".

9. Mr. Habib then recalled that the Korean negotiators had proposed the insertion in Agreed Minute #2 of the phrase "reasonable quantities of" following the word "duty". The U.S. negotiators agreed to that revision but wished to clear up any ambiguity that might exist. It was the understanding of the U.S. negotiators that the U.S. armed forces will be responsible for determining what constitutes "reasonable quantities". If the Korean authorities have any doubts or questions, they can always raise the matter in the Joint Committee.

10. Mr. Chang expressed appreciation for the agreement of the U.S. negotiators to this revision of Agreed Minute #2. The Korean negotiators agreed that the primary responsibility for determining what constitutes "reasonable quantities" would rest with the U.S. military authorities. But they also believed that the Korean authorities should have the opportunity to discuss the question whenever they thought it necessary. Since the spirit of the U.S. negotiators reflected a mood of cooperation, the Korean negotiators were sure that any difficulty which might arise with regard to this Agreed Minute would be satisfactorily resolved by the Joint Committee.

11. Mr. Habib expressed agreement and reiterated that the right of the Korean authorities to raise the matter in the Joint Committee was unquestioned. He commented that full agreement had now been reached on the Customs Article, with the exception of Agreed Minute #7. He asked whether the Korean negotiators had any views to express regarding this Agreed Minute.

0252

12. Mr. Chang replied that Agreed Minute #7 was closely related to the provisions of the article dealing with non-appropriated fund organizations. The Korean negotiators believed that final agreement on the latter article would mean automatic agreement on this Agreed Minute.

13. Mr. Habib agreed and remarked that full agreement had now been reached on the text of the Customs Article.

Invited Contractors

14. Turning to the Invited Contractors Article, Mr. Chang stated that the Korean negotiators had considered the position stated previously by the U.S. negotiators regarding the payment of taxes on vehicles. The Korean negotiators were now prepared to waive all taxes on vehicles, including those privately owned by contractors and their employees, provided the contractors and their employees would respect and obey the laws and regulations relating to registration of vehicles and issuance of driving permits. Therefore, the Korean negotiators were willing to withdraw their proposed Agreed Minute #3 if the U.S. negotiators would withdraw their proposed subparagraph (i) of Paragraph 3.

15. Mr. Habib replied that the U.S. negotiators would agree to the deletion of subparagraph (i), provided that the Korean negotiators would state for the negotiating record that the registration fees and drivers' permit regulations will be the same for contractors and their employees as for Korean nationals with due allowance for language problems. The U.S. negotiators considered this to be a reasonable request. All that they were asking for was a statement by the Korean negotiators that there would be no discrimination against the contractors and their employees.

0253

16. Mr. Chang stated that the Korean negotiators wished to outline the following procedures which would be followed with regard to the contractors and their employees:

a. Driving Permits - Anyone holding a valid driving permit issued by a foreign government or subdivision thereof would be required to take a simple test on local traffic regulations and pay a fee of Won 770. This would be handled, if the driver is located in Seoul, by the Traffic Section of the Seoul City Municipal Police Bureau;

b. Registration - Upon presentation of an appropriate certificate regarding the exemption from vehicle tax the owner of a vehicle would be required to pay registration fees totalling Won 4,355, broken down as follows:

```
Registration -     ₩1000
Inspection   -      3060
License Plates       295
                 ₩ 4355
```

17. Mr. Habib asked whether the above-outlined procedures and fees were identical with those applied to Korean citizens. Mr. Chang replied affirmatively. Mr. Habib said it was the understanding of the U.S. negotiators that these procedures applied only to vehicles owned by the contractors or by their employees and did not apply to U.S. Government-owned vehicles used by the contractors. Mr. Chang replied that this was the understanding of the Korean negotiators also. Complete agreement was thereupon reached on the text of the Invited Contractors Article, with the exception of Paragraph 8. It was agreed that further discussion of Paragraph 8 would be held after agreement had been reached on the Criminal Jurisdiction Article.

18. The next meeting was scheduled for July 16 at 3:00 p.m.

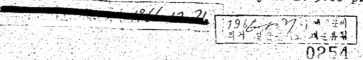

0254

<u>JOINT SUMMARY RECORD OF THE 58TH SESSION</u>

1. Time and Place: 3:00 - 5:10 P.M. July 16, 1964 at
   the Foreign Ministry's Conference
   Room (No.1)

2. Attendants:

ROK Side:

Mr. Chang, Sang Moon	Director European and American Affairs Bureau
Mr. Koo, Choong Whay	Chief, America Section Ministry of Foreign Affairs
Mr. Cho, Choong Hoon	Chief Customs Section Ministry of Finance
Mr. Hur, Hyong Koo	Chief Prosecutors Section Ministry of Justice
Col. Kim, Won Kil	Chief Military Affairs Section Ministry of National Defense
Maj. Lee, Kyo Hoon	Military Affairs Section Ministry of National Defense
Mr. Park, Sang Yong	3rd Secretary Ministry of Foreign Affairs
Mr. Ahn, Yun Gi	3rd Secretary Ministry of Foreign Affairs
X Mr. Lee, Kae Chul	3rd Secretary Ministry of Foreign Affairs
Mr. Lee, Keun Pal (Rapporteur and Interpreter)	3rd Secretary Ministry of Foreign Affairs
Mr. Hwang, Young Jae	3rd Secretary Ministry of Foreign Affairs

U.S. Side:

Mr. Philip C. Habib	Counselor American Embassy
Brig. Gen. G.G. O'Connor	Deputy Chief of Staff 8th U.S. Army
Col. Howard Smigelow	Deputy Chief of Staff 8th U.S. Army

0255

Capt. John Wayne	Assistant Chief of Staff USM/K
Col. Kenneth C. Crawford	Staff Judge Advocate 8th U.S. Army
Mr. Frank R. La Macchia	First Secretary American Embassy
Mr. Benjamin A. Fleck (Rapporteur and Press Officer)	First Secretary American Embassy
Mr. Robert A. Kinney	J-5 8th U.S. Army
Lt. Col. Charles Wright	Staff Judge Advocate's Office 8th U.S. Army
Mr. Robert A. Lewis	2nd Secretary American Embassy
Mr. David Y. C. Lee (Interpreter)	2nd Secretary American Embassy
Mr. Daniel A. O'Donohue	2nd Secretary American Embassy

1.   Mr. Chang opened the meeting by introducing Mr. Park
Sang-yong, who was attending as an Observer. Mr. Habib
in turn introduced Mr. David Y.C. Lee, and Mr. Daniel A.
O'Donohue, who were attending as Interpreter and Observer,
respectively, for the U.S. negotiators.

Non-Appropriated Fund Organizations

2.   Taking up the Non-Appropriated Funds Organizations
Article, Mr. Chang remarked that the only remaining point
at issue was the question of what persons and organizations
should be entitled to use the NAFO facilities. He said the
Korean negotiators had carefully studied the text of the
Agreed Minute proposed by the U.S. negotiators. Inasmuch as
the Status of Forces Agreement was concerned with the U.S.
armed forces, the Korean negotiators believed that persons
and organizations not connected in any way with the U.S.
armed forces or the U.S. Government could not be appropriately
included in the terms of the Agreement. Therefore, they
believed that item (f) of the U.S. draft was not an appropriate

0256

subject for discussion at the negotiating table. They
proposed the deletion of item (f). At the 36th negotiating
meeting, the U.S. negotiators had indicated that the
deletion of this item might cause problems. Nevertheless,
the Korean negotiators continued to believe that it should
be deleted.

3. Mr. Habib replied that the Korean negotiators were
taking a position that would, in effect, prevent the U.S.
armed forces or the ROK Government from exercising in the
future any flexibility with regard to this subject. The
U.S. negotiators had made it clear that the provisions
of item (f) would be applied to persons and organizations
only with the express consent of the ROK Government.

4. Mr. Habib stated that elimination of item (f)
would create problems with regard to three organizations:
the United Nations Commission for the Unification and
Rehabilitation of Korea (UNCURK); the Swiss and Swedish
members of the Neutral Nations Supervisory Commission (NNSC);
and the United Nations Memorial Cemetery in Korea (UNMCK).
He pointed out that if there were no clause in the Agreement
providing for the extension of NAFO facilities to these
organizations, the U.S. armed forces would be unable to extend
such facilities, even if they or the ROK Government wanted
to do so.

5. Mr. Habib stated that the Swiss and Swedish members
of the NNSC, given their function in terms of the Armistice
Agreement, have a direct relationship with the U.S. armed
forces. Both the U.S. Government and the ROK Government
have a substantial interest in them and the U.S. armed
forces provide them with logistical support at Pan Mun Jom.

0257

6. Mr. Habib pointed out that the members of UNCURK view their organization as being the political arm of the United Nations in Korea, even as the United Nations Command is the military arm. They have already expressed to members of the U.S. negotiating team their concern over the possibility that the SOFA might not provide for the continued extension of NAFO facilities to them. In reply, they have been told that the matter will be considered during the negotiations. The extension of NAFO facilities to UNCURK is a burden to the U.S. armed forces. Nevertheless, the U.S. negotiators believe that it is desirable to continue to do so, in view of the need to maintain harmonious relations with that organization. It is in the interest, not only of the U.S. authorities but also of the ROK Government, to remain on good terms with UNCURK. The U.S. negotiators believed that there was no difference of opinion on this question between the negotiating teams but that they were faced with a mutual problem, for which a satisfactory solution must be found.

7. Mr. Chang remarked that at previous meetings, the U.S. negotiators had already indicated that under item (f) would be included, in addition to UNCURK, the United Nations Technical Assistance Board (UNTAB), the Scandinavian Medical Mission, the American-Korean Foundation, and members of the Diplomatic Corps. Now, the U.S. negotiators were suggesting the addition of NNSC personnel and UNICK personnel. The Korean negotiators still desired the deletion of item (f) but they found the arguments of the U.S. negotiators with regard to NNSC personnel to be reasonable. Therefore, they proposed the deletion of item (f) and the inclusion of NNSC personnel under item (b).

0258

<u>Criminal Jurisdiction</u>

8. Turning to the Criminal Jurisdiction Article,
Mr. Habib stated that the U.S. negotiators would make a paragraph
by paragraph reply to the proposals made by the Korean
negotiators at the 52nd meeting.

9. Mr. Habib recalled that the Korean negotiators
had proposed the substitution in Paragraph 1(a) of the
Korean draft of the phrase "all persons subject to the
military law of the United States" for the phrase "the
members of the United States armed forces and the civilian
components". They had also expressed concern over the
possibility that the language in the U.S. draft would permit
the exercise in Korea of judicial power by some U.S. authority
other than military authorities. The U.S. negotiators wished
to give a categorical assurance that the U.S. Government
has no intention to establish civil courts which could exercise
jurisdiction in the Republic of Korea. There is no intention
that U.S. other than military authorities will exercise
jurisdiction in Korea over U.S. personnel. At the same time,
however, the U.S. negotiators would like to call attention
to the possibility that legislation may be passed eventually
in the United States which would provide that accused U.S.
civilians abroad could be returned to the United States
for trial. Paragraph 1(a) of the U.S. draft had been
drafted specifically so as not to preclude this possibility.
The U.S. negotiators, therefore, believed the U.S. draft
preferable to the proposed change in the Korean draft, since
it would not preclude the applicability of any legislation
which might be passed to bridge the present "jurisdiction
gap" over U.S. civilians abroad.

0259

10. Mr. Habib recalled that at the 52nd meeting, the Korean negotiators had stated that the ROK Government would not exercise jurisdiction over U.S. military personnel by military tribunal under any circumstances. They had also given the same assurance with regard to the civilian component. The U.S. negotiators welcomed these assurances. They wished to point out again that the language of Paragraph 1(b) of the U.S. draft plainly sets forth the ROK Government's intention, since it states that "the civil authorities of the Republic of Korea shall have the right to exercise ...". The U.S. draft of this subparagraph contained the phrase "the right to exercise", which was not contained in the Korean draft. On restudying the subparagraph, the U.S. negotiators had found the Korean phraseology to be clear and acceptable and agreed to the deletion of the phrase "the right to exercise". The only remaining difference in language in the two drafts of the subparagraph, therefore, was the inclusion of the word "civil" in the U.S. draft. Since the Korean negotiators had already given the assurances just referred to, they should be able to agree to the inclusion of this word.

11. Turning to the subject of the Duty Certificate, Mr. Habib recalled that at the 47th meeting, the Korean negotiators had proposed that the definition of official duty based on that contained in the U.S. Army, Far East, circular of January 1956 be read into the Agreed Joint Summary. At the 49th meeting, the U.S. negotiators had agreed to this proposal, provided the Korean negotiators would agree to Agreed Minute #2 Re Paragraph 3(a) of the U.S. draft. Instead of agreeing to this package proposal of the U.S. negotiators, the Korean negotiators at the 52nd meeting had proposed an alternative Agreed Minute Re Paragraph

0260

3(a) (ii). Before commenting on this Korean counter-
proposal, the U.S. negotiators wished to seek clarification
of the Korean position and, at the same time, wished to
make the U.S. position regarding duty certificates quite
clear.

12. Mr. Habib stated that in the view of the U.S.
negotiators, the duty certificate would be definitive
unless it is modified by the U.S. authorities, either as
a result of a request by the ROK authorities for modification
or otherwise. There was no intention to foreclose requests by
the Korean authorities for reconsideration of duty certificates
in specific cases where there is a justifiable basis for
questioning the correctness of the certificate. What is
important, in the view of the U.S. negotiators, is that
the certificate will be conclusive unless modification is
agreed upon. This is not made clear in the Korean draft.
A second matter of concern to the U.S. negotiators is that
the accused should not be deprived of his entitlement to a
prompt and speedy trial as a result of protracted reconsideration of the duty certificate. If agreement to modification
were not reached within a specified time, the U.S. authorities
would expect the duty certificate to be conclusive for
that case, although discussions could continue concerning the
propriety of issuing a duty certificate under similar
circumstances in a future case.

13. The U.S. negotiators had been instructed to inform
the Korean negotiators, Mr. Habib continued, that the U.S.
Government was concerned lest modification of the U.S.
position on duty certificates was being sought by the Korean
negotiators as a means of acquiring jurisdiction in cases
involving action taken by sentries to protect U.S. property.

In the absence of special circumstances, such cases would
be certified as official duty. The U.S. authorities would be
willing to reconsider the duty certificate in such a case, if
requested to do so by the Korean authorities. However, the
duty certificate would be definitive unless it were modified
as a result of the reconsideration. Mr. Habib made it clear
that the U.S. negotiators were not responding to the revised
draft of the Agreed Minute tabled by the Korean negotiators
and, before doing so, wished to clarify the views of the
Korean negotiators on the points he had mentioned.

14. Mr. Chang replied that whereas the U.S. draft
provides that the duty certificate shall be "conclusive"
(Agreed Minute #2 Re Paragraph 3(a)), the Korean draft uses
the word "sufficient" (revised Agreed Minute Re Paragraph
3(a) (ii)). The Korean draft provides for specific
procedures to be followed if the Korean authorities raise
an objection to a duty certificate, while the U.S. draft
does not outline any procedure. The Korean negotiators,
therefore, preferred the Korean draft.

15. Mr. Habib stated that the U.S. negotiators wished
to make it clear that a Korean appeal regarding a duty
certificate would not alter the conclusive nature of the
certificate unless the U.S. authorities agreed to modify
the certificate after reconsideration. He asked what
procedure the Korean negotiators had in mind.

16. Mr. Chang reviewed the position stated by the
U.S. negotiators. They held that once the duty certificate
were issued, it would remain valid unless modified by the
U.S. authorities after considering objections raised by
the Korean authorities. According to the U.S. position,

0262

there were two possibilities: the duty certificate would either be conclusive or it would be modified by the U.S. authorities. Mr. Chang stated that this was contrary to the position set forth in the revised draft tabled by the Korean negotiators. They had in mind that if the Korean authorities objected to a duty certificate, agreement would then be reached by the Joint Committee, not unilaterally by the U.S. authorities. The Korean negotiators also believed that the Joint Committee must be allowed sufficient time to reach a decision. There might be cases in which the validity of the duty certificates would be ambiguous; therefore it would take some time for both sides to reach agreement. For these reasons, the Korean negotiators could not agree to the two points made by the U.S. negotiators.

17. In reply to Mr. Habib's request for clarification of the concept of "sufficient time", Mr. Chang stated that "appropriate time" might be a better phrase. The Korean negotiators believed that agreement could be reached on a certain number of days as a time limit for Joint Committee consideration of duty certificate cases.

18. Referring to the Korean revised draft, Mr. Habib asked who would determine that "the contrary is proved" or that a decision had been reached. Mr. Chang replied that the Korean draft provided that the Korean authorities could base an objection to a duty certificate on the belief of the chief prosecutor that there was proof contrary to the certificate. Mr. Chang added that the third paragraph of the Korean revised draft of the Agreed Minute Re Paragraph 3(a) (ii) provided for referral of the case to the Korean courts if the Joint Committee were unable to reach agreement regarding modification of a duty certificate to which the Korean authorities had objected.

0263

19. Moving on to another portion of the Article, Mr. Habib recalled that the Korean negotiators had previously indicated that they did not wish to accept the concept of the combat zone, as contained in Agreed Minute #1 Re Paragraph 1(b) of the U.S. draft. They had expressed the hope that a workable arrangement could be agreed upon to satisfy the U.S. concern over assuring the combat readiness of U.S. troops without resort to the concept of a combat zone. The Korean negotiators had also requested deletion from the U.S. draft of Agreed Minute #1 Re Paragraph 3(a), which would give the U.S. authorities primary right to exercise jurisdiction over court martial offenses. Having carefully studied the Korean requests, the U.S. negotiators were prepared to make a significant counter-proposal in an effort to reach full agreement on the waiver question. The U.S. negotiators would agree to the deletion of the two Agreed Minutes just mentioned if the Korean negotiators would accept the Agreed Minute Re Paragraph 3 of the U.S. draft. This would be a substantial concession by the U.S. negotiators.

20. Regarding the subject of pre-trial custody, Mr. Habib recalled that at the 52nd meeting, the Korean negotiators had tabled a revised draft of Paragraph 5(d) and a new Paragraph 5(e). The U.S. negotiators believed the revised version of Paragraph 5(d) to be an improvement over the original language but they still considered Paragraph 5(c) of the U.S. draft to be preferable. Transfer of an accused to Korean custody is adequately covered by the last sentence of the latter paragraph. The U.S. negotiators had studied the proposed new Paragraph 5(e), regarding Korean custody of offenders against the security of the Republic of Korea.

0264

The U.S. armed forces in Korea are there to help protect
and preserve the security of the ROK and will continue to
do everything possible to carry out that mission. Therefore,
the U.S. negotiators were prepared to agree to inclusion of
the new ROK paragraph 5(e), e.i. to Korean custody in
security cases if the Korean negotiators would agree to the
following two understandings:

a. There must be mutual U.S.-ROK agreement as to
the circumstances in which such custody is appropriate;

b. Korean confinement facilities must be adequate
by U.S. standards.

21. With regard to the question of trial safeguards,
Mr. Habib recalled that the Korean negotiators had indicated
general agreement with Paragraph 9 and related Agreed
Minutes of the U.S. draft but had raised some question
regarding several of the trial safeguards enumerated in the
Agreed Minute Re Paragraph 9. In order to be responsive
to the ROK views and to facilitate early agreement on this
subject, the U.S. negotiators proposed the following changes
in the Agreed Minute Re Paragraph 9 of the U.S. draft:

a. Deletion of subparagraph (a);

b. In subparagraph (b), deletion of all language
after the words "shall have the right to appeal a conviction
or sentence".

22. Mr. Chang stated that the Korean negotiators
appreciated the extensive response which the U.S. negotiators
had made to the Korean proposals. However, the U.S. position
did not fully meet the Korean requirements. The Korean
negotiators were disappointed but would consider the U.S.
position and would respond at the next meeting.

23. The next meeting was tentatively scheduled for July
28 at 3:00 p.m.

0265

JOINT SUMMARY RECORD OF THE 59TH SESSION

1. Time and Place: 3:00 - 4:45 P.M. July 28, 1964 at
   the Foreign Ministry's Conference
   Room (No.1)

2. Attendants:

   ROK Side:

   Mr. Chang, Sang Hoon   Director
                                 European and American Affairs
                                 Bureau

   Mr. Koo, Choong Whay   Chief, America Section
                                 Ministry of Foreign Affairs

   Mr. Hur, Hyong Koo   Chief
                                 Prosecutors Section
                                 Ministry of Justice

   Maj. Lee, Kye Hoon   Military Affairs Section
                                 Ministry of National Defense

   Mr. Park, Sang Yong   3rd Secretary
                                 Ministry of Foreign Affairs

   Mr. Ahn, Yun Gi   3rd Secretary
                                 Ministry of Foreign Affairs

   Mr. Lee, Keun Pal   3rd Secretary
   (Rapporteur and   Ministry of Foreign Affairs
    Interpreter)

   Mr. Hwang, Young Jae   3rd Secretary
                                 Ministry of Foreign Affairs

   Mr. Park, Won Chul   3rd Secretary
                                 Ministry of Foreign Affairs

   U.S. Side:

   Mr. Philip C. Habib   Counselor
                                 American Embassy

   Brig. Gen. G.G. O'Connor   Deputy Chief of Staff
                                 8th U.S. Army

   Col. Howard Smigelow   Deputy Chief of Staff
                                 8th U.S. Army

   Capt. John Wayne   Assistant Chief of Staff
                                 USN/K

   Col. Kenneth C. Crawford   Staff Judge Advocate
                                 8th U.S. Army

0266

Mr. Frank R. La Macchia	First Secretary American Embassy
Mr. Benjamin A. Fleck! (Rapporteur and Press Officer)	First Secretary American Embassy
Mr. Robert A. Kinney	J-5 8th U.S. Army
Mr. Daniel A. O'Donohue	2nd Secretary American Embassy
Maj. Alton H. Harvey	Staff Judge Advocate's Office 8th U.S. Army
Mr. Kenneth Campen	Interpreter

1. Mr. Habib opened the meeting by introducing Major Harvey, who was replacing Lt. Colonel Wright as a member of the U.S. negotiating team. Mr. Chang welcomed Major Harvey to the negotiations.

Criminal Jurisdiction

2. Taking up the criminal jurisdiction article, Mr. Chang stated that at the previous session the Korean negotiators had expressed their initial disappointment at the response made by the U.S. negotiators to the proposals tabled by the Korean negotiators at the 50th and 52nd meetings. The Korean negotiators, after studying the U.S. position, would like to make a point by point comment on the U.S. response to their proposals.

3. Mr. Chang then made the following statement:

4. "a. All persons subject to the military law of the U.S., Para 1.(a)

"With respect to our proposal to substitute the phrase 'all persons subject to the military law of the United States' for the phrase 'the members of the U.S. armed forces and the civilian components,' the U.S. side gave an assurance that the U.S. Government has no intention

0267

to establish civil courts which could exercise jurisdiction in the Republic of Korea. At the same time, the U.S. negotiators indicated their preference for the language in their draft to the Korean proposal, on the grounds that legislation may be passed eventually in the U.S. which would provide that any accused U.S. civilian abroad could be taken to the U.S. for trial.

5. "We have no objection to the principle that the SOFA language should be flexible enough to accommodate all eventualities foreseen in the near future. However, it is inconceivable that such an uncertain eventuality as the legislation referred to by the U.S. negotiators should affect in any way our Status of Forces negotiations. Furthermore, decisions of the Supreme Court of the United States on the matter have been subject to reversal since 1956. Therefore, we can think not only of the possibility over which the U.S. negotiators are concerned but also of the possibility that the U.S. Supreme Court may eventually reverse its decision of 1960 so that civilian offenders may be tried by U.S. Court Martial overseas.

6. "Moreover, in our view, the proposed idea of taking the accused civilians back to the U.S. for trial is neither consonant with the established principle of judicial proceedings nor acceptable to any sovereign nation hosting foreign troops. We believe the contemporary principle and practice of trial in any given country demand that the trial should be held at the place where the offense is committed or at least at a place reasonably distant from the site of the crime. We also believe that if an accused who committed an offense in the territory of one sovereign

0268

country is brought to another sovereign country for trial
there would arise a serious question as to possible
infringement of sovereignty."

7. "b. The civil Authorities of the Republic of Korea,
Para. 1(b)

"Regarding the provision of Paragraph 1(b), the
United States negotiators stated that the language of
paragraph 1(b) of the U.S. draft, 'the civil authorities
of the Republic of Korea', sets forth the Korean Government's
intention as expressed in assurances given by the Korean
negotiators that the Korean Government will not exercise
jurisdiction over U.S. military personnel by military
tribunal under any circumstances.

8. "The assurance was intended to meet the requirement
of the U.S. negotiators, who have expressed their concern
over the possibility of subjecting their military personnel
to Korean military tribunal.

9. "Inasmuch as such a significant assurance was given
to your side, we have naturally expected that you would no
longer insist on retaining the word 'civil'. Since this
word 'civil' cannot be found in other SOFAs we wonder what
were your understandings or arrangements with other countries
in agreeing to the provision without the word 'civil'.

10. "If the Korean negotiators would accept such
unprecedented wording as appeared in the U.S. draft, this
would undoubtedly cause very delicate problems in the
Korean Government as well as with the Korean people.
Neither the sentiment of the Korean people nor the atmosphere
of the National Assembly would tolerate acceptance of such
a version.

0269

11. "c. <u>Official Duty Certificate, Agreed Minutes</u>
<u>Re para. 3(a) (ii)</u>

"Regarding the official duty certificate, the
U.S. side stated at the last session the following two
points:

(1) The certificate will be conclusive unless
modification is agreed upon;

(2) The accused should not be deprived of his
entitlement to a prompt and speedy trial as
a result of protracted reconsideration of the
duty certificate.

12. "The Korean negotiators should like to concentrate
on the first point alone at this meeting. The Korean
negotiators have studied the U.S. statement, and we have
found that the statement indicates an improvement over the
U.S. Agreed Minute re Paragraph 3(a).

13. "The provision of the U.S. Agreed Minute re
Paragraph 3(a) reads as follows: 'A certificate issued by
or on behalf of his commanding officer etc... shall be
conclusive for the purpose of determining primary jurisdiction.' However, the U.S. negotiators at the last session
stated that unless modification is agreed upon either
through request of the Korean authorities or otherwise,
the certificate will be conclusive. The indication of
possible modification at the request of the Korean authorities
is an improvement from our point of view.

14. "In our view, any possible controversy over the
duty certificate, though we do not expect to encounter many
of them, should be solved by mutual consultation and to
mutual satisfaction. Therefore, if a controversy arises

0270

over the certificate, the matter should be handed over to
the Joint Committee for reconsideration. Whatever way we
may take to solve this problem of duty certificate, we
must find a mechanism under which mutual consultation and
agreement are provided for resolution of controversy over
the validity of the official duty certificate.

15. "d. <u>The Concept of the Combat Zone and the Waiver
of the Primary Jurisdiction</u>

"At the previous session, the United States
negotiators proposed that if the Korean negotiators would
accept the Agreed Minute Re Paragraph 3 of the United
States draft with respect to the waiver of primary jurisdiction, the U.S. side would delete the clause on the combat
zone of Agreed Minute #1, Re Paragraph 1(b) and Agreed
Minute #1, Re Paragraph 3(a). At the same time, the U.S.
negotiators added that this proposal was a substantial
concession by the U.S. side.

16. "The Korean negotiators appreciate the significant
suggestion made by the U.S. side. We take the suggestion
as an indication on the U.S. part to accommodate our
concern over the proposed concept of the combat zone.
Although the suggestion was conditioned upon the acceptance
by the Korean side of the provision of the Agreed Minute
Re Paragraph 3 of the U.S. draft, we welcome the qualified
responsiveness of the U.S. side.

17. "However, to our regret, we cannot view the U.S.
proposal as a significant concession, as the U.S. negotiators
have claimed. Even if the U.S. negotiators withdraw the
concept of the combat zone, the U.S. negotiators, by retaining
the provisions of the Agreed Minute Re Paragraph 3 of the
U.S. draft, would accomplish their ultimate purpose of

0271

obtaining total waiver from the Korean authorities.
A quick review of the U.S. draft of the waiver clause would
show clearly that the contents of the clause amount to
what we call 'total waiver'.

18. "According to the provisions of U.S. draft:

(a) The Korean authorities have to waive automatically
their primary jurisdiction upon the receipt of notice
instead of the request for waiver from the U.S. side.

(b) The Korean authorities are also required to
seek agreement of the Joint Committee in case they desire
to recall the waiver for any particular case.

You have to note that the recall of waiver which
has automatically been made by the Korean side is not
granted by the U.S. side on the same automatic basis.
In other words, while the Korean waiver is automatic,
U.S. grant of recall is conditioned upon approval by the
Joint Committee.

(c) Furthermore, the U.S. draft provides that the
waiver thus granted by the Korean authorities shall be
unconditional and final for all purposes and shall bar both
the authorities and the nationals of the Republic of Korea
from instituting criminal procedures. It is extremely
unfair that the United States side, by the mere fact of
waiver granted by the Korean authorities, intends not only
to bar Korean nationals from initiating appropriate remedial
actions, but also to prevent the authorities of the Korean
Government from instituting criminal procedures even in
a case where the U.S. has not tried the waivered case.
In this regard, we are unable to find any international
precedents similar to the U.S. draft in any other SOFA.

0272

19. "We are willing to assure you that we are prepared to waive the primary jurisdiction as generously as any NATO party does under the very simple provision in NATO SOFA. However, as a matter of principle, we believe that the Korean authorities, as the authorities of the receiving state, should have the right to determine whether or not to waive primary jurisdiction.

"This right can not be replaced by the automatic waiver clause which the U.S. side seeks. We should like to reiterate our position that whatever the final agreement we may reach on this subject, the agreement has to retain the language and mechanism that would provide for the principle of self-determination by the Korean authorities on waiver of primary jurisdiction.

20. "e. Pre-trial Custody, Paragraph 5(d) and 5(e)

"Regarding the subject of pre-trial custody, the U.S. chief negotiator stated that the revised draft of Paragraph 5(d) is an improvement over the original language but they still believed Paragraph 5(c) of the U.S. draft to be preferable. At the same time he stated that the U.S. side was prepared to agree to the revised Paragraph 5(e) of the Korean draft regarding custody in security offenses.

21. "With respect to pre-trial custody in the hands of the U.S., the revised Korean version of Paragraph 5(d) is almost identical with the language of the U.S. draft and fully reflects the views of the U.S. side. However, the Korean negotiators believe that they should reserve the language which would guarantee the U.S. side's sympathetic consideration to any request for the transfer of custody which may be made by the Korean authorities in specific cases.

22. "With respect to Korean custody in security offenses,

the Korean negotiators appreciate the acceptance by the U.S. side of the revised proposal made by the Korean side. However, we have noted that the acceptance by the U.S. side is conditioned upon the acceptance by the Korean negotiators of the two understandings:

(a) The first proposed understanding is not acceptable to the Korean negotiators, since we believe that in security offenses, the Korean authorities should be the only and final authorities to determine whether or not such custody is appropriate. This does not necessarily mean that we would not consult with U.S. authorities as to the necessity of such custody. But, as a matter of principle, we believe agreement with U.S. side is not necessary in a security case.

(b) Regarding the second question, the Korean negotiators are prepared to accept the proposed understanding.

23. "f. Trial Safeguards

"The Korean negotiators appreciate the proposal made by the U.S. negotiators to effect the following changes in the Agreed Minute Re Paragraph 9 of the U.S. draft:

(a) Deletion of Subparagraph (a);

(b) In subparagraph (b), deletion of all language after the words 'shall have the right to appeal a conviction or sentence.'

24. "The Korean negotiators hope that the U.S. negotiators would consider other outstanding issues regarding trial safeguards on which the Korean negotiators made their views clear at the 50th session and respond at an early meeting."

0274

25. Mr. Habib stated that the U.S. negotiators would reserve until the next meeting a detailed reply to the remarks just made by the Korean Chief Negotiator. However, the U.S. negotiators would like to make some general observations regarding the positions stated by Mr. Chang.

26. Mr. Habib said the U.S. negotiators do not accept the principle that phraseology appearing in other status of forces agreements is definitive with regard to the Korean SOFA. The U.S. negotiators regarded precedents as useful, but not binding. In addition to the precedents found in the language of other agreements, the negotiators also had to take into account a body of experience. This experience included awareness of the way in which other status of forces agreements were actually working and accumulated knowledge of conditions in Korea. The task at hand was the negotiation of a status of forces agreement for Korea, not for Japan or any other country.

27. Mr. Habib noted that the statement made by the Korean negotiators was simply a repetition of views which they had stated previously and did not appear to take into account the expressed views of the U.S. negotiators on certain key issues. The U.S. negotiators would make detailed comments at the next meeting. Before doing so, they wished to ask a few questions and make some remarks in order to clarify certain points.

28. Regarding Paragraph 1(a), Mr. Habib noted that the Korean negotiators had expressed the wish to retain the phrase "all persons subject to the military law of the United States", despite the assurance given by the U.S. negotiators that no U.S. courts would be established in Korea and despite

한·미국 간의 상호방위조약 제4조에 의한 시설과 구역 및 한국에서의 미국군대의 지위에 관한 협정(SOFA)
전59권. 1966.7.9 서울에서 서명 : 1967.2.9 발효(조약 232호) (V.51 실무교섭회의 합의의사록, 제38-68차, 1964)

the desire of the U.S. negotiators to retain flexibility
in case legislation should be passed in the future which
would establish jurisdiction over U.S. civilians abroad.
The objections of the Korean negotiators were apparently
based on: (a) a feeling that the passage of such legislation
was inconceivable, and (b) the possibility of a reversal
of the 1960 Supreme Court decision. In stating these
objections, the Korean negotiators were attempting to
exercise the right of review of U.S. legislation, which
was certainly not relevant to the question at hand. The
Korean negotiators were seeking to differentiate between
military personnel and civilians in the application of U.S.
law. If U.S. law is to apply, it should apply equally to
military personnel and civilians, who are in Korea for the
accomplishment of the same mission under the provisions of
the Mutual Security Treaty. The U.S. negotiators were
concerned that the application of rights under the SOFA
should not be discriminatory between the military personnel
and the civilians who were in Korea under identical
conditions and for the same purpose. Mr. Habib asked what
the attitude of the Korean negotiators would be if the
Supreme Court decision of 1960 had not been made.

29. Regarding Paragraph 1(b), Mr. Habib stated that
the position of the U.S. negotiators that jurisdiction over
the U.S. armed forces by the host government should be
limited to the civil authorities of the government was a
firm U.S. position in every country in which a SOFA is in
force. The U.S. negotiators wanted to have it stated
explicitly in the SOFA with the ROK. If the Korean

0276

negotiators were willing to give the assurances that they
had given in this respect, why were they unwilling to spell
the assurances out in the Agreement? The absence of the
phrase "civil authorities" from other agreements is no
reason why it should not be included in this Agreement.
The experience of the past two years had clearly shown
that the ROK Government does not hesitate to resort to
military courts to try civil crimes. The Korean negotiators
had argued that it would be difficult to explain this
provision to the public and to the National Assembly. Why
could the National Assembly not be told simply that the
U.S. authorities were unwilling to pass jurisdiction from
U.S. military courts to Korean military courts. The U.S.
negotiators believed that such an explanation would be
palatable and acceptable to the National Assembly. They
believed the Korean objections to this provision to be
shallow and urged the Korean negotiators to reconsider.

30. With regard to the question of the duty certificate,
Mr. Habib reminded the Korean negotiators that the U.S.
negotiators had not responded specifically to the proposed
revision of the Agreed Minute Re Paragraph 3(a) (ii) of the
Korean draft. Now that the U.S. negotiators had received
further explanation of what the Korean negotiators had in
mind, they would respond in detail to this proposed revision
at the next meeting.

31. With regard to the waiver provision, Mr. Habib
said the Korean negotiators appeared to be concerned over
the question of automaticity. The concern of the U.S.
negotiators was to obtain the maximum possible degree of
waiver. The implication of the remarks made by the Korean

0277

Chief Negotiator was that the Korean authorities did not desire to try all cases that may arise and that only in special circumstances would they wish to try a case. The U.S. draft does not preclude this and provides the means whereby the Korean authorities could seek recall of their waiver.

32. With regard to pre-trial custody, Mr. Habib noted that the Korean negotiators had made no concessions to meet what the U.S. negotiators consider to be a serious problem. With respect to this subject, also, the U.S. negotiators based their position on experience. The U.S. draft was clear. It provided that defendants in the custody of the U.S. authorities would be produced promptly at the request of the Korean authorities. The U.S. negotiators did not understand the Korean desire to retain custody, except in the case of security cases, with regard to which the U.S. negotiators had made a concession. The U.S. negotiators had also pointed out that the final sentence of Paragraph 5(c) of the U.S. draft was related to this question and would permit the Korean authorities to take custody when requested to do so. In view of the assurances on presentation of the accused already given by the U.S. negotiators, the Korean authorities could exercise jurisdiction just as effectively if the U.S. military authorities retain custody.

33. Mr. Habib noted that the U.S. negotiators had considered the views of the Korean negotiators regarding trial safeguards and had given their reply. They believed there was no reason to withdraw elementary safeguards which are generally accepted as necessary under U.S. law and, in

0278

most cases, under ROK law. The trial safeguards listed in
the U.S. draft were not onerous and did not detract from
the exercise of jurisdiction by the Korean authorities.
The objections of the Korean negotiators appeared to rest on
narrow legalistic bases. A lack of safeguards for ROK
citizens was no argument for the omission of those safeguards
from an international agreement. More important criteria
for judging these provisions included the question whether
the provisions were onerous, unfair, or lacking precedents.
The U.S. negotiators believed them to be not onerous, quite
fair, and supported by sound precedents.

34. Mr. Habib asked whether the Korean negotiators
wished to make any further comments to assist the U.S.
negotiators in their consideration of the Korean position.

35. Mr. Chang replied that a wide gap separated the
positions of the two sides. Perhaps the explanation given
by the Korean negotiators had not been extensive enough or
the U.S. negotiators had misunderstood the Korean position.
The question of trial safeguards presented delicate problems.
He proposed that this subject be taken up in informal
discussions between the legal members of the negotiating teams.

36. Mr. Habib replied that the U.S. negotiators believed
that more rapid progress could be made by discussing this
question in the negotiating meetings. At the next meeting,
the U.S. negotiators would be prepared to hold a point by
point discussion of this subject.

37. Mr. Habib remarked that obviously a gap did exist
between the two positions. The Korean negotiators were
proposing that the U.S. negotiators go all the way toward
meeting the Korean position. Such a course would not meet
the U.S. requirements.

0279

38. Mr.Chang replied that the Korean negotiators did not expect the U.S. negotiators to come all the way to meet the Korean position. Each side should consider the position of the other. The Korean negotiators believed that international precedents were important. They suggested that standard language be agreed to wherever possible.

39. Mr. Habib replied that standard language should not be used if standard conditions did not exist. The language had to be modified to suit specific situations existing in the country. He suggested that both sides think about these problems.

40. The next meeting was scheduled for August 7 at 3:00 p.m.

0280

JOINT SUMMARY RECORD OF THE 60TH SESSION

1. Time and Place: 3:00 - 5:30 P.M. August 7, 1964 at the Foreign Ministry's Conference Room (No.1)

2. Attendants:

ROK Side:

Mr. Chang, Sang Moon	Director European and American Affairs Bureau
Mr. Koo, Choong Whay	Chief, America Section Ministry of Foreign Affairs
Mr. Lee, Myung Hi	Prosecutor Prosecutors Section Ministry of Justice
Maj. Lee, Kye Hoon	Military Affairs Section Ministry of National Defense
Mr. Park, Sang Yong	3rd Secretary Ministry of Foreign Affairs
Mr. Lee, Kae Chul	3rd Secretary Ministry of Foreign Affairs
Mr. Lee, Keun Pal (Rapporteur and Interpreter)	3rd Secretary Ministry of Foreign Affairs
Mr. Hwang, Young Jae	3rd Secretary Ministry of Foreign Affairs
Mr. Park, Won Chul	3rd Secretary Ministry of Foreign Affairs

U.S. Side:

Mr. Philip C. Habib	Counselor American Embassy
Capt. John Wayne	Assistant Chief of Staff USN/K
Col. Kenneth C. Crawford	Staff Judge Advocate 8th U.S. Army
Mr. Benjamin A. Fleck (Rapporteur and Press Officer)	First Secretary American Embassy
Mr. Robert A. Kinney	J-5 8th U.S. Army

0281

Mr. Robert A. Lewis	2nd Secretary American Embassy
Mr. Daniel A. O'Donohue	2nd Secretary American Embassy
Maj. Alton H. Harvey	Staff Judge Advocate's Office 8th U.S. Army
Mr. David Y.C. Lee (Interpreter)	2nd Secretary American Embassy

Criminal Jurisdiction

1. Mr. Habib opened the meeting by stating that the U.S. negotiators wished to take up the Criminal Jurisdiction Article and go through it from the beginning, discussing the differences of view which had emerged during previous discussions.

2. With regard to Paragraph 1(a), Mr. Habib continued, the Korean negotiators had objected to the concept of jurisdiction contained in the U.S. draft, which would allow for the exercise of jurisdiction by the U.S. authorities at some future time outside the Republic of Korea. The Korean negotiators had stated at the 59th meeting that any future return of accused civilians to the United States for trial would be inconsistent with judicial principles and not acceptable to any sovereign nation hosting foreign troops. They also had stated that if a person accused of committing a crime in one sovereign country was taken to another sovereign country for trial "there would arise a serious question as to possible infringement of sovereignty".

3. Mr. Habib stated that the U.S. negotiators did not agree with this interpretation of the proposed provision. He pointed out that it is a recognized principle of international law that a sovereign state retains jurisdiction over its nationals whether they are within the territorial jurisdiction of the asserting state or within that of a

0282

foreign state. This jurisdiction is based upon the personal supremacy of a sovereign state over its own nationals rather than on any question of territorial sovereignty. The rights and duties of a national are solely determined by the law of his sovereign state and he is subjected to such penal jurisdiction for acts committed abroad as is provided for in that law.

4. Jurisdiction based upon the supremacy of a state over its nationals, Mr. Habib continued, is not in derogation of the sovereignty of the foreign state in which the offense is committed. Unless there are contrary treaty provisions, the state claiming jurisdiction based on nationality is under the obligation not to infringe upon the territorial supremacy of a foreign state by performing acts of sovereignty in the foreign state. (This does not detract from the state's right under international law to punish its nationals when they are again within its territorial jurisdiction for acts committed abroad.)

5. Mr. Habib pointed out that the Republic of Korea has exercised this right through implementation of Korean law. The Korean negotiators had said that this would be contrary to international law and judicial principles. The U.S. negotiators, however, wished to point out that the laws of the Republic of Korea recognize this principle and make specific provisions for this very situation. Article 3, Criminal Code, Korean Law 293, reads as follows:

"Crimes Committed by Koreans Abroad

"This Code shall apply to all Korean nationals outside the territory of the Republic of Korea."

0283

6. In fact, Mr. Habib continued, Korean law carries the principle of jurisdiction over crimes committed abroad much further than is applicable to the issue under discussion. Article 5 of the Korean Criminal Code provides that the Code shall apply to aliens who commit certain specified crimes outside the territory of the Republic of Korea. Article 6 reads as follows:

"Crimes Committed Abroad Against the Republic of Korea and Korean Nationals

"This Code shall apply to aliens who commit, outside the territory of Korea, against the Republic of Korea or her nationals, crimes other than those specified in the preceding article, except where they do not constitute crimes at the place of commission or where their prosecution or execution of the punishment imposed has been remitted."

7. Mr. Habib stated that the United States has no counterpart to Article 3 of the Korean Criminal Code. Whether or not this will be accomplished in future legislation is a matter wholly reserved to the United States Government in the exercise of its sovereign right of supremacy over its own nationals. If such legislation is passed, it would not derogate from the unquestioned sovereignty of the Republic of Korea. It is difficult to understand, he continued, why the ROK negotiators are concerned over a principle recognized by international law and specifically provided for in their own Criminal Code.

8. Mr. Habib said the U.S. negotiators had clearly stated the purpose of the language in the U.S. draft, which was to provide for the possibility of future legislation in the United States. The Korean negotiators had objected on the grounds that there was no basis in judicial practice for such a provision and that it would derogate against the sovereignty of the Republic of Korea. The U.S. negotiators

0284

had clearly demonstrated that there was no lack of precedents in judicial practice and that the provision would not derogate against the sovereignty of the Republic of Korea.

9. Mr. Habib added that the U.S. negotiators believed the Korean negotiators might be basing their objection also on the fact that this provision does not appear in this form in other status of forces agreements. He reiterated the frequently expressed view of the U.S. negotiators that this agreement was being negotiated on the basis of accumulated experience and not on the basis of language in other agreements. There was nothing in this provision which was inconsistent with the spirit of other status of forces agreements, nor with the exercise of sovereignty by either government, nor with judicial precedents, including those contained in Korean law. Mr. Habib asked whether the Korean negotiators wished to comment.

10. Mr. Chang replied that the U.S. negotiators had quoted articles of the Korean Criminal Code to justify their position that an accused could be taken from one country to another for trial without causing any infringement upon the territorial jurisdiction of the former. The spirit underlying them was that the Government of the Republic of Korea would exercise jurisdiction over the accused when the accused come within reach of ROK sovereignty or under an extradition agreement. In other words, the Korean articles do not call for unilateral and involuntary waiver of territorial jurisdiction, while the U.S. draft in question and the explanation of the U.S. negotiators clearly demand unconditional waiver, voluntary or involuntary, of territorial jurisdiction on the part of the Republic of Korea. The

Korean negotiators did not believe that the U.S. Government
would automatically waiver jurisdiction over a Korean
offender in the United States. In the absence of an extradition
agreement between the two countries, which is the case at
present, if the ROK Government tried to extradite a Korean
civilian or soldier accused of an offense in the United
States for trial in the Republic of Korea, the U.S. Government
not only could, but would probably object. In case the
U.S. Government feels, for one reason or another, that the
territorial jurisdiction can not be waived, the accused
Korean can not be brought to Korea for trial. In brief,
waiver of territorial jurisdiction is traced to the consent
of the territorial sovereign.

11. Mr. Habib replied that the negotiators were not
arguing on the specifics of Korean law. Nor were they
discussing the subject of extradition. They were discussing
the principle of the right of each government to exercise
its sovereignty, a principle which the Korean negotiators
had questioned at the last meeting. The U.S. negotiators
were not questioning the way in which the Korean authorities
applied ROK law. With regard to the attitude of the U.S.
Government, Mr. Habib reminded the Korean negotiators of the
recent case of a member of the ROK Navy who had got into
trouble in Guam. Although the charges against him had
been of a very serious nature, including manslaughter, the
U.S. Government, acting in response to the request of the
ROK Government, had agreed to permit him to be returned to
the Republic of Korea for trial.

12. Mr. Habib reiterated that the provision in question
would result in no derogation of sovereignty and was based
on judicial precedents. The Korean negotiators had raised

0286

the question of comparability with other status of forces agreements. In this case, the U.S. negotiators were not arguing in favor of their language on the basis of the existence of a different set of conditions in Korea than in other countries where U.S. armed forces are stationed. They wished to point out that at the time when the status of forces agreements with Japan and with the NATO governments were negotiated, the Supreme Court decision of 1960 had not yet been handed down. At the time when the agreement with Japan was negotiated, the U.S. negotiators had believed that U.S. military courts had jurisdiction over certain U.S. civilians. Therefore, in this respect the two agreements were not comparable.

13. Mr. Habib stated that similar reasoning lay behind the language of Paragraph 1(b) of the U.S. draft. The U.S. negotiators of the status of forces agreements with Japan and the NATO governments had not conceived of the possibility that military authorities of the host country could exercise jurisdiction. Inasmuch as that possibility does exist in the Republic of Korea, the U.S. negotiators, in drafting this more modern agreement, wish to make the language of the provision quite clear by having it read "the civil authorities of the Republic of Korea." This is not an unreasonable provision and should be fairly easy to explain. It is fully consistent with the statements of the Korean negotiators for the negotiating record that the Korean authorities have no intention of subjecting U.S. personnel covered by this SOFA to military courts. The objection of the Korean negotiators to this provision appeared to be solely the fact that such language does not

0287

appear in the SOFA with Japan. The U.S. negotiators were of the opinion that this was not a valid objection.

14. Reverting to Paragraph 1(a), Mr. Chang stated that when an accused is taken from the host country to another country for trial, the host country voluntarily waives its jurisdiction. If such a case arose in the Republic of Korea and the ROK authorities were not prepared to waive ROK jurisdiction, the accused could not be taken to another country for trial. In effect, the language of the U.S. draft called for a voluntary waiver of jurisdiction over dependents by the ROK Government.

15. Mr. Chang asked whether the United States, following the 1960 Supreme Court decision, had received assurances from other governments with whom it has negotiated status of forces agreements that civilians may be taken to the United States for trial. Mr. Habib replied that, to his knowledge, the question had not arisen.

16. With regard to Paragraph 1(b), Mr. Chang stated that the Korean negotiators had given an unequivocal assurance for the negotiating record that under no circumstances would members of the U.S. armed forces be subject to trial by Korean military authorities, in the hope that the U.S. negotiators would agree to the deletion of the word "civil". Mr. Habib replied that the simplest way of handling this question was to leave the word "civil" in the text of the paragraph.

17. Mr. Chang stated that the Korean negotiators believed both sides were trying to negotiate an agreement that would be acceptable to their respective citizens and legislatures. They were trying to find acceptable wording regarding this question. The Korean negotiators believed that the effect would be the same, whether the assurance appeared in the text

0288

of the Agreement or in the Agreed Joint Summary. Inasmuch
as the effect was same, the U.S. negotiators should and
could be responsive to the concern of their counterparts.
Utter disregard by the U.S. side of the Korean concern was
not a constructive way of conducting negotiation. The
Korean negotiators could not understand the U.S. insistance
on the inclusion of the word "civil" in the text.

18. In an attempt to clarify the Korean position,
Mr. Habib asked whether the Korean negotiators were proposing
to include their assurance in the Agreed Joint Summary
or as an Agreed Minute. Mr. Chang replied that they were
neither making any suggestion nor proposal. They merely
wished to clarify the U.S. position whether the U.S.
negotiators would accept the assurance as an Agreed Minute
and delete the word "civil" from the text.

19. Mr. Habib stated that the U.S. negotiators wished
to clarify further the U.S. position with regard to the duty
certificate and to bring to the attention of the Korean
negotiators certain precedents and other factors of which
they might not be aware. The U.S. negotiators had stated
their view that the duty certificate is conclusive. The
Korean negotiators had taken the position that if the Korean
authorities objected to a duty certificate, they should be
able to refer the matter to the Joint Committee. If the
Joint Committee could not reach agreement, the matter would
then be referred to the Korean courts, under the terms of the
third paragraph of the revised Agreed Minute Re Paragraph
3(a)(ii) of the Korean draft. The Korean negotiators had
expressed the hope that the U.S. military authorities would
be prepared to entertain requests for modification of duty

certificates. The U.S. negotiators, Mr. Habib continued, did not wish to mislead the Korean negotiators regarding the firmness of the U.S. belief in the conclusive nature of the duty certificate. This belief was based on a lengthy body of experience. The U.S. negotiators wished to call the attention of the Korean negotiators to the following information.

20. In Belgium, Mr. Habib stated, duty certificates are prepared by the unit commanding officer and submitted to the Army Attache at the U.S. Embassy in Brussels. The Army Attache either submits the duty certificate to the local authorities or advises them informally regarding the duty status of the accused. The Belgian authorities have never questioned U.S. determinations regarding duty status of an accused.

21. In Denmark, Mr. Habib continued, no formal procedures have been established for the determination of official duty status and no official duty cases have arisen to date. If such a case should occur, the determination would be made by the U.S. Representative on the Joint Committe, who would advise appropriate Danish authorities.

22. In France, the U.S. Staff Judge Advocate notifies the French prosecutor of official duty cases. The French Ministry of Justice issued a circular in 1956, which recognized the primary responsibility of the United States, as sending state, to determine the duty status of the accused. The French Court of Cassation in the case of James Martin (a _partie_ _civile_ prosecution brought by an injured claimant) decided that only the sending state may make the determination of the performance of official duty referred to in Article VII of the NATO Status of Forces Agreement and that the sending state's duty certificate is conclusive as a matter of law.

0290

23. In Germany, Mr. Habib continued, criminal jurisdiction over U.S. personnel is exercised by the sending state only. However, the Agreement to Supplement the NATO Status of Forces Agreement in Germany provides as follows:

"1. Whenever, in the course of criminal proceedings against a member of a force or of a civilian component, it becomes necessary to determine whether an offence has risen out of any act or omission done in the performance of official duty, such determination shall be made in accordance with the law of the sending State concerned. The highest appropriate authority of such sending State may submit to the German Court or authority dealing with the case a certificate thereon.

"2. The German court or authority shall make its decision in conformity with the certificate. In exceptional cases, however, such certificate may, at the request of the German court or authority, be made the subject of review through discussions between the Federal Government and the diplomatic mission in the Federal Republic of the sending State."

24. Mr. Habib went on to point out that in Greece official duty certificates are issued by the Staff Judge Advocate and, if approved by the U.S. Representative on the Joint Committee, are submitted through diplomatic channels to the Ministry of Foreign Affairs. Greek authorities have never questioned official duty status determinations made by U.S. authorities.

25. In Italy, Mr. Habib continued, the determination of official duty status is made by a service Legal Officer or by the command Staff Judge Advocate on the basis of information provided by the unit commander. The determination is then submitted to the appropriate Italian official with a statement that the command will exercise its primary right of jurisdiction over the accused. It is well established in Italy that official duty certificates submitted by U.S. authorities are accepted without question by Italian authorities, including those issued with regard to acts or omissions which occur during travel incident to temporary duty

0291

or permanent change of station or while traveling between residence and place of duty in privately-owned vehicles.

26. In Luxembourg, official duty determinations are made by the U.S. Representative on the Joint Committee on the basis of information provided by the immediate commander of the individual concerned and are transmitted by him to the Chief Public Prosecutor of the appropriate arrondisse- ment. Authorities of Luxembourg in all cases have accepted United States official duty determinations.

27. Mr. Habib stated that he could go on, relating the precedents established in the Netherlands, Norway, Portugal, the United Kingdom, and the United States. Without taking the time to do that, he could state that again and again, in the countries cited, duty certificates are not questioned but are accepted as conclusive. In view of the many precedents he had cited and others which he had not cited, the U.S. negotiators did not believe that their requirement that the duty certificate be considered conclusive was an extraordinary requirement. He suggested that further discussion on this question be deferred until the U.S. negotiators responded specifically to the revised Agreed Minute Re Paragraph 3(a)(ii) proposed by the Korean negotiators.

28. Turning to the waiver provisions, Mr. Habib recalled that the Korean negotiators had rejected the idea of an automatic waiver on the grounds that no precedent existed for such a provision. In the view of the U.S. negotiators, there was general agreement on the desirability of some sort of waiver provision. The U.S. negotiators had proposed a general waiver by the ROK Government, with the

0292

power to recall that waiver in special circumstances; the ROK negotiators had proposed that the U.S. authorities be given the power to request a waiver in special circumstances. Mr. Habib asked whether the Korean negotiators could elaborate on, or restate, their position in the light of the discussions which had taken place since these positions had first been stated.

29. Mr. Chang replied that the provisions regarding waiver were more important than those regarding the duty certificate because the waiver provisions would play a heavier role in determining which side would exercise jurisdiction than the other provisions would. This was a very sensitive subject. The Korean negotiators could not accept the automaticity of waiver provided for in the U.S. draft. They wished to reserve to the Korean authorities the right to determine whether or not to waive when requested to do so by the U.S. authorities. The Korean position was based not on a lack of precedents but on principle. The principle is that the waiver is granted by the authorities who hold the jurisdiction and could not be exercised by the authorities lacking the jurisdiction. The automatic waiver provisions proposed by the U.S. negotiators are diametrically opposite to this principle. Under the system of automatic waiver, the U.S. authorities, who lack the original jurisdiction, are to exercise waiver, while the Korean authorities are to ask for recall of waiver. The Korean negotiators had already stated, and wished to state again, that the Korean authorities would waive in as many cases as possible but they must retain the discretion whether or not to waive.

한·미국 간의 상호방위조약 제4조에 의한 시설과 구역 및 한국에서의 미국군대의 지위에 관한 협정(SOFA)
전59권. 1966.7.9 서울에서 서명 : 1967.2.9 발효(조약 232호) (V.51 실무교섭회의 합의의사록, 제38-68차, 1964) 299

The Korean negotiators therefore could not think of a SOFA
with a waiver clause providing for an automatic waiver.

30. Turning to the question of pre-trial custody,
Mr. Habib recalled that the remaining difference of opinion
pertains to the question of custody in security cases.
The U.S. negotiators had indicated their willingness to
agree to Paragraph 5(e) of the Korean draft, provided the
Korean negotiators would agree to the inclusion in the
Agreed Joint Summary of the following two understandings:

    a. There must be mutual U.S.-ROK agreement as to
    the circumstances in which such custody is appropriate;
    and

    b. Korean confinement facilities must be adequate
    by U.S. standards.

The Korean negotiators had accepted the second of these two
understandings but had rejected the first on the grounds
that the Korean authorities should be the only and final
authorities to determine whether or not such custody is
appropriate. Earlier, the Korean negotiators had stated
that the Korean authorities required custody of individuals
charged with security offenses in order to prevent further
threats to the security of the Republic of Korea or to prevent
destruction of evidence. It was inconceivable, Mr. Habib
stated, that the United States Government would be a party
to threats to the security of the Republic of Korea. The
U.S. armed forces were not present in the Republic of Korea
to pose a threat to its security. The U.S. authorities
desired to participate in the determination of the circumstances
under which Korean custody of the accused would be appropriate.
This position did not reject the right of the Korean authorities to hold custody. As a matter of practical implementation, mutual discussion would be called for in a security
case. Let both sides consider this question further.

0294

31. Mr. Chang replied that in the light of the special and close relationship existing between the two countries, the Korean negotiators were not unprepared to reconsider this matter. They viewed it as a matter of principle, however. The Korean authorities were prepared to consult with U.S. military authorities concerning a security case and to recognize the U.S. right to participate in the determination of circumstances leading to custody by the Korean authorities but the final decision concerning custody must be made by the Korean authorities, not the U.S. authorities. Agreement between them was not necessary.

32. Mr. Habib replied that the U.S. negotiators believed that agreement was necessary - agreement as to the circumstances in which custody would be appropriate. In order to preclude the temptation to the Korean authorities to make a unilateral decision, there should be consultation. The U.S. negotiators were proposing these two understandings for inclusion in the Agreed Joint Summary in view of the importance of the Joint Summary as a document providing specific guidelines for those who will be charged with implementing the Agreement. Mr. Chang replied that the Korean negotiators fully shared the views of the U.S. negotiators concerning the importance of the Agreed Joint Summary and its function as a guide for implementation of the Agreement.

33. Turning to the subject of trial safeguards, Mr. Habib stated that the Agreed Minute Re Paragraph 9(a) in the U.S. draft, which would provide for a public trial, would not rule out the possibility of the public being excluded from a trial in which morals or state secrets are involved. Mr. Habib recalled that the Korean negotiators had proposed

한·미국 간의 상호방위조약 제4조에 의한 시설과 구역 및 한국에서의 미국군대의 지위에 관한 협정(SOFA)
전59권. 1966.7.9 서울에서 서명 : 1967.2.9 발효(조약 232호) (V.51 실무교섭회의 합의의사록, 제38-68차, 1964)

the deletion of the first sentence of this Agreed Minute, which calls for public trial by an impartial tribunal composed of judges who have completed their probationary period. The U.S. negotiators were aware of the fact that Paragraph 3 of Article 24 of the ROK Constitution provides that "all citizens shall have the right to a speedy trial" and "shall have the right to a public trial ... without delay in the absence of justifiable reasons". They were also aware of Paragraph 1 of Article 24, which provides that a citizen has the right to be tried" in conformity with the law by competent judges as qualified by the Constitution and law". Although these points are covered in the ROK Constitution, the U.S. negotiators believe that, in view of their importance, they should be included also in the Status of Forces Agreement. With regard to the competency of judges, there is no inconsistency between the ROK Constitution and the proposed Agreed Minute. The U.S. negotiators assume that "competent" judges, as the term is used in the Constitution, are judges who have completed their probationary period. Nor is the language of the proposed Agreed Minute inconsistent with practice in the United States, where the public may be excluded from a public trial if morals or state secrets are at issue. What the U.S. negotiators were seeking to ensure was the right of a representative of the United States Government to be present at all sessions of a trial, whether or not under special circumstances it was closed to the general public.

34. Mr. Habib noted that the second sentence of the proposed Agreed Minute would prohibit the trial of U.S. personnel by a Korean military tribunal. This provision was directly related to the question of including the word "civil" in Paragraph 1(b), which the negotiators had already discussed.

0296

35. Mr. Chang stated that the Korean negotiators recognized that there was a difference of opinion over the question of public trials. The Korean negotiators would take the comments of the U.S. negotiators under consideration. They had no objection in principle to the U.S. negotiators statement regarding the composition of the court. They agreed that the second sentence of the proposed Agreed Minute Re Paragraph 9(a) was related to the question of including or deleting the word "civil" from Paragraph 1(b).

36. Turning to the proposed Agreed Minute Re Paragraph 9(b) of the U.S. draft, Mr. Habib noted that the Korean negotiators had proposed deletion of the second paragraph on the grounds that there is no counterpart in the Korean criminal procedures and that the paragraph is contrary to the spirit of existing ROK laws. Mr. Habib pointed out that this paragraph guarantees the counsel of an accused the right to examine and copy the statements of witnesses prior to trial when these statements are contained in the file of the case. The Korean negotiators had argued that under the Korean code of criminal procedure the accused is given the opportunity to know the nature of the evidence against him and that this is sufficient. In the view of the U.S. negotiators, the right provided to the accused by the provisions of the second paragraph of this proposed Agreed Minute is a common sense right. Justice is not achieved by keeping the evidence from the accused or his counsel until the time of trial.

37. Mr. Habib stated that the U.S. negotiators believed that the provision in question was comparable to the provisions of ROK law. He referred specifically to Article 273 of the ROK Code of Criminal Procedure, which states:

0297

"273. (Investigation of Evidence Before the Date of Public Trial)

"(1) The court may, upon application, permit the prosecutor or the accused or his counsel to examine the accused or other witnesses and to inspect evidence before the date fixed for trial...."

The right sought by the U.S. negotiators is comparable to, and consistent in spirit with, this provision of the Korean code. Therefore, the U.S. negotiators urged the Korean negotiators to reconsider their objections to this provision.

38. Mr. Chang replied that the Korean negotiators wished to study this matter further.

39. It was agreed to adjourn the meeting at this point. The next meeting was scheduled for August 14 at 3:00 p.m.

0298

JOINT SUMMARY RECORD OF THE 61ST SESSION

1. Time and Place: 3:00 – 5:00 P.M. August 14, 1964 at
   the Foreign Ministry's Conference
   Room (No.1)

2. Attendants:

ROK Side:

Mr. Chang, Sang Moon	Director European and American Affairs Bureau
Mr. Koo, Choong Whay	Chief, America Section Ministry of Foreign Affairs
Mr. Oh, Jae Hee	Chief, Treaty Section Ministry of Foreign Affairs
Col. Kim, Won Kil	Chief, Military Affairs Section Ministry of National Defense
Mr. Choo, Moon Ki	Chief Legal Affairs Section Ministry of Justice
Mr. Hur, Hyong Koo	Chief Prosecutors Section Ministry of Justice
Mr. Lee, Keun Pal (Rapporteur and Interpreter)	3rd Secretary Ministry of Foreign Affairs
Mr. Hwang, Young Jae	3rd Secretary Ministry of Foreign Affairs
Mr. Park, Won Chul	3rd Secretary Ministry of Foreign Affairs

U.S. Side:

Mr. Philip C. Habib	Counselor American Embassy
Brig. Gen. Carroll H. Dunn	Deputy Chief of Staff 8th U.S. Army
Col. Howard Smigelow	Deputy Chief of Staff 8th U.S. Army
Capt. John Wayne	Assistant Chief of Staff USN/K

0299

Col. Kenneth C. Crawford	Staff Judge Advocate 8th U.S. Army
Mr. Franic R. La Macchia	First Secretary American Embassy
Mr. Benjamin A. Fleck (Rapporteur and Press Officer)	First Secretary American Embassy
Mr. Robert A. Kinney	J-5 8th U.S. Army
Mr. Robert A. Lewis	2nd Secretary American Embassy
Maj. Alton H. Harvey	Staff Judge Advocate's Office 8th U.S. Army
Mr. Kenneth Campen	Interpreter

1. Mr. Habib opened the 61st meeting by introducing
Brigadier General Carroll H. Dunn, who was replacing Brigadier
General G.G. O'Connor on the U.S. negotiating team. Mr.
Chang warmly welcomed General Dunn on behalf of the Korean
negotiators.

Claims

2. Taking up the Claims Article, Mr. Habib recalled
that at the 51st meeting, the Korean negotiators had tabled
proposed Agreed Minutes to this article. The first of these
would provide that the decisions of the Korean claims
authorities shall be final and conclusive. If the U.S.
authorities disagree on the amount of a claim decided upon
by the Korean claims authorities, the latter will reexamine
the case but the results of their reexamination shall be final.
According to the provisions of the second Agreed Minute
proposed by the Korean negotiators, the ROK Government Claims
Service would replace the U.S. Claims Service in the processing
of claims six months from the date of entry into force of the
Agreement, regardless of the state of readiness of the ROK
Government Claims Service to assume such responsibilities.

0300

3. Mr. Habib stated that the U.S. negotiators had carefully reviewed these proposals and had found them to be unacceptable. The primary objective in negotiating this article is to ensure an effective system of settling legitimate claims against the U.S. armed forces in Korea. The present system functions promptly and equitably. The Korean proposals would require changing from the present procedures, which have worked well for the past five years, to the recently established and as yet relatively untried ROK Government Claims Service procedures. The Korean negotiators had proposed that this change be made within six months of the effective date of the Agreement.

4. The United States Government, Mr. Habib continued, has accumulated a great deal of experience over the past eleven years with the operation of claims machinery in other countries. It has found that the formula concept of settling claims, as proposed by the Korean negotiators, is time-consuming and difficult to administer. This system compels the host nation to establish an expensive bureaucracy and often generates ill-will between the host nation and the United States. In Japan, the formula system is currently being administered in a manner much different from that described in the SOFA with Japan. Not one claim has yet been paid in Japan without prior concurrence of U.S. authorities.

5. The U.S. negotiators believe, Mr. Habib continued, that there is no question but that continuation of the present system, which is meeting the problem to the general satisfaction of all concerned, is infinitely preferable to switching over to the new, untried, and relatively complicated system proposed by the Korean negotiators. The U.S. negotiators

0301

believe that continued operation of the present U.S. Claims
Service, with the U.S. Government underwriting the entire cost
of the operation, will be in the best interests of both the
ROK and U.S. Governments. Continuation of the present system
will be much more likely to result in equitable and prompt
settlement with legitimate Korean claimants than would the
alternative system proposed by the Korean negotiators.

6. Mr. Chu replied that he would like to give a
supplementary explanation of the Korean proposals. The
U.S. negotiators had expressed the view that the reexamination
system to be set up under the first Agreed Minute proposed
by the Korean negotiators would delay final disposition of
claims. It was true, he said, that the ROK Claims Service
has no reexamination system at present as proposed in the
Agreed Minute. However, the ROK authorities had proposed
the first Agreed Minute, considering that establishment of
the reexamination system would be necessary not only for final
and prompt disposition of the cases but also for opening a way
to reconsider any disagreement by the U.S. authorities on the
amount of a claim decided upon by the Korean authorities.
They had also stated that the second proposed Agreed Minute
would establish an untried system. The U.S. negotiators had
expressed concern about the six-month provision in the
Korean proposals. The Korean negotiators considered six
months to be sufficient time to enable the Korean authorities
to establish an efficient system. Some of the U.S. negotiators
had visited the Ministry of Justice in the autumn of 1963
and had witnessed the procedures then in effect. They had
stated at that time that they believed no practical difference
existed between the two systems. Therefore, the Korean

0302

negotiators urged the U.S. negotiators to take into account the proposed mechanism envisaged in the Korean proposals.

7. Mr. Habib replied that perhaps in theory no difference existed between the two claims sytems. In practice, however, there was a great difference. It was a fact, he continued, that at the present time the Korean authorities had no effective claims service. The Korean negotiators had proposed the establishment of one within a given period of time but the U.S. negotiators believed this would be quite difficult to accomplish, in view of the possibility of the use of haphazard methods. In addition, there was the possibility that a case might be influenced unduly by public attention, which would result in a lack of adherence to standards.

8. Mr. Habib said that in order to assist them in considering the Korean position, the U.S. negotiators wished to have the answers to the following questions: concerning the operation of the State Compensation Committee, promulgated under law number 231, December 24, 1962, and established on April 27, 1963:

a. How many attorneys, investigators, interpreters, and translators are employed by the Committee?

b. Who pays the salaries of the personnel employed by the Committee?

c. How many claims have been processed by the Committee in 1963 and in 1964?

d. Does the amount of an award include attorneys' fees?

e. Has the ROK Government appropriated any money to settle claims awards in 1963 and 1964? If so, what was the appropriation act for each year and how much money was appropriated?

0303

f. How many offices, including central and regional offices, have been established? How many employees are there in each office?

g. Have rules and regulations been set forth by the Committee for the administration of the Act and the guidance of the employees administering the Act? If so, may the U.S. negotiators have a copy?

9. Mr. Habib stated that the U.S. negotiators believed the answers to the questions which he had just asked would demonstrate that the Korean authorities did not have an effective claims service. That is why the U.S. negotiators preferred to continue the present system. They were not suggesting that the U.S. authorities do not have an obligation to pay claims. Nor were they trying to seek means to avoid payment of claims.

10. Mr. Chu replied that the Korean negotiators would answer as many of the questions asked by the U.S. negotiators as possible. Last year, members of the U.S. negotiating team had visited the Ministry of Justice, had been given a briefing, and had closely examined the Korean procedures. They had been given the relevant Korean laws and other documents, as well as statistics regarding claims lodged, claims paid, and claims otherwise disposed of. The Korean authorities would be glad to provide these materials again, if necessary.

11. Mr. Habib replied that the U.S. negotiators wanted this material to be introduced officially so that it might be discussed officially.

12. Mr. Chu stated that the present Korean claims system was not inefficient for the number of cases currently being received. However, the Korean authorities were already taking the necessary steps for reorganizing and enlarging

0304

the system in order to improve it and enable it to handle an increase in cases. Present payments, he said, are based on accumulated experience and on decisions of the Korean courts. The questions asked by the U.S. negotiators would be answered at a later negotiating session.

13. Mr. Habib asked whether the Korean negotiators could give some indication of the amount of time currently required to process a claim under the existing ROK claims procedures. Mr. Chu replied that the average length of time was about three months.

Criminal Jurisdiction

14. Turning to the Criminal Jurisdiction Article, Mr. Habib recalled that at the previous meeting, the U.S. negotiators had begun a detailed discussion of the Agreed Minutes of the U.S. draft which enumerated the trial safeguards sought by the U.S. authorities. He proposed that that discussion be resumed at the point at which it had been halted at the last meeting.

15. Mr. Habib recalled that at the 50th meeting, the Korean negotiators had proposed deletion of the Agreed Minute Re Paragraph 9(c) and (d). In subsequent discussion, they had not mentioned this proposal again. The U.S. negotiators, therefore, were uncertain of the Korean position regarding this Agreed Minute, which was an important paragraph in the view of the U.S. negotiators. It would guarantee to the accused the right of confrontation, one of the oldest concepts of the Anglo-Saxon legal system, which is recognized in Articles 161 through 164, 291, 293 and 294 of the ROK Code of Criminal Procedure.

한·미국 간의 상호방위조약 제4조에 의한 시설과 구역 및 한국에서의 미국군대의 지위에 관한 협정(SOFA)
전59권. 1966.7.9 서울에서 서명 : 1967.2.9 발효(조약 232호) (V.51 실무교섭회의 합의의사록, 제38-68차, 1964)

16. Mr. Chang replied that this Agreed Minute, as well as others which provided safeguards guaranteed by the ROK Constitution and relevant laws, should be deleted from the Agreement. To include them would be unnecessarily repetitive and redundant.

17. Mr. Habib replied that inclusion of such safeguards in the Agreement might be redundant insofar as Korean law is concerned but not with regard to the Agreement. In the case of safeguards not guaranteed by Korean law, it is not inconceivable that the law could be amended. The trial safeguards were important and their inclusion in the Agreement was an important factor in enabling the U.S. Government to agree to the conclusion of the Agreement. Pointing out that this was a fundamental question, Mr. Habib asked whether the Korean negotiators were now questioning the listing of trial safeguards. Previously, the Korean negotiators had seemed to accept the problem of the U.S. negotiators and the U.S. negotiators had assumed that the Korean negotiators had agreed in principle to a listing of trial safeguards. Unless the Korean negotiators agreed to such a listing, there was little point in discussing the safeguards individually and in detail, as the U.S. negotiators had planned to do at this meeting.

18. Mr. Chang replied that the Korean draft clearly stated that all trial safeguards enumerated in Paragraph 9 of the U.S. draft were guaranteed by the ROK Constitution and relevant laws. At the 50th meeting, the Korean negotiators had stated that it was not necessary to repeat in the Agreed Minutes the trial safeguards listed in Paragraph 9 or to include those safeguards which are consonant with the

spirit of the ROK Constitution and relevant laws. The U.S. negotiators had expressed concern over the possibility that the laws and the Constitution might be changed. Even if they were changed, the Korean negotiators were sure that the changes would result in better protection and benefit for the accused. The U.S. negotiators had no reasonable grounds for listing all of these safeguards. If they did not agree with the position of the Korean negotiators, no satisfactory solution was possible. If the U.S. negotiators would indicate which of the proposed safeguards were of particular importance, the Korean negotiators were prepared to negotiate with regard to those Agreed Minutes.

19. Mr. Habib stated that the U.S. negotiators had not intimated that they believed changes in Korean laws would not be for the better. They accepted the statement of the Korean negotiators in this regard but it was not relevant to the question under discussion. He pointed out that the first sentence of the Agreed Minute Re Paragraph 9 of the U.S. draft specifically refers to ROK law, where it reads that the accused "shall be accorded every procedural and substantive right granted by law to the citizens of the Republic of Korea". The U.S. negotiators believed that the Status of Forces Agreement should provide certain fundamental rights as trial safeguards. These are not incompatible with ROK law. The Korean negotiators had agreed that they were compatible. The Korean negotiators had asked for a specific enumeration of those safeguards which the U.S. authorities believed to be most important. The U.S. draft provided this enumeration. If the Korean negotiators objected to

certain of the safeguards listed in the U.S. draft, the
U.S. negotiators were prepared to discuss them. However,
there was no chance whatsoever that the U.S. negotiators
would abandon the principle of enumerating trial safeguards
in the Agreement. There is nothing in the safeguards listed,
he added, which derogates from the sovereignty of the ROK
Government.

20. Mr. Chang replied that a difference of opinion
existed regarding those safeguards which were already
guaranteed by the ROK constitution and the relevant Korean
Laws and that the Korean negotiators would present their
views at a later meeting. If the U.S. negotiators wished to
discuss those safeguards which were not covered by the ROK
Constitution or Korean law, the Korean negotiators were
prepared to do so. Mr. Habib said that such discussion
might be useful.

21. As already indicated, Mr. Habib said, the proposed
Agreed Minute Re Paragraph 9(c) and (d) was not incompatible
with the ROK Constitution.

22. The Korean negotiators, Mr. Habib continued, had stated
that the Agreed Minute Re Paragraph 9(e) would be acceptable
if the word "confidentially" were deleted. They had argued
that the present Korean legal system requires the accused
to remain under surveillance of competent officers during an
interview. However, the U.S. negotiators believed that if a
counsel is to be effective, he must be able to have his
client confide in him without fear of being overheard. The
only apparent basis for the restrictive provisions of the
Penal Administrative Law is to prevent escape and the
stifling of evidence. The same objective could be accomplished

0308

by locking the accused and his counsel in a room with a guard outside. In this regard, although the Code of Criminal Procedure is compatible with the right of confidential communication, the Penal Administration Law should be changed for cases involving U.S. personnel, either by legislation or through administrative practice. Mr. Habib pointed out that a ranking Korean prosecutor, in an article in the Law Times of August 28, 1963, had stated:

"It may be argued that the rights of the defense counsel to meet the arrested without any participation (by the warden) and communicate directly should be legislated to prevent such troubles."

Finally, Mr. Habib continued, the principle of confidential communication is recognized as a "customary" rule of international law, for example in the Geneva Prisoner of War Convention.

23. Regarding the Agreed Minute Re Paragraph 9(f), Mr. Habib stated that there was no difference of opinion, since its provisions were consistent with the ROK Code of Criminal Procedure.

24. Regarding the Agreed Minute Re Paragraph 9(g), Mr. Habib stated that the Korean negotiators had expressed disagreement with that portion which reads: "no statement of the accused taken in the absence of such a representative shall be admissable as evidence in support of the guilt of the accused". The U.S. negotiators wished to point out that an official U.S. representative would be on duty and available at all times to be present at preliminary investigations, examinations, pre-trial hearings, the trial, and post-trial proceedings. The Korean negotiators appeared to wish to limit the right of this representative to be present at such sessions. The U.S. position was that an official

0309

representative should be able to attend all such sessions, including in camera sessions. The obvious reason for the inclusion of this provision in the Agreement is to ensure that no confession is obtained by coercion.

25. Mr. Habib stated that the U.S. negotiators believed the Agreed Minute Re Paragraph 9 to be fully compatible with ROK law. They had already agreed to delete subparagraph (a), since other ways could be arranged to maintain appropriate trial records. There was no question about the compatibility with the ROK Code of Criminal Procedure of the remaining portion of subparagraph (b). General provisions similar to those of subparagraphs (c) and (d) were contained in the Code of Criminal Procedure and the Constitution.

26. With regard to subparagraph (e) of the Agreed Minute Re Paragraph 9, the Korean negotiators had proposed a counter-draft which brought into discussion the whole question of the prosecution appealing sentences. The Korean proposal would place the accused in the unfair position of the prosecutor having a "second chance", after becoming aware of the arguments used by the defense at the first trial. Increasing a sentence on appeal by the prosecution is contrary to the fundamental legal principles familiar to all American personnel and protection against such an eventuality is an essential right which should be included in the SOFA.

27. Mr. Habib noted that there was no incompatibility with the Korean laws and the ROK Constitution with regard to subparagraphs (f), (g) and (h).

28. Mr. Habib recalled that the Korean negotiators had stated that they interpreted subparagraph (i) as meaning that U.S. offenders should not be subject to punishment

0310

other than by decisions of a judicial court. This interpretation was correct. The provision is a prohibition
against the enactment by a legislature of a bill which
convicts a person of a crime without giving him a trial.
Obviously, the U.S. negotiators believed that a judicial
tribunal should be available to every offender.

29. Mr. Habib noted that there was no incompatibility
between subparagraph (j) and the ROK Constitution.

30. With regard to subparagraph (k), Mr. Habib recalled
that the Korean negotiators had proposed alternative language.
There was a difference in language between the two versions
but no difference in legal basis. The language proposed by
the Korean negotiators was not specific enough, since under
a strict reading of the Korean proposal, a trial could
proceed without the accused being present.

31. With regard to subparagraph (l), Mr. Habib stated
that there was no inconsistency in the legal basis of this
provision with the Korean laws.

32. Mr. Habib recalled that the Korean negotiators had
proposed the deletion of the word "improper" from the third
unnumbered paragraph of the Agreed Minute Re Paragraph 9.
The U.S. negotiators believed that it was important to
retain this word in the draft, since there are a number of
improper actions that are not necessarily illegal. The ROK
Code of Criminal Procedure provides that a confession shall be
received in evidence" only when the statement was made under
such circumstances that it is undoubtedly believed to be true".
The circumstances covered by this provision include improper
acts.

0311

33. Mr. Habib recalled that the Korean negotiators had proposed the deletion of the fourth unnumbered paragraph of the Agreed Minute Re Paragraph 9, which would limit appeals by the prosecution. The U.S. negotiators were aware of Article 361 of the Code of Criminal Procedure. They have no objection to appeals made by the prosecution for errors of law. They do object, however, to the prosecution making an appeal based on a "mistake of fact" or on the "unreasonableness of the sentence". Such appeals would allow the prosecution a number of chances to argue the same case. If such a provision were adopted, the accused would not be entitled to the advantage which is rightfully his if the prosecution is lax in its efforts and the prosecution would have a second chance after knowing the nature of the defense.

34. Mr. Chang stated that the Korean negotiators appreciated the extensive explanations given by the U.S. negotiators. They would consider the U.S. position on trial safeguards and express their views at a later meeting.

35. The next meeting was tentatively scheduled for August 28 at 3:00 p.m.

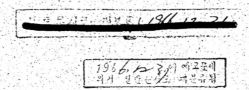

0312

JOINT SUMMARY RECORD OF THE 62ND SESSION

1. Time and Place: 4:00 - 5:20 P.M. August 28, 1964 at
   the Foreign Ministry's Conference
   Room (No.1)

2. Attendants:

   ROK Side:

   Mr. Chang, Sang Moon   Director
                                      European and American Affairs
                                      Bureau

   Mr. Koo, Choong Whay   Chief, America Section
                                      Ministry of Foreign Affairs

   Mr. Oh, Jae Hee   Chief
                                      Treaty Section
                                      Ministry of Foreign Affairs

   Col. Kim, Won Kil   Chief
                                      Military Affairs Section
                                      Ministry of National Defense

   Mr. Choo, Moon Ki   Chief
                                      Legal Affairs Section
                                      Ministry of Justice

   Maj. Lee, Kye Hoon   Military Affairs Section
                                      Ministry of National Defense

   Mr. Lee, Keun Pal   3rd Secretary
   (Rapporteur and   Ministry of Foreign Affairs
    Interpreter)

   Mr. Hwang, Young Jae   3rd Secretary
                                      Ministry of Foreign Affairs

   Mr. Park, Won Chul   3rd Secretary
                                      Ministry of Foreign Affairs

   U.S. Side:

   Mr. Philip C. Habib   Counselor
                                      American Embassy

   Brig. Gen. Carroll H. Dunn   Deputy Chief of Staff
                                      8th U.S. Army

   Col. Howard Smigelow   Deputy Chief of Staff
                                      8th U.S. Army

   Col. Kenneth C. Crawford   Staff Judge Advocate
                                      8th U.S. Army

0313

Mr. Franic R. La Macchia	First Secretary American Embassy
Mr. Robert A. Kinney (Rapporteur and Press Officer)	J-5 8th U.S. Army
Maj. Alton H. Harvey	Staff Judge Advocate's Office 8th U.S. Army
Mr. Kenneth Campen	Interpreter
Lt. Col. Martin S. Drucker	Observer
Lt. Col. Charles Thompson	Observer

1. Mr. Habib opened the 62nd meeting by introducing Lt. Col. Martin S. Drucker and Lt. Col. Charles Thompson, of the US Armed Forces Claims Service in Korea. Mr. Chang welcomed them on behalf of the Korean negotiators.

Claims

2. Taking up the Claims Article, Mr. Chang stated that Mr. Chu would make a statement on the Claims Article. Mr. Chu stated that the Korean negotiators had already given a thorough explanation of the Korean claims compensation system and of its practical implementation at the 30th session. They felt that the US negotiators had grasped the whole picture of the Korean claims system, which functions efficiently at present. However, in order to respond to the questions raised at the 61st session by the Chief US negotiator regarding the Korean claims system, the Korean negotiators were ready to present the following additional explanations on those matters which had not been covered at the 30th session:

a. Employees of the Compensation Committee.

No significant change has been made in the organization of the State Compensation Committee or in personnel employed either for administrative or for investigational purposes of the claims service, since the detailed explanation which

0314

had been given to the US negotiators at the 30th session. At present, there are 9 investigators (2 legal officers, 2 class three officials, and 5 other officers), and 5 clerks (3 for payment administration and 2 for general administration). Interpreters and translators are currently not employed since there has been no necessity for such personnel for settlement of the civil claims currently received.

b. Salaries of Employees.

All of the employees of the Korean claims authorities are employees of the Korean Government. Therefore, their salaries are paid by the Government in accordance with the relevant laws and regulations.

c. Claims Processed in the Years 1963 and 1964.

In 1963, 283 cases had been received and processed during the period from May 1 to December 31, 1963.

As of 30 June 1964, 207 cases had been received and 139 cases had been processed thus far in 1964, 68 cases were under consideration on 30 June 1964.

In other words, during the past 14 months, 490 claims cases have been received and processing of 422 has been completed. Detailed tabulation of the claims which have been received and considered by the Committee are as shown on the table.

Number of Claims Processed in 1963 and 1964

YEAR	NO. OF CLAIMS RECEIVED	DISPOSITION				
		AWARDED	REJECTED	WITHDREW	TOTAL	PENDING
1963 (1 May-31 Dec.)	283	189	81	13	283	-
1964 (1 Jan.-30 Jun.)	207	91	27	21	139	68
TOTAL	490	280	108	34	422	68

0315

d. Fees for Attorney.

In the claims awards made by the Committee, attorney's fees are not included.

e. Appropriations for awards in 1963 and 1964.

In the 1963 and 1964 budgets, 30,390,000 Won and 25,910,200 Won, respectively, were appropriated for awards. Although the amount of the budget for fiscal year 1964 is a little less than that for 1963, this will not affect the payment of claims awards. If additional appropriations should be necessary, the Korean authorities would take appropriate measures.

f. Number of Claims Offices.

As had been explained at the 30th session, there is one central office in the Ministry of Justice. However, as the Korean negotiators pointed out at the 61st session, actions designed to improve the central office as well as enlarge the system are now being taken by the Korean authorities.

g. Rules and Regulations.

In order to implement the State Compensation Law, No. 231, promulgated on September 8, 1951, there are following laws and regulations:

    (1) Law relating to Procedures for Claims on Damages by the State, No. 1223, promulgated on Dec. 24, 1962.

    (2) Regulations relating to the Application of the Law No. 1223, Cabinet Ordinance No. 1187, promulgated on February 5, 1963, and amended by Presidential Decree No. 1773, April 21, 1964.

    (3) Regulations relating to the Application of the Law No. 1223, Ministry of Justice Regulation No. 63, April 27, 1964, amended by Ministry of Justice Regulation No. 79, May ___, 1964.

0316

Mr. Chu also presented the US negotiators with Korean
language copies of ROK Government laws and regulations on
claims.

3.   Mr. Chu further stated that, as the Korean
negotiators explained in detail at the 30th session, in
addition to these laws and regulations, the Korean Civil
Code, decisions of the courts, and other data serve as
guidance for reasonable settlement of claims. At the 61st
session, the Chief US negotiator had stated that the US
negotiators believed the answers to the questions which
they had raised would demonstrate that the Korean authorities
did not have an effective claims service. However, the Korean
negotiators believe that the foregoing answers, and their
explanation of the State Compensation Committee at the 30th
session, surely demonstrate the effectiveness of the present
Korean claims system. The Korean claims authorities have
been settling, promptly, equitably, and efficiently, the
claims for various damages arising out of acts or omissions
of 600,000 members of the Korean Armed Forces and more than
200,000 officials of the Government done in the performance
of their official duties, as well as for other damages
arising out of acts, omissions, or occurrences for which the
Korean Government is legally responsible. The Korean
negotiators wish to remind the US negotiators of the fact
that some of the US negotiators visited the Ministry of
Justice last Fall, and were given two briefings on the
Korean State Compensation Committee system and its operation,
they also observed an actual State Compensation Committee
meeting dealing with civil claims, and recognized the
efficiency of the system.

한·미국 간의 상호방위조약 제4조에 의한 시설과 구역 및 한국에서의 미국군대의 지위에 관한 협정(SOFA)
전59권. 1966.7.9 서울에서 서명 : 1967.2.9 발효(조약 232호) (V.51 실무교섭회의 합의의사록, 제38-68차, 1964) 323

4. The Korean negotiators believe, Mr. Chu continued, that after the Status of Forces Agreement comes into force, the possible increase in number of claims which would be filed with the Korean authorities could be efficiently processed by the Korean authorities, without imposing any excessive administrative burden on the Korean authorities, with some improvement and enlargement of the present Korean system.

5. The Korean negotiators also wish to point out, Mr. Chu stated, that the Korean claims agencies are staffed with judges, prosecutors, and attorneys, with profound experience and abundance of knowledge of judicial precedents accumulated over the past ten years. Therefore, the Korean negotiators are confident that the Korean authorities, with the help of the experienced personnel available in the field of civil claims, could promptly and equitably dispose of claims arising out of the stationing of the comparably not too large number of the US military personnel in Korea.

6. Mr. Chu said that the Korean legal experts had met informally several times with members of the US negotiating team and exchanged their views regarding their respective positions. As the result of these meetings, the Korean negotiators had made their position clear at the 51st session by proposing three agreed minutes, after carefully studying the views expressed by the US negotiators in these informal discussions. The Korean negotiators wish to ask the US negotiators to study further the proposals made by the Korean negotiators and respond favorably at a later meeting.

7. With regard to the statement made by the Chief US negotiator at the 61st session in connection with the US Claims Service in Korea, Mr. Chu asked the US negotiators the following questions:

0318

a. The US negotiators stated that the formula system
in the Japan SOFA worked much differently in practice
than as indicated in the text of the US-Japan
Claims Article. Could the US negotiators present
detailed information on the working procedures
for settlement of claims in Japan?

b. The US negotiators had stated that the present US
Claims Service meets the problem to the general
satisfaction of all concerned. Does this mean that
there are no claimants who have been dissatisfied so
far? How does the US Claims Service dispose of
claims which are not settled to the satisfaction of the
claimant at present? Does the US Claims Service
have a reexamination system? If so, who participates
in the reexamination? Are they the same personnel
who participate in the original decision? How many
cases have been reexamined? Could the US negotiators
give a detailed contents of the cases reexamined?

c. How many persons are there in the US Claims Service
in Korea who hold qualifications as attorneys,
prosecutors and judges?

d. How many claims were processed by the US Claims
Service in Korea since its activation? Are there
detailed statistics on individual claims cases of
various types, including amounts involved?

e. The Korean negotiators would also like to have
information regarding the cases for which the highest
and the lowest amount were paid, including the
copies of the claim files thereof.

f. How long does it take, on the average, to process
a claim by the US Claims Service in Korea?

0319

a. The US negotiators stated that the formula system in the Japan SOFA worked much differently in practice than as indicated in the text of the US-Japan Claims Article. Could the US negotiators present detailed information on the working procedures for settlement of claims in Japan.

b. The US negotiators had stated that the present US Claims Service meets the problem to the general satisfaction of all concerned. Does this mean that there are no claimants who have been dissatisfied so far? How does the US Claims Service dispose of claimant at present? Does the US Claims Service have a reexamination system? If so, who participates in the reexamination? Are they the same personnel who participate in the original decision? How many cases have been reexamined? Could the US negotiators give a detailed contents of the cases reexamined?

c. How many persons are there in the US Claims Service in Korea who hold qualifications as attorneys, prosecutors and judges?

d. How many claims were processed by the US Claims Service in Korea since its activation? Are there detailed statistics on individual claims cases of various types, including amounts involved?

e. The Korean negotiators would also like to have information regarding the cases for which the highest and the lowest amount were paid, including the copies of the claim files thereof.

f. How long does it take, on the average, to process a claim by the US Claims Service in Korea?

0320

8. Mr. Habib thanked Mr. Chu for his explanation and for the copies of the ROK Government claims materials. The US negotiators will reply in detail at the next meeting.

9. Mr. Habib asked if the documents in the Korean language just provided by Mr. Chu contained information on ROK standards used in determination of the amounts of claims awards. Mr. Chu answered that the materials do not contain such standards, or guidelines, but as explained in detail at the 30th session, the ROK claims official used the Hofmann formula in deciding the amount of awards.

10. Mr. Habib stated that the US Armed Forces Claims Service has a published set of awards for various claims, and that such a standard set of regulations and guidelines tends to prevent discrimination, or wide variation in claims awards. Mr. Chu asked if the U.S. side could furnish the Korean negotiators with the copies of such a published set of standards used by the U.S. Armed Forces Claims Service. He explained that the ROK State Compensation Committee determined the amount of awards, not by their own arbitrary decisions, but by the Hofmann formula, using the precedents established by the ROK civil courts. He emphasized that there was no room for discrimination in the operation of the Korean claims system. Mr. Habib asked if this could be demonstrated through example? It was agreed this subject would be discussed more fully at a later meeting.

11. Mr. Habib indicated that, while the ROK negotiators had supplied general statistics on total claims, detailed statistics on individual claims cases of various types would also be useful. The ROK negotiators indicated such information would be supplied at a later meeting.

Security Measures

12. Mr. Habib indicated he wanted to clarify the present US position on the Security Measures Article, since the two sides had discussed three different drafts of this Article, formally and informally, as well as related articles in other SOFA's and a proposed understanding for the Agreed Joint Summary.

13. Mr. Habib said that the only US draft now under consideration is the one tabled at the 25th negotiating session on 26 June 1963.

14. The ROK negotiators, at the 46th session on 13 March 1964, stated that they would agree to the inclusion of the phrase "the persons who are present in the Republic of Korea pursuant to Article ____ (Invited Contractors)", and the phrase "consistent with Article ____ (Criminal Jurisdiction Article)", as desired by the US, if the US negotiators would agree to delete the phrase "of the persons referred to in this paragraph, and their property", as desired by the ROK side. The US negotiators are willing to agree to the deletion from the US draft of the phrase "of the persons referred to in this paragraph and their property", as proposed by the ROK negotiators, if the ROK negotiators agree to the inclusion in the Agreed Joint Summary of the mutual understanding first tabled at the 55th negotiating session on 19 June 1964.

15. Mr. Habib stated that both ROK and US authorities are fully aware that the defense of Korea is a joint effort involving Americans as well as Koreans, and it is believed both ROK and US officials want to insure that the US and ROK forces have the capability to discharge effectively their mutual obligations under the US-ROK Mutual Security Pact. The first sentence of the Security Measures Article to which we have both agreed, demonstrated this fact by stating that:

0322

"The United States and the Republic of Korea will cooperate in taking such steps as may from time to time be necessary to ensure the security of the United States armed forces, the members thereof, the civilian component, the persons who are present in the Republic of Korea pursuant to Article ____ (Invited Contractors), their dependents and their property."

16. Mr. Habib stated that the US negotiators feel that it is entirely proper and correct for the confidential negotiating record to show clear agreement between ROK and US Governments on the following understanding:

"In cooperating with each other under this Article, the two Governments agree that each will take such measures as may be necessary to ensure the security and protection of the US armed forces, the members thereof, the civilian component, the persons who are present in the Republic of Korean pursuant to Article ____ (Invited Contractors), their dependents and their property."

17. Mr. Habib stated that the foregoing language means just what it says and no more. The US negotiators wish to assure the Korean negotiators that such an understanding does not envisage the passage of legislation which would be applicable only to offenses against US personnel. Any legislation would of course be equally applicable to Koreans as well as Americans. We seek no special privileges in this regard. At the same time, the US cannot believe that the ROK Government would knowingly fail to take any measures that would be necessary to assist in accomplishment of our mutual defense objectives. This, of course, would include the passage of legislation if such were necessary. This does not mean that the US is implying that current ROK legislation

0323

his area is deficient. But times and conditions do change. The US simply wishes ROK assurance for the record that in the event of changed conditions the ROK will, in cooperation with the US, take such measures as the then existing circumstances dictate to be necessary. This is the sort of understanding which underlies the basic fabric of ROK-US defense agreements and cooperative efforts, and which surely reflects the views of both of our Governments.

18. Mr. Habib concluded his statement by emphasizing that the two sides now appeared to be in agreement on the text of the article, and at least on the spirit behind the understanding for the agreed record. Therefore, it is hoped that with this elaboration of the US views, the Koreans and US negotiators can achieve early agreement on this Article and go on to discussion of other articles where real differences in US-ROK views still exist.

19. Mr. Chang thanked the US side for their review of the status of this Article and for the US statement, which he felt took a very constructive approach toward resolving this problem. He indicated that the Korean negotiators would take this question under advisement and reply at the next meeting. However, Mr. Chang pointed out that the last phrase of the Article was not still agreed upon, as the Korean draft reads "for the punishment of offenders under the applicable laws of the ROK" while the US draft reads "to ensure the punishment ... " the Korean negotiators, Mr. Chang continued, prefer their draft on the ground that it is the responsibility borne soly by the Korean Government to ensure the punishment of certain offenses under the applicable law and the responsibility could not properly be placed as a negotiable subject. Mr. Habib

0324

explained that, of course, offenders could only be punished "under the applicable laws of the Republic of Korea", and that there was o intent in the proposed language to prejudge the case of such offenders.

20. It was agreed that the secretaries for the ROK and US sides, respectively, would meet later to decide the date for the next meeting.

0325

JOINT SUMMARY RECORD OF THE 63RD SESSION

1. Time and Place: 3:00 - 4:30 P.M. September 11, 1964 at
   the Foreign Ministry's Conference
   Room (No.1)

2. Attendants:

   ROK Side:

   Mr. Chang, Sang Moon   Director
                                 European and American Affairs
                                 Bureau

   Mr. Koo, Choong Whay   Chief, America Section
                                 Ministry of Foreign Affairs

   Mr. Oh, Jae Hee   Chief
                                 Treaty Section
                                 Ministry of Foreign Affairs

   Col. Kim, Won Kil   Chief
                                 Military Affairs Section
                                 Ministry of National Defense

   Mr. Choo, Moon Ki   Chief
                                 Legal Affairs Section
                                 Ministry of Justice

   Mr. Kim, Se Kwon   Prosecutor
                                 Claims Section
                                 Ministry of Justice

   Maj. Lee, Kye Hoon   Military Affairs Section
                                 Ministry of National Defense

   Mr. Hwang, Young Jae   3rd Secretary
                                 Ministry of Foreign Affairs

   Mr. Park, Won Chul   3rd Secretary
                                 Ministry of Foreign Affairs

   Mr. Kim, Yoon Taik   3rd Secretary
   (Interpreter)   Ministry of Foreign Affairs

   U.S. Side:

   Mr. Philip C. Habib   Counselor
                                 American Embassy

   Brig. Gen. Carroll H. Dunn   Deputy Chief of Staff
                                 8th U.S. Army

   Col. Howard Smigelow   Deputy Chief of Staff
                                 8th U.S. Army

0326

Capt. John Wayne	Assistant Chief of Staff USN/K
Mr. Benjamin A. Fleck (Rapporteur and Press Officer)	First Secretary American Embassy
Mr. Robert A. Kinney	J-5 8th U.S. Army
Mr. Robert A. Lewis	Second Secretary American Embassy
Maj. Alton H. Harvey	Staff Judge Advocate's Office 8th U.S. Army
Mr. Kenneth Campen	Interpreter
Lt. Col. Charles Thompson	Claims Service 8th U.S. Army

1. Mr. Chang opened the meeting by introducing Mr. Kim Se-kwon, a Prosecutor from the Ministry of Justice, and Mr. Kim Yun-taik, who would serve as interpreter for the Korean negotiators in the place of Mr. Yi Kun-pal. Mr. Habib welcomed these gentlemen to the negotiations and, in turn, introduced Lt. Colonel Charles Thompson, of the U.S. Claims Service, who would participate in the discussion of the Claims Article. Mr. Chang welcomed Lt. Colonel Thompson.

Correction of Summary Record

2. Mr. Habib stated that before proceeding with the agenda agreed upon, the U.S. negotiators would like to correct an error which they had discovered in the Agreed Joint Summary of the 60th meeting. The first sentence of paragraph 23 of that Summary reported a statement that in Germany criminal jurisdiction over U.S. personnel is exercised by the sending state only. This, of course, was untrue, as both the U.S. and Korean negotiators were well aware. The topic under discussion at the time had been duty certificates and the discussion which followed the statement in question

0327

had made it plain that the United States does not have
exclusive criminal jurisdiction in the Federal Republic
of Germany. Accordingly, the U.S. negotiators proposed that
the two secretaries amend the Agreed Joint Summary of the
60th meeting by deleting from paragraph 23 the words:
"criminal jurisdiction over U.S. personnel is exercised by
the sending state only. However", Mr. Chang replied that
the Korean negotiators agreed to the proposed correction.

Claims

3. Taking up the Claims Article, Mr. Habib stated that
he would like to make a few remarks related to the previous
discussion of this article. The U.S. negotiators had
shought to make clear that the U.S. Government is determined
to continue to meet its recognized responsibilities to
provide prompt and equitable settlement of any justified
claims against the U.S. armed forces in Korea. The U.S.
Armed Forces Claims Service, Korea, is currently fulfilling
these responsibilities in an efficient and effective manner.
The U.S. armed forces wish to continue this operation in order
to fulfill the legal obligations of the U.S. Government in
the settlement of claims. The U.S. Claims Service has
operated in such a manner as to insure the continuance of
the current friendly relations between the Korean people and
the U.S. armed forces. The U.S. negotiators are convinced
that this friendly relationship is, in part, a result of the
fact that the Korean people know that legitimate claims
against the U.S. armed forces will be speedily and fairly
settled. At the previous meeting, the U.S. negotiators had
promised to try to answer specific questions. Lt. Colonel

0328

Thompson would now answer the questions posed by the Korean negotiators.

4. Lt. Colonel Thompson stated that with reference to the first question asked by the Korean negotiators, concerning the operation of the claims system in Japan, it is the understanding of the U.S. negotiators that the U.S. armed forces and the Japanese authorities each conducts a separate claims investigation. When these investigations have been concluded, the Japanese claims agency and the U.S. claims agency reach agreement as to the liability and the amount of any award.

5. With reference to the Korean inquiry regarding the settlement of claims in Korea, Lt. Colonel Thompson stated that there are some dissatisfied claimants. However, objections are received only in 5 percent of the cases. Obviously, not all claims are justified nor can they all be settled by payment of the amount claimed. Claims are thoroughly re-examined upon the receipt of a complaint made by a claimant. This re-examination is made by the commissioner who originally acted on the claim. If the same commissioner is not available, the review will be made by another commissioner. He is authorized to change a prior determination upon the receipt of new and material evidence, or to correct manifest errors in calculation, or because of fraud or collusion. It is estimated that ten cases are re-examined each month. This includes cases re-examined for the first time and those being re-examined for the second and subsequent times. Detailed contents of all cases are not immediately available, as the files are sent to the United States within 60 days after settlement or 120 days after disapproval or receipt of the last letter from the claimant requesting review. It may be noted that the principal complaints of claimants are based

on findings of negligence on the part of the claimants to
a degree which prevents payment of the claim.

6. In response to the third question posed by the
Korean negotiators, Lt. Colonel Thompson stated that four members
of the U.S. Claims Service are qualified attorneys and three
of these serve as Claims Commissioners. There are no Claims
Commissioners who are not attorneys. Furthermore, these
four attorneys at present have a combined total of fifty-
nine years of legal experience. In addition, the services
of seven U.S. attorneys and one Korean attorney assigned
to the office of the Staff Judge Advocate, Eighth United
States Army, are available for general legal advice.

7. Regarding the number of claims made against the
U.S. armed forces, Lt. Colonel Thompson tabled the following
data showing the number of claims processed during 1963 and
up to September 1, 1964:

	Claims Adjudicated	Claims Allowed	Claims Disallowed	Claims Paid	Amount Paid Won	Dollars
1963	839	680	159	649	19,264,162	148,185.0
1964 (as of Sept.1)	911	589	322	576	25,865,548	101,433.5

Lt. Colonel Thompson stated that statistical reports for the
period from June 1, 1959, through 1962 have been sent to the
United States and are not immediately available. The largest
amount paid on a claim was Won 627,376 ($4,844.60), paid to
Mr. Na In-duk, who had been assaulted and shot in the leg by
two U.S. soldiers who were absent without leave from their
units. Mr. Na's leg had to be amputated. The lowest payment
had been Won 200 ($1.54), paid to Mr. Yi Chong-hwa for damage
to his barley field by a U.S. tank. The files on both of these
cases have been sent to the United States and details,
therefore, are not available at this time. Lt. Colonel Thompson

0330

said that individual files can be made available for review by the Korean authorities, upon request. However, if the cases have been completed, it will take approximately 30 days to obtain the records from the United States.

8. Regarding the time it takes to process a claim, Lt. Colonel Thompson stated that this varies, based on the complexity of the investigation and the factual situation. He pointed out that there may be delays caused by difficulties in investigation or by the claimant's failure to provide promptly required documents. These variables make it impossible to fix an absolute time of processing. It may be fairly estimated, however, that normally a claim is settled and the claimant notified within sixty days after the claim has been received by the Claims Service.

9. Regarding the question of the standards adhered to by the Claims Service, Lt. Colonel Thompson stated that the allowable compensation normally represents the cost of repairing the property or the cost of restoring it to the condition it was in immediately prior to the damage. The claimant establishes these costs by presenting receipts for amounts expended to repair or estimates of the cost of repair submitted by reputable contractors or other qualified repairmen. Compensation for lost or completely destroyed property is computed at the actual value of the property at the time of the loss or destruction. The value of growing crops and trees is similarly computed. The compensation payable for personal injury and death, Lt. Colonel Thompson continued, is not as amenable to mathematical calculation as are the costs of property damage. To obtain as much consistency as possible, standard elements are utilized to form a sound basis on which to compute awards. In this regard, the Claims

0331

Service follows the disability grades and compensation tables set forth in the Korean Labor Standards Act and implementing Presidential Decree No. 889, used by the Republic of Korea Workman's Compensation Board. Such tables can be obtained readily from the appropriate ROK Government offices. The Claims Commissions are charged with the responsibility of evaluating each case in the light of standard elements to arrive at a fair settlement.

10. Mr. Chu replied that the Korean negotiators would study the statements made by Lt. Colonel Thompson and perhaps would ask further questions at a later meeting. Mr. Chu said that he wished to make a few remarks in addition to those which he had made at the previous meeting.

11. Mr. Chu recalled that the U.S. negotiators had asked what criteria the Korean Claims Service used for computation of claims payments. In reply, he had explained the Korean practices. It was true that there were no Korean legal provisions for settling claims. However, when the payment of claims against the U.S. armed forces was turned over to the Korean Claims Service, such claims would be handled effectively and without prejudice. He said that the highest amount paid by the Korean Claims Service in settlement of a claim was Won 450,000, in a traffic accident case resulting in death. More detailed data on cases handled by the Korean Claims Service would be provided as soon as compiled.

12. Mr. Chu said he would like to acquaint the U.S. negotiators with the personal backgrounds of members of the Korean Claims Settlement Commission. The Chairman was Mr. Kwon, the present Vice Minister of Justice, formerly a

0332

law professor for 7 years, a lawyer for 3 years, and a public prosecutor for 15 years. Mr. Lee, the Director of the Bureau of Legal Affairs, had been a law professor for 6 years and a prosecutor for 13 years. Member Yun had been a prosecutor for 19 years, as had member Lee, the present Director of the Bureau of Correction. Member Lim, head of the Appellate Court, had served for 15 years as a judge. Member Kim, currently Vice Chief of the Staff Judge Advocate's Section, ROK Army Headquarters, had served previously for 11 years as a Judge Advocate. Member Kim, a lawyer and formerly a Justice of the Supreme Court, had served as a lawyer for 20 years and a judge for 10 years. In view of the backgrounds of these people, who could doubt that claims would be handled by them in an equitable and just manner? Handling of claims against the U.S. armed forces by the Korean Claims Service would not compromise U.S. interests.

13. Mr. Chu stated that in case a claimant was dissatisfied, he could file an objection with a Korean court for decision of the matter through legal procedures. As the U.S. negotiators knew, there were three levels of courts in the ROK judicial system. Thus, a claimant could file his objection three separate times.

14. On the basis of the information which the Korean negotiators had provided concerning the Korean claims system, Mr. Chu asked the U.S. negotiators to reconsider their position. Mr. Habib asked if the Korean negotiators could provide any examples of cases which had been appealed to the courts. What had been the findings of the court? Mr. Chu replied that only one such case had occurred to date, and that adjudication in that case had not yet been completed.

15. Mr. Habib recalled that Mr. Chu had stated that
at present there were no fixed legal provisions for the
payment of claims but that the Korean authorities intended
to settle claims equitably. Mr. Habib pointed out that
the lack of legal standards leaves open the possibility of
settlement of individual claims on bases not related to any
standards. He asked whether the Korean negotiators could
furnish any data which would indicate the range of payments
actually made for claims of the same type. Mr. Chu replied
that these data would appear in the statistics which the
Korean authorities were in the process of compiling.

16. Mr. Habib said he wished to ask a more fundamental
question. To date, the Korean negotiators had not indicated
why they wished to make a change from the claims system which
is in operation. The U.S. negotiators had explained how the
U.S. Claims Service operates. They had indicated that the
U.S. armed forces are prepared to continue to operate this
system, which imposes no financial burden whatsoever on the
Korean authorities. Did the Korean negotiators find anything
wrong in the operation of U.S. Claims Service? The only
argument against its continuation which they had made to
date was that this problem was handled differently in other
countries. The U.S. negotiators did not believe that was a
good argument. They believe it to be significant that in
only 5 percent of the cases have claimants objected to the
manner in which their claim has been handled by the U.S.
Claims Service. The U.S. negotiators would be interested
in knowing what the similar figure was with regard to claims
handled by the Korean Claims Service. As the U.S. negotiators
had previously pointed out, the U.S. armed forces were
not trying to evade their responsibility with regard to the
payment of claims. They and the U.S. negotiators preferred
not to exchange a system which was working effectively and

0334

equitably and obviously to the satisfaction of the claimants
for one which was only in its beginning stages.

17. Mr. Chu replied that the Korean negotiators were
well aware that the two claims systems under discussion
were similar. Mr. Habib pointed out that the U.S. negotiators
had not expressed any such judgment and did not believe the
two systems to be similar. Mr. Chu said this was the belief
of the Korean negotiators. He added that the absence of
objections, as indicated by the 5 percent figure cited by
the U.S. negotiators, does not necessarily mean that all of
the remaining 95 percent of the claimants were satisfied.
They had to contend, after all, with such things as the
language barrier and lack of knowledge of how the system
worked.

18. Mr. Habib demurred. In the absence of objections,
he said, one can only assume satisfaction. He pointed out
that the U.S. Claims Service provides interpreters, explains
fully the procedures to be followed, and gives whatever
other assistance may be necessary to claimants.

19. Mr. Chu then stated that, as a matter of principle,
what happens in a given country should be settled by the
authorities of that country. Mr. Habib again demurred.
He pointed out that the matters under discussion involved
two countries and that how matters involving the two
countries were settled was a question to be settled by
agreement between the two governments. He reminded the
Korean negotiators that the U.S. armed forces were in Korea
under the terms of an international agreement.

20. Mr. Chu said the Korean negotiators understood the
position stated by the U.S. negotiators and that the two
sides were in the process of negotiating an agreement which

0335

would make an exception to the principle which he had just stated. The Korean negotiators believed there were no differences between the two systems but the Korean system contained more remedies for handling objections by dissatisfied claimants. The Korean Claims Service personnel understand their own people better than U.S. personnel and can more easily persuade claimants to accept the payments awarded.

21. Mr. Chang added that the Korean negotiators believed that by now the U.S. negotiators realized that the Korean Claims Service was an efficient, working system. However, the U.S. negotiators appeared still to have misgivings regarding the lack of legal standards. Claims were paid by the Korean Claims Service on the basis of practices developed over many years. Lack of legal standard on the part of the Korean Claims system does not necessarily mean that the awards were given without any standard. The U.S. negotiators had not indicated that the U.S. Claims Service had any legal standards either.

22. Mr. Habib pointed out that Lt. Colonel Thompson had covered this subject as the last point in the statement which he had made earlier in the meeting. Mr. Chang replied that the Korean authorities had standards but they were not standards which had been promulgated as law by the National Assembly. He asked what legally promulgated standards were followed by the U.S. Claims Service. He pointed out that the matters under discussion involved Korean nationals and that the Korean negotiators believed it to be ridiculous that Korean nationals should be dealt with under procedures that were not Korean. However, the Korean negotiators agreed that the interest of the foreign government involved must be recognized. How that interest could be expressed was open to negotiation.

0336

23. Mr. Habib remarked that the negotiators appeared to have exhausted the possibilities for discussion of this article at this time and suggested that further discussion be deferred until a later meeting, after each side had the opportunity for further study. Mr. Chang agreed.

Security Measures

24. Turning to the Security Measures Article, Mr. Chang stated that the Korean negotiators had studied the position expounded by the U.S. negotiators at the 62nd meeting. As a result, the Korean negotiators had reached the conclusion that the last phrase of the Article must read as in the Korean draft, "... for the punishment of ...", as the Korean negotiators had indicated at the 62nd meeting. With regard to the understanding proposed by the U.S. negotiators for the Agreed Joint Summary at the 55th meeting, the Korean negotiators believed the understanding is not necessary in the light of the content of the text and the representation made by the U.S. negotiators at the last meeting, as the U.S. negotiators had stated that they seek no special privileges with regard to the security measures for U.S. personnel and that they fully recognize that the Korean authorities would not fail to cooperate with the U.S. armed forces in taking necessary measures for security of the U.S. military personnel.

25. Mr. Chang stated that the Korean negotiators still found objectionable points in the proposed understanding. First, the phrase "... each will take such measures as may be necessary..." seems to involve some possible factor of misunderstanding that the United States authorities might institute unilateral measures without prior agreement with

the Korean authorities. The Korean negotiators did not think that the United States negotiators intended the proposed understanding to bring about such an effect. If the interpretation of the Korean negotiators was correct and the U.S. negotiators were seeking prior agreement with the Korean authorities to effect mutual cooperation, the Korean negotiators believed that the provisions of the Article itself would be sufficient and that no such ambiguous understanding should be included as a confidential agreement in the Agreed Joint Summary.

26. Secondly, Mr. Chang continued, while the proposed understanding provides that each side may institute measures for "persons" as well as for the U.S. armed forces, it was noted that the second sentence of the text already provides that the ROK Government will take legislative measures regarding the U.S. armed forces, if necessary. With regard to "persons", the Korean position still stood, as the Korean negotiators had repeatedly explained it in the past. The ROK Government is prepared to take legislative measures for them only when it considers such measures necessary. Accordingly, inclusion of the phrase "such measures" in the understanding is not acceptable to the Korean side, if the term includes legislative measures for persons. Moreover, should any problem arise in the course of implementing the Article, the Korean negotiators believe that the Joint Committee could deal with it effectively. The Korean authorities will take such measures as they deem necessary and other, joint measures may be taken if such are necessary. As the Korean negotiators are convinced that the Korean authorities will ask the United States for its cooperation whenever such is deemed

necessary and that the United States will respond favorably, the Korean negotiators believed that such mutual cooperation is sufficiently provided for in the text of the Article. Therefore, the Korean negotiators suggested that the U.S. negotiators, taking the Korean position into consideration, withdraw their proposal for a separate understanding.

27. Mr. Habib replied that the U.S. negotiators had attempted to make clear that what they were proposing was not discriminatory legislation for U.S. "persons" only, but legislation which would include Korean and U.S. persons alike. Mr. Chang stated that the Korean negotiators understood this. Mr. Habib then stated that the U.S. negotiators would study the Korean position, as just explained by Mr. Chang.

28. It was agreed that the two secretaries would meet and fix the date of the next meeting.

0339

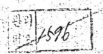

JOINT SUMMARY RECORD OF THE 64TH SESSION

1. Time and Place: 4:00 - 5:00 P.M. October 16, 1964 at
   the Foreign Ministry's Conference
   Room (No.1)

2. Attendants:

   ROK Side:

Mr. Chang, Sang Moon	Director European and American Affairs Bureau
Mr. Hu, Sung John	Director Labor Administration Bureau Office of Labor Affairs
Mr. Koo, Choong Whay	Chief, America Section Ministry of Foreign Affairs
Mr. Kim, Dai Chung	Chief Labor Administration Section Office of Labor Affairs
Col. Kim, Won Kil	Chief Military Affairs Section Ministry of National Defense
Mr. Lee, Keun Pal (Rapporteur and Interpreter)	3rd Secretary Ministry of Foreign Affairs
Mr. Hwang, Young Jae	3rd Secretary Ministry of Foreign Affairs

   U.S. Side:

Mr. Philip C. Habib	Counselor American Embassy
Brig. Gen. Carroll H. Dunn	Deputy Chief of Staff 8th U.S. Army
Col. Howard Smigelow	Deputy Chief of Staff 8th U.S. Army
Capt. John Wayne	Assistant Chief of Staff USN/K
Col. Kenneth C. Crawford	Staff Judge Advocate 8th U.S. Army
Mr. Frank R. LaMacchia	First Secretary American Embassy

0340

Mr. Benjamin A. Fleck (Rapporteur and Press Officer)	First Secretary American Embassy
Mr. Robert A. Kinney	J-5 8th U.S. Army
Mr. Robert A. Lewis	Second Secretary American Embassy
Maj. Alton H. Harvey	Staff Judge Advocate's Office 8th U.S. Army
Mr. David Y.S. Lee (Interpreter)	Second Secretary American Embassy
Mr. Julio Hernandez (Observer)	Labor Adviser 8th U.S. Army

1. Mr. Habib opened the discussion by recalling that the Labor Article had been discussed previously in formal negotiating sessions and in subsequent informal discussions, during which the respective positions of the two sides had been clarified. The U.S. negotiators had studied the views expressed by the Korean negotiators in the light of the situation in Korea and the requirements of the U.S. armed forces in the joint defense of the Republic of Korea. He said the U.S. negotiators would now table several proposed changes in the U.S. draft of this article which were designed to meet the needs of the Korean negotiators and to be consistent with the joint U.S.-ROK defense requirements.

2. Mr. Habib recalled that the U.S. negotiators had tabled a revised Paragraph 2 at the 45th meeting. This revised paragraph would provide for assistance by the ROK authorities in recruitment of USFK Korean employees. At that meeting a new Agreed Minute had also been tabled, which would provide that the ROK Government be reimbursed for

0341

direct costs incurred in providing the assistance requested
pursuant to Paragraph 2. At the 46th meeting, the ROK
negotiators had indicated their desire that the U.S.
military authorities, when accomplishing direct recruitment
and employment of personnel, should provide the ROK Government with relevant information required for labor administration. During subsequent discussion of this point in
informal sessions, the ROK negotiators had indicated that
the relevant information would be information required
mainly for administrative and planning purposes, covering
such details as the number of employees hired, the places
of employment, and the job classifications. The U.S.
negotiators wish to cooperate, Mr. Habib continued, with
the ROK Government in meeting its requirements for ROK
labor administration. Therefore, they wished to table
at this time the following proposed revision of Paragraph 2,
which includes an entirely new second sentence:

> "2. Employers may accomplish the recruitment,
> employment and management of employees directly, and
> upon request of the employer, with the assistance
> of the authorities of the Republic of Korea. In case
> employers accomplish direct recruitment of employees,
> employers will provide available relevant information
> as may be required for labor administration to the
> Office of Labor Affairs of the Republic of Korea."

3. With regard to Paragraph 3 of the Labor Article,
Mr. Habib said the U.S. negotiators believe that USFK
personnel standards parallel or exceed those of the ROK
Labor Standards Act, a fact which they believe the ROK
Office of Labor Affairs would be happy to confirm. The
U.S. armed forces will continue to conform to Korean labor
standards and practices and to Korean labor laws as they
are generally observed by Korean employers, subject to
the basic management needs of the U.S. armed forces. In

0342

order to make this commitment more explicit, Mr. Habib continued, the U.S. negotiators were tabling at this time the following entirely new proposed Paragraph 3:

"3. To the extent not inconsistent with the provisions of this article or the basic management needs of the United States Armed Forces, the conditions of employment, compensation, and labor-management practices established by the United States Armed Forces for their employees will conform with the labor laws, customs, and practices of the Republic of Korea."

4. Mr. Habib recalled that the ROK negotiators had requested the U.S. negotiators to agree to the withholding of income taxes of Korean employees of the U.S. armed forces, in accordance with ROK law. The United States Government recognizes the general soundness of the principle of the employer withholding employee contributions for income taxes. Assuming the responsibility for withholding such contributions of the 33,000 Korean employees of the U.S. armed forces will be a major administrative burden. However, the U.S. armed forces desire to cooperate with the ROK Government in every possible way. Therefore, the U.S. negotiators wished to table the following new Agreed Minute:

"Employers will withhold from the pay of their employees, and pay over to the Government of the Republic of Korea, withholdings required by the income tax legislation of the Republic of Korea."

5. Mr. Chang replied that the Korean negotiators appreciated the action of the U.S. negotiators in tabling these proposed revisions. He recalled that both sides had met informally and exchanged views on these matters. The proposed new Paragraph 2 and the Agreed Minute tabled by the U.S. negotiators were apparently based on these exchanges of views but the Korean negotiators noted that there were some changes in wording. They would study the tabled revisions and comment at a later meeting.

6. With regard to Paragraph 3, Mr. Chang said the Korean negotiators felt no hesitation in accommodating U.S. needs for defense purposes to the extent practicable. The basic position of the Korean negotiators was that laborers employed by the U.S. armed forces should enjoy all the rights guaranteed by the relevant Korean labor laws for other Korean employees, including the right to strike if disputes cannot be resolved satisfactorily. There appeared to be a continuing difference between the positions of the two sides.

7. Mr. Habib replied that the U.S. negotiators had made clear that the U.S. armed forces will conform to the ROK Labor Standards Act. They had pointed out that present USFK practice parallels or exceeds the basic standards set forth in that Act. At the same time, the U.S. negotiators have emphasized that the United States Government cannot submit to the jurisdiction of a foreign court or labor tribunal. In previous discussions, the negotiators had explored possible procedures for settling labor disputes. Obviously, the U.S. armed forces would like to see disputes settled as amicably as possible. In formulating their position, the Korean negotiators should take into account two factors. First, the U.S. negotiators have made quite clear that the U.S. armed forces will conform to the basic standards of Korean law. Secondly, the U.S. Government cannot submit to jurisdiction of foreign courts or labor tribunals. The U.S. negotiators believed that their position on these two points is not inconsistent. They also believe that in practice, any problems will be taken care of, since both sides intend to work together in good faith.

0344

8. Mr. Chang replied that the Korean negotiators fully understood the two basic points of the U.S. position, as described by Mr. Habib. They did not doubt that the U.S. armed forces would conform to the basic standards set forth in Korean law and they agreed that some aspects of the personnel procedures of the U.S. armed forces exceed those basic standards. Also, Mr. Chang continued, the ROK authorities have no intention of subjecting U.S. authorities to the jurisdiction of Korean courts in connection with labor disputes. Reaching agreement on this point would be much simpler if the U.S. negotiators would agree to a provision that the U.S. armed forces would conform to ROK laws with the understanding that disputes would be solved by the Joint Committee instead of being taken to court. In the informal discussions, the Korean negotiators had suggested that in case a dispute arises, it be referred to the Office of Labor Affairs, ROK Ministry of Health and Social Affairs. If not settled by the Office of Labor Affairs, it would then be referred to a Special Labor Committee. If the Labor Committee could not settle it, the dispute would then be referred to the Joint Committee, whose decision would be final and binding.

9. Mr. Habib replied that obviously, the U.S. armed forces stand ready to be advised and helped by the relevant ROK Ministries in the event of a dispute. Nothing in the U.S. draft of the Labor Article would prevent this. Nor does it prevent discussion of disputes by the Joint Committee. The U.S. draft does provide for conformance. If the ROK authorities were not satisfied that the U.S.

armed forces are conforming, the presumption is that they
would raise the matter in the Joint Committee or in a
subcommittee. There was nothing in the U.S. draft which
would prevent such discussion. The U.S. negotiators had
indicated that the U.S. armed forces could not conform to
those provisions of ROK law which would subject the U.S.
Government to ROK courts or labor tribunals. The Korean
negotiators had indicated their understanding that such
subjection would not be in keeping with the normal relationship between sovereign governments. It appeared to the
U.S. negotiators, therefore, that agreement has been reached
on the provisions of the text of this paragraph and that
what the negotiators were now discussing was how best to
implement those provisions. All agreed that the Joint
Committee was the implementing body. Therefore, it
should be left to the Joint Committee to decide how to
implement those provisions.

10. Mr. Chang replied that the U.S. negotiators had
misunderstood the comments of the Korean negotiators if
they believed that the latter had agreed to the language
of the proposed revision of Paragraph 3. He said there
still existed a wide gap between the positions of the two
sides with regard to the solution of labor disputes which
was directly related to agreement on Paragraph 3. The
Korean negotiators felt that the words "the basic management
needs" were ambiguous. However, they would study the
drafts and comment at a later meeting.

11. The next meeting was scheduled for October 23
at 3:00 p.m.

0346

JOINT SUMMARY RECORD OF THE 65TH SESSION

1. Time and Place: 4:00 - 5:00 P.M. October 23, 1964 at
   the Foreign Ministry's Conference
   Room (No.1)

2. Attendants:

ROK Side:

Mr. Chang, Sang Moon	Director European and American Affairs Bureau
Mr. Hu, Sung John	Director Labor Administration Bureau Office of Labor Affairs
Mr. Koo, Choong Whay	Chief, America Section Ministry of Foreign Affairs
Mr. Kim, Dai Chung	Chief Labor Administration Section Office of Labor Affairs
Mr. Oh, Jae Hee	Chief Treaty Section Ministry of Foreign Affairs
Maj. Lee, Kye Hoon	Military Affairs Section Ministry of National Defense
Mr. Lee, Keun Pal (Rapporteur and Interpreter)	3rd Secretary Ministry of Foreign Affairs
Mr. Hwang, Young Jae	3rd Secretary Ministry of Foreign Affairs
Mr. Park, Won Chul	3rd Secretary Ministry of Foreign Affairs

U.S. Side:

Mr. Philip C. Habib	Counselor American Embassy
Brig. Gen. Carroll H. Dunn	Deputy Chief of Staff 8th U.S. Army
Col. Howard Smigelow	Deputy Chief of Staff 8th U.S. Army
Capt. John Wayne	Assistant Chief of Staff USN/K

0347

Col. Kenneth C. Crawford	Staff Judge Advocate 8th U.S. Army
Mr. Frank R. LaMacchia	First Secretary American Embassy
Mr. Benjamin A. Fleck (Rapporteur and Press Officer)	First Secretary American Embassy
Mr. Robert A. Kinney	J-5 8th U.S. Army
Maj. Alton H. Harvey	Staff Judge Advocate's Office 8th U.S. Army
Mr. David Y.S. Lee (Interpreter)	Second Secretary American Embassy
Mr. Ogden C. Reed	Civilian Personnel Director 8th U.S. Army

1. Mr. Chang opened the meeting by stating that the Korean negotiators had studied the revisions of the U.S. draft of the Labor Article which the U.S. negotiators had proposed at the previous meeting.

2. Regarding Paragraph 2, although the Korean negotiators believed there was no great substantive difference, they did wish to include language providing for recruitment with the assistance of ROK authorities "to the maximum extent practicable". Therefore, they wished to table at this time the following proposed Paragraph 2:

> "2. The employers provided for in paragraph 1 shall recruit and employ to the maximum extent practicable with the assistance of the authorities of the Republic of Korea. In case employers exercise direct recruitment and employment of employees, employers shall provide such relevant information as may be necessary for labor administration to the Office of Labor Affairs of the Republic of Korea."

0348

Mr. Chang stated that the Korean draft could fully meet the U.S. requirement to hire employees directly.

3. Mr. Chang stated that the question of adding an Agreed Minute regarding the withholding of income tax payments had been discussed previously. Although its language differed from the language originally proposed by the Korean negotiators, they found no substantial difference. Therefore, they accepted the Agreed Minute tabled by the U.S. negotiators at the 64th meeting.

4. Mr. Chang remarked that the most important paragraph to be discussed at this meeting was Paragraph 3. The revised draft tabled by the U.S. negotiators states that the United States armed forces will conform with the labor laws, customs, and practices of the Republic of Korea "to the extent not inconsistent with the provisions of this article or the basic management needs of the United States Armed Forces." The Korean negotiators found the term "basic management needs of the United States Armed Forces" to be ambiguous. They feared that the use of this phraseology could be the source of disputes over interpretation of this paragraph. Mr. Chang remarked that when the U.S. negotiators had tabled this revised draft, they had said that the U.S. armed forces will conform with the basic standards of Korean law and that the United States Government cannot submit to the jurisdiction of foreign courts or labor tribunals.

5. The Korean negotiators, Mr. Chang continued, had made it clear that the ROK authorities had no intention of trying to force agencies of the U.S. Government to submit to Korean courts or labor tribunals. In order to provide for other means of settling labor disputes, the Korean negotiators wished to table the following proposed

0349

revision of Paragraph 3 and a related Agreed Minute:

"3. The conditions of employment and work, such as those relating to wages and supplementary payments, the conditions for the protection and welfare of employees, compensations, and the rights of employees, concerning labor relations shall, unless otherwise agreed upon in this Article, conform with those laid down by the legislation of the Republic of Korea."

"Agreed Minute

"With regard to any dispute between the employers except the persons referred to in Paragraph 1, Article _____, and employees or labor unions which cannot be settled through the use of existing procedures of the U.S. armed forces, settlement shall be accomplished in the following manner.

"(a). The dispute shall be referred to the Office of Labor Affairs, Ministry of Health and Social Affairs, Republic of Korea, for conciliation.

"(b). In the event that the dispute is not settled by the procedure described in (a) above, the matter may be referred to a Special Labor Committee appointed by the Office of Labor Affairs, Ministry of Health and Social Affairs, Republic of Korea, for mediation. This committee shall be tri-partite in composition and shall be consisted of equal representation from Labor Unions, the Office of Labor Affairs, and the United States armed forces.

"(c). In the event that the dispute is not settled by the procedures described in (a) and (b) above, the dispute shall be referred to the Joint Committee, or such sub-committee as may be established thereunder for arbitration to resolve the dispute. The decisions of the Joint Committee or sub-committee thereunder shall be binding."

The Korean negotiators, Mr. Chang continued, were convinced that the detailed procedures which were designed to resolve disputes outside of the jurisdiction of Korean courts or labor tribunal could fully meet the U.S. concern over the possibility of subjecting the U.S. Government to Korean courts or labor tribunals.

0350

6. Mr. Habib stated that the U.S. negotiators would give the Korean proposals careful study. At this time, he wished to make some preliminary remarks concerning them. With regard to Paragraph 2, the U.S. negotiators had tabled a draft which was intended to indicate that in recruiting personnel, the U.S. armed forces are prepared to use the ROK Labor Offices whenever practicable. This use would be dependent on the ability of the Labor Offices to provide labor of the type needed by the U.S. armed forces. The Korean negotiators had previously indicated that the ROK Labor Offices are now prepared to recruit only unskilled and semi-skilled labor. At present, the requirement of the U.S. armed forces is for skilled labor and specially-trained technical personnel. Use of the Labor Offices would also be limited by the fact that there is a low attrition rate among employees of the U.S. armed forces and the fact that there is a large group of former employees who have reemployment rights and whose reemployment would be effected outside of the procedure of using the Labor Offices. The U.S. draft provides that when the armed forces need the assistance of the ROK authorities in hiring personnel, they will ask for such assistance and it will be provided. The U.S. draft quite clearly provides for direct hire while the language proposed by the Korean negotiators, "to the maximum extent practicable", authorizes direct hire only by implication. A clear statement of the procedures to be followed would be greatly preferable to a statement granting authority to the U.S. armed forces only by implication.

0351

7. In addition, Mr. Habib continued, the language proposed by the Korean negotiators omits any statement of the right of the employer to manage his employees. The U.S. proposal contains such a statement. The U.S. negotiators considered this an important point because a literal reading of the Korean draft could lead to the interpretation that the U.S. armed forces would manage their employees with the assistance of ROK authorities.

8. Mr. Habib said that he hoped that the Korean negotiators were not under any misapprehension that the U.S. armed forces in Korea were just an ordinary employer.

9. Turning to Paragraph 3, Mr. Habib said that the revised draft proposed by the U.S. negotiators made it clear that the U.S. armed forces in Korea were prepared to conform not only with Korean labor laws but also with customs and practices. The Korean negotiators had objected to the phrase "basic management needs of the U.S. armed forces." The U.S. negotiators wished to point out that the needs of the U.S. armed forces in connection with the accomplishment of their mission could involve management decisions which are unforeseeable. The U.S. negotiators had thought that the primary need of the Korean negotiators was the inclusion in this article of an explicit statement of the willingness of the U.S. armed forces to conform with Korean labor laws and practices. They had not thought that the Korean negotiators wished to place a straightjacket on the U.S. armed forces, which have a unique function and unique needs. The U.S. negotiators saw no ambiguity in the phrase "basic management needs", which was directly related to the question of conformity. If the U.S. armed forces were committed to conformity with Korean laws and practices, as proposed in the U.S. draft, any question regarding the fulfillment of that commitment would be the subject of discussion and

0352

amicable settlement in the Joint Committee. The U.S.
negotiators believed the language proposed by the Korean
negotiators would establish a requirement which was too
rigid for a subject which is much more complicated in
practice than the Korean draft would indicate. The U.S.
draft is explicit enough to meet the needs of the Korean
authorities and would leave implementation to the Joint
Committee.

10. Taking up the Agreed Minute tabled by the Korean
negotiators, Mr. Habib said that although the U.S.
negotiators believed that spelling out in the SOFA procedures
for the settlement of labor disputes was unnecessary, they
did not disagree in principle. In order to assist them in
their study of the Korean proposal, Mr. Habib continued,
he wished to ask a few preliminary questions.

11. With regard to labor disputes, Mr. Habib pointed
out that the U.S. armed forces now informally receive
advice and assistance from the ROK Office of Labor Affairs.
Subparagraph (a) of the Korean draft, therefore, appeared
to be consistent with current practice. However, the U.S.
negotiators felt misgivings about subparagraph (b) because,
by introducing mediation procedures, it appeared to border
on a requirement that the U.S. armed forces be brought before
a Korean tribunal. As the Korean negotiators were aware,
the U.S. negotiators could not agree to any such requirement.
The proposal contained in subparagraph (b) would place
the employer at a disadvantage. The U.S. negotiators
would give their considered views regarding this Agreed
Minute at a later meeting. Their preliminary reaction was
that if inclusion of detailed procedures for settlement

0353

of disputes were ultimately agreed to, it would be preferable
to omit any reference to mediation procedures by providing
that an unsettled dispute be taken directly from unsuccessful
conciliation efforts by the Office of Labor Affairs to
consideration by the Joint Committee. The negotiators
might profitably seek to draft a simpler statement of
procedures which would lead to the submission of an unsettled
dispute to the Joint Committee.

12. Mr. Chang replied that the Agreed Minute tabled
by the Korean negotiators had been based on the procedures
followed in the Republic of Korea, in keeping with the
provisions of Korea law, which, in principle, provided for
the three steps of conciliation, mediation, and arbitration.
However, under Korean law there were no grounds for enforcement of settlements arrived at through conciliation or
mediation. Only in the case of arbitration awards was
there any legal ground for enforcement. The Korean
negotiators would take into account the views just expressed
by the U.S. negotiators.

13. Mr. Chang said the U.S. negotiators had suggested
that the Korean draft of Paragraph 2 might prohibit the
direct hire of civilian employees by the U.S. armed forces.
The Korean negotiators could not conceive that the Korean
draft in any way would prohibit direct hire. They believed
this to be a technical question of wording rather than one
of substance. They would study the comments of the U.S.
negotiators.

14. Mr. Habib replied that he had said that the Korean
draft provided for direct hire only by implication, whereas

0354

the U.S. negotiators desired an explicit authorization.

15. Referring to Mr. Habib's comment that the Korean draft of Paragraph 2 omitted any statement of the right of the employer to manage his employees, Mr. Chang stated that this omission had been intentional because the Korean negotiators needed clarification by the U.S. negotiators of what the latter meant when they referred to "management". The Korean negotiators believed that the extent of management in terms of labor relations is a highly technical subject, especially when disputes are involved. They were fearful, however, that if the concept of management were included in this paragraph, it might be interpreted to include disciplinary measures, including the right to fire employees in certain circumstances. Therefore, the Korean negotiators had purposely omitted any reference to management from their draft in order to hold further discussion on the subject.

16. Mr. Habib pointed out that, as in many other instances throughout the SOFA, one paragraph (Paragraph 2) is designed to grant certain authority to the U.S. armed forces and the following paragraph (Paragraph 3) explains how the authority is to be exercised. Unless granted the authority to manage their employees, the U.S. armed forces would find it difficult to carry out the managerial functions referred to in Paragraph 3. Mr. Reed then explained that the U.S. armed forces defined management as including hire, placement, promotion, and separation of employees.

한·미국 간의 상호방위조약 제4조에 의한 시설과 구역 및 한국에서의 미국군대의 지위에 관한 협정(SOFA)
전59권. 1966.7.9 서울에서 서명 : 1967.2.9 발효(조약 232호) (V.51 실무교섭회의 합의의사록, 제38-68차, 1964) **361**

17. Mr. Chang mentioned that Mr. Habib had pointed out that the U.S. armed forces were not an ordinary employer. The Korean negotiators were well aware of this. If the U.S. armed forces were an ordinary employer, this discussion would be unnecessary. The Korean negotiators had expressly stated that the U.S. armed forces would not be subjected to Korean courts or labor tribunals. They had also said that, in view of the uniqueness of the U.S. armed forces as an employer, they would consider omitting mediation procedures from the provisons for settlement of disputes. If it could be said that the Korean draft does not seem to take into account the uniqueness of the U.S. armed forces as an employer, it could also be said that the U.S. draft does not take into consideration the general labor practices provided for by Korean laws. Each side, therefore, should study the matter carefully.

18. Mr. Habib remarked that the Korean draft of Paragraph 3 covered the same ground as the U.S. draft but used more words in doing so. Mr. Chang replied that it was necessary to be specific because the Korean negotiators would have great difficulty in explaining to the National Assembly the meaning of the words "basic management needs of the United States armed forces." Mr. Habib reiterated that while the U.S. armed forces were prepared to commit themselves to conform to Korean laws and practices, it was necessary to include a qualification which provided for unforeseeable contingencies. Mr. Chang replied that the qualification suggested by the U.S. negotiators was much too general, for it could be applied to any situation.

0356

Mr. Habib replied that implementation of the Agreement
must be left to the Joint Committee. If the ROK authorities
believed that the U.S. armed forces were not carrying out
their commitment, they retained the right to raise the
question in the Joint Committee.

19. The meeting was adjourned after the U.S. negotiators
indicated that they would give careful study to the Korean
proposals.

1966. 12. 31

1966. 12. 31

0357

1. Time and Place: 3:00 - 4:15 P.M. November 24, 1964 at
   the Foreign Ministry's Conference
   Room (No.1)

2. Attendants:

ROK Side:

Mr. Chang, Sang Moon	Director European and American Affairs Bureau
Mr. Yoon, Woon Young	Director Prosecutors Bureau Ministry of Justice
Mr. Koo, Choong Whay	Chief, America Section Ministry of Foreign Affairs
Mr. Lee, Nam Ki	Chief America Section Ministry of Foreign Affairs
Col. Kim, Won Kil	Chief Military Affairs Section Ministry of National Defense
Mr. Choo, Moon Ki	Chief Legal Affairs Section Ministry of Justice
Mr. Oh, Jae Hee	Chief Treaty Section Ministry of Foreign Affairs
Mr. Lee, Myung Hi	Prosecutor Prosecutors Section Ministry of Justice
Mr. Lee, Keun Pal (Rapporteur and Interpreter)	3rd Secretary Ministry of Foreign Affairs
Mr. Hwang, Young Jae	3rd Secretary Ministry of Foreign Affairs

U.S. Side:

Mr. Philip C. Habib	Counselor American Embassy
Brig. Gen. Carroll H. Dunn	Deputy Chief of Staff 8th U.S. Army
Col. Howard Smigelow	Deputy Chief of Staff 8th U.S. Army
Capt. John Wayne	Assistant Chief of Staff USN/K

0358

Col. Kenneth C. Crawford	Staff Judge Advocate 8th U.S. Army
Mr. Frank R. LaMacchia	First Secretary American Embassy
Mr. Benjamin A. Fleck (Rapporteur and Press Officer)	First Secretary American Embassy
Mr. Robert A. Kinney	J-5 8th U.S. Army
Mr. Goodwin Shapiro	Second Secretary American Embassy
Maj. Alton H. Harvey	Staff Judge Advocate's Office 8th U.S. Army
Mr. David Y.S. Lee (Interpreter)	Second Secretary American Embassy

1. Mr. Chang opened the meeting by introducing Mr. Yun Un-yong, who has replaced Mr. Yun Tu-sik as Director of the Prosecutors' Bureau, Ministry of Justice. Mr. Chang stated that Mr. Yun Un-yong would play the major role for the Ministry of Justice in the negotiations. Mr. Chang then announced the impending departure of Mr. KU Chung-hoe for an overseas assignment. Remarking that Mr. Ku had participated in the negotiations for a longer period than anyone else on the Korean negotiating team, Mr. Chang stated that his Korean colleagues would sorely miss Mr. Ku's contributions to the negotiations. He then introduced as Mr. Ku's successor on the negotiating team and as Chief of the Foreign Ministry's America Section, Mr. YI Ham-ki.

2. Mr. Habib welcomed Mr. Yun and Mr. Yi to the negotiations on behalf of the American negotiating team. He then expressed the appreciation of the American negotiators for the cooperation and understanding which Mr. Ku had consistently displayed and for Mr. Ku's great devotion to achieving a successful outcome of the negotiations. The U.S. negotiators greatly regretted that Mr. Ku would not be present for the signing of the

0359

Agreement. Mr. Habib then introduced Mr. Goodwin Shapiro, who was replacing Mr. Robert Lewis as a member of the U.S. negotiating team.

3. Mr. Chang welcomed Mr. Shapiro. Mr. Ku then expressed his personal regret at having to leave the negotiations before they were successfully concluded.

Criminal Jurisdiction

4. Mr. Chang stated that the Korean negotiators wished to review the positions of the two sides regarding the three most important unresolved issues, namely the provisions regarding waiver, and duty certificates, in the Criminal Jurisdiction Article and certain aspects of the Claims Article.

5. Taking up first the use in Paragraph 1(b) of the U.S. draft of the phrase "civil authorities of the Republic of Korea", Mr. Chang made the following statement:

"a. With respect to the phrase 'civil authorities of the Republic of Korea' in the U.S. draft, the U.S. negotiators had previously stated that the position that jurisdiction over the U.S. armed forces by the host government should be limited to the civil authorities of the government was a firm U.S. position in every country in which a SOFA is in force. The U.S. negotiators wanted to have it stated explicitly in the SOFA with the ROK Government. At the 60th session, the U.S. negotiators had again reiterated that the U.S. negotiators of the Agreements with Japan and the NATO governments had not conceived of the possibility that military authorities of the host country could exercise jurisdiction. Inasmuch as that possibility does exist in the Republic of Korea, the U.S. negotiators wished to make the language of the provision quite clear by having it read 'the civil authorities of the Republic of Korea'.

0360

"b. To accommodate the oft-repeated U.S. concern above, and to meet the Korean requirement, the Korean negotiators had given to the U.S. negotiators an unqualified assurance for the negotiating record that under no circumstances would members of the U.S. armed forces and civilian components be subject to trial by Korean military authorities, in the hope that the U.S. negotiators would agree to the deletion of the word 'civil' from the draft.

"c. The Korean negotiators had further wished at the 60th session to clarify the U.S. position by asking whether the U.S. position was to accept the assurance as an agreed minute and delete the world 'civil' from the text. Although the U.S. side declined to respond to the question on the ground that the question was a hypothetical one, we wish to reiterate our position that the assurance made for the Joint Summary Record should be sufficient to settle the problem. In other words, we cannot accept the word 'civil', either in the text or in an agreed minute, but are prepared to negotiate to meet the U.S. requirement through assurances in a form other than text or agreed minute. We wonder what still keeps the U.S. negotiators from accepting the Korean assurances which squarely meet the U.S. requirement. If the U.S. negotiators have in mind any other reasons for insisting on the word 'civil' in the text, we have so far no way of knowing them.

"d. The Korean negotiators ask the U.S. negotiators to take into consideration the position of the Korean negotiators and accept it."

6. Turning to the question of duty certificates, Mr. Chang made the following statement:

0361

"a. With respect to the issuance of official duty certificates, the Korean negotiators had proposed at the 52nd session a revised draft which recognized the U.S. military authorities as the authorities to issue a certificate, and had further stated that a certificate issued by the U.S. military authorities would be sufficient evidence in determining the primary jurisdiction over offenses and any objection which might be raised by the Korean authorities should be decided by the Joint Committee.

"b. At the 58th session, the U.S. negotiators had in return proposed as the basis of discussion of the Korean draft the following two understandings:

  (1) The certificate will be conclusive unless modification is agreed upon.

  (2) The accused should not be deprived of his entitlement to a prompt and speedy trial as a result of protracted reconsideration of the duty certificate.

With regard to the 2nd understanding, the Korean negotiators had in principle no objection to the U.S. proposal. Accordingly, the Korean negotiators had expressed their willingness to set any number of days to meet the U.S. concern.

"c. Regarding the first understanding, the Korean negotiators had stated that although we believed that the certificate issued by the U.S. military authorities would in most of the cases be honored, in case any objection is raised by the Korean authorities, the problem of validity of a duty certificate should be solved by consultation and agreement between the representatives of both sides at the Joint Committee. We are firmly opposed to any idea which would entertain the possibility that the decision may be made unilaterally by the U.S. military authorities.

0362

"d. The Korean negotiators have carefully studied
the precedents presented by the U.S. negotiators at the
60th session. In fact, we would be most willing to comply
with international precedents. However, we also believe
that any dispute in international society should be
amicably settled through agreement between the parties
concerned and settlement of any controversy over duty
certificates should be no exception.

"e. We request the U.S. negotiators to reconsider
the Korean proposal and present their views at the earliest
possible date."

7. Turning to the question of waiver of jurisdiction,
Mr. Chang made the following statement:

"a. The Korean negotiators wish to review their
position on the draft regarding the waiver of primary right
to exercise jurisdiction, thereby reminding the U.S.
negotiators of outstanding issues and difficulties which
confront us in connection with the waiver problem.

"b. According to the U.S. draft, even though we consider it absolutely necessary to try an accused in specific
cases, we would be obliged to hand him over to the U.S.
authorities and then undergo afterwards necessary procedures
to recall the waived case by seeking agreement at the Joint
Committee. Furthermore, the U.S. draft does not guarantee
any assurance which enables us to obtain successful recall
in specific cases.

"c. In the past, the U.S. negotiators had emphasized
that it was the intention of the U.S. negotiators to obtain
maximum waiver from the Korean authorities. To meet the
U.S. concern, the Korean negotiators had reiterated that
we would waive as many cases as other countries do under
their SOFA's. Nevertheless, we firmly maintain that our

0363

position is to retain the principle so that we could waive primary right to the U.S. authorities except when we determine that it is of particular importance to try an accused in the Korean court.

"d. Time and again, we are ready to assure the U.S. negotiators that the Korean authorities will waive as generously as other SOFA countries do; however, we wish to retain discretion on our part as to whether or not to waive. In this connection, we believe that we are asking the U.S. negotiators not any new or unique provisions "but only universal ones which have been generally accepted by other SOFA's so so that we could reserve as a hosting country primary right to exercise jurisdiction not in general but in specific cases under special circumstances.

"e. We ask once again that the U.S. negotiators reconsider our difficulties toward this problem and accept the Korean views."

8. Mr. Habib replied that Mr. Chang had given a clear recapitulation of the views of the Korean negotiators on key issues remaining in the Criminal Jurisdiction Article. He assured the Korean negotiators that their views have received and will continue to receive the full consideration of the U.S. negotiators.

Claims

9. Turning to the Claims Article, Mr. Chang stated that the Korean negotiators had studied the position of the U.S. negotiators carefully and wished to make their own position quite clear. He then made the following statement:

"a. The U.S. negotiators have stated throughout the past discussions of this Article that they preferred the present system of the U.S. Armed Forces Claims Service in Korea to the system proposed by the Korean negotiators, because the formula concept envisaged by the latter is proved to be

0364

time-consuming and expensive to administer.

"b. However, on those concerns of the U.S. negotiators regarding the Korean proposal, the Korean negotiators have fully explained that the existing Korean claims system is operated efficiently, equitably, and would overcome the problems envisaged by the U.S. negotiators without any difficulty.

"c. In this regard, the U.S. negotiators indicated that the present U.S. system was operated efficiently, equitably and to the general satisfaction of the claimant concerned, whereas the Korean system had relatively shorter experience than the U.S. Armed Forces Claims Service in Korea and had no legally published standard of awards for various claims. Particularly, the U.S. negotiators pointed out that the lack of legal standards would leave open the possibility of settlement of individual claims on bases not related to any standard.

"d. The Korean negotiators believe that the foregoing U.S. negotiators' concerns are neither called for nor well-founded, and they would like to point out the reasons why they believe so.

"e. The U.S. authorities, in the settlement of claims in Korea as military authorities of a sending state, would not deny the significance of the following views: that the award should be paid in a just and reasonable manner, and that the settlement of claims should not adversely affect the promotion and maintenance of friendly relations between the people of the ROK and the United States.

한·미국 간의 상호방위조약 제4조에 의한 시설과 구역 및 한국에서의 미국군대의 지위에 관한 협정(SOFA)
전59권. 1966.7.9 서울에서 서명 : 1967.2.9 발효(조약 232호) (V.51 실무교섭회의 합의의사록, 제38-68차, 1964)

"f. It is, therefore, believed that, for the settlement of claims, the U.S. authorities would not hesitate in providing just and reasonable procedures as well as maximum convenience for the claimant in Korea.

"g. The claims system proposed by the Korean negotiators, particularly with regard to the procedures for the settlement of the claims arising out of acts or omissions of members or employees of the U.S. armed forces done in the performance of official duty, or out of any other act, omission or occurrence for which the U.S. armed forces are legally responsible, and causing damage to the third parties other than the Government of the ROK, at which the U.S. negotiators expressed a deep concern, is so provided that all the claimants could enjoy the full protection guaranteed by the Korean laws. The Government of the ROK will be responsible for the settlement of all the claims arising out of the above acts or omissions. And in case the claimant is dissatisfied with the disposition of the Korean Government, he would be able to have recourse to the Korean court so that all the claims arising within the ROK could be settled by the same procedures regardless of whether the loss or damage is caused by the U.S. armed forces or all the other claims normally arising out of acts or omissions of the ROK armed forces and officials of the Korean Government.

"h. Therefore, there is left no room for the claimant to express discontent with the settlement of claims to the Government of the U.S. or the U.S. military authorities in Korea. This procedure will certainly prevent the national emotion of the Korean people from turning

0366

to the direction which both the Governments and people do not desire, and will, in fact, contribute to the furtherance of the friendly relations now existing between both sides.

"i. However, if the claims were to be settled by the procedures proposed by the U.S. negotiators, awards would have to be paid only in accordance with the military regulations of the U.S. armed forces, specifically, the AR 25-90 of 1957, "Claims Arising in Foreign Countries". In this procedure, the claimants are not duly protected from the legal point of view. When the claimants are not satisfied with the award decided by the U.S. authorities, all they could do would be an appeal to the same authorities for reconsideration. And the claimants have no chance for redress through a competent court.

"j. The Korean negotiators also believe that the U.S. negotiators will fully realize the short-comings of the appeal system of the U.S. claims service in which the same persons who initially decided the award consider the same case again.

"k. For the claimant concerned, it would be hard to approve of procedures whereby the loss or damage caused by his own Government should be given a chance to be tried fairly in the court and the similar loss or damage caused by the foreign authorities should not.

"l. The U.S. negotiators might be concerned at the possibility that the proposed Korean system would not work as it should, and that the Korean authorities would make unjust and discriminatory decisions. The concern is based on the premise that the Korean system lacks the so-called 'legally published standard'. To the knowledge of

0367

한·미국 간의 상호방위조약 제4조에 의한 시설과 구역 및 한국에서의 미국군대의 지위에 관한 협정(SOFA)
전59권. 1966.7.9 서울에서 서명 : 1967.2.9 발효(조약 232호) (V.51 실무교섭회의 합의의사록, 제38-68차, 1964) 373

the Korean negotiators, the U.S. side has so far failed to present its system of the legally published standard.

"m. However, such a possibility is not existing anywhere in the Korean draft as well as in the existing Korean Claims System as witnessed by some of the U.S. negotiators. In fact, the Korean Government would be in the paying side of an award like the U.S. Government because it has to share a considerable portion of the award. And this, we believe, is a sufficient guarantee to the U.S. Government that illegitimate, unreasonable, and inequitable awards will not be paid as well as a firm determination of the Korean Government that the settlement of claims should be made without prejudice by the authorities of the ROK.

"m. Therefore, the Korean negotiators sincerely request the U.S. negotiators to reconsider their position and to proceed with the discussion of the Claims Article based on the Korean draft."

10. Mr. Habib stated that the U.S. negotiators understood the position of the Korean negotiators. The meeting was then adjourned.

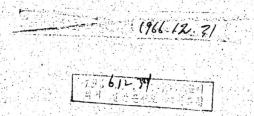

0368

JOINT SUMMARY RECORD OF THE 67TH SESSION

1. Time and Place: 4:00 - 5:00 P.M. December 16, 1964 at
   the Foreign Ministry's Conference
   Room (No.1)

2. Attendants:

   ROK Side:

   Mr. Chang, Sang Moon   Director
                                 European and American Affairs
                                 Bureau

   Mr. Yoon, Woon Young   Director
                                 Prosecutors Bureau
                                 Ministry of Justice

   Mr. Lee, Nam Ki   Chief
                                 America Section
                                 Ministry of Foreign Affairs

   Mr. Oh, Jae Hee   Chief
                                 Treaty Section
                                 Ministry of Foreign Affairs

   Mr. Lee, Myung Hi   Prosecutor
                                 Prosecutors Section
                                 Ministry of Justice

   Mr. Kim, Kee Joe   3rd Secretary
                                 Ministry of Foreign Affairs

   Mr. Lee, Keun Pal   3rd Secretary
   (Rapporteur and   Ministry of Foreign Affairs
    Interpreter)

   Mr. Hwang, Young Jae   3rd Secretary
                                 Ministry of Foreign Affairs

   Mr. Park, Won Chul   3rd Secretary
                                 Ministry of Foreign Affairs

   U.S. Side:

   Mr. Philip C. Habib   Counselor
                                 American Embassy

   Brig. Gen. Carroll H. Dunn   Deputy Chief of Staff
                                 8th U.S. Army

   Capt. John Wayne   Assistant Chief of Staff
                                 USN/K

Col. Kenneth C. Crawford	Staff Judge Advocate 8th U.S. Army
Mr. Frank R. LaMacchia	First Secretary American Embassy
Mr. Benjamin A. Fleck (Rapporteur and Press Officer)	First Secretary American Embassy
Mr. Robert A. Kinney	J-5 8th U.S. Army
Mr. Goodwin Shapiro	Second Secretary American Embassy
Maj. Alton H. Harvey	Staff Judge Advocate's Office 8th U.S. Army
Mr. David Y.S. Lee (Interpreter)	Second Secretary American Embassy

1. Mr. Chang opened the meeting by introducing Mr. KIM Kee Joe, of the America Section, Ministry of Foreign Affairs, a newly-appointed member of the Korean negotiating team. Mr. Habib welcomed Mr. Kim to the negotiations on behalf of the American negotiators.

Criminal Jurisdiction

2. Taking up the Criminal Jurisdiction Article, Mr. Habib said the U.S. negotiators wished to resume the presentation of their views. A review of the negotiating record showed that the views of both sides had been explored in great depth. Both sides realize that this article is the key to the entire Agreement. The U.S. negotiators believe that considerable progress has been made in reconciling the views of the two negotiating teams. In some respects, the U.S. negotiators have already made a number of substantial concessions to the Korean position. At this meeting, the U.S. negotiators would table a comprehensive package proposal designed to provide solutions to the four major outstanding

0370

issues in this article: waiver of jurisdiction, duty
certificates, pre-trial custody, and trial safeguards.
Resolution of these issues would leave a number of additional
points to be clarified but these four issues are the key
elements in the article. U.S. willingness to agree to each
of the four positions set forth in the package is contingent
on the agreement of the Korean negotiators to accept all
four positions.

3. Mr. Habib stated that the U.S. negotiators were
prepared to table significant modifications of the U.S.
positions on the waiver and duty certificate issues, which
were designed to be responsive to views previously expressed
by the Korean negotiators, consistent with essential U.S.
requirements. The U.S. negotiators had previously tabled
modified positions on the pre-trial custody and trial
safeguards issues. They believed that some agreement in
principle had been reached on the latter two issues.

4. Mr. Habib then tabled the following revision of
the Agreed Minute Re Paragraph 3, U.S. draft:

"The Republic of Korea, recognizing that it is
the primary responsibility of the United States authorities to maintain good order and discipline where persons
subject to United States law are concerned, waives
its primary right to exercise jurisdiction under
paragraph 3(b). In accordance therewith, the United
States authorities shall notify the authorities of
the Republic of Korea of their intention to exercise
jurisdiction in such cases through the Joint Committee.
When the authorities of the Republic of Korea, after
consultation with United States authorities, are of the
opinion that, by reason of special circumstances in a
specific case involving an offense against the security
of the Republic of Korea, or of forcible rape, or of a
malicious killing, the exercise of Korean jurisdiction
is of vital importance to the Republic of Korea in that
case, they will notify the United States authorities
of that opinion within fifteen days after receipt of
notification that the United States intends to exercise
jurisdiction. The United States shall not have the
right to exercise jurisdiction within those fifteen
days. If any question arises concerning who is to

exercise jurisdiction the United States diplomatic
mission will be afforded an opportunity to confer with
the proper authorities of the Republic of Korea before
a final determination of this matter is made.

"Trials of cases in which the authorities of the
Republic of Korea waive the primary right to exercise
jurisdiction, and trials of cases involving offenses
described in Paragraph 3(a) (ii) committed against
the state or nationals of the Republic of Korea will
be held within a reasonable distance from the place where
the offenses are alleged to have taken place unless
other arrangements are mutually agreed upon. Representatives of the Republic of Korea may be present at such
trials.

"In the implementation of the provisions of Article
___ and this Minute, and to facilitate the expeditious
disposal of offenses, arrangements may be made between
the authorities of the United States and the Republic
of Korea to dispense with notification."

5. Mr. Habib explained that the Agreed Minute just
tabled would combine an automatic waiver with a right of
recall by the Korean authorities under the circumstances
specified in the Minute. When the Korean authorities,
after consultation with United States authorities, decided
that, due to special circumstances in a particular case
involving the security of the Republic of Korea, a forcible
rape, or a malicious killing, the exercise of Korean
jurisdiction was of vital importance, they would so notify
the United States authorities. If any question should
arise concerning the exercise of jurisdiction, the United
States diplomatic mission would be afforded the opportunity
to confer with authorities of the Republic of Korea before
a final determination was made. This formula, Mr. Habib
emphasized, recognizes the right of the Government of the
Republic of Korea to determine when under the specified
circumstances a waiver may be recalled.

6. Mr. Habib recalled that the Korean negotiators have
always stated that the exercise of Korean jurisdiction was
contemplated only in those cases which were deemed to be

0372

of particular importance. The formula proposed by the U.S. negotiators provides for this and includes those serious crimes committed against either the Government of the Republic of Korea or Korean individuals. In those cases, the ROK Government would determine whether or not the waiver should be recalled, although the right of U.S. authorities to confer on such recall is provided. Mr. Habib called the attention of the Korean negotiators to the fact that the second paragraph of the tabled Agreed Minute is a new addition to the U.S. draft. This provision was added in order to incorporate the position set forth in the third paragraph of the Agreed Minute Re Paragraph 3(c) of the Korean draft. The U.S. negotiators view these provisions as desirable and are pleased to be able to accede to the wishes of the Government of the Republic of Korea by incorporating them in the U.S. draft.

7. Mr. Habib recalled that at the 52nd negotiating meeting, the Korean negotiators had tabled a proposed Agreed Minute to Paragraph 3(a) (ii) pertaining to duty certificates. As understood by the U.S. negotiators, the major objection of the Korean negotiators to Agreed Minute #2 Re Paragraph 3(a) of the U.S. draft was its provision that the duty certificate issued by a commanding officer would be conclusive. The U.S. negotiators continued to believe that the duty certificate must be controlling but they were now prepared to make a major concession by tabling a revised Agreed Minute #2 Re Paragraph 3(a) which they believe embodies certain essential principles previously tabled by the Korean negotiators.

8. Mr. Habib then tabled the following revised Agreed Minute #2 Re Paragraph 3(a):

0373

"2. Where a member of the United States armed forces or civilian component is charged with an offense, a certificate issued by competent authorities of the United States forces stating that the alleged offense, if committed by him, arose out of an act or omission done in the performance of official duty shall be sufficient evidence of the fact for the purpose of determining primary jurisdiction.

"In those exceptional cases where the chief prosecutor for the Republic of Korea considers that there is proof contrary to a certificate of official duty, it may be made the subject of review through discussions between appropriate officials of the Government of the Republic of Korea and the diplomatic mission of the United States in Korea."

9. Mr. Habib recalled that the Korean draft defined the duty certificate as "sufficient evidence" rather than as being conclusive. The Korean draft also had contained a distinction regarding the issuing authority. The revised U.S. Agreed Minute would provide that the duty certificate will be issued by "competent authorities of the United States" rather than by the Staff Judge Advocate. This change is deemed necessary because many major units of the U.S. forces do not have a Staff Judge Advocate assigned to them, even though such units may always request any legal advice from their superior headquarters. Another modification in the revised Agreed Minute relates to the body to whom the ROK Chief Prosecutor would refer if he determined that there was proof contrary to the duty certificate. Under the terms of the revision, the question would be reviewed by the appropriate authorities of the Republic of Korea and the United States diplomatic mission rather than by the Joint Committee. The U.S. negotiators regard this as a better system since it will result in reaching a final determination more quickly.

0374

10. Regarding the duty certificate itself, Mr. Habib
continued, the U.S. negotiators continue to hold strong views.
Both sides recognize the fact that the accused should not
be deprived of his entitlement to a prompt and speedy trial
as a result of a prolonged review by officials of the two
governments. The U.S. negotiators believe also that the
duty certificate must be controlling. Therefore, if
agreement is not reached within a specified time on a specific
case, the duty certificate would be conclusive for that
case but discussions could continue concerning the propriety
of issuing a duty certificate under similar circumstances
in future cases. The U.S. revised Agreed Minute would
provide the ROK Chief Prosecutor the right to question
the duty certificate. It would provide the means for
discussing the matter and the possibility of modifying
the certificate. However, unless modified, the duty
certificate would be controlling. This is fully consistent
with practice and precedents elsewhere.

11. Mr. Habib stated that the U.S. negotiators were
offering the foregoing amendments to important provisions
of the Article with the understanding that they were part of
a package which also contained additional proposals which
he would now explain.

12. First, Mr. Habib continued, the U.S. negotiators
continued to deem necessary sub-paragraph 5(c) of the U.S.
draft, pertaining to pre-trial custody. The U.S. negotiators
would agree to the adoption of sub-paragraph 5(e) proposed
by the Korean negotiators (which would provide for ROK
custody in security cases) if the Korean negotiators would
agree to the inclusion in the Joint Agreed Summary of the
understanding proposed at the 58th meeting, i.e.:

0375

a. Mutual agreement must be reached as to the circumstances in which custody is appropriate in security cases; and

b. Confinement facilities must be adequate by U.S. standards.

13. Secondly, Mr. Habib stated, it is essential to U.S. needs that the trial safeguards be enumerated in the SOFA. Therefore, the enumeration of trial safeguards contained in Paragraph 9 and the related Agreed Minutes must be accepted. This subject had already been discussed at length and in detail and the U.S. negotiators did not believe further discussion was necessary.

14. Mr. Habib stated that the U.S. negotiators believe that the Korean negotiators are well aware of the special importance that the United States Government attaches to the custody provisions and the fair trial guarantees. The U.S. negotiators, like the Korean negotiators, must be able to justify the provisions of the Agreement before their legislature and the Korean negotiators surely realize the great importance which the U.S. Congress places on guarantees of a fair trial.

15. Mr. Habib pointed out that the package proposal also included deletion of the provisions of the U.S. draft relating to the combat zone (Agreed Minute No.1 Re Paragraph 1(b)) and to the primary right of jurisdiction in those cases in which a ROK court-martial would be appropriate if a Korean serviceman were the accused (Agreed Minute No. 1 Re Paragraph 3(a)). In recognition of the dislike for these provisions previously expressed by the Korean negotiators, the U.S. negotiators had already agreed to their deletion.

0376

16. Mr. Habib stated that the U.S. negotiators presented this comprehensive package proposal with the objective of achieving an early, successful conclusion to the negotiations. They had made major concessions on the issues of waiver of jurisdiction and duty certificates, subject to Korean acceptance of the U.S. positions on custody and trial safeguards. The U.S. negotiators hoped that the Korean negotiators and the authorities of the ROK Government, in considering the U.S. proposals, would keep in mind that these proposals represent the carefully formulated views of the U.S. Government and reflect the desire on the part of U.S. Government authorities to be as responsive as possible to ROK views, consistent with essential U.S. requirements. Other questions remain to be settled in this Article but the U.S. negotiators believe that they can be settled expeditiously if agreement is reached on the four major issues. The U.S. negotiators, therefore, asked the ROK negotiators to give these proposals the most careful consideration.

17. Mr. Chang replied that the Korean negotiators appreciated the intensive and comprehensive package proposal made by the U.S. negotiators. They recognized that the proposal was made by the U.S. negotiators with a view to expediting the negotiations. Although the U.S. negotiators had said that the proposals regarding waiver and duty certificates constituted significant modifications of the U.S. position, a considerable gap still remained between the U.S. and Korean positions on those subjects. The Korean negotiators would study the U.S. proposals and comment on them at a subsequent meeting.

18. It was agreed to hold the next meeting on December 23 at 3:00 p.m.

JOINT SUMMARY RECORD OF THE 68TH SESSION

1. Time and Place: 3:00-4:10 P.M. December 23, 1964 at the Foreign Ministry's Conference Room (No.1)

2. Attendants:

ROK Side:

Mr. Chang, Sang Moon	Director European and American Affairs Bureau
Mr. Hu, Sung Joon	Director Labor Administration Bureau Office of Labor Affairs
Mr. Lee, Nam Ki	Chief America Section Ministry of Foreign Affairs
Mr. Oh, Jae Hee	Chief Treaty Section Ministry of Foreign Affairs
Maj. Lee, Kye Hoon	Military Affairs Section Ministry of National Defense
Mr. Kim, Kee Joe	3rd Secretary Ministry of Foreign Affairs
Mr. Lee, Keun Pal (Rapporteur and Interpreter)	3rd Secretary Ministry of Foreign Affairs
Mr. Hwang, Young Jae	3rd Secretary Ministry of Foreign Affairs
Mr. Park, Won Chul	3rd Secretary Ministry of Foreign Affairs

U.S. Side:

Mr. Philip C. Habib	Counselor American Embassy
Brig. Gen. Carroll H. Dunn	Deputy Chief of Staff 8th U.S. Army
Capt. John Wayne	Assistant Chief of Staff USN/K
Col. Kenneth C. Crawford	Staff Judge Advocate 8th U.S. Army

0378

Mr. Frank R. LaMacchia	First Secretary American Embassy
Mr. Benjamin A. Fleck (Rapporteur and Press Officer)	First Secretary American Embassy
Mr. Robert A. Kinney	J-5 8th U.S. Army
Mr. Goodwin Shapiro	Second Secretary American Embassy
Maj. Alton H. Harvey	Staff Judge Advocate's Office 8th U.S. Army
Mr. David Y.S. Lee (Interpreter)	Second Secretary American Embassy

Labor Article

1. The discussion was begun by Mr. Habib, who stated that since the Labor Article was last discussed (at the 65th negotiating meeting), the U.S. authorities had carefully reviewed the status of this article, including the views expressed by the Korean negotiators at the formal and informal negotiating sessions during the past ten months. The U.S. negotiators were now prepared to table significant modifications of the U.S. draft, which were designed to be responsive to the views of the Korean authorities to the maximum extent consistent with the essential requirements of the U.S. armed forces in carrying out their important defense mission in Korea. For the convenience of the negotiators, the U.S. negotiators were tabling a fresh draft of the entire article, in which the modifications being proposed at this meeting were underlined. The U.S. negotiators hoped that early agreement could be reached on the article on the basis of the modified U.S. positions now being tabled. Mr. Habib then tabled the revised U.S. draft and said he would explain the modifications.

0379

2. With regard to Paragraph 2, Mr. Habib explained, the U.S. negotiators propose revision of the first sentence, dividing it into two separate sentences. The first sentence of the revision is a simple and direct statement that the U.S. armed forces, as the employers of over 33,000 Korean personnel, may recruit, employ, and administer such personnel. The new second sentence had been included in response to Korean desires and explicitly states that the recruitment services of the Government of the Republic of Korea will be utilized insofar as is practicable. The third sentence in the revised paragraph was included earlier at the request of the ROK authorities. The U.S. negotiators believe that this revised Paragraph 2 fully takes into account the views of the ROK authorities, as expressed at both formal and informal negotiating meetings, and therefore should be acceptable to the Korean negotiators.

3. With regard to Paragraph 3, Mr. Habib said the U.S. negotiators were proposing a modification of this paragraph in response to the objections expressed by the Korean negotiators at the 65th meeting to the phrase "the basic management needs" in the earlier U.S. draft. This phrase was said to be too broad and ambiguous and therefore it has been replaced by the words "the military requirements". The U.S. armed forces, which are in Korea pursuant to the U.S.-ROK Mutual Defense Treaty of November 17, 1954, are here to assist in the defense of the Republic of Korea. The U.S. armed forces have tried to be good employers to their Korean employees and expect to continue to conform generally to ROK labor laws and practices. Under the present conditions

of armistice, the U.S. armed forces must be prepared to meet any military contingencies, including developments which are unforeseeable. The U.S. negotiators believe that the ROK authorities, including the National Assembly, recognize the realities of the military situation in Korea and will be prepared, therefore, to agree that the words "the military requirements" are necessary in this context in Paragraph 3.

4. Mr. Habib recalled that the ROK negotiators had expressed a strong desire to append an Agreed Minute to the Labor Article which would establish procedures for the settlement of labor disputes which cannot be settled internally by the U.S. armed forces. In response to this desire, the modified U.S. draft contained a new Agreed Minute 5, along the lines proposed by the Korean negotiators at the 65th negotiating meeting. This new Agreed Minute would provide for a three-stage procedure for settling any labor dispute which cannot be settled internally by the U.S. armed forces. The first step would be to refer the dispute to the ROK Office of Labor Affairs, Ministry of Health and Social Affairs, for conciliation. If the dispute cannot be settled through the conciliation efforts of the Office of Labor Affairs, the Minute would provide that the dispute may then be referred to the Joint Committee. At that time, the Joint Committee might refer the matter to a labor sub-committee or to a specially designated committee for further fact-finding, review, and conciliation efforts. If the dispute cannot be settled by the procedures outlined above, the proposed Agreed Minute provides that the Joint Committee will resolve the dispute and its decisions shall be binding. The U.S. Government believes that the ROK and U.S. authorities should be able to

0381

resolve any labor dispute through these procedures.

5. Mr. Habib pointed out that if the disputes machinery is to be effective, every settlement must be adhered to. Therefore, the proposed Agreed Minute stipulates that neither an employee organization nor employees shall engage in any practice disruptive of normal work requirements while the settlement procedures are in progress. This is a normal characteristic of conciliation procedures. The U.S. negotiators believed that agreement had already been reached that the decisions of the Joint Committee must be binding. Therefore, failure of any recognized employee organization or employee to abide by decisions of the Joint Committee in the settlement of disputes should be considered to be just cause for withdrawal of recognition of that employee organization and/or the discharge of that employee. It is the firm view of the U.S. Government, Mr. Habib continued, that the Korean employees of the U.S. armed forces, like the American civilian employees of those forces and the civilian employees of the ROK armed forces, are a vital factor in the defense of the Republic of Korea. In this regard, such employees are considered to be in a comparable position to the civilian employees of the ROK armed forces and the American civilian employees of the U.S. armed forces. It is the intention of the U.S. armed forces to do everything possible to promote and maintain good employer-employee relations with their Korean employees and, in cooperation with the ROK Government, as provided in Agreed Minute 5, to resolve labor disputes which cannot be settled internally.

6. Mr. Habib pointed out that the revised U.S. draft also contained a revised Agreed Minute #2. The first sentence of the Minute, identical with that in the previous version,

0382

would make clear that the undertaking of the U.S. armed forces to conform to Korean labor laws, customs, and practices does not imply and waiver of the immunities of the U.S. Government under international law. ROK Government authorities have indicated agreement with this principle. The second sentence would stipulate that the U.S. Government may terminate employment at any time that the continuation of such employment is inconsistent with the military requirements of the U.S. armed forces. As the U.S. negotiators had previously explained, the military requirements of the U.S. armed forces make it necessary for them to have this authority in order to insure that essential defense and security requirements can be met.

7. Mr. Habib concluded his presentation of the revised U.S. draft by saying that the U.S. negotiators believed the Korean negotiators would find the revisions generally responsive to their views and consistent with joint U.S.-ROK defense requirements. The U.S. negotiators believed that the revised U.S. draft of the Labor Article would aid materially in maintaining and enhancing the effective employer-employee relations which currently exist between the U.S. armed forces and their Korean employees. The U.S. negotiators had tabled this draft with the full understanding that the U.S. armed forces highly value their Korean employees and the existing relationship with them. The U.S. armed forces believed that they had established a good reputation as an employer and were determined to continue their efforts to promote the well-being and training of those employees.

0383

한·미국 간의 상호방위조약 제4조에 의한 시설과 구역 및 한국에서의 미국군대의 지위에 관한 협정(SOFA)
전59권. 1966.7.9 서울에서 서명 : 1967.2.9 발효(조약 232호) (V.51 실무교섭회의 합의의사록, 제38-68차, 1964)　389

8. Mr. Chang replied that the Korean negotiators
would comment in detail on the revised U.S. draft at a subsequent meeting. However, he wished to make some preliminary
comments. The U.S. negotiators had said that their revised
draft contained significant modifications. The Korean
negotiators recognized this to be the case with respect to
the substitution of "military requirements" for "basic
management needs". However, the Korean negotiators expressed
their view that the addition of a new sentence to Agreed
would be
Minute 2/unnecessary duplication of the revised Paragraph 3,
and that the U.S. negotiators had retreated to a rigid
position in the application of the phrase "military requirements". With regard to Agreed Minute #5, the revised draft
appeared to be not significantly different from the views
expressed by the U.S. negotiators at the 65th meeting.

9. Mr. Chang stated that even the phrase "military
requirements" was still ambiguous and too broad. The Korean
negotiators would like to have it defined or explained.
Mr. Habib replied that "military requirements" were those
requirements which contributed to the accomplishment of
the military mission of the U.S. armed forces. The interpretation of the phrase in individual cases would be up to the
Joint Committee, which therefore would have a very important
role to play in this regard. Mr. Chang replied that the
Korean negotiators believed interpretation of the phrase
should not be left to the Joint Committee. The phrase
should be defined before reaching agreement on this Article.

10. Mr. Habib replied that if a specific case arose,
presumably it would be referred to the Joint Committee.

0384

Basically, the U.S. armed forces are in Korea to fulfill
certain defense and security requirements. Whatever actions
they perform should be consistent with those requirements.
The same rule should apply to the Korean employees of those
forces. Paragraph 3 of the U.S. draft states "to the
extent not inconsistent with .... the military requirements."

11. Mr. Chang replied that the Korean negotiators viewed
the revision of Paragraph 3 as the only major change
proposed by the U.S. negotiators. However, the phrase
"military requirements" was ambiguous. If this revised
draft were agreed to, the Korean employees of the U.S.
armed forces would be denied rights which they now enjoy.
The purpose of the labor article is to safeguard their rights.
Therefore, the Korean negotiators called on the U.S. negotiators
to take into consideration the rights which the Korean
employees presently enjoyed and the comments of the Korean
negotiators.

12. Mr. Habib replied that the U.S. negotiators doubted
very much that this language would deny the rights of the
Korean employees. This was not the intent nor did the language
have this meaning. The remarks of the Korean negotiators
called into question the sincerity of the U.S. negotiators
with regard to the other portions of the article. This
paragraph had been carefully drafted with the military
mission of the U.S. armed forces in mind. The Korean
negotiators were raising unjustified questions and finding
differences where they did not exist.

13. Mr. Chang replied that the Korean negotiators did
not mean to question the sincerity of the U.S. negotiators.
The introduction of the phrase "military requirements"

0385

was the major modification proposed by the U.S. negotiators.
If the Korean negotiators accepted the U.S. revised draft
the privileges presently enjoyed by the Korean employees of
the U.S. armed forces would be diminished.

14. When asked to explain how the privileges would be
diminished, Mr. Chang replied that subparagraph (d) of Agreed
Minute #5 would eliminate the right of the employees to
strike. Mr. Habib replied that the provisions of subparagraph (d) were normal procedures which were provided for
in ROK labor laws. Mr. Chang said that the ROK law provided
that disruptive practices were not allowed for a specific
number of days. However, argument concerning a labor dispute
could drag on and on in the Joint Committee.

15. Mr. Reed stated that it was his understanding that
the ROK law provided that during mediation and arbitration
procedures, there was no right to strike, even after the 20-day
and 30-day cooling-off periods. Mr. Chang replied that if
conciliation failed, the right to strike after a certain
number of days existed. Mr. Reed pointed out that the concept
of a limited period was not contained in the U.S. draft.
Article 7, Chapter 2 of the ROK Labor Disputes Act provides
that there shall be no disruptive action unless mediation
or arbitration efforts fail. The procedures proposed
by the U.S. negotiators were intended to lead to the settlement of disputes. The U.S. negotiators did not believe that
any strike would be justified if these procedures were followed.

16. Mr. Chang replied that the Korean negotiators would
study the U.S. proposals. The meeting was then adjourned with
the understanding that the Korean negotiators would call the
next meeting.

1967. 1. 6.

도총문서로 분류 (1966. 12. 31)

0386

기록물종류	문서-일반공문서철	등록번호	950	등록일자	2006-07-27
			9623		
분류번호	741.12	국가코드	US	주제	
문서철명	한.미국 간의 상호방위조약 제4조에 의한 시설과 구역 및 한국에서의 미국군대의 지위에 관한 협정 (SOFA) 전59권. 1966.7.9 서울에서 서명 : 1967.2.9 발효 (조약 232호) *원본				
생산과	미주과/조약과	생산년도	1952 - 1967	보존기간	영구
담당과(그룹)	조약	조약		서가번호	--
참조분류					
권차명	V.52 실무교섭회의 합의의사록, 제69-82차, 1965-66				

내용목차

* 일지 :
1953.8.7	이승만 대통령-Dulles 미국 국무장관 공동성명
	- 상호방위조약 발효 후 군대지위협정 교섭 약속
1954.12.2	정부, 주한 UN군의 관세업무협정 체결 제의
1955.1월, 5월	미국, 제의 거절
1955.4.28	정부, 군대지위협정 제의 (한국측 초안 제시)
1957.9.10	Hurter 미국 국무차관 방한 시 각서 수교 (한국측 제의 수락 요구)
1957.11.13, 26	정부, 개별 협정의 단계적 체결 제의
1958.9.18	Dawling 주한미국대사, 형사재판관할권 협정 제외 조건으로 행정협정 체결 의사 전달
1960.3.10	정부, 토지, 시설협정의 우선적 체결 강력 요구
1961.4.10	장면 국무총리-McConaughy 주한미국대사 공동성명으로 교섭 개시 합의
1961.4.15, 4.25	제1, 2차 한.미국 교섭회의 (서울)
1962.3.12	정부, 교섭 재개 촉구 공한 송부
1962.5.14	Burger 주한미국대사, 최규하 장관 면담 시 형사재판관할권 문제 제기 않는 조건으로 교섭 재개 통고
1962.9.6	한.미국 간 공동성명 발표 (9월 중 교섭 재개 합의)
1962.9.20~	제1-81차 실무 교섭회의 (서울)
1965.6.7	
1966.7.8	제82차 실무 교섭회의 (서울)
1966.7.9	서명
1967.2.9	발효 (조약 232호)

마/이/크/로/필/름/사/항

촬영연도	*롤 번호	화일 번호	후레임 번호	보관함 번호
2006-11-24	I-06-0072	05	1-205	

0001

JOINT SUMMARY RECORD OF THE 69TH SESSION

1. Time and Place: 3:00 - 4:00 P.M. January 25, 1965 at
   the Foreign Ministry's Conference
   Room (No.1)

2. Attendants:

ROK Side:

Mr. Chang, Sang Moon	Director European and American Affairs Bureau
Mr. Hu, Sung Joon	Director Labor Administration Bureau Office of Labor Affairs
Mr. Lee, Nam Ki	Chief America Section Ministry of Foreign Affairs
Maj. Lee, Kye Hoon	Military Affairs Section Ministry of National Defense
Mr. Kim, Kee Joe	3rd Secretary Ministry of Foreign Affairs
Mr. Lee, Keun Pal (Rapporteur and Interpreter)	3rd Secretary Ministry of Foreign Affairs
Mr. Hwang, Young Jae	3rd Secretary Ministry of Foreign Affairs
Mr. Park, Won Chul	3rd Secretary Ministry of Foreign Affairs

U.S. Side:

Mr. Philip C. Habib	Counselor American Embassy
Brig. Gen. Carroll H. Dunn	Deputy Chief of Staff 8th U.S. Army
Col. Howard Smigelow	Deputy Chief of Staff 8th U.S. Army
Capt. John Wayne	Assistant Chief of Staff USN/K
Mr. Frank R. LaMacchia	First Secretary American Embassy

0002

Mr. Benjamin A. Fleck (Rapporteur and Press Officer)	First Secretary American Embassy
Mr. Robert A. Kinney	J-5 8th U.S. Army
Mr. Goodwin Shapiro	Second Secretary American Embassy
Maj. Alton H. Harvey	Staff Judge Advocate's Office 8th U.S. Army
Mr. David Y.S. Lee (Interpreter)	Second Secretary American Embassy
Mr. Ogden C. Reed	Civilian Personnel Director 8th U.S. Army

Labor Article

1. Opening the meeting, Mr. Chang recalled that the Labor Article had been discussed during the past ten months at eight negotiating meetings. The Korean negotiators believe that considerable progress has been made toward agreement on certain points. The Korean negotiators appreciated the endeavors of the U.S. negotiators in contributing to that progress and particularly in proposing modifications at the previous meeting.

2. Mr. Chang stated that the Korean negotiators had reviewed the revised U.S. draft and had carefully considered the views expressed by the U.S. negotiators when they tabled that draft. As the Korean negotiators had clearly stated in the past, the Korean position is that the rights and privileges currently enjoyed by the Korean employees of the U.S. armed forces should be improved through the conclusion of the Status of Forces Agreement. However, the Korean negotiators do not intend to be inflexible in negotiating this article. Rather, they are prepared to compromise, at least to the extent that the Korean employees can continue to have the rights and privileges which they are presently enjoying.

0003

3. With this basic position and these requirements in mind, Mr. Chang continued, the Korean negotiators had made most significant modifications in the Korean draft. He then tabled a revision of the Korean draft, noting that the revised portions were underlined. Mr. Chang stated that he would explain the revisions, paragraph by paragraph, and at the same time would comment on the U.S. revised draft.

4. With regard to Paragraph 1, Mr. Chang said the Korean position remains the same but the new draft had been designed to streamline the text. Excluded from the revised text were the phrases "the contractors", "the Korean Service Corps", and "a domestic employed by an individual member of the U.S. Armed Forces". As for the contractors, Mr. Chang pointed out that the standing position of the Korean negotiators, as had been clearly stated during discussion of the Contractors Article, is that the terms and conditions of employment of the Korean employees by invited contractors shall be governed by the applicable Korean labor legislation. As regards the Korean Service Corps, the U.S. negotiators would recall that the Korean negotiators had already proposed that this subject not be raised within the framework of the SOFA negotiations. The phrase relating to a domestic employed by an individual member of the U.S. armed forces, civilian component, or dependent thereof, had been deleted because a domestic is not covered by the Korean labor laws.

5. Mr. Chang stated that the Korean negotiators were now prepared to accept the language of Paragraph 2 of the revised U.S. draft, with a minor change of wording.

6. Turning to Paragraph 3, Mr. Chang noted that there had been no substantial difference of opinion with regard to the principle that the conditions of employment should

0004

conform with those laid down by Korean labor legislation.
At previous negotiating sessions, the Korean negotiators had
expressed the view that the implication of the phrase
"military requirements", as well as that of the phrase
"basic management needs" which it replaced, was ambiguous
and too broad. In that regard, Mr. Habib had stated that
the interpretation of the phrase in individual cases would be
referred to the Joint Committee. With these views in mind,
the Korean negotiators were now proposing this revised
draft of Paragraph 3 and a new Agreed Minute #4. The revised
portion of Paragraph 3 reads "except as may otherwise be
mutually agreed" in place of the phrase "to the extent
not inconsistent with the provisions of this Article or
the military requirements of the United States Armed Forces".
The proposed Agreed Minute #4, which meets the substance of
the U.S. requirements in principle, reads as follows:

> "4. In case where it is impossible for the
> employers to conform, on account of the military
> requirements of the United States Armed Forces, with
> the Korean labor legislation under the provisions
> of Paragraph 3, the matter shall in advance be referred
> to the Joint Committee for mutual agreement.

> "The Republic of Korea will give due consideration
> to the military requirements of the United States
> Armed Forces."

Mr. Chang stated that the revised draft which he had just
read had been designed to meet fully the requirements of
the U.S. negotiators. In their sincere efforts to reach
agreement on this article, the Korean negotiators now
accepted the phrase "the military requirements of the United
States Armed Forces." Under the provisions of the revised
draft, the Korean negotiators clearly recognize the possibility
of deviation by the U.S. authorities from Korean labor legislation on the grounds of "military requirements". The

0005

Korean negotiators were further proposing that such U.S. deviation should be referred to the Joint Committee for mutual agreement. They believed the U.S. negotiators would have no objection to this proposal.

7. With regard to Paragraph 4 of the U.S. draft, Mr. Chang said that the Korean negotiators were of the opinion that the provisions of subparagraph (a) relating to the right to strike, organization of labor unions, etc., were covered by Paragraph 3 of the revised Korean draft, which stipulates that employer-employee relations must conform with the existing Korean labor legislation. The Korean negotiators believed that subparagraph (a) was unnecessary duplication and therefore they proposed its deletion from this article. They were prepared to accept subparagraph (b) of the U.S. draft with a minor change of wording. This appeared as Paragraph 4 of the revised Korean draft.

8. With regard to Paragraph 5, Mr. Chang stated that the Korean negotiators accepted subparagraph (a) of the U.S. revised draft, substituting "allocation privileges" for "employment privileges". They believed the change to be readily understandable from a logical point of view. With regard to subparagraph (b), Mr. Chang stated that all eligible Korean youths cannot be exempted from their military service, for it is the solemn duty of all youths under the provisions of the Constitution to serve in the armed forces. However, some may be granted deferment, not exemption, from their military service under very special circumstances in accordance with the Korean draft law. This law provides that "exemption" is granted only to those who are disabled or crippled. Therefore, the Korean negotiators propose the adoption of sub-paragraph (b), as amended in the revised Korean draft.

0006.

9. Mr. Chang said the Korean negotiators accept Paragraph 6 of the revised U.S. draft.

10. Turning to the Agreed Minutes, Mr. Chang noted that Agreed Minute #1 of the U.S. draft had been deleted from the Korean revised draft. The deletion was self-explanatory in the light of the Korean position regarding Paragraph 1.

11. Mr. Chang said the Korean negotiators agreed to the first sentence of Agreed Minute #2 of the U.S. draft, which appears as Agreed Minute #1 of the revised Korean draft. But, he continued, the Korean negotiators are firmly against inclusion of the second sentence. At the previous meeting, the Korean negotiators had expressed the view that this sentence constituted unnecessary duplication of Paragraph 3 of the revised U.S. draft. In this connection, they believed that Agreed Minute #4 of the revised Korean draft would provide proper procedures.

12. Mr. Chang noted that Agreed Minutes #2 and #3 were identical with Agreed Minutes #3 and #4 of the U.S. revised draft.

13. Mr. Chang stated that full explanation of Agreed Minute #4 had been included in the explanation given of Paragraph 3.

14. Turning to Agreed Minute #5, which would establish procedures for the settlement of labor disputes which cannot be settled through the use of existing procedures of the U.S. armed forces, Mr. Chang stated that the Korean negotiators were now ready to agree in principle to the adoption of a three-stage procedure for the settlement of disputes, as proposed by the U.S. negotiators at the 68th meeting. However, they thought subparagraph (b) of the revised U.S. draft was unnecessarily complicated in providing for-

0007

reference of a dispute to the Joint Committee and then
to a special committee designated by the Joint Committee,
for subparagraph (c) provides for reference once again to
the Joint Committee. In order to simplify those steps, the
Korean negotiators were proposing that the Joint Committee
designate a special committee to which a labor dispute would
be referred before reference to the Joint Committee. They
had modified subparagraph (b) in their revised draft and
hoped that the U.S. negotiators would agree. With regard
to the third step in the settlement process, the Korean
negotiators had no objection to the revised U.S. draft.

15. With regard to subparagraph (d), relating to the
prohibition of act of dispute during the settlement procedures,
Mr. Chang stated that the Korean negotiators maintained
their position that the Korean employees may conduct act
of dispute in accordance with the spirit of the Korean laws
while no practice disruptive of normal work requirements
should be permitted in violation of the cooling-off period
set forth in the relevant Korean labor legislation. The
Korean negotiators cannot accept any provision that precludes
the exercise of fundamental rights of laborers for an
indefinite period. However, the Korean negotiators do not
maintain that the employees should be able to engage in
disruptive practices at any time they feel like it. Therefore,
the Korean negotiators proposed subparagraph (d) of their
revised draft and subparagraph (e) which is almost identical
with subparagraph (d) of the U.S. draft. The Korean negotiators
hoped that the U.S. negotiators would find their proposals
acceptable. They had tried their best to meet the U.S.
requirements and urged the U.S. negotiators to study the
revised Korean draft carefully and respond at an early date.

0008

16. Mr. Habib replied that the U.S. negotiators would study the Korean draft and comment on it at a later meeting. At present, they would like to ask a few questions in order to clarify the Korean position.

17. With regard to Agreed Minute #1, the Korean negotiators had said that it was equivalent to Agreed Minute #2 of the U.S. draft. This was not the case, however, as the Korean draft contained the language "to conform with those laid down by the legislation of the Republic of Korea" while the U.S. draft reads "to conform to Korean labor laws, customs, and practices". The U.S. negotiators failed to understand what the language of the Korean draft meant. Mr. Chang replied that the Korean negotiators understood that the basic intention of the U.S. negotiators is that the U.S. authorities will not conform with decisions of the Korean courts or labor committees. The Korean negotiators believed that customs and practices are not related to court decisions or to Korean law and therefore need not be mentioned. Mr. Habib remarked that the intent of the Korean negotiators appeared to be to exclude reference to customs and practice from the language of this Agreed Minute. Mr. Chang confirmed this and it was agreed to change the language of the Agreed Minute in the Korean draft to read: "to conform with the labor legislation of the Republic of Korea."

18. Mr. Reed inquired about the reference in Agreed Minute #5 subparagraph (d) of the revised Korean draft to Article 14 of the Korean Labor Dispute Law. Mr. Chang thereupon read Article 14, as follows:

"Article 14. (Cooling Period). No act of dispute shall be conducted unless 20 days have elapsed in the case of general enterprise and 30 days in the case of public utility after a lawful adjudication of the labor

0003

committee prescribed in Article 16 has been rendered."
There then followed a discussion as to whether subparagraph
(d) of the Korean draft was consistent with Article 14 of
the Labor Dispute Law. Mr. Chang confirmed that while
Article 14 refers to a 30-day cooling off period following
adjudication by the labor committee, subparagraph (d)
refers to a 30-day cooling off period following referral
to the Office of Labor Affairs. Mr. Habib stated that the
U.S. negotiators would study this question, as well as
the rest of the revised Korean draft. The meeting was then
adjourned.

0010

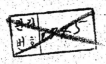

JOINT SUMMARY RECORD OF THE 70TH SESSION

1. Time and Place: 3:00 - 4:30 p.m. February 12, 1965 at
   the Foreign Ministry's Conference
   Room (No.1)

2. Attendants:

ROK Side:

Mr. Chang, Sang Moon	Director European and American Affairs Bureau
Mr. Yoon, Woon Young	Director Prosecutors Bureau Ministry of Justice
Mr. Lee, Nam Ki	Chief America Section Ministry of Foreign Affairs
Col. Kim, Won Kil	Chief Military Affairs Section Ministry of National Defense
Maj. Lee, Kye Hoon	Military Affairs Section Ministry of National Defense
Mr. Im, Du Bin	Prosecutor Ministry of Justice
Mr. Choi, Sang Yup	Prosecutor Ministry of Justice
Mr. Kim, Kee Joe	3rd Secretary Ministry of Foreign Affairs
Mr. Lee, Keun Pal (Rapporteur and Interpreter	3rd Secretary Ministry of Foreign Affairs
Mr. Hwang, Young Jae	3rd Secretary Ministry of Foreign Affairs

U.S. Side:

Mr. Philip C. Habib	Counselor American Embassy
Brig. Gen. Carroll H. Dunn	Deputy Chief of Staff 8th U.S. Army
Col. Kenneth C. Crawford	Staff Judge Advocate 8th U.S. Army
Mr. Frank R. LaMacchia	First Secretary American Embassy

0011

Mr. Benjamin A. Fleck (Rapporteur and Press Officer)	First Secretary American Embassy
Mr. Robert A. Kinney	J-5 8th U.S. Army
Mr. Goodwin Shapiro	Second Secretary American Embassy
Maj. Alton H. Harvey	Staff Judge Advocate's Office 8th U.S. Army
Mr. David Y.C. Lee (Interpreter)	Second Secretary American Embassy

1. Mr. Chang opened the meeting by introducing Mr. Im Tu-pin and Mr. Choi Sang-yup, both prosecutors of the Ministry of Justice. Mr. Habib welcomed them to the negotiations on behalf of the U.S. negotiators.

Criminal Jurisdiction

2. Taking up the Criminal Jurisdiction Article, Mr. Chang stated that, as a result of most careful study with the appropriate authorities of the Korean Government of the package proposal which had been tabled by the U.S. negotiators at the 67th negotiating meeting, the Korean negotiators had found that there still exists a wide gap between the drafts tabled by each side regarding major points at issue, particularly with regard to the provisions concerning waiver of the primary right to exercise jurisdiction and pre-trial custody. However, in an attempt to meet the requirements of the U.S. negotiators and to be consistent with their own basic position, the Korean negotiators now wished to propose most significant modifications, designed to be responsive to the U.S. package proposal. Mr. Chang said he would explain the Korean package proposal paragraph by paragraph.

0012

<u>Official Duty Certificate</u>

3. The Korean negotiators tabled the following proposed Agreed Minutes Re Paragraph 3(a) (ii):

"<u>Agreed Minute #1 Re Paragraph 3(a) (ii)</u>

"Where a member of the United States armed forces or civilian component is charged with an offense, a certificate issued by a staff judge advocate on behalf of his commanding officer stating that the alleged offense, if committed by him, arose out of an act or omission done in the performance of official duty shall be sufficient evidence of the fact for the purpose of determining primary jurisdiction.

"In those exceptional cases where the chief district prosecutor of the Republic of Korea considers that there is proof contrary to a certificate of official duty, it shall be made the subject of review through discussions between appropriate officials of the Government of the Republic of Korea and the diplomatic mission of the United States."

"<u>Agreed Minute #2 Re Paragraph 3(a) (ii)</u>

"The term 'official duty' as used in Article _____ and the Agreed Minute is not meant to include all acts by members of the United States armed forces and the civilian components during periods when they are on duty, but is meant to apply only to acts which are required to be done as functions of those duties the individuals are performing. Thus, any departure from the acts a person is required to perform in a particular duty usually will indicate an act outside of his official duty."

4. Mr. Chang stated that with regard to the provisions concerning the official duty certificate, the Korean negotiators believe the latest U.S. proposal to be considerably different from the position of the Korean negotiators. Nevertheless, in order to facilitate the negotiations, and to meet the concern expressed in the past over this problem by the U.S. negotiators, the Korean negotiators were now prepared to make one of their most significant concessions by accepting the U.S. version with minor changes of wording and subject to certain conditions which he would enumerate.

0013

5. With regard to the authority to issue the duty certificate, the Korean negotiators preferred the wording "by a Staff Judge Advocate on behalf of his commanding officer", Mr. Chang continued. The U.S. negotiators had proposed at a previous meeting the wording "by competent authorities of the U.S. armed forces", on the grounds that many major units of the U.S. armed forces do not have a Staff Judge Advocate assigned to them, although such units may always request legal advice from their superior headquarters. In view of the importance which they attached to the validity of the duty certificate and complicated problems of a legal nature which may follow the issuance thereof, the Korean negotiators prefer their wording to that of the U.S. draft. In the actual implementation of the language which the Korean negotiators proposed, they believe some arrangement could easily be worked out so that if there is no Staff Judge Advocate assigned to a particular unit, as explained by the U.S. negotiators, a Staff Judge Advocate assigned to a superior headquarters, from whom that unit requests legal advice, may be able to issue the duty certificate on behalf of his commanding officer, thus solving this problem.

6. In short, Mr. Chang said, the basic position of the Korean negotiators is that in the light of the very decisive role which the duty certificate plays in most cases in determining primary jurisdiction, the scope of the issuing authority should be limited to a Staff Judge Advocate assigned to a unit equivalent to or higher than an army division.

0014

7. In the interest of preciseness, Mr. Chang noted that the Korean negotiators also propose to substitute the language "chief district prosecutor of the Republic of Korea" for the language "chief prosecutor of the Republic of Korea".

8. Mr. Chang pointed out that the Korean negotiators also propose inclusion of the definition of official duty in the Agreed Minutes, along with the provisions regarding issuance of the duty certificate. They believe that including the definition in the Agreed Minutes would provide the authorities concerned with a guide line in determing whether or not an offense was committed in the performance of official duty.

9. Mr. Chang said the Korean negotiators were prepared to accept the two understandings which had been proposed by the U.S. negotiators for inclusion in the Joint Summary record. However, the Korean negotiators believe that in case the chief district prosecutor raises any objection regarding the validity of the duty certificate, full consideration of his objection by the U.S. authorities should be guaranteed. Therefore, they propose to include an additional sentence in the first understanding. The two understandings would then read as follows:

"a. The certificate will be conclusive unless modification is agreed upon. The United States authorities shall give due consideration to any objection which may be raised by the chief district prosecutor of the Republic of Korea.

"b. The accused shall not be deprived of his entitlement to a prompt and speedy trial as a result of prolonged reconsideration of the duty certificate."

10. Mr. Chang said that the Korean negotiators believed the conditions, which he had just enumerated, to acceptance of the U.S. provisions regarding the duty certificate were

of a modest nature and therefore would be acceptable to the U.S. negotiators.

Trial Safeguards

11. Mr. Chang said that, after giving very careful consideration to the importance which the U.S. negotiators attach to guarantees of a fair trial, and in order to expedite discussions of safeguards and other major points at issue, the Korean negotiators were now going to make one of their most significant concessions by accepting the principle of enumeration of all of the trial safeguards proposed by the U.S. negotiators. However, this concession was made on condition that the U.S. negotiators accept the following proposed modifications of some of the safeguards in the U.S. draft. The Korean negotiators believe the suggested modifications are most essential to the efficient operation of the Korean judicial system.

12. Agreed Minute Re Paragraph 9(a). Mr. Chang said the second sentence of this Agreed Minute, regarding trial of U.S. personnel by Korean military tribunals, is closely related to the subject of jurisdiction by Korean authorities in Paragraph 1(b) of the Article. Therefore, decision regarding the second sentence of the Agreed Minute should await agreem nt on the provisions of Paragraph 1(b) of the text. In this connection, the basic Korean position regarding Paragraph 1(b) is that the language should read "the authorities of the Republic of Korea" instead of the present language in the U.S. draft: "the civil authorities of the Republic of Korea". Mr. Chang said the Korean negotiators would appreciate early comment on this matter by the U.S. negotiators.

0016

13. Mr. Habib said he wished to obtain clarification of the Korean position. Were the Korean negotiators proposing that if the word "civil" were deleted from the text of Paragraph 1(b) the second sentence of the Agreed Minute be retained? Mr. Chang replied that the Korean negotiators had already stated that no U.S. personnel would be subject to trial by Korean military tribunal. They wished that statement, which had been recorded in the Agreed Joint Summary, to be accepted by the U.S. negotiators. Both the word "civil" and the second sentence of the Agreed Minute should be deleted. Mr. Habib thanked Mr. Chang for his explanation and said that the Korean position was understood by the U.S. negotiators.

14. _Agreed Minute Re Paragraph 9_. Mr. Chang referred to the third (unnumbered) paragraph of the Agreed Minute Re Paragraph 9 of the U.S. draft, which deals with the non-admissibility of confessions, admissions, or real evidence obtained by illegal or improper means. The Korean negotiators had already pointed out the possibility that actual implementation of this portion of the Agreement might be confused as a result of ambiguous interpretation of the language to the effect that certain means taken by the Korean authorities were illegal or improper. Therefore, the Korean negotiators wished to propose the following more specific language:

"No confession, admission, or other statement, obtained by torture, violence, threat, deceit, or after prolonged arrest or detention, or which has been made involuntarily, will be considered by the courts of the Republic of Korea as evidence in support of the guilt of the accused under this Article."

As the U.S. negotiators might notice, Mr. Chang continued, the proposed revision omits the term "real evidence". The Korean negotiators propose this omission not because the Korean authorities are not hesitant to resort to illegal

0017

means to obtain real evidence but simply because of the
fact that even if the evidence should be obtained by
illegal means that would not necessarily affect the validity
of that evidence in support of the guilt of the accused.

15. Agreed Minute Re Paragraph 9(g). Mr. Chang
referred to the language of the Agreed Minute Re Paragraph
9(g) of the U.S. draft regarding the non-admissibility as
valid evidence of a statement taken in the absence of
a representative of the Government of the United States.
At the 50th negotiating meeting, the Korean negotiators had
emphasized that since a representative of the Government,
a counsel, an interpreter, and the accused himself are
all given the right to be present at all of the judicial
proceedings, it is entirely within the discretion of the
Government representative whether or not to appear in such
cases. Furthermore, the absence of the Government representative from the judicial proceedings should not impair the
admissibility of a statement in view of the revised language
which the Korean negotiators had just proposed for the
third paragraph of the Agreed Minute Re Paragraph 9.
Accordingly, Mr. Chang continued, the Korean negotiators
propose the deletion of all of the first sentence of the
Agreed Minute Re Paragraph 9(g) following the word "detention".

16. With regard to the provisions of subparagraph (e)
of the second (unnumbered) paragraph of the Agreed Minute
Re Paragraph 9 and the fourth (unnumbered) paragraph of
that Agreed Minute, Mr. Chang recalled that the Korean
negotiators at the 50th negotiating meeting had proposed
an alternative draft reading as follows: "shall not be
subject to a heavier penalty than the one that was applicable at the time the alleged criminal offense was committed

0018

or was adjudged by the court of the first instance as the original sentence when an appeal of a case is made by or on behalf of the accused."

17. The Korean judicial system, Mr. Chang continued, is based upon the right to appeal to a High Court or to the Supreme Court by a prosecutor or an accused either on the grounds of "errors of law" or of mistakes of fact. According to the provisions of the fourth paragraph and subparagraph (e) of the second paragraph of the Agreed Minute Re Paragraph 9 of the U.S. draft, appeal by the prosecutor is limited to such an extent that appeal to a higher court can not be made except in the case of errors of law.

18. Because a trial is conducted by a judge or a group of judges, Mr. Chang stated, it is readily understandable that in spite of all the efforts on the part of the court, judgments of the court cannot always be free from human mistakes. Accordingly, it is necessary to establish a safeguard which is designed to review and ultimately preclude any misjudgement resulting from errors of law as well as mistakes of fact. In this connection, it becomes apparent that a sort of reviewing system is necessary to correct misjudgements for the accused as an interested party in particular and for the prosecutor as a guardian of legal justice and uniform application of law in general. To serve this end, the provisions of Article 361-V of the Korean Code of Criminal Procedure clearly enumerate reasons for appeal to a High Court on grounds of errors of law as well as mistakes of fact. Article 383 of the same Code, although somewhat restrictive, stipulates reasons for appeal to the Supreme Court on the grounds of mistakes of fact.

0019

19. Since the United States negotiators have expressed their sincerity and willingness to subject the U.S. military personnel to the jurisdiction of the Republic of Korea, Mr. Chang continued, the Korean negotiators wish to point out that it would be much more efficient if the U.S. negotiators would generously accept the basic principles of the Korean judicial system, such as the appeal system, rather than try to reshape that system along the lines of a system which is alien to the Korean judiciary. Therefore, the Korean negotiators propose that the U.S. negotiators accept the revised Korean draft of subparagraph (e) of the second paragraph of the Agreed Minute Re Paragraph 9 and agree to deletion of the fourth paragraph of that Agreed Minute.

20. Mr. Chang stated that the position of the Korean negotiators remains unchanged with regard to subparagraph (k) of the second (unnumbered) paragraph of the Agreed Minute Re Paragraph 9. He recalled that at the 50th meeting, the Korean negotiators had pointed out that the U.S. draft does not preclude the possibility of abuse by the accused of the right provided for in the subparagraph. Moreover, the Korean negotiators believe it is appropriate to leave the question up to the court for decision, after its examination of the accused's request. The Korean negotiators had no hesitation in assuring the U.S. negotiators that, in spite of the concern of the latter, implementation of the language proposed by the Korean negotiators at the 50th meeting would be mutually satisfactory.

21. With regard to other provisions of the U.S. draft concerning trial safeguards, Mr. Chang said the Korean

negotiators accepted the following Agreed Minutes to which the Korean negotiators had raised initial objection; the second paragraph of first sentence of/the Agreed Minute Re Paragraph 9(b); the Agreed Minute Re Paragraph 9(e); and subparagraphs (f) and (i) of the second (unnumbered) paragraph of the Agreed Minute Re Paragraph 9.

Pre-Trial Custody

22. Mr. Chang tabled the following proposed revisions of portions of Paragraph 5:

"(c) The military authorities of the United States shall promptly notify the authorities of the Republic of Korea of the arrest of a member of the United States armed forces, the civilian component, or a dependent in any case in which the Republic of Korea has the primary right to exercise jurisdiction.

"(d) An accused member of the United States armed forces or civilian component, or of a dependent over whom the Republic of Korea is to exercise jurisdiction will, if he is in the hands of the military authorities of the United States, be in the custody of the military authorities of the United States during all judicial proceedings and until custody is requested by the authorities of the Republic of Korea.

"If an accused is in the hands of the Republic of Korea, he will, on request, be handed over to the military authorities of the United States, unless the authorities of the Republic of Korea consider that there is adequate cause and necessity to retain him. Such accused will be in the custody of the military authorities of the United States during all judicial proceedings and until custody is requested by the authorities of the Republic of Korea.

"(e) In respect of offenses solely against the security of the Republic of Korea provided in Paragraph 2(c), an accused shall be in the custody of the authorities of the Republic of Korea.

"(f) Where an accused has been in the custody of the military authorities of the United States under Paragraph 5(d), the military authorities of the United States may transfer custody to the authorities of the Republic of Korea at any time, and shall give sympathetic consideration to any request for the transfer of custody which may be made by the authorities of the Republic of Korea in specific cases.

한·미국 간의 상호방위조약 제4조에 의한 시설과 구역 및 한국에서의 미국군대의 지위에 관한 협정(SOFA) 전59권. 1966.7.9 서울에서 서명 : 1967.2.9 발효(조약 232호) (V.52 실무교섭회의 합의의사록, 제69-82차, 1965-66) 413

"The military authorities of the United States shall promptly make any such accused available to the authorities of the Republic of Korea upon their request for purposes of investigation and trial.

"The authorities of the Republic of Korea will give sympathetic consideration to a request from the military authorities of the United States for assistance in maintaining custody of an accused member of the United States armed forces, the civilian component, or a dependent."

23. Mr. Chang recalled that at the 49th negotiating meeting, the U.S. negotiators had stated that Paragraph 5(c) of the Korean draft had no counterpart in the U.S. draft nor any precedents in the NATO Agreement or the SOFA with Japan, the reason being that it imposes on the U.S. military forces an onerous requirement which serves no fundamental purpose. With these remarks of the U.S. negotiators in mind, the Korean negotiators wished to substitute the words "in any case in which the Republic of Korea has the primary right to exercise jurisdiction" for the words "unless the United States authorities have the right to exercise exclusive jurisdiction over such a person". The language proposed by the Korean negotiators is based not only on precedents elsewhere but also on the belief of the Korean negotiators that since Paragraph 5(b) stipulates the obligation of the Korean authorities to notify the U.S. military authorities of the arrest of U.S. personnel, the obligation of the U.S. authorities likewise to notify the Korean authorities of the arrest of U.S. personnel over whom the Republic of Korea has the primary right to exercise jurisdiction is no longer onerous but only reciprocal.

24. Regarding pre-trial custody of persons in the hands of the U.S. military authorities, Mr. Chang went on,

0022

Paragraph 5(d) of the Korean draft is practically identical with the similar provisions in Paragraph 5(c) of the U.S. draft. Therefore, the Korean negotiators foresee no difficulty in the U.S. negotiators accepting the Korean version.

25. However, regarding pre-trial custody of persons in the hands of the Korean authorities, Mr. Chang said, the position of the Korean negotiators remains unchanged. Although the Korean negotiators would be willing to assure the U.S. negotiators that custody will be turned over to the U.S. military authorities unless there is a specific reason and necessity to retain custody in the hands of the Korean authorities, the Korean negotiators are unable to accept the U.S. version which requires prompt and unconditional transfer of custody to the U.S. military authorities.

26. Mr. Chang recalled that the U.S. negotiators had stated at the 45th negotiating meeting that they had proposed the language of the U.S. draft partly because examination of the Korean pre-trial detention facilities had indicated that they are not satisfactory places for an American soldier, member of the civilian component, or dependent to be confined while awaiting trial, and partly because of the many cases reported in Korean newspapers in which persons awaiting trial in Korean courts have been subject to torture and compulsion to incriminate themselves. However, the concern of the U.S. negotiators is neither well-founded nor necessary because the Korean negotiators have expressed not only their readiness to accept the proposed U.S. understanding that Korean confinement facilities should be adequate by U.S. standards, but also their willingness to accept the principle of enumerating almost all of the trial safeguards the U.S. negotiators

have felt necessary for a fair trial for U.S. personnel, thereby precluding all the anxieties expressed in the past by the U.S. negotiators. The Korean negotiators believe, therefore, that there is no reason why the U.S. negotiators cannot now accept Paragraph 5(d) of the Korean draft.

27. Mr. Chang noted also that the Korean negotiators had made another significant concession regarding the timing of the re-transfer of custody to the Korean authorities after completion of criminal proceedings.

28. With regard to Korean custody under the provisions of Paragraph 5(e) of the Korean draft in the case of an offense against the security of the Republic of Korea, Mr. Chang stated that the Korean negotiators still believe that mutual agreement is not necessary since they believe that in security offenses the Korean authorities should be the sole authorities to determine whether or not such custody is appropriate. However, the Korean authorities are ready to consult with the U.S. authorities whenever such custody is deemed imperative in security cases, as well as in cases where there is adequate cause and necessity to retain such custody, as provided for in Paragraph 5(d) of the Korean draft. In this connection, therefore, the Korean negotiators proposed two understandings for inclusion in the Agreed Joint Summary:

"a. There shall be mutual ROK-US consultation as to the circumstances in which such custody of the authorities of the Republic of Korea as provided for in paragraphs 5(d) and 5(e) is appropriate;

"b. Korean confinement facilities shall be adequate by U.S. standards."

0024

29. Mr. Chang said the Korean negotiators believe their proposal regarding Paragraph 5(f) to be self-explanatory. If the U.S. military authorities do not desire to retain custody under special circumstances, this provision would enable them to transfer at any time the custody of the accused. When an accused has been under custody of the U.S. military authorities or when an arrested person has been handed over to them, a situation may arise in which the Korean authorities may have to request transfer of custody for efficient trial proceedings. Since this possibility exists, the Korean negotiators believe the Korean version is preferable, which would guarantee sympathetic consideration by the U.S. military authorities to a request by the Korean authorities.

30. In accepting the U.S. language regarding the obligation of the U.S. authorities to make an accused in U.S. custody available to the Korean authorities upon their request for investigation and trial, Mr. Chang continued, the Korean negotiators consider it essential that the U.S. should make the arrested person available without delay. The Korean negotiators were pleased to incorporate into the Korean draft the U.S. language regarding Korean assistance in maintaining custody of an accused member of the U.S. armed forces.

Waiver of the Primary Right to Exercise Jurisdiction

31. Mr. Chang tabled the following revised draft of the Agreed Minute Re Paragraph 3:

> "The authorities of the Republic of Korea, recognizing that it is the primary responsibility of the United States military authorities to maintain good order and discipline where persons subject to United States military law are concerned, will, upon the request of the military authorities of the United States pursuant to Paragraph 3(c), waive their primary

"right to exercise jurisdiction under Paragraph 3(b) except when they determine that it is of particular importance that jurisdiction be exercised by the authorities of the Republic of Korea. In case where any question arises concerning such determination as may be made by the authorities of the Republic of Korea in accordance with the foregoing provisions, the United States diplomatic mission will be afforded an opportunity to confer with the proper authorities of the Republic of Korea.

"Trials of cases in which the authorities of the Republic of Korea waive the primary right to exercise jurisdiction, and trials of cases involving offenses described in Paragraph 3(a) (ii) committed against the state or nationals of the Republic of Korea will be held within a reasonable distance from the place where the offenses are alleged to have taken place unless other arrangements are mutually agreed upon. Representatives of the Republic of Korea may be present at such trials.

"To facilitate the expeditious disposal of offenses of minor importance, arrangements may be made between the United States military authorities and the competent authorities of the Republic of Korea to dispense with notification."

32. Mr. Chang stated that when the U.S. negotiators had tabled their latest version of the waiver provisions, at the 67th negotiating meeting, they had said that they were tabling significant modifications of the waiver of the primary right to exercise jurisdiction. After carefully studying the U.S. draft, the Korean negotiators regretted to state that although the revised U.S. language indicates some progress from the original U.S. position, it is unacceptable to the Korean negotiators since it is still diametrically opposed to the formula which the Korean negotiators have been trying to retain in the Agreed Minute.

33. Mr. Chang recalled that the U.S. negotiators in the past had stated that their position was to obtain a maximum degree of waiver from the Korean authorities. To accommodate the U.S. requirements, the Korean negotiators had already

0026

418 주한미군지위협정(SOFA) 서명 및 발효 21

given assurances that the Korean authorities would waive
in as many cases as other countries do under their very
simple waiver provisions. Nevertheless, the Korean
negotiators firmly maintain the position that the language
of the Agreed Minute should be "the standard language"
which would enable the Korean authorities to waive except
when they determine that it is of particular importance
to them to try an accused in a Korean court. The Korean
negotiators wonder why the U.S. negotiators, "after all
those years of obtaining a considerably high degree of
waiver under their standard wording with many other countries",
refuse to accept similar language in the draft proposed by
the Korean negotiators.

34. Mr. Chang noted that the texts of both drafts
clearly enumerate certain categories of offenses which are
supposed to be subject to the jurisdiction of the United
States. They further provide that any other offenses are
to be subject to the jurisdiction of the Republic of Korea
as the host country. In addition to listing those offenses
which fall under U.S. jurisdiction, the U.S. negotiators
in their proposed Agreed Minute, go even further, to the
extent that they are practically asking waiver of all
offenses over which the Republic of Korea, under the provisions of the Article itself, has the primary right of
jurisdiction. In view of the U.S. position, the Korean
negotiators are unable to see any merit in differentiating
the primary jurisdiction of the receiving state from that
of the sending state. In other words, Mr. Chang continued,
the Korean negotiators believe the U.S. is trying to exact
onerous concessions from the Republic of Korea. As the

0027

government of a state playing host to a friendly foreign army, the Korean authorities are trying to retain only a small portion of the primary right to exercise jurisdiction over offenses which are subject to their jurisdiction. In summing up their position, the Korean negotiators are unable to think of any principle or formula for deciding whether or not to waive jurisdiction in specific cases other than that based upon self-determination by the Republic of Korea as a sovereign country acting as host to the U.S. army.

35. Mr. Chang said the Korean negotiators were pleased to incorporate into their draft of the Agreed Minute that sentence in the U.S. draft which would give the U.S. diplomatic mission in the Republic of Korea an opportunity to make representations to the appropriate Korean authorities in case any question arises concerning the Korean determination to exercise jurisdiction.

36. Mr. Chang stated that the Korean negotiators are prepared to agree to enumeration of offenses over which the Korean authorities are to exercise jurisdiction, not in the Agreed Minutes but in the Agreed Joint Summary. Accordingly, the Korean negotiators wished to propose the following understanding for inclusion in the Agreed Joint Summary:

"It is understood that offenses falling under the categories of cases in which it is determined that exercise of jurisdiction by the Republic of Korea is of particular importance include the following:

"a. An offense against the security of the Republic of Korea;

"b. An offense causing the death of a human being;

"c. Rape;

"d. Robbery;

0028

"e. Any other offenses of malicious nature which the authorities of either Government consider to be of particular importance as the result of examination thereof;

"f. An attempt to commit foregoing offenses or participation therein."

Mr. Chang said the Korean negotiators not only opposed enumeration of offenses in the Agreed Minutes but also believed the enumeration proposed by the U.S. negotiators to be too restrictive.

37. The Korean negotiators, Mr. Chang continued, are also prepared to recognize the primary responsibility of the U.S. military authorities to maintain good order and discipline where persons subject to United States military law are concerned. Therefore, they had incorporated that portion of the U.S. draft into their revised draft.

38. Mr. Chang noted that the Korean negotiators were also accepting the final portion of the U.S. draft regarding arrangements to dispense with notification with respect to disposal of offenses of minor importance. The Korean negotiators believe that such arrangements should be limited to offenses of minor importance, leaving major offenses to deliberation by both sides. The Korean negotiators also believe that any other detailed arrangements for efficient implementation of this Article can be worked out between the appropriate authorities of each side in the Joint Committee, restricting the text of the Article and the Agreed Minutes to the stipulation of important principles.

39. Mr. Chang remarked that after a year of sincere discussion of the Criminal Jurisdiction Article, following the tabling of their respective drafts by both sides on February 14, 1964, the Korean negotiators believe beyond all

0029

doubt that ultimate agreement on this Article, particularly on the subject of waiver, hinges on the very key question as to whether or not the formula of self-determination is adopted in the Agreed Minute Re Paragraph 3. The Korean negotiators wished to emphasize once again what they had already stated, namely that the Republic of Korea is unable to accept any other formula than the one guaranteeing discretion to the host country as to whether or not to waive its primary jurisdiction.

40. Mr. Chang said the Korean negotiators sincerely hope that the U.S. negotiators, taking into account the concessions made to meet U.S. requirements with respect to official duty and trial safeguards, would accept the Korean package proposal, thereby paving the way toward early conclusion of the current negotiations to which the people and the National Assembly of the Republic of Korea attach very great importance and the progress of which they are following with keen interest.

41. Mr. Chang stated that the Korean negotiators believed that their presentation had covered all the subjects which had been included in the earlier package proposal tabled by the U.S. negotiators. With regard to other remaining issues of major or minor nature, not mentioned at this meeting, the position of the Korean negotiators remained the same. The Korean negotiators would appreciate an early and favorable reply from the U.S. negotiators regarding both the proposals just tabled by the Korean negotiators and the remaining issues.

42. Mr. Habib replied that the Korean negotiators had presented extensive material for the consideration of the U.S. negotiators. They would study the Korean proposals and, if necessary, would seek clarification at a later meeting.

0030

It was agreed to adjourn without setting a date for the
next meeting.

0031

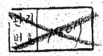

JOINT SUMMARY RECORD OF THE 71ST SESSION

1. Time and Place: 4:00-6:00 P.M., February 26, 1965 at
                   the Foreign Ministry's Conference
                   Room (No.1)

2. Attendants:

   ROK Side:

   Mr. Chang, Sang Moon   Director
                                   European and American Affairs
                                   Bureau
                                   Ministry of Foreign Affairs

   Mr. Huh, Sung Joon   Director
                                   Labor Administration Bureau
                                   Office of Labor Affairs

   Mr. Lee, Nam Ki   Chief
                                   America Section
                                   Ministry of Foreign Affairs

   Mr. Hur, Hyong Koo   Chief
                                   Prosecutors Section
                                   Ministry of Justice

   Col. Kim, Won Kil   Chief
                                   Military Affairs Section
                                   Ministry of National Defense

   Maj. Lee, Kye Hoon   Military Affairs Section
                                   Ministry of National Defense

   Mr. Kim, Kee Joe   3rd Secretary
                                   Ministry of Foreign Affairs

   Mr. Lee, Keun Pal   3rd Secretary
   (Rapporteur and   Ministry of Foreign Affairs
    Interpreter)

   Mr. Hwang, Young Jae   3rd Secretary
                                   Ministry of Foreign Affairs

   Mr. Park, Won Chul   3rd Secretary
                                   Ministry of Foreign Affairs

   U.S. Side:

   Mr. Philip C. Habib   Counselor
                                   American Embassy

   Brig. Gen. Carroll H. Dunn   Deputy Chief of Staff
                                   8th U.S. Army

0032

Capt. John Wayne	Assistant Chief of Staff USN/K
Col. Kenneth C. Crawford	Staff Judge Advocate 8th U.S. Army
Mr. Robert A. Kinney	J-5 8th U.S. Army
Mr. Goodwon Shapiro	2nd Secretary American Embassy
Lt. Col. Charles K. Wright Jr.	Staff Judge Advocate's Office 8th U.S. Army
Mr. Jack Friedman	8th U.S. Army
Mr. Edward Hurwitz (Interpreter)	2nd Secretary American Embassy
Mr. G. W. Flowers	Observer

Criminal Jurisdiction

1. Taking up the Criminal Jurisdiction Article, Mr. Chang
stated that the Korean negotiators believe that the U.S.
side is giving the most careful consideration to the comprehensive package proposal which they had tabled at the 70th
negotiating session. In the meantime, the Korean negotiators
would like to reiterate their positions on the most important
issue: that is, waiver of primary jurisdiction.

2. As explained at the 70th negotiating session, the
Korean negotiators had made the most significant concessions
to the U.S. side regarding trial safeguards because guarantees
of a fair trial to the U.S. personnel seemed to be a major
concern of the U.S. negotiators. Further Korean concessions
with respect to the official duty certificate were made in
the belief that discretion with regard to determination on
whether an offense arises out of performance of official
duty or not rests primarily with the military authorities
of the United States. At the same time, the Korean negotiators

0033

had made those concessions in the hope that the U.S. negotiators would naturally reciprocate their concessive approach in turn by providing the Korean side with discretion on the issue of waiver of primary jurisdiction.

3. The U.S. negotiators had stated previously that under the standard wording of the SOFA with Japan, the U.S. military authorities have been obtaining waiver in a high percentage of cases from the Japanese authorities. In view of such U.S. statements, the Korean negotiators are unable to understand the reason why the U.S. side, while generously granting complete discretion to Japan, has been reluctant to accept the Korean proposal, which is definitely more favorable and cooperative toward the United States.

4. Mr. Chang indicated that in view of the brotherly relationship which exists between our two countries, the ROK Government is confident that it would be more lenient toward offenses committed by U.S. military personnel than any other Government could be. He noted that this fact deserves careful consideration by the U.S. side. The Korean people can hardly expect to understand why they should accept any discriminatory treatment regarding criminal jurisdiction, or why they should be asked to accept a version of this article which is far inferior to those granted to other countries, particularly to Japan, which once was a defeated enemy of the United States.

5. Mr. Chang stated that the Korean negotiators are well aware of the concern expressed by the U.S. side over the fact that the Korean judicial system is entirely different from the U.S. system. On this point, however, the ROK negotiators would like to point out that the ROK judicial system is similar to the Japanese system under which the U.S. side had, as previously explained, accumulated satis-

0034

factory experiences in the past. Furthermore, since the
Korean side had made its position clear by meeting all the
U.S. requirements in the field of trial safeguards, previous
U.S. expressions of concern are no longer valid.

6. Mr. Chang emphasized that, inasmuch as the U.S.
side had expressed its sincerity by agreeing to subject
its military personnel to the Korean jurisdiction, the
Korean negotiators believe that it would be logical to
recognize Korean discretion in determining whether or not
to waive primary jurisdiction in specific cases.

7. The Korean negotiators wish to make it clear,
Mr. Chang stated, that they have already conceded to the
U.S. side to such an extent that they are unable to think
of any further concessions in connection with the problem
of waiver. To be specific, the Korean negotiators have
reached the final limit of their concessions in the proposed
waiver formula presented at the 70th negotiating session,
namely the version containing the following clause in the
first sentence of the Agreed Minute Re Paragraph 3:

"except when they determine that it is of particular
importance that jurisdiction be exercised by the
authorities of the Republic of Korea."

8. Therefore, Mr. Chang emphasized, the Korean
negotiators sincerely hope that the U.S. side will accept
the ROK package proposal on Criminal jurisdiction, thereby
clearing the way for an early conclusion of the agreement
on the US-ROK SOFA. The U.S. negotiators have stressed
that the U.S. Congress and the American people are concerned
about the outcome of the negotiations. We would like also
to emphasize that the Korean people and the ROK National
Assembly are also concerned and been following with keen
interest the slow progress of the SOFA negotiations since
they resumed in September 1962.

0035

9. In summary, Mr. Chang stated that the Korean
negotiators believe it is high time for the U.S. side to
reevaluate its position in order to resolve the problem
of waiver as well as other pending issues by accepting the
ROK package proposal and to expedite discussion of remaining
problems relating to the criminal jurisdiction article.

Labor Article

10. Mr. Habib stated that the U.S. negotiators would
like to discuss the Labor Article, in order to exchange
views on the recently tabled revised US and ROK drafts
and seek clarification and expression of the Korean positions
on certain aspects of the new ROK draft. The US negotiators
propose to concentrate the discussion at this time mainly
on questions of principle in which there appears to be a
significant divergence of views between the two sides and
to leave minor differences for later discussion and resolution.

11. Mr. Habib noted that Invited Contractors are
included in the definition of "employers" in paragraph 1,
while the ROK draft, by omission, excludes them from the
definition of employers. Invited Contractors are American-
based firms which are utilized to perform functions in
Korea solely for the U.S. military forces. Although these
functions could be performed directly by the U.S. military,
the U.S. has found from experience that certain functions
and work can be more effectively and efficiently performed
under contract with Invited Contractors. American firms
are utilized as Invited Contractors only when technical
or security considerations dictate, or when the materials
or services required by United States standards are unavailable in Korea; otherwise, USFK utilizes Korean contractors.
In the interests of uniformity and good labor relations,

0036

the U.S. negotiators consider it highly important that Invited Contractors are subject to the same obligations undertaken by the U.S. in the Labor Article. This can only be accomplished by including the "Invited Contractors" as employers by definition. The Invited Contractors - whose Korean employees are represented by the same union as other USFK employees - are thus obliged to adhere to wage scales, and grievance and disputes procedures established for employees working directly for an agency of the U.S. Government. This situation insures that every Korean, whether employed by a private American firm working for the USFK under contract or by an agency of the U.S. Government, receive similar rights and advantages. Such an arrangement is now in effect and is practical, since Invited Contractors are limited to working solely for the U.S. Government in Korea.

12. Mr. Chang stated that the ROK draft omitted Invited Contractors because the Koreans felt such employees should be differentiated from direct-hire employees of the U.S. military. The ROK negotiators felt Invited Contractors should be subject to Korean labor laws, just as Korean employees of other foreign business firms. Mr. Habib emphasized that the Invited Contractors operate in Korea for only one purpose - to assist in the defense of Korea - and therefore they are not like other foreign business firms. Mr. Chang agreed that this question deserves further consideration and he asked for information on the number and role of Invited Contractors and of their Korean employees. Mr. Habib replied that there are about 40 USFK Invited Contractors, who employ about 5,000 Koreans. It was agreed

0037

that the US negotiators would provide additional information about the role of the USFK Invited Contractors and their Korean employees, outside the meeting, and that the ROK negotiators would reconsider their position on this subject.

13. Mr. Habib also questioned the second sentence of the ROK para 1, which states: "Such civilian personnel shall be nationals of Korea." Mr. Habib pointed out that the Labor Article provides the only authorization in the entire agreement for the U.S. to hire civilian employees. If this sentence in the ROK draft were accepted, it would render meaningless the definition of "Civilian Component" as being persons of U.S. nationality, agreed to on 19 March 1963 at the 17th meeting. Under this ROK language, all of USFK's civilian employees would have to be Korean. He indicated that he did not think this was their intention. The question of nationality of USFK employees is covered in previously agreed portions of the SOFA, i.e., Article 1, Definitions Article (paras (b) and the Agreed Minute) and in the Invited Contractors Article (para 1 and Agreed Minute 2). The reference to the nationality of USFK Korean employees in para 1 of the ROK draft appears to be in contradiction to these previously agreed portions of the SOFA. Mr. Chang indicated that the ROK negotiators understand the point being made by Mr. Habib, and indicated that they would reconsider the matter.

14. Mr. Habib pointed out that the US draft provides that the US will conform to ROK labor laws, customs and practices "to the extent not inconsistent with the provisions of this Article or the military requirements of the USFK," while the ROK draft stipulates conformance to ROK labor

0038

legislation, "except as may otherwise be mutually agreed."
With regard to the phrase in Para 3 of the US draft, "To
the extent not inconsistent with the provisions of this
Article," the US as a sovereign nation, cannot be subject
to the jurisdiction of ROK labor courts. This fact had
been recognized by the ROK negotiators, as reflected in
Agreed Minute No. 1 of the revised ROK draft, which
indicates the US undertaking to conform with ROK labor
laws "does not imply any waiver by the United States Government of its immunities under international law." This phrase
in the US draft of Para 3 is also directly related to the
Agreed Minute No.5, as proposed by both sides, which
establishes joint ROK Government-US Government procedures
for resolving labor disputes between USFK and its Korean
employees. These procedures were proposed by the U.S. to
provide for fair and equitable ROK-US settlement of such
labor disputes, while not subjecting the U.S. Govt to the
ROK Labor Dispute Adjustment Law. On that basis, the phrase
in Para 3 of the US draft, "to the extent not inconsistent
with the provisions of this Article," must be included in
the Labor Article to be consistent with Agreed Minute No. 1
of the ROK draft, Agreed Minute No.2 of the USFK draft,
and Agreed Minute No.5 of both the US and ROK drafts. Mr.
Chang indicated that the ROK negotiators would be prepared
to reconsider the Korean position relating to inclusion
of the phrase, "to the extent not inconsistent with the
provisions of this Article."

15. Regarding the words, "military requirements" in
para 3, Mr. Habib stated that both the U.S. and ROK sides
a ree to the properity of Joint Committee review of any

0039

action contrary to ROK labor laws which is taken in connection with US-ROK defense requirements. However, the ROK draft which requires that non-conformance based on military requirements be mutually agreed upon in advance by the Joint Committee is too inflexible. As the ROK side knows, military requirements are not of such a nature as to always be foreseeable. The fulfillment of the defense mission in Korea is made more difficult by the existing armistice situation, which requires the United States and the ROK Forces to be prepared at any time to meet any military contingency. In this uncertain environment, unforeseeable military requirements may necessitate immediate solutions. The provisions of the ROK draft could place the United States Forces in the untenable position of either delaying action until agreement was reached in the Joint Committee, possibly jeopardizing the mission, or taking immediate necessary action without approval of the Joint Committee, in violation of the agreement. Neither of these alternatives is acceptable. USFK must have authority to vary from the ROK labor laws when necessary to satisfy the military requirements, which are paramount. The failure to do so could seriously hamper military operations in an emergency.

16. Mr. Chang emphasized that the language of the US draft would make it possible for the USFK to take any action in non-conformance with ROK labor laws without seeking agreement of ROK authorities. The ROK side considers this language too broad. The ROK negotiators are not seeking an absolute commitment of US conformity to ROK labor laws, but they desire the inclusion of the clause "except as may otherwise be mutually agreed." In any emergency situation

0040

short of hostilities, the ROK negotiators feel that there would be sufficient time for both sides to consult in the Joint Committee. In the event of hostilities, of course, such advance consultation may not be feasible or possible, and enforcement of the Article would be ineffective.

17. Mr. Habib pointed out that this Article was being negotiated to cover all contingencies, to be effective in time of peace as well as at a time of national emergency. The ROK response has clarified the Korean position, and the US negotiators will further consider this issue.

18. Mr. Habib pointed out that the US draft of para 4 consists of two subparas, while the ROK draft includes only the second subpara, and that subpara is worded differently. Omitted from the ROK draft is the US subpara which gives the USFK Korean employees the same right to strike as an employee in a comparable position with the ROK Armed Forces, and which provides USFK employees the right to organize and join a Union "whose objectives are not inimical to the U.S. interests." Mr. Habib emphasized that the U.S. side considers this to be one of the most significant paragraphs in the Labor Article. Korean employees of USFK, like the ROK armed forces civilian employees, have a vital role in the effective defense of the Republic. ROK Ministry of National Defense and USFK Korean employees work in direct support of the same objective – the defense of the Republic. The Korean people, in developing their present constitution, wisely provided in Article 29 that public officials shall not be accorded the right to strike. This ROK Government position is the same as the U.S. Government position on the problem of the right of government workers to strike. We

0041

tabled the new Agreed Minute No.5 on 23 December 1964 in order to provide effective machinery for full US-ROK cooperation and close collaboration in equitably and fairly resolving labor disputes involving Korean employees. We believe it is in our mutual interests to provide effective means to resolve labor disputes without disruptive actions which could jeopardize the joint defense efforts.

19. Mr. Habib pointed out that the USFK currently maintains and will continue to "maintain procedures designed to assure the just and timely resolution of employee grievances." Such grievance procedures have been significantly refined and improved, and they are believed to be operating effectively to resolve employee grievances. Both sides understand that one party in a dispute cannot formally "insure" what the actions of the other party will be. Therefore, we believe that the U.S. language, i.e., "maintain procedures designed to assure" employees grievances is more realistic than the proposed ROK language that "Employers shall insure the just and timely resolution of employee grievances."

20. Mr. Chang indicated that the Korean negotiators would give further consideration to the point raised about varia- tions in language regarding the resolution of employee grievances. With regard to the strike question, Mr. Chang emphasized that all laborers are guaranteed the right of collective action under the ROK constitution and the ROK negotiators cannot agree to the proposed language of the U.S. draft.

21. Mr. Habib pointed out that the provisions of para 4(a) of the U.S. draft are closely related to Agreed Minute

0042

No. 5. The fundamental difference in the two drafts of this Agreed Minute relates to whether or not USFK Korean employees or organized employee organizations can engage in practices disruptive of normal work requirements. The tabled U.S. draft of the Labor Article would conserve and expand the rights of the USFK employee, and provide the basis for sound employer-employee relationships as well as for joint ROK-US procedures for resolving labor disputes.

22. Mr. Habib emphasized that the procedures established by Agreed Minute No.5 would insure that the interests and views of USFK Korean employees will be given full consideration and their rights protected. With regard to reference in the ROK draft to utilizing procedures in Article 14 of the Labor Dispute Adjustment Law, it should be clearly understood that the US Government cannot be subject to the provisions of this law. Every USFK Korean employee, at the time of employment signed an affidavit which states:

"Any employee who engages in any strike against the Government of the United States or who is a member of an organization which asserts the right to strike against the Government shall be immediately removed from employment."

In addition, the labor union of the USFK Korean employees, the Foreign Organizations Korean Employees Union (FOKEU) pledged in 1961 as a basic requirement for USFK recognition that it "shall not assert the right of collective action (strike or slow down) of direct hire employees against the United States Government." This pledge was the basis on which the USFK agreed to recognize and cooperate with the union. The US Government is convinced that the best

0043

interests of both the ROK and US Government, as well as of
USFK Korean employees, require that the SOFA provide for an
equitable means of resolving labor disputes as provided
in Agreed Minute No.5. We firmly believe that granting
USFK defense employees the right to engage in disruptive
activities would be contrary to joint US-ROK defense interests,
as well as the best long-term interests of these employees.
USFK employees are not ordinary employees, but are comparable
in importance in the defense of the Republic to civilian
defense employees working for the ROK Government, and we
are not prepared to concede that they have the right to
strike.

23. Mr. Chang reiterated the ROK objection to the no-
strike provisions of the US draft, and indicated that the
US side was misinterpreting Article 29 of the ROK Constitution. Both sides agreed they would review ROK legislation
relating to this subject, and Mr. Chang indicated he would
reply in more detail at an early meeting.

24. It was agreed that the next meeting will be held
on March 2 at 3:00 P.M.

0044

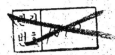

JOINT SUMMARY RECORD OF THE 72ND SESSION

1. Time and Place: 3:00-4:30 P.M., March 2, 1965 at
the Foreign Ministry's Conference
Room (No.1)

2. Attendants:

ROK Side:

Mr. Chang, Sang Moon	Director European and American Affairs Bureau
Mr. Huh, Sung Joon	Director Labor Administration Bureau Office of Labor Affairs
Mr. Lee, Nam Ki	Chief America Section Ministry of Foreign Affairs
Mr. Choo, Moon Ki	Chief Legal Affairs Section Ministry of Justice
Maj. Lee, Kye Hoon	Military Affairs Section Ministry of National Defense
Mr. Kim, Kee Joe	3rd Secretary Ministry of Foreign Affairs
Mr. Lee, Keun Pal (Rapporteur and Interpreter)	3rd Secretary Ministry of Foreign Affairs
Mr. Hwang, Young Jae	3rd Secretary Ministry of Foreign Affairs

U.S. Side:

Mr. Philip C. Habib	Counselor American Embassy
Brig. Gen. Carroll H. Dunn	Deputy Chief of Staff 8th U.S. Army
Capt. John Wayne	Assistant Chief of Staff USN/K
Col. Howard Smigelow	Deputy Chief of Staff 8th U.S. Army
Col. Kenneth C. Crawford	Staff Judge Advocate 8th U.S. Army
Mr. Benjamin A. Fleck	First Secretary American Embassy

0045

Mr. Robert A. Kinney	J-5 8th U.S. Army
Mr. Goodwin Shapiro	Second Secretary American Embassy
Maj. Alton H. Harvey	Staff Judge Advocate's Office 8th U.S. Army
Mr. David Y.C. Lee (Interpreter)	Second Secretary American Embassy

Claims Article

1. The ROK Chief Negotiator, Mr. Chang Sang-mun, stated that the Korean negotiators, with a view to expediting negotiations, would like to call the U.S. negotiators attention to the Claims Article. The drafts on the subject of claims for the both sides were tabled at the 28th negotiating session on August 8, 1963, more than 18 months ago. Since the exchange of the two sides' respective drafts on this subject, the Korean negotiators have made many attempts to accommodate the expressed concern of the U.S. side. Unfortunately, there still exist fundamental differences in the positions of the two sides.

2. Therefore, the Korean negotiators would like to reiterate their position briefly today regarding the focal point of the past discussions for settlement of claims arising out of acts or omissions of members or employees of the U.S. armed forces done in the performance of official duty, or out of any other act, omission or occurrence for which the U.S. armed forces are legally responsible, and causing damage to third parties other than the Government of the Republic of Korea.

3. The U.S. side maintained on this matter that the claims should be settled in accordance with the "Foreign

0046

Claims Act" of the U.S., which is implemented by regulations
of the U.S. Army, Navy, and Air Force. This system,
however, has a serious defect in view of the principle of
equity and justice as expounded by the Korean negotiators
at the 66th negotiating session. The U.S. side stated at
the 29th session that a claimant could appeal, under its
present system, from the Claims Commission of the U.S.
Claims Service in Korea up through to Headquarters, U.S.
Armed Forces Claims Service, located in the United States.

4. Nevertheless, the unilateral Claims Service decisions
could hardly be supported as a rational treatment for the
claimant. Although the Korean negotiators believe that
most of the claims would be settled amicably without resorting
to court decisions, the Korean negotiators take the view that
the only way to overcome the aforementioned defect involved
in the proposed U.S. system is to provide the claimant with
a chance for a fair trial by a competent court. Furthermore,
the Korean negotiators believe that all the claims arising
within the territory of the ROK should be settled by the
relevant laws of the ROK.

5. Therefore, the Government of the ROK is willing
to undertake the responsibility for the processing of the
claims for the benefit of the U.S. armed forces in Korea,
as proposed in the Korean draft. The Korean proposal
guarantees just and equitable settlement of all the claims
arising out of death, injury, or property damage caused
by the U.S. armed forces in Korea without infringing upon
the best interests of both the U.S. and the claimant
concerned. Therefore, the Korean negotiators request the
U.S. side to reconsider its position and accept the standard

language of other Status-of-Forces Agreements regarding
the claims article, as proposed by the Korean side, and
respond within the earliest date practicable.

6. Mr. Habib indicated that the U.S. side would take
this ROK statement on the Claims Article under consideration and would reply later.

Labor Article

7. Mr. Habib indicated that he would resume discussion
of the Labor Article with paragraph 5, where the negotiators
left off at the 71st meeting. He indicated that he would
discuss only the most important points which required
further explanation and elaboration.

8. Mr. Habib pointed out that Paragraph 5 of both
drafts deals with important topic of the key USFK Korean
employees for their assigned defense tasks in time of
emergency. The U.S. draft of this paragraph states such
employees "shall" be available to continue to perform
their key roles in the joint US-ROK defense effort. The
ROK draft states only that essential USFK employees "may"
be deferred.

9. Mr. Habib indicated that the comments of the
ROK negotiators at our 71st negotiating session, as well
as the proposed ROK draft of para 5, indicates that ROK
Government authorities apparently do not fully realize
the important role that the Korean civilian employees of
the United States Forces in Korea play in the joint US-
ROK defense of the Republic of Korea. It is true that
during the years of the Korean War, the USFK Korean
employees were used mainly in jobs requiring unskilled
labor. But this situation has greatly changed in recent

0048

years and most USFK Korean employees are employed in important defense work essential to the security of the Republic of Korea. Less than 5 percent of the present USFK Korean employees are in the unskilled labor-pool category. The majority of USFK Korean employees are in responsible administrative, technical, industrial, or professional-type positions. About 750 USFK Korean employees now occupy management-type positions. Most USFK employees possess special training and a wide variety of skills and many of them hold vital positions in the support and backup of the joint US-ROK defense effort.

10. Mr. Habib stated that both the U.S. and ROK drafts provide that lists of essential employees will be provided. The U.S. draft of this paragraph assures the U.S. and ROK defense planners that, in time of emergency, essential USFK employees shall be available to continue to perform their important roles in the joint US-ROK defense effort. Effective defense planning requires that the USFK must be assured in advance that its essential Korean employees _shall_ be available to continue their defense work in the event of a national emergency. If the ROK SOFA authorities can only agree that such essential employees "may" be deferred, the USFK cannot then make realistic plans that definitely count on the continued use of such employees in the joint US-ROK defense of Korea in an emergency.

11. The U.S. side emphasized that it is on the basis that such employees would be available in an emergency that the USFK has been promoting policies of upgrading its Korean employees into important defense positions and replacing third-state nationals and U.S. personnel with skilled Korean personnel. In view of the relative abundance of manpower in the ROK and the relatively modest demands on

'0043

the ROK manpower pool by the USFK, we doubt that you really
desire to deny USFK deferment of essential Korean workers
in an emergency. If this should prove to be the case,
however, the USFK might have to reconsider its policies
of expanding utilization of Korean nationals, and of
replacing third-state and U.S. nationals with Koreans in
essential defense positions within the U.S. military establishment in Korea. Perhaps the explanation for the variation
between the ROK and US drafts can be found in the remarks
of the Korean negotiators at the 71st meeting, that they felt
in time of national emergency the provisions of the Labor
Article might not be enforced. But Para 5 is written to
enable the US and ROK authorities to do sound, advance
planning for just such a national emergency. Therefore,
USFK's essential employees must be available to continue
to serve in their defense roles in any emergency which
would threaten the security of the Republic of Korea.

12. At the 69th negotiating session, the Korean side
stated that no eligible Korean youth can be exempted from
his military service, for it is the solemn duty of all
Korean youths to serve in the Armed Forces. Mr. Habib
emphasized that the U.S. side agrees with these sentiments
and does not intend to place on its list of essential
employees to be exempted or deferred, eligible Korean
youths who have not yet served their basic term of military
service. However, the USFK has many Korean employees who
are veterans of the military service and who now occupy
essential positions with the U.S. forces. In a national

0050

emergency, the USFK must retain such essential Korean personnel. The USFK plans to give the Ministry of National Defense its lists of such personnel in advance, as indicated in the revised ROK draft. It is agreed that if the ROK military establishment, in reviewing the USFK lists against its own mobilization plans for an emergency, desires that individual reserve officers be subject to recall to key positions in the ROK military service, such arrangements can be worked out amicably by Korean and American authorities.

13. In summation, Mr. Habib indicated that both sides apparently were in agreement that lists of essential USFK Korean employees should be prepared in advance of an emergency. In addition, we want assurances that once the lists are submitted, these essential employees will be available in times of emergency. The U.S. side would appreciate an explanation of the ROK position in light of the foregoing factors.

14. Mr. Chan noted that the U.S. side indicated that less than five percent of the present USFK exployees are in the unskilled labor-pool category. Therefore, almost 90 percent must be skilled or managerial. What is the approximate number who are considered essential and should be exempt from military service? The ROK draft clearly envisages the availability of these employees to the U.S. forces in any emergency, even though the ROK draft uses the words "may be deferred." But the U.S. draft clearly contradicts the spirit of the ROK Constitution. The US-ROK differences are only differences in expression.

0051

15. Mr. Chang continued that the ROK side cannot accept the word "exempt" as used in the U.S. draft. Once the U.S. list of essential Korean employees is submitted, there should be US-ROK consultations and agreement on the list, including the number, types, and skills of employees to be made available to the U.S. forces. Such agreements should be reached in advance, and then the ROK side would do its best to defer the required personnel.

16. Mr. Habib replied that Para 5 provides the basis for effective advance planning for an emergency, and that the U.S. must have assurances in advance that the U.S. forces' essential Korean employees will be available in an emergency to continue in their important defense work. The U.S. side will give the Korean side an estimate of the number of essential employees at a later meeting.

17. Turning to consideration of Agreed Minute No. 2, Mr. Habib noted that the first sentence of Agreed Minute No. 2 of the U.S. draft, and Agreed Minute No. 1 of the ROK draft are essentially similar, with only minor differences in wording. The ROK draft does not include the second sentence of the U.S. draft of this Agreed Minute, but the U.S. negotiators consider it important to include the sentence which makes clear the right of the USFK to terminate employment of its employees. The USFK follows procedures to assure just and timely resolution of employee grievances, and provides severance pay to terminated employees in accordance with Korean law, custom, and practice. We have every intention of continuing to be a good employer, but since the only reason for USFK being in Korea is to assist in the joint US-ROK defense effort, USFK must maintain its right to terminate employment as required.

0052

18. Mr. Habib pointed out that unless this sentence is included, the USFK has no clear-cut right anywhere in the agreement to terminate employment. We have a very carefully conceived labor program. We are going to continue to be a good employer. What is objectionable about this second sentence which the ROK draft omits?

19. Mr. Chang indicated that although the ROK side believes the USFK in principle may terminate employment whenever it wishes, it also believes the USFK should conform to the relevant provisions of the ROK laws in such matters. This includes advance notification and showing due cause, etc. He pointed out that Article 27 of the ROK Labor Standards Law provides that there can be no termination of employment without justifiable reason. The ROK side has provided - in paragraph 3 and the Agreed Minutes No.4 - for cases in which it is impossible for the employers to conform to ROK laws because of military requirements.

20. Mr. Habib emphasized that paragraph 3 deals with conformity while Agreed Minute No. 2 deals with the right to terminate employment. The ROK negotiators were apparently confusing conditions of termination with the right to terminate. The former was covered in Para 3, in which U.S. armed forces pledged to conform with ROK labor laws, customs, and practices. It was emphasized that the right to terminate, as distinct from conditions of termination, must be spelled out in the agreement. Mr. Habib stated that the USFK will conform to ROK practices and customs relating to termination of employment, and if the ROK Government questions any USFK action in this regard, it can take it up with the Joint Committee.

0053

21. Mr. Chang replied that the ROK Government is
prepared to assure the U.S. side of the right to terminate
for justifiable reasons. The ROK para 3 gives the U.S.
enough authority to terminate. Mr. Chang indicated that the
ROK side would study the U.S. statements and reply at an
early meeting.

0054

JOINT SUMMARY RECORD OF THE 73RD SESSION

1. Time and Place: 10:30-11:30 A.M., April 20, 1965 at
   the Foreign Ministry's Conference Room
   (No.1)

2. Attendants:

ROK Side:

Mr. Chang, Sang Moon	Director European and American Affairs Bureau
Mr. Huh, Sung Joon	Director Labor Administration Bureau Office of Labor Affairs
Maj. Lee, Kye Hoon	Military Affairs Section Ministry of National Defense
Mr. Kim, Kee Joe	3rd Secretary Ministry of Foreign Affairs
Mr. Lee, Keun Pal (Rapporteur and Interpreter)	3rd Secretary Ministry of Foreign Affairs
Mr. Hwang, Young Jae	3rd Secretary Ministry of Foreign Affairs
Mr. Park, Won Chul	3rd Secretary Ministry of Foreign Affairs

U.S. Side:

Mr. Philip C. Habib	Counselor American Embassy
Brig. Gen. Carroll H. Dunn	Deputy Chief of Staff 8th U.S. Army
Col. Allan G. Pixton	Deputy Chief of Staff 8th U.S. Army
Capt. George Hagerman	Assistant Chief of Staff USN/K
Col. Kenneth C. Crawford	Staff Judge Advocate 8th U.S. Army
Mr. Benjamin A. Fleck	First Secretary American Embassy
Mr. Robert A. Kinney	J-5 8th U.S. Army
Mr. Jack Friedman	Second Secretary American Embassy
Maj. Alton H. Harvey	Staff Judge Advocate's Office 8th U.S. Army

0055

Mr. David Y.C. Lee   Second Secretary
(Interpreter)   American Embassy

Mr. Ogden C. Reed   Civilian Personnel Director
                            8th U.S. Army

Mr. G. W. Flowers   Observer

1. Mr. Habib opened the meeting by introducing two
new members of the U.S. negotiating team: Colonel Allan G.
Pixton, replacing Colonel Smigelow, and Captain George
Hagerman, replacing Captain Wayne. Mr. Chang welcomed
Colonel Pixton and Captain Hagerman to the negotiations on
behalf of the Korean negotiators.

2. Taking up the Labor Article, Mr. Habib tabled a
revised draft of the entire article. He stated that the
U.S. negotiators were tabling this draft, in a spirit of
compromise, in order to reach early full agreement on this
article. As revised, the U.S. draft would provide continued
fair and equitable treatment for Korean employees of the
U.S. armed forces, as well as sound and just procedures
for the resolution of labor grievances and disputes. Mr. Habib
said he would discuss the changes in the draft on a paragraph
by paragraph basis. The principal revisions related to
Paragraphs 3,4,5 and their Agreed Minutes.

3. Paragraph 1 and related Agreed Minute #1 - In
Paragraph 1, Mr. Habib said, the word "paramilitary" had
been added to differentiate clearly the paramilitary Korean
Service Corps from the direct hire employees of the U.S.
armed forces covered by this article. The U.S. armed forces
plan to discuss the status of the Korean Service Corps,
which is commanded by ROK Army officers on active duty
and in reserve (and which has operated outside ROK labor
laws and courts) directly with authorities in the Ministry

0056

of National Defense. In order to expedite agreement regarding
the language relative to domestic servants, the U.S. negotiators had deleted the second sentence of the previous draft
of Agreed Minute #1, subject to an understanding that the
present situation with regard to domestics employed by
individual members of the U.S. armed forces and civilian
component shall continue. As the Korean negotiators were
aware, Mr. Habib continued, individual members of the
United States armed forces, civilian component, and dependents
hire and pay domestic servants directly, subject only to USFK
security and health checks and general guidance. Applicable
Korean laws would govern employment of such domestics.

4. <u>Paragraph 2</u> - Mr. Habib noted that the U.S. and
Korean negotiators are in agreement regarding Paragraph 2,
except for minor differences of wording. The U.S. negotiators
concurred in the Korean proposal to substitute the word
"such" for the word "available" in the second sentence,
subject to Korean understanding that we cannot furnish
information not available to us as part of our normal
operating procedure. The U.S. negotiators foresee no problems
in supplying the information desired by the Korean authorities,
as indicated in Paragraph 20 of the Agreed Joint Summary
of the 46th negotiating meeting.

5. <u>Paragraph 3 and related Agreed Minute #5</u> - Mr. Habib
stated that the U.S. negotiators believe that they are in
essential agreement with the Korean negotiators regarding
Paragraph 3, except for possible differences in interpretations
of the phrase "military requirements". In order to be
responsive to the Korean desire for review and consideration
by the Joint Committee of situations in which the U.S.
armed forces cannot conform to the ROK Labor legislation

0057

because of military requirements, the U.S. negotiators
were tabling a new Agreed Minute #5. The U.S. negotiators
believe, Mr. Habib continued, that the U.S. armed forces only
rarely, if ever, will not be able to conform to ROK labor
legislation applicable under this Article, except in emergency
situations. The new Agreed Minute #5 would provide that when
the U.S. armed forces cannot conform to ROK labor legislation
on account of military requirements, the matter shall
be reported, in advance whenever possible, to the Joint
Committee for its consideration and review. The U.S.
negotiators believe that the Agreed Minute demonstrates the
good faith of the U.S. armed forces, in pledging to conform
to the ROK labor laws, customs, and practices, to the
extent not inconsistent with the provisions of this article,
and to agree to this type of Joint Committee consideration
of possible situations in which military requirements may
be at variance with ROK labor legislation. In this regard,
the ROK negotiators had mentioned the possibility that in
an emergency the provisions of the Labor Article might be
suspended. The U.S. negotiators believe that the new U.S.
language is the best way to take care of unforeseeable
situations in which military necessity may require non-
conformance to ROK labor legislation.

6. Paragraph 4 - Mr. Habib stated that the U.S.
negotiators were tabling a new Paragraph 4 which sets forth
clearly the positive U.S. commitments to be a good employer,
pursuing enlightened policies and procedures relating to employer-
employee relationships. Subparagraph (a) would provide
that employers will maintain procedures designed to assure the
just and timely resolution of employee grievances. Subparagraph
(b) would provide the employees the right to organize and
join a union. Under its terms, membership or non-membership
in such groups would not be a factor in employment or in
other actions affecting employees.

0058

Subparagraph (c) would assure recognized unions the
right of consultation with U.S. military authorities.
Such labor-management consultations are currently an
established part of the U.S. armed forces' relations
with the recognized union.

7. Subparagraph (d) of Paragraph 4, Mr. Habib
continued, incorporates much of the previously tabled
Agreed Minute #5, setting forth procedures for settling
labor disputes which cannot be settled by use of
established USFK procedures. These procedures closely
parallel the previously-tabled Korean proposals, and
provide the disputes which cannot be settled by use
of USFK procedures shall be referred to the ROK Office
of Labor Affairs for conciliation. If a dispute cannot
be settled by the Office of Labor Affairs, it would be
referred to the Joint Committee, which might refer it
to a Labor Sub-Committee or to a specially designated
committee or take it under consideration directly.
The Joint Committee would be the final arbiter of any
such labor disputes. The U.S. and Korean negotiators
were in agreement that its decisions shall be binding
upon employers, employees, and the union.

8. As stated in subparagraph (e) of Paragraph 4,
Mr. Habib continued, the U.S. negotiators firmly maintain

0059

that a Korean working for the U.S. armed forces in the joint
U.S.-ROK defense effort shall be subject to the same legal
provisions concerning strikes and other work stoppages
as an employee in a comparable position in the employment
of the armed forces of the Republic of Korea. Both categories
of Korean employees of our two governments are working
directly in the defense of their country. The U.S.
negotiators believe firmly in the principle that our
employees must be subject to the same ROK legal provisions
with regard to strikes or work stoppages as comparable employees
working for the ROK armed forces. This is a basic and
unchanging U.S. position, which is related directly to the
effectiveness of the U.S. armed forces in the defense of
the Republic of Korea.

     9. Paragraph 5 - Mr. Habib pointed out that
Paragraph 5 of both drafts deals with the important topic of
the availability of essential Korean employees of the U.S.
armed forces for their assigned defense tasks in time of
emergency. The newly-tabled Paragraph 5 of the U.S. draft
had been patterned after the language of the Korean draft
tabled at the 69th negotiating session. It is almost
identical with the Korean Paragraph 5 except for the use
of the word "shall" instead of "may" in subparagraph (b).
The use of the word "shall" would assure U.S. and Korean
defense planners that in time of emergency, essential
employees of the U.S. armed forces in Korea would be available
to continue to perform their essential roles during the
emergency. USFK requirements for Korean manpower, Mr. Habib
continued, are very small in comparison to Korean manpower
availabilities. On the other hand, the role of the U.S.
forces in a war emergency in the Republic of Korea would be

0060

of an extremely important and probably decisive nature.
Their essential civilian employees are basic to the
effectiveness of the U.S. armed forces. Therefore, the U.S.
negotiators wished to emphasize that deferment of essential
USFK personnel in advance must be provided for. This vital
matter cannot be left to consideration and decision in
time of emergency. There would be a great deal of paper
work in listing and processing essential employees who
would be deferred. This work must be accomplished to our
mutual satisfaction before the emergency arises, if
implementation is to be effective. The U.S. negotiators
believe that the details can be worked out in consultation
between the U.S. armed forces and officials of the Ministry
of National Defense in advance, to the mutual satisfaction
of both parties.

10. Mr. Habib noted that the Agreed Minutes in the new
U.S. draft had been renumbered so that they now appear
in the same order as the paragraphs to which they refer.

11. Mr. Habib stated that the revised U.S. draft was
the result of many hours of discussion of this Article by
both sides over the past 15 months. The U.S. negotiators
urged early accpetance of the revised draft by the Korean
negotiators. The U.S. negotiators believe that it fully
protects the legitimate rights and interests of Korean
employees of the U.S. armed forces and, at the same time,
is consistent with joint U.S.-ROK defense requirements.

12. Mr. Chang replied that the Korean negotiators
appreciated the compromising spirit in which the U.S.
negotiators had presented their revised draft in the
hope for full agreement as soon as possible. The Korean
negotiators would carefully consider the U.S. draft and
respond in a few days. However, the Korean negotiators

0061

believed that considerable differences still existed
between the positions of the two sides. They wished,
therefore, to make some preliminary comments to indicate
the basic Korean position.

13. With regard to Paragraph 1, Mr. Chang said the
Korean negotiators still wished to settle the question
of the Korean Service Corps outside the framework of the
SOFA negotiations, since U.S. side had insited that the
KSC is a semi-military or paramilitary organization,
while the Korean side had maintained otherwise, and
agreement on the question was not foreseeable.

14. With regard to subparagraphs (a), (b), and (c)
of Paragraph 4, Mr. Chang recalled that the U.S. negotiators
had stated that the U.S. armed forces will conform
to ROK labor laws to the maximum extent possible. The
Korean negotiators believe, therefore, that the detailed
provisions set forth in these subparagraphs were unnecessary.
However, they had no objection if the U.S. negotiators
felt it necessary to include them, subject to agreement on
the other outstanding problems of the Labor Article.

15. Regarding Paragraph 4(e), which had to do with
the right to strike, Mr. Chang said the Korean negotiators
believed that if they accepted the U.S. language, the
Government of the Republic of Korea would be obliged to
enact a law prohibiting the employees of the U.S. armed
forces from resorting to strikes. The Korean negotiators
doubted that the language of the U.S. draft was in
accordance with ROK labor legislation.

16. Regarding Paragraph 5(b), Mr. Chang noted two
main points. First, employees shall be deferred on the

0062

request of the U.S. armed forces. Secondly, a list of
essential employees is to be furnished in advance. The
U.S. proposal did not appear to provide for the mutual
satisfaction desired by the Korean negotiators. If they
accepted the U.S. language, the ROK authorities would have
to defer everyone whose name appeared on the list furnished
in advance. They believed that the ROK authorities should
have discretion, in consultation with the U.S. armed forces,
to decide who would be deferred.

17. Mr. Habib pointed out that what the Korean
negotiators wanted was implied in the U.S. language.
The U.S. negotiators believed that there would be mutual
satisfaction, since there must be agreement on the attain-
ment of essential skills by the employees whose names would
appear on the list furnished by the U.S. armed forces.
The Joint Committee would be the mechanism for attaining
mutual satisfaction. If the Korean authorities questioned
that any person named on the list had actually attained
the required skills, they could raise the question in the
Joint Committee.

18. Mr. Chang said the Korean negotiators still felt
that the language regarding this question could be more
specific. He said they would propose such language.

19. Mr. Chang noted that the U.S. negotiators had
modified the language of Agreed Minute #5, by providing
for notification "in advance whenever possible." The
phrase "whenever possible" should be omitted, however, since
the Korean negotiators believed that it would always be possible
to report in advance. Furthermore, if the U.S. armed forces
found that they could not conform to the ROK labor laws, they

0063

should always refer the matter to the Joint Committee in advance.

20. Mr. Habib replied that if it is always possible to report in advance, then the Korean position was met by the U.S. language and no problem existed. The U.S. armed forces did not intend this provision to be a means of avoiding conformity to the Korean labor laws. They did believe, however, that in times of emergency it might not always be possible to notify the Joint Committee in advance of non-conformity. There had to be some qualifying phrase; otherwise the provision would be unreasonable.

21. Mr. Chang said he wished to close his preliminary remarks by stating that the Korean negotiators noted and appreciated the sincerity of the U.S. negotiators in submitting their revised draft.

22. Mr. Habib said that he wished to reply briefly to Mr. Chang's comments regarding Paragraph 4(e). The U.S. negotiators wished to reiterate that neither the U.S. armed forces nor the ROK armed forces are ordinary employers. The phraseology of the revised U.S. draft of this subparagraph had been carefully chosen from the standpoint of the Korean requirements as well as those of the U.S. armed forces. The language is not unreasonable, given the unusual nature of the employers. Neither employer is an ordinary business enterprise. They are not in business to make money but to defend the Republic of Korea.

23. Regarding Paragraph 1, Mr. Habib pointed out that in revising the language, the U.S. negotiators had done exactly what the Korean negotiators had desired - they had excluded members of the Korean Service Corps from the definition of employees and, therefore, from the coverage provided by this article. It appeared that both sides were substantially in agreement regarding this issue.

0064

24. It was agreed that the Korean negotiators would call the next meeting as soon as they were prepared to comment in detail on the U.S. draft.

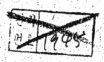

JOINT SUMMARY RECORD OF THE 74TH SESSION

1. Time and Place: 10:00 - 11:00 A.M., April 23, 1965 at the Foreign Ministry's Conference Room (No. 1)

2. Attendants:

ROK Side:

Mr. Chang, Sang Moon	Director European and American Affairs Bureau
Mr. Lee, Nam Ki	Chief America Section Ministry of Foreign Affairs
Mr. Hur, Hyong Koo	Chief Prosecutors Section Ministry of Justice
Maj. Lee Kye Hoon	Military Affairs Section Ministry of National Defense
Mr. Kim, Kee Joe	3rd Secretary Ministry of Foreign Affairs
Mr. Lee, Keun Pal (Rapporteur and Interpreter)	3rd Secretary Ministry of Foreign Affairs
Mr. Lee, Chung Bin	3rd Secretary Ministry of Foreign Affairs
Mr. Hwang, Young Jae	3rd Secretary Ministry of Foreign Affairs

U.S. Side:

Mr. Philip C. Habib	Counselor American Embassy
Mr. Brig. Gen. Caroll H. Dunn	Deputy Chief of Staff 8th U.S. Army
Col. Allan G. Pixton	Deputy Chief of Staff 8th U.S. Army
Capt. George Hagerman	Assistant Chief of Staff USMK/K
Col. Kenneth C. Crawford	Staff Judge Advocate 8th U.S. Army
Mr. Benjamin A. Fleck	First Secretary American Embassy

0066

Mr. Robert A. Kinney	J-5 8th U.S. Army
Mr. Goodwin Shapiro	Second Secretary American Embassy
Maj. Alton H. Harvey	Staff Judge Advocate's Office 8th U.S. Army
Mr. David Y.C. Lee (Interpreter)	Second Secretary American Embassy

1. Mr. Habib opened the meeting by stating that the U.S. negotiators wished to speak at this meeting on the subjects of waiver of jurisdiction, pre-trial custody, and duty certificate. In order to expedite the negotiations and enable the two governments to reach full agreement on the Status of Forces Agreement, he said, the U.S. Government was now prepared to make a major and final concession on the waiver issue by offering what is generally called the German NATO waiver formula. This is the heart of the final U.S. position on the Criminal Jurisdiction Article. Noting that the U.S. and Korean negotiators are in essential agreement regarding paragraph 3 and 4, Mr. Habib said that the U.S. negotiators wished to table at this time a new Agreed Minute Re Paragraph 3(b) to replace the previous Agreed Minute Re Paragraph 3 of the U.S. draft. The draft of the Agreed Minute was tabled.

2. With regard to the waiver issue, Mr. Habib continued, the U.S. negotiators have proceeded on the basis of the Korean conception that the Korean authorities will seek to exercise jurisdiction only when, by reason of special circumstances in a special case, major interests of the Korean administration of justice make imperative the exercise of Korean jurisdiction. The new U.S. waiver

0067

formula, he pointed out, is similar to this proposal, for
in special circumstances in a specific case where major
interests of Korean administration of justice make imperative
the exercise of Korean jurisdiction the ROK Government can
recall its waiver and exercise its jurisdiction.

3. Mr. Habib stated that the U.S. negotiators were
offering this formula because the Korean negotiators had clearly
indicated the intention of the Korean authorities to
exercise restraint. In the light of these repeated
assurances, the U.S. negotiators do not expect the ROK
Government to seek frequent recall of waiver. On the
contrary, they expect that restraint in recall of waiver will
be exercised in all cases, except where special circumstances
of fundamental interest apply. This is not, Mr. Habib
continued, an unusual expectation. For example, the U.S.
negotiators would like to present the following German waiver
statistics which point up the host country's restraint in
recalling waivers under this formula. The following tabulation, he pointed out, presents the percentage of U.S.
servicemen subject to German jurisdiction for the latest
reporting period, the 12-month period from December 1, 1963
to November 30, 1964, by various categories of offenses:

Cases of Murder	50% tried by Germany
Rape	4%
Manslaughter	10%
Robbery	0.6%
Burglary	0%
Arson	0%
Assault	0%
Forgery	0%
Economic Control Laws	0%
Disorderly Conduct	0%

0068

Mr. Habib stated that these statistics show that the Federal Republic of Germany has exercised its right of recall of waiver in only a small percentage of cases. The U.S. negotiators are reassured by the ROK negotiators' emphasis in the Agreed Joint Summary that, if given the right of jurisdiction, they would show great restraint in exercising jurisdiction over U.S. servicemen.

4. The U.S. negotiators believe, Mr. Habib said, that this new U.S. Agreed Minute provides a sound basis for early conclusion of the negotiations. The new language on waiver of jurisdiction is fully consistent with the ROK Government's desire for a clearcut exposition of its right to exercise jurisdiction over U.S. servicemen. This waiver formula meets the needs of both the host state and the sending state. It reserves to the Republic of Korea the right to exercise jurisdiction in cases where it believes exercise of jurisdiction is imperative. At the same time, the formula defers to the needs of the sending state for necessary control and disciplinary authority over its armed forces. The U.S. negotiators believe that this formula should be a positive factor in promoting friendly U.S.-ROK relations. After the Korean negotiators had had an opportunity to study this proposal in detail, Mr. Habib said, the U.S. negotiators would be glad to provide any further desired explanations.

5. Turning to the subject of pre-trial custody, Mr. Habib declared that the proposals made by the Korean negotiators at the 70th negotiating meeting had brought the two sides closer to agreement on this portion of the Criminal Jurisdiction Article. In response to those proposals, the U.S. negotiators now wished to table a revised Paragraph 5 which is responsive to the Korean views. They hoped that this revised draft will result in full agreement on this question.

0069

6. Mr. Habib noted that the subparagraph (c) proposed by the Korean negotiators, which provides that the U.S. military authorities will promptly notify the Korean authorities of the arrest of personnel of the U.S. armed forces in any case in which the Republic of Korea has primary jurisdiction, had been incorporated verbatim as an additional sentence in subparagraph (b) of the U.S. draft. The Korean negotiators had pointed out that the first sentence of Paragraph 5(b) stipulates the obligation of the Korean authorities to notify the U.S. military authorities of the arrest of U.S. personnel. They believed, therefore, that there should be a reciprocal obligation on the part of the U.S. authorities. The U.S. negotiators agreed with this position and had incorporated the proposed Korean language into the U.S. draft.

7. Mr. Habib noted that the Korean negotiators had urged several times that language be included in the Article which would provide for sympathetic consideration by the U.S. military authorities of requests by the Korean authorities for transfer of custody in specific cases. The U.S. negotiators now accepted this proposals to provide the languages desired by the Korean negotiators, and an additional sentence was now included in subparagraph (c) of the U.S. draft. This sentence provides that the U.S. military authorities will give sympathetic consideration to any request for transfer of custody which may be made by the Korean authorities in specific cases. Mr. Habib noted that the last two sentences of subparagraph (c) are also similar to the last two sentences of subparagraph (b) of the Korean draft, tabled at the 70th negotiating meeting.

0070

8. Mr. Habib said that the U.S. negotiators were prepared to incorporate verbatim subparagraph (e) of the Korean draft as subparagraph (d) in the U.S. draft, provided that the Korean negotiators would accept the two understandings tabled by the U.S. negotiators at the 58th meeting. These proposed understandings were as follows:

a. There must be mutual U.S.-ROK agreement as to the circumstances in which such custody is appropriate;

b. Korean confinement facilities must be adequate by U.S. standards.

Noting that the U.S. armed forces are in Korea to help protect and preserve the security of the Republic, Mr. Habib stated that the U.S. negotiators had the obligation to protect the legitimate rights of American military personnel. Therefore, there should be mutual agreement as to the circumstances in which such custody is appropriate. It is obvious, he continued, that before this subparagraph can be effective, there must be agreement between the two sides. Otherwise, the subparagraph has no meaning.

9. Mr. Habib then took up the question of duty certificates. On this subject, he noted, the two sides are not far apart. The U.S. negotiators were proposing several changes in the U.S. position which should expedite full agreement on Paragraph 3 and the Agreed Minute Re Paragraph 3(a).

10. The Korean negotiators had tabled language at the 70th meeting, Mr. Habib recalled, which provided that the duty certificate should be issued by a Staff Judge Advocate. The U.S. negotiators agreed that a Staff Judge Advocate would usually be in the best position to avoid legal

0071

problems which could follow errors in issuing duty
certificates. However, such an officer, regardless of his
technical qualifications, is not in a position of command
and does not have command responsibilities. In order to
be responsive to the Korean viewpoint and to assure the
Korean negotiators that the Staff Judge Advocate will be
consulted with regard to duty certificates, the U.S.
negotiators wished to make a proposal. If the Korean
negotiators would accept the provision in the U.S. draft
that the duty certificate will be issued by "competent authorities" of the U.S. armed forces, the U.S. negotiators will
agree to the inclusion of the following understanding in
the Agreed Joint Summary:

"A duty certificate will be issued only upon the
advice of a Staff Judge Advocate."

11. Mr. Habib stated that the U.S. negotiators were
puzzled by the substitution in the Korean draft of the
phrase "Chief District Prosecutor" for the previously
used phrase "Chief Prosecutor". The U.S. negotiators
agreed that the district prosecutors undoubtedly would make
recommendations to the Chief Prosecutor. However, the
U.S. negotiators believed that it would be quite improper
for the District Prosecutors to initiate discussions directly
with U.S. diplomatic officials regarding duty certificates.
This should be done only by the Chief Prosecutor in Seoul.
The U.S. draft provides that the Chief Prosecutor may raise
the issue with U.S. diplomatic officials when he considers
that there is proof contrary to a duty certificate. Whether
or not he does raise the issue is up to him. Therefore,
the word "may" is preferable to the word "shall". The

0072

initiative would still lie with the ROK Government to
raise the issue at the diplomatic level if it thought it
necessary.

12. Mr. Habib recalled that the Korean negotiators, at
the 70th negotiating session, had proposed the addition of
a second sentence to the first of two understandings
originally proposed by the U.S. negotiators regarding the
issuance of duty certificates. Under the provisions of
Agreed Minute #2 Re Paragraph 3(a) of the U.S. draft,
the U.S. authorities will give consideration to any points
raised by the ROK Chief Prosecutor. To make this point
clear in the first agreed understanding, the U.S. negotiators
wished to propose modification of the understanding by adding
a phrase to the version originally suggested by them.
The modified understanding would then read as follows:

"a. The certificate will be conclusive unless
modification is agreed upon under procedures outlined
in Agreed Minute No.2 Re Paragraph 3(a)."

13. Mr. Habib recalled that the Korean negotiators,
at the 47th negotiating meeting, had stated that if the
definition of official duty based on that contained in
the U.S. Army, Far East, Circular of January 1956 were read
into the Agreed Joint Summary, existing differences over the
language of the Agreed Minute #2 Re Paragraph 3(a) could be
resolved on the basis of the U.S. draft. This definition
of official duty, which clearly spells out that a substantial
departure from the acts a person is required to perform in
a particular duty usually will indicate an act outside of
"official duty", was tabled at the 49th meeting. A modified
version of this definition was tabled by the Korean negotiators
at the 70th meeting as Agreed Minute #2 Re Paragraph 3(a)(ii).

0073

The U.S. negotiators remain willing to agree to the original Korean proposal, Mr. Habib continued, that the U.S. Army definition, as tabled at the 49th meeting, be incorporated into the Agreed Joint Summary when agreement is reached on the duty certificate issue.

14. Mr. Habib said that the U.S. negotiators were prepared to discuss a few additional issues in connection with the Criminal Jurisdiction Article but would reserve such discussion until a later meeting.

15. Mr. Chang expressed the appreciation of the Korean negotiators for the tabling by the U.S. negotiators of revisions of certain portions of the Criminal Jurisdiction Article. He said that Korean negotiators would carefully consider the proposed revisions and would respond at a later meeting.

16. It was agreed to hold the 75th meeting on April 27 to discuss the Labor Article and the 76th meeting on April 28 to discuss the Criminal Jurisdiction Article.

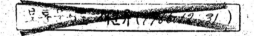

0074

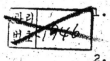

1. Time and Place: 3:30-4:30 P.M., April 28, 1965 at
                     the Foreign Ministry's Conference
                     Room (NO.1)

2. Attendance:

ROK Side:

Mr.	Chang, Sang Moon	Director European and American Affairs Bureau
Mr.	Huh, Sung Joon	Director Labor Administration Bureau Office of Labor Affairs
Mr.	Lee, Nam Ki	Chief America Section Ministry of Foreign Affairs
Maj.	Lee, Kye Hoon	Military Affairs Section Ministry of National Defense
Mr.	Kim, Kee Joe	3rd Secretary Ministry of Foreign Affairs
Mr.	Lee, Keun Pal (Interpreter)	3rd Secretary Ministry of Foreign Affairs
Mr.	Hwang, Young Jae	3rd Secretary Ministry of Foreign Affairs
Mr.	Park, Won Chul	3rd Secretary Ministry of Foreign Affairs

U.S. Side:

Mr.	Philip C. Habib	Counselor American Embassy
Brig. Gen.	Carroll H. Dunn	Deputy Chief of Staff 8th U.S. Army
Col.	Allan G. Pixton	Deputy Chief of Staff 8th U.S. Army
Capt.	George Hagerman	Assistant Chief of Staff USN/K
Col.	Kenneth C. Crawford	Staff Judge Advocate 8th U.S. Army
Mr.	Frank R. LaMacchia	First Secretary American Embassy
Mr.	Benjamin A. Fleck	First Secretary American Embassy
Mr.	Robert A. Kinney	J-5 8th U.S. Army
Mr.	Goodwin Shapiro	Second Secretary American Embassy
Maj.	Alton H. Harvey	Staff Judge Advocate's Office 8th U.S. Army
Mr.	David Y.C. Lee (Interpreter)	Second Secretary American Embassy
Mr.	Ogden C. Reed (Observer)	Civilian Personnel Director 8th U.S. Army
Mr.	G. W. Flowers (Observer)	8th U.S. Army

0075

Labor Article

1. Mr. Chang opened the meeting by stating that the Korean negotiators, as they had promised at the 73rd negotiating session, had carefully considered the revised draft of the Labor Article tabled by the U.S. negotiators at that meeting. They would now table a revised draft of the entire article, in which the underlining indicates modifications of the draft which they had tabled at the 69th session. Mr. Chang said he would discuss the new revised draft on a paragraph by paragraph basis.

2. Paragraph 1 - Mr. Chang said the Korean negotiators accepted the U.S. formula for defining an "employer", except as regards invited contractors. The Korean negotiators continued to maintain their position that invited contractors should be subject to Korean laws with regard to local employment relations and, therefore, they should be excluded from the provisions of this Article.

3. With regard to the definition of an "employee", Mr. Chang continued, the Korean negotiators similarly had modified the language of their draft, taking into account the U.S. suggestion of excluding members of the civilian component. They believed that it is unnecessary to mention domestics in this paragraph because domestics are not covered by Korean labor legislation (e.g. Article 10, Labor Standards Law). The Korean negotiators believed that members of the Korean Service Corps should be considered as employees coming under the provisions of this Article. KSC personnel have been recruited from the free labor market as manual laborers serving for the U.S. Army since September, 1955, said Mr. Chang.

4. Referring to Agreed Minute #1, Mr. Chang said that the Korean negotiators consider that its provisions are already covered in Paragraph 2 of the Article. Under the terms of Paragraph 2, the ROK Government, as it has done

0076

in the past, will make available, on the request of the
U.S. armed forces, Korean personnel not only for the
Korean Service Corps but also for any employment, insofar
as possible, to meet the requirements of the U.S. armed forces.

5. _Paragraph 3 and Agreed Minute #4_ - Mr. Chang
said that the Korean negotiators had made some self-explanatory
modifications of the language in Paragraph 3 to satisfy the
needs of the U.S. negotiators. There had also been some
changes in Agreed Minute #4. The Korean negotiators believe
it is reasonable to provide that any deviation from Korean
law shall be referred to the Joint Committee in advance for
mutual agreement. In this regard, the Korean negotiators
recalled that the U.S. negotiators had in mind deviation
from Korean law during times of emergency. In order to
cover such situations, the Korean negotiators had drafted
a new Paragraph #5, which they would explain shortly.
They did not foresee any difficulty on the part of the
U.S. authorities in referring in advance any deviation
from Korean law to the Joint Committee for mutual agreement.

6. _Paragraph 4_ - Mr. Chang said the Korean revised
draft had deleted subparagraph (a) of the U.S. draft,
regarding the resolution of employee grievances, for such
provisions are fully described in Korean legislation.
Also, the Korean negotiators could not accept the U.S.
versions of subparagraphs (b) and (c) because the employees'
rights of union organization and consultation are provided
for to a satisfactory extent in Korean labor legislation.
Also, in a sense, any formula of recognizing the organization
of labor unions is against the spirit of Korean labor legislation.

7. Regarding the issue of settlement of disputes,
Mr. Chang said that the Korean negotiators had made a
significant concession by providing in subparagraph (a)(4)

0077

of Paragraph 4 that the cooling-off period shall begin
after the dispute is referred to the second stage, i.e.
the specially-designated committee. This implies, he
continued, prolongation by many more days of the prohibition
against disruptive practices by the employees. The Korean
negotiators believed this formula would satisfy the U.S. desires.

8. Mr. Chang said the Korean negotiators had drawn
up a new formula with regard to the right to strike.
This was contained in subparagraph (b) of Paragraph 4,
which would provide that the right to strike shall be accorded
to employees except those whose exercise of this right is
prohibited by the Joint Committee. There had been a
great many deliberations on the right to strike and now
the Korean negotiators were proposing to settle the matter
by providing in their draft that the Joint Committee
would resolve the question. (The U.S. negotiators had held the
position that certain employees should not exercise the right
to strike. The Korean negotiators agree that there would
be some employees of the U.S. armed forces who should not
exercise that right. Therefore, Mr. Chang said, the Korean
negotiators were proposing that the Joint Committee designate
such persons.)

9. _Paragraph 5_ - Mr. Chang said that the Korean
negotiators, taking into account the worries of the U.S.
negotiators concerning deviation from Korean law during
times of emergency, had introduced a new paragraph which
would provide that the application of the Labor Article
may be suspended, in whole or in part, in accordance with the
extent promulgated in the emergency measures taken by the
Government of the Republic of Korea. The Korean negotiators
believed that this formula would relieve the worries of the
U.S. negotiators and that they would accept Paragraph 3

0078

and Agreed Minute #4 of the Korean draft without any
objection.

10. Mr. Chang said the Korean negotiators had no
problems with regard to subparagraph (a) of Paragraph 5
of the U.S. draft. In subparagraph (b), the Korean
negotiators had inserted the words "through mutual
agreement" in order to clarify the points agreed upon at the
previous meeting.

11. Mr. Chang said that the Korean negotiators'
final comments were directed toward the second sentence of
Agreed Minute #3 of the U.S. draft. The U.S. negotiators
held the view that nowhere in the Article is there provision
for the right of employers to terminate employment of
employees. The Korean negotiators wished to call the
attention of the U.S. negotiators to the first sentence of
Paragraph 2, which reads: "Employers may recruit, employ
and administer their personnel". The Korean negotiators
understand that the word "administer" indicates the stages
of personnel administration from hire to fire, as explained
by the U.S. negotiators at the 65th meeting. The U.S.
authorities would have the right to terminate employment
under the provisions of Paragraph 2, when, under the provisions
of Paragraph 3, there were justifiable reasons. If the
U.S. negotiators insist on the inclusion of the second
sentence of Agreed Minute #3, then many more rights of employers
in the field of personnel administration should be
specifically spelled out in the Article. For that reason,
the Korean negotiators maintain that this provision is
unnecessary.

12. Mr. Habib stated that the U.S. negotiators would
reserve discussion of the revised Korean draft of the
Labor Article until the next meeting.

0079

Criminal Jurisdiction Article

13. Turning to the Criminal Jurisdiction Article, Mr. Chang stated that the draft tabled by the U.S. negotiators at the previous meeting, which included the so-called German NATO waiver formula, was being given the most careful consideration by the Korean negotiators and competent ROK authorities. The Korean negotiators, therefore, would respond to the U.S. negotiators' presentation at a later meeting. Meanwhile, the Korean negotiators wished to seek clarification of a few points with regard to the U.S. draft.

14. First, with regard to the provisions of Paragraph 3 and 4, the Korean negotiators wished clarification of the phrase "major interests of Korean administration of justice make imperative the exercise of Korean jurisdiction". Specifically, they wished to know if this phrase had the same meaning as the phrase in the Korean draft that "it is of particular importance that jurisdiction be exercised by the authorities of the Republic of Korea".

15. The Korean negotiators would also like to know, Mr. Chang continued, whether, whenever the Korean authorities consider that in a specific case major interests of Korean administration of justice make imperative the exercise of Korean jurisdiction, that particular case can be recalled automatically, regardless of whether or not an understanding is reached between the Korean and American authorities. Does the initiative and discretion whether or not to recall waiver rest with the Korean authorities when they consider it to be necessary?

16. Mr. Habib replied that the answer to the second question was yes. The discretion whether or not to recall waiver would rest with the Korean authorities. However, he pointed out, the language of the U.S. draft illustrates and is responsive to the statement of the

0080

Korean negotiators that they would waive in as many cases as other countries do under their very simple waiver provisions. There is no automaticity involved in the process provided for in the U.S. draft. The right of recall of waiver is granted to the Government of the Republic of Korea. However, discussion between the Korean authorities and the U.S. authorities is provided for. Moreover, the illustrative list of offenses is further intended to emphasize the restraint which the U.S. negotiators have been told that the Korean authorities would exercise. The list of offenses is illustrative; it is not intended to provide for automatic recall of waiver in every case involving an offense included in the list.

17. In response to the first question asked by the Korean negotiators, Mr. Habib said that the U.S. negotiators hoped that what the Korean negotiators had in mind when they drafted the phrase "it is of particular importance that jurisdiction be exercised" was the same as what the U.S. negotiators had in mind in proposing the phrase "major interests of Korean administration of justice make imperative the exercise of Korean jurisdiction". The U.S. negotiators believe, however, that the language in the U.S. draft was a more specific response to the Korean intent. The U.S. negotiators assumed that if the Korean authorities indicated a desire to exercise jurisdiction, there would be discussion, including consideration of why it was necessary to recall the waiver in that particular case. To put it another way, the right of recall is granted; the circumstances of recall can be the subject of discussion. The U.S. negotiators expect that the Korean authorities would use restraint in the recall of waivers which would be fully consistent with the spirit expressed by the Korean negotiators.

18. Mr. Ho said the Korean negotiators wished to know whether the provisions of Paragraph 3(a) of the Agreed Minute Re Paragraph 3(b) would permit the Korean authorities to exercise jurisdiction over offenses other than those enumerated in subparagraphs (i)(ii), and (iii) of Paragraph 3(a) of that Agreed Minute. Mr. Habib replied that the language of the U.S. draft would permit the Korean authorities to exercise jurisdiction over cases involving offenses not listed specifically, provided the Korean authorities could show that it was imperative that Korean jurisdiction be exercised. The words "in particular" in the U.S. draft did not mean "exclusively" and the list is intended to be illustrative, not definitive.

19. With regard to the U.S. proposal on duty certificates, Mr. Ho asked the U.S. negotiators to specify the categories of U.S. authorities who would be included in the phrase "competent authorities of the U.S. armed forces". In particular, they wished to know whether the phrase should be construed to include the commanding officer of a company -size unit. In reply, Colonel Crawford explained that the U.S. proposal envisaged that a Staff Judge Advocate would be consulted in each case before a duty certificate was issued, but the certificate would be issued by an officer with command responsibility. Staff Judge Advocates have no command responsibility but they do have the legal expertise and experience needed to insure the legal soundness of actions taken by commanding officers. Since there are only five Staff Judge Advocates assigned to the U.S. armed forces in Korea and since the lowest-ranking one is assigned at the division level, issuence of duty certificates would take place at the division level or higher and the lowest-ranking competent authority issuing a duty certificate would be Brigadier General.

20. It was agreed to hold the next meeting on April 30.

0082

JOINT SUMMARU RECORD OF THE 76TH SESSION

1. Time and Place: 2:30-4:00 P.M., April 30, 1965 at the
Foreign Ministry's Conference Room(No.1).

2. Attendance:

ROK Side:

Mr.	Chang, Sang Moon	Director European and American Affairs Bureau
Mr.	Choo Moon Ki	Chief Legal Affairs Section Ministry of Justice
Maj.	Lee Kye Hoon	Military Affairs Section Ministry of National Defense
Mr.	Kim, Kee Joe	3rd Secretary Ministry of Foreign Affairs
Mr.	Lee, Keun Pal (Interpreter)	3rd Secretary Ministry of Foreign Affairs
Mr.	Hwang, Young Jae	3rd Secretary Ministry of Foreign Affairs
Mr.	Park, Won Chul	3rd Secretary Ministry of Foreign Affairs

U.S. Side:

Mr.	Philip C. Habib	Counselor American Embassy
Brig. Gen.	Carroll H. Dunn	Deputy Chief of Staff 8th U.S. Army
Col.	Allan G. Pixton	Deputy Chief of Staff 8th U.S. Army
Capt.	George Hagerman	Assistant Chief of Staff USN/K
Col.	Kenneth C. Crawford	Staff Judge Advocate 8th U.S. Army
Mr.	Benjamin A. Fleck	First Secretary American Embassy
Mr.	Robert A. Kinney	J-5 8th U.S. Army
Maj.	Alton H. Harvey	Staff Judge Advocate's Office 8th U.S. Army
Mr.	David Y.C. Lee (Interpreter)	Second Secretary American Embassy
Mr.	Lt. Col. Charles M. Thompson (Observer)	Claims Service 8th U.S. Army

0083

CLAIMS ARTICLE

1. Mr. Habib opened the meeting by stating that the
U.S. negotiators had given careful consideration to the
points raised by the Korean negotiators at previous sessions
regarding the Claims Article. The U.S. negotiators believed
that the point had now been reached where a solution of the
problem must be found. Not only should that solution be
satisfactory to both sides, but it must provide for an
equitable and timely settlement of all justified claims.
In an effort to expedite agreement on this article, the
U.S. negotiators were now prepared to accept the Korean
draft, subject to some important modifications which
would be explained.

2. In order to make the terminology of this article
consistent with that of other articles of the Agreement,
Mr. Habib continued, the U.S. negotiators wished to propose
some minor changes in language. These would not affect the
meaning of the article. They would apply throughout the
article, wherever appropriate, as follows:

a. Change "armed services" to armed forces"
(Paragraphs 1, 4, 5(e)(ii);

b. Change "execution of its official duty" to
"performance of his official duties" (Paragraph 1(a);

c. Change "in the execution of its official duty"
to "for official purposes" (Paragraph 1(b));

d. Change "counter-measures" to "counter-claims"
(Paragraph 2(a)).

3. Mr. Habib noted that Paragraph 2(a) pertains to claims
for damage to property owned by either government other than
that to which Paragraph 1 applies.
The U.S. negotiators proposed the deletion of the phrase
"and located in the Republic of Korea". The forces of the
United States and the Republic of Korea are jointly present

0084.

in foreign countries and also on the high seas. Therefore, the U.S. negotiators believe that it would be mutually advantageous to make the terms of the paragraph applicable on a world-wide basis. With this modification, Paragraph 2(a) of the Korean draft would be acceptable to the U.S. negotiators.

4. Mr. Habib noted that Paragraph 2(f) would provide for the waiver of government claims, other than those covered by the provisions of Paragraph 1, up to $800.00 or Won 104,000. Through long experience, the U.S. authorities have found this amount to be too small. Therefore, the U.S. negotiators proposed that this paragraph be re-written as follows:

> "2(f). Each party waives its claim in any such case up to the amount of 1,400 United States dollars or its equivalent in Korean currency at the rate of exchange provided for in the Agreed Minute to Article ------ at the time the claim is filed."

5. Mr. Habib noted that Paragraph 5(e)(i) of the Korean draft deals with the proportionate cost in satisfying claims. The U.S. negotiators proposed that the amounts be changed to provide for the standard distribution of 25% chargeable to the host nation and 75% chargeable to the visiting nation.

6. Mr. Habib noted that Paragraph 5(e)(iii) provides for reimbursement of the Republic of Korea for claims settled. The U.S. negotiators wished to change the language of the Korean draft by inserting the words "liability, amount and " before the words "proposed distribution" and by deleting the word "accepted" and inserting in its place the words "approved by the United States." The subparagraph would then read as follows:

> "5(e)(iii). Every half year, a statement of the sums paid by the Republic of Korea in the course of the half-yearly period in respect of every case regarding which the liability, amount, and proposed distribution on a percentage basis have been approved by the United States shall be sent to the appropriate authorities of

한·미국 간의 상호방위조약 제4조에 의한 시설과 구역 및 한국에서의 미국군대의 지위에 관한 협정(SOFA) 전59권. 1966.7.9 서울에서 서명 : 1967.2.9 발효(조약 232호) (V.52 실무교섭회의 합의의사록, 제69-82차, 1965-66) 477

the United States, together with a request for reimbursement. Such reimbursement shall be made in won within the shortest possible time."

7. Mr. Habib noted that the Korean draft of the Paragraph 5(e)(iii) would require mutual agreement only on the distribution. At the 61st and 62nd negotiating sessions, the U.S. negotiators had pointed out that the actual practice under the SOFA with Japan is to obtain mutual agreement as to liability, amount and proposed distribution. As the U.S. negotiators had explained at that time, no claims has been paid in Japan unless approval of the U.S. authorities was obtained. This practice allows each side to determine liability and propriety of the award prior to settlement. Thereafter, mutual agreement is reached. The U.S. negotiators consider this a good system and one that fulfills the requirements of each country. It should be affirmatively stated in the text of the article. Therefore, the U.S. negotiators were proposing the modifications in the text of this subparagraph which they had just tabled.

8. With regard to Paragraph 5(f) of the Korean draft, Mr. Habib continued, the U.S. negotiators proposed the substitution of the word "including" for the word "excluding". This change is designed to accomplish two objectives. First, it would make the language of the subparagraph consistent with the rest of the article. Secondly, it would protect a Korean employee of the U.S. armed forces from becoming the subject of a civil action when he is already subject to claims pursuant to this paragraph. Therefore, the change propsed by the U.S. negotiators is designed to meet the requirements of consistency and fairness.

9. With regard to Paragraph 9(a) of the Korean draft, the U.S. negotiators believe that it would be preferable to

0086

state specifically the basis for an authorized claim
of immunity from the civil jurisdiction of the courts
of the Republic of Korea. The exceptions allowed in the
modification proposed by the U.S. negotiators would permit
a claim of immunity if the matter arose from the
performance of official duty or if there has been full
satisfaction of the claim in question. The U.S. negotiators
believe this to be consistent with the intent of the
Korean draft and urge, therefore, that the paragraph be
modified as follows:

> "9(a). The United States shall not claim
>
> immunity from the jurisdiction of the courts of the
> Republic of Korea for members or employees of the
> United States armed forces in respect of the civil
> jurisdiction of the courts of the Republic of Korea
> except in respect of proceedings for the enforcement
> of any judgment given against them in the Republic
> of Korea in a matter arising from the performance
> of their official duties or except after payment in
> full satisfaction of claim."

10. Mr. Habib noted that Paragraph 9(b) of the Korean
draft would require U.S. authorities to "possess and turn
over" personal movable property subject to compulsory
execution under Korean law and located within United States
facilities and areas. The Korean negotiators were aware,
Mr. Habib continued, that provisions of the United States
Constitution and laws restrict the power of the military
commanders over personal property. At the same time, the
U.S. authorities wished to be of maximum assistance to the
Korean authorities in this regard. Therefore, they proposed
that Paragraph 6(b) of the U.S. draft, which covers the
same subject matter, be substituted for Paragraph 9(b)
of the Korean draft. The U.S. negotiators wished to assure
the Korean negotiators that U.S. authorities would render
all possible assistance to the Korean courts.

11. Mr. Habib then turned to Paragraph 9(c) of the
Korean draft, dealing with U.S. and Korean cooperation

한·미국 간의 상호방위조약 제4조에 의한 시설과 구역 및 한국에서의 미국군대의 지위에 관한 협정(SOFA) 479
전59권. 1966.7.9 서울에서 서명 : 1967.2.9 발효(조약 232호) (V.52 실무교섭회의 합의의사록, 제69-82차, 1965-66)

in the procurement of evidence. The Korean draft implies that a hearing must be held in every case. The United States authorities have every intention of cooperating in procuring any necessary evidence but the U.S. negotiators doubted that the Korean negotiators were proposing that a hearing would be required in the disposition of every claim under this article. Therefore, the U.S. negotiators proposed that Paragraph 7 of the U.S. draft be substituted for Paragraph 9(c) of the Korean draft. This paragraph would provide for mutual cooperation in the procurement of evidence for fair disposition of a claim, regardless of whether a hearing, or some other procedure, is utilized. The U.S. negotiators believed that this would eliminate any possibility of misinterpretation while still meeting the requirements of the Korean negotiators.

12. Mr. Habib said the U.S. negotiators wished to propose that Paragraph 10 of the U.S. draft be incorporated into the Korean draft as a new Paragraph 12. This paragraph would make clear the status of KATUSA and KSC personnel for claims purposes. This subject had been discussed at length; the U.S. negotiators wished to point out that it provides for nothing more than a continuation of the present practices and policies. These individuals do generate claims. It is essential and only common sense to clarify in this article their status with respect to these claims.

13. Mr. Habib pointed out that the Korean draft contains no provision establishing liability for prior claims. To ensure that all parties understand what claims fall within the scope of the agreement, this article should clearly spell out the fact that it does not apply to claims which arise before the Agreement comes into force. Therefore, the U.S. negotiators wished to propose a new Paragraph 13, reading as follows:

0088

"13. The provisions of this Article shall not apply to any claims which arose before the entry into force of this Agreement."

14. Mr. Habib said that he had now come to the most important question of when the responsibility for settlement of claims would be transferred to the authorities of the Republic of Korea. The U.S. negotiators believe that the present claims system has been performing this task in an efficient and timely fashion, with equitable awards made for all justified claims. As the Korean negotiators know, the U.S. authorities are deeply concerned with their obligation to settle these claims equitably and speedily. The U.S. negotiators, in previous meetings, have questioned the capability of the recently established Korean Claims Service to assume this task without an extended period for expansion and training of new employees. At previous meetings, the Korean negotiators had consistently maintained that the task could be efficiently accomplished "with some enlargement and improvement of the present Korean system". In response to the Korean position, the U.S. negotiators were now prepared to make a major concession by tabling a new Agreed Minute to replace those previously tabled by the Korean negotiators. This Agreed Minute would read as follows:

<u>Agreed Minute</u>

A. Unless otherwise provided,

1. The provisions of paragraphs five, six, seven and eight of this article will become effective six months from the date of entry into force of this agreement as to claims arising from incidents in the Seoul Special City area.

2. The provisions of paragraphs five, six, seven and eight will be progressively extended to other areas of Korea as determined and defined by the Joint Committee.

B. Until such time as the provisions of paragraphs five, six, seven and eight become effective in any given area

1. The United States shall process and settled claims (other than contractual claims) arising out of the acts or omissions of members or employees of the United States armed

0089

forces done in the performance of official duty or out of any other act, omission or occurence for which the United States armed forces are legally responsible, which cause damage in the Republic of Korea to parties other than the two governments;

2. The United States shall entertain other noncontractual claims against members or employees of the armed forces and may offer an ex gratia payment in such cases and in such amount as is determined by the appropriate United States authorities; and

3. Each party shall have the right to determine whether a member or employee of its armed forces was engaged in the performance of official duties and whether property owned by it was being used by its armed forces for official purposes.

C. For the purposes of subparagraph 2(d), subparagraph 5(e) shall be effective throughout Korea from the date of entry into force of this agreement.

15. Mr. Habib stated that Paragraph A1 of the proposed Agreed Minute would provide for transfer of claims settlement within the Seoul Special City area to the Korean Claims Service six months after the effective date of the Agreement. Approximately, 20% to 25% of the claims currently processed by the U.S. Claims Service arise in the Seoul Special City area. The extension of this responsibility to the Korean Claims Service in other areas would then depend upon the effectiveness of the Service in processing claims in the Seoul Special City Area. At previous sessions, the Korean negotiators had asserted that the Korean Claims Service would overcome the problems envisaged by the U.S. negotiators without difficulty. If this proved correct, the extension of Korean Claims Service jurisdiction to other areas would take place at an early date. The U.S. negotiators wished to assure the Korean negotiators that the U.S. authorities would agree to transfer claims settlement authority as soon as the capability of the Korean Claims Service was demonstrated to the satisfaction of the Joint Committee.

16. Mr. Habib noted that Paragraph B of the Agreed Minute pertains to claims arising prior to the time

0090

the settlement authority is transferred to the Korean Claims Service in the particular area concerned. Paragraph C covers "other government claims", which will be settled in accordance with Paragraph 2 of the Article, which will come into effect immediately when the Agreement becomes effective. Since Paragraph 5(e), which pertains to the proportionate shares of the cost incurred in settling these claims, is essential to the operation of Paragraph 2(d), it must also come into force as soon as the Agreement becomes operative.

17. Mr. Habib said he wished to summarize the position of the U.S. negotiators with regard to this article. At this meeting, they had presented a comprehensive proposal designed to meet the major requirements of both sides and to expedite agreement on this article. Their proposals would meet the desires expressed by the Korean negotiators to the maximum extent possible consistent with the obligations which the U.S. authorities and negotiators feel to the Korean people. The modifications proposed by the U.S. negotiators are essential. The U.S. negotiators hope that the Korean negotiators, after careful study, will accept the compromise proposal made by the U.S. negotiators.

18. Mr. Chang replied that the Korean negotiators appreciated the comprehensive nature of the U.S. proposals. They would give them careful consideration and respond at a later meeting.

19. It was agreed to hold the next meeting on May 7, 1965.

한·미국 간의 상호방위조약 제4조에 의한 시설과 구역 및 한국에서의 미국군대의 지위에 관한 협정(SOFA) 483
전59권. 1966.7.9 서울에서 서명 : 1967.2.9 발효(조약 232호) (V.52 실무교섭회의 합의의사록, 제69-82차, 1965-66)

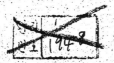

JOINT SUMMARY RECORD OF THE 77TH SESSION

1. Time and Place: 3:00-4:30 P.M., May 6, 1965 at the
   Foreign Ministry's Conference Room
   (No.1)

2. Attendance:

ROK Side:

Mr. Chang, Sang Moon	Director European and American Affairs Bureau
Mr. Lee, Nam Ki	Chief America Section Ministry of Foreign Affairs
Mr. Hur, Hyong Koo	Chief Prosecutors Section Ministry of Justice
Mr. Kim, Dong Hwi	Chief Treaty Section Ministry of Foreign Affairs
Maj. Lee, Key Hoon	Military Affairs Section Ministry of National Defense
Mr. Kim, Kee Joe	3rd Secretary Ministry of Foreign Affairs
Mr. Lee, Keun Pal (Interpreter)	3rd Secretary Ministry of Foreign Affairs
Mr. Hwang, Young Jae	3rd Secretary Ministry of Foreign Affairs
Mr. Park, Won Chul	3rd Secretary Ministry of Foreign Affairs

U.S. Side:

Mr. Philip C. Habib	Counselor American Embassy
Brig. Gen. Carroll H. Dunn	Deputy Chief of Staff 8th U.S. Army
Col. Allan G. Pixton	Deputy Chief of Staff 8th U.S. Army
Capt. George Hagerman	Assistant Chief of Staff USN/K
Col. Kenneth C. Crawford	Staff Judge Advocate 8th U.S. Army

0092

Mr. Frank R. LaMacchia	First Secretary American Embassy
Mr. Benjamin A. Fleck	First Secretary American Embassy
Mr. Robert A. Kinney	J-5 8th U.S. Army
Mr. Goodwin Shapiro	Second Secretary American Embassy
Maj. Alton H. Harvey	Staff Judge Advocate's Office 8th U.S. Army
Mr. David Y.C. Lee (Interpreter)	Second Secretary American Embassy

1. Mr. Chang opened the meeting by stating that
the Korean negotiators, together with competent authorities
of the Korean Government, had given very careful consideration to the U.S. proposals regarding the waiver formula,
duty certificates, and pre-trial custody. As the result
of this deliberation, the Korean negotiators, with a
view to reaching early agreement on this, the most
important article in the SOFA, were about to make most
significant concessions by meeting the requirement of
the U.S. and accepting in principle, with minor modifications, the drafts tabled by the U.S. negotiators at the
74th negotiating session.

2. However, Mr. Chang continued, before giving a
detailed presentation of their views, the Korean negotiators
wished to seek clarification by the U.S. negotiators
regarding the provisions of Paragraph 4 of the Agreed
Minute Re Paragraph 3(b) tabled by the U.S. negotiators.
In case the Korean Government, in resolving disagreement
in accordance with the provisions of Paragraph 4, determines
to exercise its jurisdiction, can the determination be
final and conclusive?

0093

3. Mr. Habib replied that the answer to Mr. Chang's question was yes. However, in presenting this draft, the U.S. negotiators had taken into account repeated statements by the Korean negotiators that due restraint would be observed by the Korean authorities in exercising their jurisdiction under their waiver clause when they considered that it was of particular importance that jurisdiction be exercised by the Korean authorities.

4. Mr. Chang expressed appreciation for Mr. Habib's reply. During the course of the negotiations, he said, the Korean negotiators had repeatedly stressed that under the terms of waiver discretion provided for in the original draft tabled by them, the Korean authorities would exercise utmost restraint in implementing the waiver provision. In other words, the Korean negotiators had given assurances that the Korean authorities would waive in as many cases as other countries do under their very simple status of forces agreements. However, the Korean negotiators had firmly held their position that the Korean authorities would waive except when they determined that it is of particular importance that jurisdiction be exercised by the authorities of the Republic of Korea, whereas the U.S. negotiators had held the position that the primary right to exercise jurisdiction should be waived to the U.S. authorities, with the right of recall retained by the Korean authorities.

5. Having received the affirmative answer which the U.S. negotiators had just given to the Korean negotiators' question, Mr. Chang said, the Korean negotiators were now prepared to accept the waiver formula.

0094

proposed by the U.S. side at the 74th meeting. However,
this concession by the Korean negotiators was made on
condition that the U.S. negotiators accept the following
modifications which were felt to be most essential by
the Korean negotiators.

6. Noting again the affirmative answer of the U.S.
negotiators with regard to the provisions of Paragraph 4
of the Agreed Minute Re Paragraph 3(b), and believing
that the following minor modification would be acceptable
to the U.S. negotiators, the Korean negotiators proposed
the addition of the following sentence to Paragraph 4:

"The recall of waiver shall be final and conclusive
unless the statement for recall referred to in
Paragraph 3 of this Minute is withdrawn by the
Government of the Republic of Korea through consultation between both Governments."

Mr. Chang said the Korean negotiators firmly believe the
above sentence to be absolutely necessary not only to
enable the ROK Government to obtain the understanding
of the National Assembly and the Korean people but also
for mutually satisfactory implementation of the waiver
formula.

7. Mr. Chang referred to Paragraph 1 of the Agreed
Minute Re Paragraph 3 (b) and said that the Korean
negotiators believe that the waiver of the primary right
of jurisdiction should be made following a request by the
United States. Therefore, the Korean negotiators proposed
the insertion at the beginning of the paragraph of the
phrase "At the request of the United States."

8. Mr. Habib asked for clarification of this proposal.
Did the phrase refer to a one-time request for a blanket
waiver or were the Korean negotiators proposing that the
United States authorities request waiver in each individual

0095

case? Mr. Chang replied that the Korean proposal was
that the United States authorities make a separate
request for waiver in each case.

9. Resuming his discussion of the drafts tabled
by the U.S. negotiators at the 74th meeting, Mr. Chang
turned to Paragraph 6 of the Agreed Minute Re Paragraph
3(b). He recalled that at the 67th meeting the U.S.
negotiators had tabled a revision of what was then their
Agreed Minute Re Paragraph 3. They had stated that the
second paragraph of that revision was a new paragraph
incorporated into the U.S. draft in order to include the
position set forth in the third paragraph of the Agreed
Minute Re Paragraph 3 of the Korean draft. They had
further stated that they viewed these provisions as
desirable and were pleased to be able to accede to the
wishes of the ROK Government by incorporating them into
the U.S. draft. Mr. Chang said that the Korean negotiators
were completely at a loss to understand the reasons why
the U.S. negotiators, after agreeing to the Korean
language at the 67th meeting, had now substituted a new
Paragraph 6 in place of that language. Accordingly, the
Korean negotiators, in the light of the trend of the
past negotiations, proposed that in place of the Paragraph
6 contained in the U.S. draft, the following portion of
the previous draft be adopted as Paragraph 6:

> "Trials of cases in which the authorities of
> the Republic of Korea waive the primary right
> to exercise jurisdiction, and trials of cases involving
> offenses described in Paragraph 3(a)(ii) committed
> against the state or nationals of the Republic
> of Korea shall be held promptly in the Republic
> of Korea within a reasonable distance from the place
> where the offenses are alleged to have taken place
> unless other arrangements are mutually agreed upon.
> Representatives of the Republic of Korea may be
> present at such trials.

0096

Mr. Chang said that any detailed arrangements in addition
to the above provisions should be left to deliberation
by the Joint Committee.

10. Mr. Habib replied that the new Paragraph 6,
which was based on Article 26 of the German Supplementary
Agreement, was necessary because with the tabling by
the U.S. negotiators of the German waiver formula there
now existed an entirely different basis for the exercise
of waiver.

11. Mr. Habib explained that subparagraph (a)(i)
of Paragraph 6 related to trials of transitory offenses -
offenses triable in the United States Federal Courts
regardless of where committed. Under the existing U.S.
laws, this provisions would be operative only upon
civilians, since any offense by personnel of the armed
forces may be tried by court-martial in the Republic
of Korea. The number of offenses classified as transitory
is very limited. Therefore, it is anticipated that
there would be only rare instances when this provision
would be applicable. Transitory offenses, Mr. Habib
continued, would include treason and conspiracy against
the United States. They would only involve Korean
interests in a very exceptional case. An example would
be a case in which a member of the civilian component
committed an act of treason against the United States
and in the process injured a Korean national. Jurisdiction
to try this case would rest only with a United States
Federal Court located in the United States. Such a case
would be rare and this provision, therefore, would rarely
be utilized.

한·미국 간의 상호방위조약 제4조에 의한 시설과 구역 및 한국에서의 미국군대의 지위에 관한 협정(SOFA)
전59권. 1966.7.9 서울에서 서명 : 1967.2.9 발효(조약 232호) (V.52 실무교섭회의 합의의사록, 제69-82차, 1965-66) 489

12. Explaining the terms of subparagraph (a)(ii) of Paragraph 6, Mr. Habib stated that this provision meant that in a few cases, military requirements or the necessity of assuring a fair trial might require the trial to be held elsewhere than in Korea. For example, if all the witnesses in a given case had returned to the United States, it might be necessary to try the case in the United States in order to secure testimony, for if the witnesses were civilians, the U.S. armed forces could not compel them to return to Korea to testify. Also, if a division were rotated to the United States, it might be more suitable or feasible to try the case of a member of the division in the United States. This provision, Mr. Habib explained, would cover unforeseen situations which would make the trial of a case in the Republic of Korea impractical.

13. With regard to subparagraph (b) of Paragraph 6, Mr. Habib said that the presence of a representative of the Republic of Korea would be incompatible with the rules of the court in only very rare cases. If, by chance, the representative were to be called as a witness, he might be excluded from the trial. The U.S. negotiators seriously doubted whether such a very exceptional circumstance, precluding the attendance of the ROK Government representative from the trial, would ever arise, except in cases involving security. However, it might arise; thus it must be provided for in the Agreement.

14. Mr. Habib said that to the knowledge of the U.S. negotiators, no problem had been encountered in connection with the similar provisions in the German Agreement.

0098

15. Mr. Chang thanked Mr. Habib for his thorough explanation of these provisions. He said the Korean negotiators were concerned only with crimes against Korean nationals or interests. The alternative language proposed by the Korean negotiators provided for "other arrangements". Disposition of the rare types of cases mentioned by Mr. Habib could be settled by the Joint Committee.

16. Mr. Habib replied that the U.S. draft provided for the same result, but in more exact legal terminology. The U.S. negotiators were trying to provide for every conceivable circumstance.

17. Mr. Chang said the Korean negotiators were now prepared to accept the U.S. proposals regarding official duty certificates, with the following minor conditions:

a. With regard to the question of who should be designated as issuing authorities, the Korean negotiators would accept the phrase "competent authorities of the United States armed forces", provided the U.S. negotiators would accept the following of the understanding to be included in the Agreed Joint Summary:

"A duty certificate shall be issued only upon the advice of a Staff Judge Advocate, and the competent authority issuing a duty certificate shall be a General grade officer."

b. The Korean negotiators accept the wording "the Chief Prosecutor for the Republic of Korea" as the definition of the Korean authority who will raise objection if he considers that there is proof contrary to a certificate of official duty.

0089

c. The Korean negotiators are ready to accept the definition of official duty proposed by the U.S. negotiators at the 49th meeting. However, they still believe the definition should be included in an Agreed Minute so that it would serve as a guide line for those authorities concerned in determining whether or not an offense was committed in the performance of official duty.

d. The Korean negotiators believe that if the Chief Prosecutor of the Republic of Korea raises any objection, it should be made obligatory for the authorities of both countries to review the case. Accordingly, they propose the substitution of the word "shall" for the word "may" in the last sentence of Agreed Minute #2 Re Paragraph 3(a) of the U.S. draft.

e. With regard to the understanding proposed by the U.S. negotiators regarding the validity of the duty certificate, both sides are in essential agreement as to intention. Thus the question is how to incorporate the Korean requirements into the understanding. The Korean negotiators still believe that the Korean proposal is preferable to that of the U.S. negotiators. They continue to support the following version of the understanding, the language of which is distinct and self-explanatory:

"The certificate will be conclusive unless modification is agreed upon. The United States authorities shall give due consideration to any objection which may be raised by the Chief Prosecutor for the Republic of Korea."

0100

18. Mr. Habib said that he wished to revert for a moment to the Korean proposal regarding the Paragraph 1 of the Agreed Minute Re Paragraph 3(b). Did the Korean negotiators really intend that the provision should require a U.S. request for waiver in every individual case? Mr. Chang replied that this was a correct interpretation of the Korean proposal. Mr. Habib stated that such a proposal was unacceptable to the U.S. Government.

19. Mr. Chang then referred to the reference to the notification of individual cases by the U.S. military authorities in Paragraph 2 of the Agreed Minute. If the U.S. authorities were obliged to notify the Korean authorities of the occurrence of each offense, why could they not at the same time request a waiver of the exercise of jurisdiction by the Korean authorities.?

20. Mr. Habib replied that the provisions of Paragraph 2 would impose on the U.S. authorities the obligation not to conceal offenses from the Korean authorities. To require the U.S. authorities to request a waiver in each case would completely alter the nature of the waiver formula, was in no way similar to the German waiver formula which the U.S. negotiators had proposed, and was unacceptable to the U.S. negotiators.

21. Turning to the provisions regarding pre-trial custody, Mr. Chang said that although there still existed substantial differences between the two drafts, the Korean negotiators, with a view to expediting the negotiations and in order to be responsive to the U.S. requirements, were now prepared to accept the U.S. draft. However, in order to be consistent with the basic needs of the Korean negotiators, they proposed that the following minor modifications be incorporated into the U.S. draft:

0101

a. The words "the authorities of the United
States" should read "the military authorities of
the United States", pending final agreement on the
definition of authorities of both sides exercising
jurisdiction in the provisions of Paragraph 1 of
the Article.

b. It has been the firm position of the Korean
negotiators that an accused, if he is in the hands
of the authorities of the Republic of Korea, will be
handed over to the military authorities of the United
States, if the latter so request and unless there
is adequate cause or necessity to retain him.
Nevertheless, in order to reach prompt and final
agreement, the Korean negotiators are prepared
to make one of their major concessions by accepting
the U.S. draft, provided that the U.S. authorities
take full account of any special request for transfer
of custody which may be made by the Korean authorities.
The Korean negotiators propose that the words "on
request" be inserted between the words "shall" and
"be" in the second sentence of subparagraph (c).
They also propose the insertion in the third sentence
of the wording "They shall take full account of any
special request regarding custody made by the
authorities of the Republic of Korea." The Korean
negotiators also propose that the U.S. military
authorities exert their best efforts to maintain
custody and to prevent any prejudice against the
course of criminal proceedings, such as the destruction of valuable evidence or the escape of an accused
from confinement. Of course, the U.S. negotiators

0102

may, if and whenever they so desire, transfer the custody of an accused to the Korean authorities.

    c. With regard to the custody of an accused in the hands of the Korean authorities in connection with security offenses, the Korean negotiators accept the following two understandings proposed by the U.S. negotiators for inclusion in the Agreed Joint Summary:

    (1) There must be mutual ROK-US agreement as to the circumstances in which such custody is appropriate;

    (2) Korean confinement facilities must be adequate by U.S. standards.

22. Mr. Chang summarized his presentation by stating that, as he had said in the beginning, the Korean negotiators, in order to meet the requirements of the U.S. negotiators and at the same time to be consistent with the minimum needs of the Korean Government, were accepting the U.S. proposals with minor modifications which they hoped the U.S. negotiators would accept. Moreover, the Korean negotiators, believing that any further delay in the conclusion of the negotiations would be in the interest of neither the Korean side or the U.S. side, requested the U.S. negotiators to take into full account the positions outlined by the Korean negotiators and to accept them, thus paving the way for an early conclusion of the negotiations.

23. Mr. Habib replied that the U.S. negotiators would consider the Korean proposals very carefully. He believed that the negotiators were very close to agreement on these provisions of the Criminal Jurisdiction Article.

24. The next meeting was scheduled for May 7 at 3:00 p.m.

한·미국 간의 상호방위조약 제4조에 의한 시설과 구역 및 한국에서의 미국군대의 지위에 관한 협정(SOFA)
전59권. 1966.7.9 서울에서 서명 : 1967.2.9 발효(조약 232호) (V.52 실무교섭회의 합의의사록, 제69-82차, 1965-66)   495

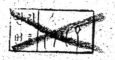

JOINT SUMMARY RECORD OF THE 78TH SESSION

1. Time and Place: 4:30-5:30 P.M., May 7, 1965 at the
    Foreign Ministry's Conference Room
    (No.1)

2. Attendance:

ROK Side:

Mr. Chang, Sang Moon	Director European and American Affairs Bureau Ministry of Foreign Affairs
Mr. Yoon, Woon Young	Director Prosecutors Bureau Ministry of Justice
Mr. Hur Hyong Koo	Chief Prosecutors Section Ministry of Justice
Mr. Lee, Nam Ai	Chief America Section Ministry of Foreign Affairs
Maj. Lee, Kye Hoon	Military Affairs Section Ministry of National Defense
Mr. Kim, Kee Joe	3rd Secretary Ministry of Foreign Affairs
Mr. Lee, Keun Pal (Interpreter)	3rd Secretary Ministry of Foreign Affairs
Mr. Lee, Chung Bin	3rd Secretary Ministry of Foreign Affairs
Mr. Hwang, Young Jae	3rd Secretary Ministry of Foreign Affairs
Mr. Cho, Yong Si (Observer)	Office of Labor Affairs

U.S. Side:

Mr. Philip C. Habib	Counselor American Embassy
Brig. Gen. Carroll H. Dunn	Deputy Chief of Staff 8th U.S. Army
Col. Allan G. Pixton	Deputy Chief of Staff 8th U.S. Army
Capt. George Hagerman	Assistant Chief of Staff USN/K

0104

Col. Kenneth C. Crawford	Staff Judge Advocate 8th U.S. Army
Mr. Benjamin A. Fleck	First Secretary American Embassy
Mr. Robert A. Kinney	J-5 8th U.S. Army
Mr. Goodwin Shapiro	Second Secretary American Embassy
Maj. Alton H. Harvey	Staff Judge Advocate's Office 8th U.S. Army
Mr. David Y.C. Lee (Interpreter)	Second Secretary American Embassy
Mr. Ogden C. Reed (Observer)	Civilian Personnel Director 8th U.S. Army
Mr. G.W. Flower (Observer)	8th U.S. Army

Labor Article

1. Mr. Habib opened the meeting by stating that at
this session the U.S. negotiators wished to concentrate on
the principal remaining point at issue in the Labor Article.
There were a number of differences still unresolved but at
this meeting the U.S. negotiators wished to present their
views on the question of the status of the Korean employees
of the U.S. armed forces. The U.S. negotiators have been
seeking to establish in this Article a relationship between
the U.S. armed forces and their employees which would
support the mission of the armed forces and at the same time
safeguard the rights and privileges of their employees.
The U.S. draft of the Labor Article would protect and preserve
all of the basic rights currently enjoyed by those employees.
The principal difference between the two drafts centers
on the question of the right to strike.

0105

2. This question, Mr. Habib continued, should be viewed in connection with the disputes settlement procedures established in the U.S. draft. Through these procedures, the U.S. negotiators have sought to provide for the amicable settlement of any disputes which may arise. They would establish a consultative and conciliation process which would operate at the governmental and Joint Committee level. Provision would be made for representation of the employees through recognition of the right to organize.

3. The Korean negotiators recognize the necessity for procedures for the settlement of disputes but the Korean draft goes beyond this, Mr. Habib continued. The Korean draft contradicts the settlement procedures provided for by quoting the Korean Labor Dispute Adjustment Law, which, in effect, says that a decision of the Joint Committee would not be binding. The Korean draft also provides that employees of the U.S. armed forces shall have the right to strike. Nowhere in their draft have the Korean negotiators recognized what the U.S. negotiators have been trying to stress - that Korean employees of the U.S. armed forces are not comparable to ordinary employees of commercial enterprises.

4. Mr. Habib reiterated the position of the U.S. negotiators that the Korean employees of the U.S. armed forces have a status and importance comparable to that of employees of the Korean armed forces. The U.S. armed forces in Korea have exactly the same mission as the ROK armed forces - the defense of the Republic of Korea.

5. Mr. Habib pointed out that the paragraph in the U.S. draft dealing with strikes (Paragraph 4(e)) simply

0106

states that "an employee shall be subject to the same
legal provisions concerning strikes and other work stoppages
as an employee in a comparable position in the employment
of the armed forces of the Republic of Korea". This
provision is not only sound with respect to the mission of
the U.S. armed forces. It is also justifiable, not only
in terms of military requirements but also in comparability
with Korean procedures. Korean recognition that certain
operations require special provisions extends beyond the
armed forces, for employees of certain utilities in the
Republic of Korea do not have the right to strike. The
U.S. negotiators would also like to point out that staff
functions of certain of the Korean employees of the
U.S. armed forces serve the Korean armed forces as well as
the U.S. armed forces, particularly in the fields of supply
and transport. The U.S. negotiators do not understand why
the Korean negotiators attempt to apply different sets of
rules to employees of the U.S. armed forces and employees
of the Korean armed forces when the mission, functions,
and command of the two armed forces are identical.

6. Mr. Habib stated that the U.S. negotiators agree
with the reasoning that leads the Korean negotiators to the
conclusion that a requirement exists to restrict the rights
of Korean employees of the ROK armed forces. The U.S.
armed forces desire the same treatment, not discriminatory
treatment, so that the achievement of the mission of the
U.S. armed forces is not interfered with. The position of
the U.S. negotiators is consistent with the past and
present practice and rules of both the U.S. and ROK
governments.

0107

7. Mr. Habib pointed out that the U.S. negotiators were not attempting to deny the rights of labor to organize and to be dealt with through established procedures. They were trying to preserve rights equivalent to those held by employees of the Korean armed forces in order to permit the U.S. armed forces to fulfill their mission without unnecessary interference. The mission of the U.S. armed forces is all-important.

8. The U.S. negotiators believe that disputes should be conciliated, Mr. Habib continued. The formula contained in the U.S. draft permits the U.S. armed forces to meet their requirements and enables the Korean negotiators to justify these provisions to the Korean authorities and people. That justification is found in the phraseology which provides for resolution of the issue in the same fashion in both armed forces.

9. Mr. Habib remarked that the principal argument of the Korean negotiators has been that the right to strike exists elsewhere. This argument is not persuasive for a number of reasons. The primary mission of the U.S. armed forces in Korea is considerably different than that of such forces elsewhere. The U.S. negotiators believe that the procedures set forth in the U.S. draft will fully meet the requirements of both sides for amicable relations. For all of the reasons which he had just cited, Mr. Habib concluded, the U.S. negotiators are unable to agree to the Korean proposal to delete Paragraph 4(e) from the U.S. draft.

10. Mr. Chang replied that the Korean negotiators would consider the position stated by the U.S. negotiators and would respond at a later meeting.

0108

Criminal Jurisdiction Article

11. Turning to the Criminal Jurisdiction Article,
Mr. Chang said the Korean negotiators were waiting to hear
the views of the U.S. negotiators regarding the latest
proposals made by the Korean negotiators. In the
meantime, the Korean negotiators wished to clarify their
position and propose a minor modification of their latest
proposal. In order to eliminate possible ambiguity, they
wished to alter the sentence which they had proposed for
addition to Paragraph 4 of the Agreed Minute Re Paragraph
3(b). The phrase "through consultation between both governments" should be deleted and in its place should be added
the phrase "within a period of 21 days after such statement
for recall is made."

12. With regard to the phrase "At the request of the
United States" which they had proposed for insertion in
Paragraph 1 of the Agreed Minute Re Paragraph 3(b), Mr. Chang
said that this proposal had been made in order to meet the
basic requirements of the Korean negotiators as well as the
requirements of the U.S. negotiators. The additional phrase
was absolutely necessary to permit the ROK Government to
maintain its dignity as a sovereign government and to enable
the Korean negotiators to explain the provisions of this
Agreed Minute to the National Assembly.

13. Mr. Habib replied that the U.S. negotiators had
presented a formula which provided for the waiver of jurisdiction and the right of recall of that waiver in extremely
important cases. They were not prepared to accept any
requirement that the U.S. authorities should request waiver
in every case. The question of waiver had nothing to do with
sovereignty. The German waiver formula in operation has
not detracted from German sovereignty. It will not detract

from the sovereignty of the Republic of Korea. The formula proposed by the U.S. negotiators had been designed to meet the often-repeated indication by the Korean negotiators of the Korean requirement to exercise jurisdiction when it was imperative to do so in the interests of Korean justice. The additional phrase proposed by the Korean negotiators would completely reverse the formula proposed by the U.S. negotiators. Paragraph 4 of the proposed Agreed Minute Re Paragraph 3(b) would give the ROK Government the final determination of the exercise of jurisdiction. This is what the Korean negotiators had repeatedly said at past meetings they needed. The waiver formula was a fundamental issue. The U.S. negotiators hoped, therefore, that the Korean negotiators would reconsider their position with regard to their proposed additional phrase in Paragraph 1 of the Agreed Minute.

14. Mr. Chang again referred to the necessity of being able to explain the waiver provision to the National Assembly and reiterated the Korean position that the Korean authorities would be prepared to waive when requested to do so by the U.S. authorities. Mr. Habib reminded the Korean negotiators that not only the National Assembly but also the U.S. Congress was interested in this Agreement and would examine its provisions carefully. He pointed out to the Korean negotiators that the present U.S. draft was actually a compromise between the earlier Korean position and the earlier U.S. position. The U.S. negotiators believed it to be a workable compromise which could be satisfactorily explained to the legislatures of both countries.

0110

15. Mr. Chang then referred to Article 19 of the
German Supplementary Agreement, which begins "At the request
of the sending state,...". Mr. Habib, in reply, explained
the significance of this language in connection with the
related Agreed Minute. He explained that, in reality,
this was a provision for a blanket waiver which was made
by the German Government, insofar as the U.S. armed forces
were concerned, at the time when the German Supplementary
Agreement became operative. He assured the Korean negotiators
that the formula which the U.S. negotiators had presented
was the German waiver formula.

0111

JOINT SUMMARY RECORD OF THE 79TH SESSION

1. Time and Place: 4:00-5:30 P.M., May 12, 1965 at the
    Foreign Ministry's Conference Room
    (No.1)

2. Attendance:

ROK Side:

Mr. Chang, Sang Moon Director
 European and American Affairs
 Bureau

Mr. Kim, Dong Hwi Chief
 Treaty Section
 Ministry of Foreign Affairs

Mr. Choo, Moon Ki Chief
 Legal Affairs Section
 Ministry of Justice

Mr. Kim, Tai Chung Chief
 Labor Administration Section
 Office of Labor Affairs

Maj. Lee, Key Hoon Military Affairs Section
 Ministry of National Defense

Mr. Kim, Kee Joe 3rd Secretary
 Ministry of Foreign Affairs

Mr. Lee, Keun Pal 3rd Secretary
(Interpreter) Ministry of Foreign Affairs

Mr. Hwang, Young Jae 3rd Secretary
 Ministry of Foreign Affairs

Mr. Park, Won Chul 3rd Secretary
 Ministry of Foreign Affairs

U.S. Side:

Mr. Philip C. Habib Counselor
 American Embassy

Brig. Gen. Carroll H. Dunn Deputy Chief of Staff
 8th U.S. Army

Col. Allan G. Pixton Deputy Chief of Staff
 8th U.S. Army

Capt. George Hagerman Assistant Chief of Staff
 USN/K

Col. Kenneth C. Crawford Staff Judge Advocate
 8th U.S. Army

0112

Mr. Frank R. LaMacchia	First Secretary American Embassy
Mr. Benjamin A. Fleck	First Secretary American Embassy
Mr. Robert A. Kinney	J-5 8th U.S. Army
Mr. Goodwin Shapiro	Second Secretary American Embassy
Maj. Alton H. Harvey	Staff Judge Advocate's Office 8th U.S. Army
Mr. David Y.C. Lee	Second Secretary American Embassy
Mr. Ogden C. Reed	Civilian Personnel Director 8th U.S. Army

Labor Article

1. Mr. Chang opened the 79th meeting by indicating that the Korean negotiators have carefully reviewed the position taken by the U.S. negotiators at the 78th session in order to pave a way for resolving the stalemate, with a view to concluding the SOFA negotiations as early as possible. To this end, intensive consultation has taken place among the responsible authorities of the Korean Government with respect to the labor problem. As a result of this consultation, the new ROK proposal is ready to present. This proposal is honest evidence of Korean side's desire to make a significant concession with regard to the Labor Article.

2. Prior to explaining the new proposal, Mr. Chang stated that the Korean negotiators would like to make two principles clear to the U.S. negotiators. First, the two sides are now negotiating to decide the status of Korean laborers working for the United States armed forces. Such laborers should not be considered either as Korean

0113

Government employees or military personnel of any state.
Secondly, since they are simple laborers working for
emoluments, their rights concerning labor relations should
be protected along the lines of established and world-wide
standards. The Korean negotiators, however, are prepared
to cooperate with the U.S. Armed Forces to enable them to
carry out our common defense mission to the maximum extent
possible on the basis of the foregoing two basic principles.
Therefore, the ROK negotiators have already agreed to
possible deviation of the U.S. armed forces from ROK
labor legislation on account of the military requirements
under normal situation as well as in time of emergency.

3. Mr. Chang stated, that, in this spirit of cooperation and with the foregoing two principles in mind, the
Korean side now wishes to make further significant
concessions relating to procedures to settle labor disputes
and concerning the exercise of the right to strike.

4. With regard to procedures to settle any labor
dispute, the ROK side proposes amendments to paragraph 4(a),
as follows:

Paragraph 4(a)

"(2) In the event that the dispute is not settled
by the procedures described in (1) above within
twenty (20) days, the dispute shall be referred
to the Joint Committee, which may refer the matter
to the Labor Sub-Committee or to a specially-
designated committee, for further conciliation
efforts."

"(4) Neither employee organizations nor employees
shall engage in any practice disruptive of normal
work requirements unless a period of seventy (70)
days has elapsed without settlement after the

0114

dispute is referred to the Office of Labor
Affairs mentioned in (1) above."

5. Mr. Chang explained that this new language provides
for a complete prohibition of disruptive practices for
a maximum period of 70 days while any dispute is referred
for settlement to the ROK Labor Office and to the Joint
Committee. This new proposal is based on the ROK belief
that there would be no dispute which could not be settled
during 70 days. Under this formula, the ROK negotiators
envisage no dispute would lead to a strike in a practical
sense, although employees would retain the ultimate, but
almost non-practical, right to strike.

6. Concerning the right to strike, Mr. Chang said
that the Korean side holds the view that there would be no
need to set forth special provisions on this right, because
the exercise of this right had heretofore been prohibited
for 70 days under the provisions of Paragraph 4(a). As
the ROK negotiators have already committed themselves at
the 75th session, they are prepared to agree with the US
side to prohibit the exercise of the right to strike by
certain categories of Korean employees working for the
US Armed Forces, when such disruptive practices would be
greatly detrimental to the military mission of the US
Armed Forces.

7. In conclusion, Mr. Chang emphasized that the
Korean negotiators believe that the foregoing proposal will
meet the requirements of the US Armed Forces, and they
hope that the US side will accept these new proposals as
a whole.

8. Mr. Habib asked to have the two principles enunciated
in paragraph 2 above repeated and then he asked if these
principles were consistent with paragraph 4(b) of the ROK

0115

draft? Mr. Chang stated that these principles are subject
to modification, and in paragraph 4(b) the ROK Government
agrees that the right to strike shall be accorded to
employees, except those whose exercise of this right is
prohibited by the Joint Committee.

9. Mr. Habib asked if these two principles are
consistent with US-ROK military requirements for the defense
of the Republic of Korea? The US has consistently maintained
the position that the US military are in Korea solely to
assist in the defense of the Republic of Korea, and that the
USFK Korean employees are a vital part of this defense.
The Korean negotiators refer to these USFK employees
as laborers, but as explained at the 72nd negotiating
session, less than 5 percent of the present USFK employees
are in the unskilled labor-pool category, while most are
skilled workers performing functions important to the
joint defense position on the US and ROK armed forces.

10. Mr. Habib emphasized that it was in the mutual interest
of our two governments to establish procedures for settling
labor disputes amicably and without adversely affecting
the defense of the Republic of Korea. That is what the
US draft is designed to accomplish. We seek non-discrimina-
tion against USFK employees. We compare the USFK employees
with ROK armed forces employees because they are similar
employees performing similar functions for similar
objectives. The US has agreed to conform to ROK labor
legislation, taking into consideration special military
requirements. We recognize the right of USFK employees to
have a union and the USFK deals with it on matters of
mutual concern. We have proposed comprehensive procedures

0116

for the amicable settlement of disputes. All the US is
asking is that the ROK Government apply the same legal
provisions in the one area of strikes and work stoppages
to USFK employees working in the defense of their country
as the ROK applies to Korean Government armed forces employees.
We do not think this position is unreasonable.

11. Mr. Chang replied that the ROK negotiators had
agreed that special conditions and procedures would be
applicable to USFK employees in the Labor Article because
of the role of such employees in the defense of the
Republic. But the ROK Government cannot agree that such
USFK employees are comparable to ROK army employees including the
civilian components (Mun-Kwan) and Government officials
or employees and it cannot agree that such employees will
be denied their constitutional rights. Mr. Chang emphasized
that, in providing for 70 days for the arbitration procedures
to operate, the Korean negotiators firmly believe that chances
of strikes would be almost non-existent in practical sense.
In the past the ROK Office of Labor Affairs has cooperated
with USFK authorities to prevent strikes and this office
will continue to do so. Furthermore, the ROK Government
has provided that the Joint Committee can establish categories
of essential employees who will be prohibited from exercising
the right to strike. Thus, although the ROK draft avoids
any particular provision which specifically denies all
USFK workers the right to strike, the ROK proposal in
effect limits the possibility of strikes to the extent
reasonable. Mr. Chang urged that the US side give careful
consideration to these Korean proposal and views.

한·미국 간의 상호방위조약 제4조에 의한 시설과 구역 및 한국에서의 미국군대의 지위에 관한 협정(SOFA)
전59권. 1966.7.9 서울에서 서명 : 1967.2.9 발효(조약 232호) (V.52 실무교섭회의 합의의사록, 제69-82차, 1965-66) 509

12. Mr. Habib answered that the Korean views would be carefully considered. He asked in turn, for the ROK Government's understanding of the role of USFK's Korean employees. The US side firmly believes that the long term interests of both the US and ROK Governments, as well as the welfare of USFK employees, requires that both sides accept the realities of their important role in the defense of the Republic of Korea.

Claims Article

13. Mr. Chang stated that the Korean negotiators have given the most careful consideration to the proposal of the United States negotiators regarding the Claims Article made at the 76th session.

14. Mr. Chang indicated that the Korean negotiators agree with the views of the United States negotiators, expressed at the previous session, that the point has now been reached where a solution of the problem with respect to this Article must be found. Accordingly, the Korean negotiators are prepared to accept the proposed changes in Korean draft as proposed by the United States side as well as the new paragraphs and Agreed Minute tabled by the United States side, subject to the following conditions and modifications as set forth below.

15. Regarding paragraph 5(e)(i), the Korean negotiators still stand on their original position that the Korean Government should share 15% of the cost of satisfying the claims for which the United States alone is responsible.

16. Regarding paragraph 5(e)(iii), Mr. Chang stated that the changes proposed by the United States negotiators are unacceptable. The proposed changes in this subparagraph

0118

directly contradict the basic principles of the claims
settlement procedures laid down by the subparagraphs (a),
(b) and (c) of paragraph 5, which the United States
negotiators have already accepted at an earlier session.
However, to accommodate the concern of the United States
side to the maximum extent practicable, the Korean
negotiators are prepared to propose the following sentences
as an Agreed Minute for paragraph 5 of this Article:

> "Regarding the claims falling under the
> provisions of paragraph five of this Article, the
> authorities of the Republic of Korea and the
> United States shall seek mutual agreement as to
> the liability for damages and compensation to be
> awarded prior to the settlement by the authorities
> of the Republic of Korea. However, any adjudication
> of the case by a competent court of the Republic of
> Korea as a result of a suit which may be instituted
> by the claimant shall be binding and conclusive upon
> the Parties of this Agreement."

17. This new Agreed Minute, the Korean negotiators
believe, would fully meet the requirements of both sides.
This system would allow each side to review the liability
and propriety of the award, and guarantee mutual agreement
between the two parties prior to the settlement by the
authorities of the Republic of Korea.

18. Regarding any case which would be decided by a
competent court, Mr. Chang emphasized that it is logical that
the judgement of such a court and payment of an award in
accordance with the judgement should be binding upon both
parties in the light of the principle agreed upon by the
provisions set forth in subparagraph 5(c).

19. Regarding paragraph 12 of the United States
draft, Mr. Chang stated that the Korean negotiators still
believe that the Korean Service Corps (KSC) employees
should be considered to be employees of the United States
armed forces for the purposes of this Article, as proposed

0119

in Agreed Minute 3 of the Korean draft. The Korean negotiators would like to point out that it is not the present practice or policy of the Korean Government, to assume responsibility for any claims which arise out of the acts or omissions of the KSC in the course of their performance of the duties which are directed by the United States armed forces.

20. Regarding paragraph 13, the Korean negotiators accept the United States proposal with the addition of a few more words which will more clearly spell out the liability for claims which arose before the Agreement comes into force. Therefore, the Korean negotiators wish to propose an additional sentence so that the revised paragraph 13 should read as follows:

"The provisions of this Article shall not apply to any claims which arose before the entry into force of this Agreement. Such claims shall be processed and settled by the authorities of the United States."

21. Regarding the Agreed Minute A2, Mr. Chang indicated that the Korean negotiators wished to clearly set forth a definite effective date of the provisions of the paragraphs covered in the Agreed Minute. Therefore, the Korean negotiators propose to modify the paragraph A2 of the proposed Agreed Minute of the United States negotiators as follows:

"As to claims arising from incidents in the other areas of the Republic of Korea, the provisions of paragraphs five, six, seven and eight of this Article will become effective twelve months from the date of entry into force of this Agreement. However, in case the authorities of the Republic of Korea are not prepared to assume the responsibility provided for in the preceding paragraphs within the twelve-month period, the authorities of the Republic of Korea may notify additional period required for the preparation to the Joint Committee for extention of the responsibility of the United States."

22. Mr. Chang stated that the Korean negotiators believe that the twelve-month period provided for in the Korean proposal is long enough to adopt the system in the other areas of the Republic of Korea. Nevertheless, the Korean negotiators would be willing to postpone the effective date of those provisions until such time as the Korean authorities are prepared to take over the claims responsibilities. This, the Korean negotiators believe, would suffice to meet the expressed concern of the United States negotiators.

23. Mr. Habib replied that the United States side would take these proposals under consideration, but that he could say right now he was sure some of the proposed ROK modifications of the Claims Article draft were not acceptable. For example, the payment of claims on a 75% - 25% has become standard for almost all such agreements and he could see no reason to make an exception in Korea.

24. Mr. Habib inquired about the meaning of the new ROK proposed Agreed Minute Re Para 5. Mr. Chang explained the new proposal was designed to respond to the U.S. requirement to the maximum extent practicable by insuring that while ROK and US authorities shall seek mutual agreement as to the liability and propriety of the award prior to the settlement by claims authorities of the Government of ROK, any adjudication by a competent ROK court shall be binding upon both parties to this agreement. Mr. Habib indicated that such language was unnecessary, for this point was covered in paragraph 5.(c). The new Agreed Minute creates a problem where none previously existed. However, deletion of the US Paragraph 5(e) (iii), as proposed by the ROK, was unacceptable, Mr. Habib emphasized. Mr. Chang replied that the Agreed Minute was

0121

proposed with a view to replacing the U.S. proposal regarding
Para 5(e)(iii). Mr. Habib reminded the ROK negotiators
that the new ROK language did not provide for mutual agreement on the liability, amount, and proposed distribution
as is the actual practice under the US-Japan SOFA. Mr.
Habib indicated that the US side would make a formal
response to the new ROK proposals regarding Claims Article
at an early meeting, after studying them in detail.

0122

JOINT SUMMARY RECORD OF THE 80TH SESSION

1. Time and Place: 2:00-4:40 P.M., May 28, 1965 at the
   Foreign Ministry's Conference Room
   (No.1)

2. Attendance:

ROK Side:

Mr. Chang, Sang Moon	Director European and American Affairs Bureau Ministry of Foreign Affairs
Mr. Huh, Suhg Joon	Director Labor Administration Bureau Office of Labor Affairs
Mr. Hur, Hyong Koo	Chief Prosecutors Section Ministry of Justice
Mr. Lee, Nam Ki	Chief America Section Ministry of Foreign Affairs
Mr. Kim, Dong Hwi	Chief Treaty Section Ministry of Foreign Affairs
Mr. Choo, Moon Ki	Chief Legal Affairs Section Ministry of Justice
Col. Kim, Won Kil	Chief Military Affairs Section Ministry of National Defense
Maj. Lee, Kye Hoon	Military Affairs Section Ministry of National Defense
Mr. Kim, Kee Joe	3rd Secretary Ministry of Foreign Affairs
Mr. Lee, Keun Pal (Interpreter)	3rd Secretary Ministry of Foreign Affairs
Mr. Hwang, Young Jae	3rd Secretary Ministry of Foreign Affairs
Mr. Park, Won Chul	3rd Secretary Ministry of Foreign Affairs

U.S. Side:

Mr. Benjamin A. Fleck	First Secretary American Embassy

0123

Brig. Gen. Carroll H. Dunn	Deputy Chief of Staff 8th U.S. Army
Col. Allan G. Pixton	Deputy Chief of Staff 8th U.S. Army
Capt. George Hagerman	Assistant Chief of Staff USN/K
Col. Kenneth C. Crawford	Staff Judge Advocate 8th U.S. Army
Mr. Frank R. LaMacchia	First Secretary American Embassy
Mr. Robert A. Kinney	J-5 8th U.S. Army
Mr. Goodwin Shapiro	Second Secretary American Embassy
Maj. Alton H. Harvey	Staff Judge Advocate's Office 8th U.S. Army
Mr. David Y.C. Lee (Interpreter)	Second Secretary American Embassy
Mr. G.W. Flower (Observer)	8th U.S. Army

1. Mr. Fleck opened the 80th meeting by stating that the US negotiators would like to table and distribute at this time the full text of the US draft of the US-ROK Status of Forces Agreement, including the Preamble and 30 articles. Article numbers had been tentatively assigned for the mutal convenience of the two sides in the negotiations, but of course are subject to change as agreed. He noted that this full text includes the US draft of the Articles on the Duration and Ratification of the Agreement, the last two Articles which were being tabled for the first time at this session.

2. Then Mr. Fleck stated that the leaders of the two Governments, at their recent conferences in Washington, had reached agreement in principle on the major outstanding issues of this Agreement. Therefore, the US negotiators proposed that consideration of the over-all agreement be expedited and that minor differences remaining in several

0124

articles be resolved soon. Thereby, it is hoped that the expectations of the President of the Republic of Korea, who was reported to have predicted on May 23rd at Cape Kennedy that the SOFA would be concluded in two or three weeks, will be fulfilled.

3. Mr. Fleck indicated that the US negotiators, in addition to tabling the final two articles, also was submitting modifications of the text of the US drafts of the Criminal Jurisdiction, Labor, and Claims Articles. The US drafts of these key articles had been substantially modified in recent weeks, in response to Korean desires, thereby enabling the leaders of the two Governments to reach agreement in principle on the major unresolved issues. Since the US negotiators had made the major concessions necessary to reach accord on the major unresolved issues, they hoped that the ROK negotiators would now respond in kind and accept the revised US draft of the agreement as a whole being tabled at this meeting.

Claims Article

4. Mr. Fleck pointed out that, at the 76th meeting, the US Government had made a major concession by accepting the Korean draft of the Claims Article subject to certain important modifications. At the 79th meeting, the Korean negotiators had proposed certain changes which would now be briefly discussed.

5. With reference to the proposed percentages of distribution contained in Paragraph 5(e)(i), Mr. Fleck said, the US negotiators can see no reason to vary the standard 25% - 75% distribution that has been accepted by almost all other countries. Regarding paragraph 5(e)(iii), the US side is unable to accept the Korean proposal, which would only require the parties to "seek mutual agreement." The United States regards the U.S. language requiring

0125

mutual agreement on liability, amount and proposed distribution as essential. There is no necessity for restating in an agreed minute that decisions of Korean courts will be binding since this is already provided for in paragraph 5(c). The United States recognizes that if a claimant rejects the settlement and takes his case to court, the decision of a competent tribunal of the Republic of Korea would be binding. The proposed ROK changes are unnecessary and unacceptable.

6. Regarding Paragraph 12, Mr. Fleck pointed out that the Korean negotiators contended that KSC personnel should be considered employees of the United States; also, that the Republic of Korea does not assume responsibility for claims generated by these individuals. The US position has always been that KSC personnel are not considered US employees and that the US does not assume responsibility for claims caused by their actions. The status of KSC personnel is now being negotiated in separate discussions. Therefore, the US negotiators had deleted the last clause of Paragraph 12. In view of the separate discussions which are taking place, it is appropriate that there be an understanding in the Joint Agreed Summary that:

"This article is not applicable to claims generated by KSC personnel. The status of the KSC members will be determined by other negotiations between the United States and the Republic of Korea."

By this means, neither the United States nor the Korean position is changed. The entire question is left for future determination.

7. With reference to Paragraph 13, Mr. Fleck stated
that the US negotiators accept the new second sentence
proposed by the Korean negotiators. This sentence pertains
to claims arising prior to the effective date of the SOFA
and states: "Such claims shall be processed and settled
by the authorities of the United States."

8. Regarding Paragraph A2 of the Agreed Minute,
Mr. Fleck stated that the US negotiators have carefully
considered the Korean proposal that ROK claims settlement
authority be automatically extended throughout Korea twelve
months after the effective date of the Agreement. The
twelve-month period may be sufficiently long to adapt
the system throughout Korea. However, this is not certain.
Twelve months may not be long enough for the Korean Claims
Service to make preparations to take over these functions.
Mr. Fleck emphasized that the US draft provides the
necessary flexibility to enable the transfer to take place
in an efficient manner. The US negotiators do not see any
reason to eliminate this flexibility by incorporating
language providing for a specific time frame.

9. The United States negotiators, Mr. Fleck said,
had made a major concession in accepting the Korean draft
as the basis of negotiations and had made further concessions
at this meeting. Mr. Fleck urged the Korean negotiators
to consider carefully and to accept these US proposals.

10. Mr. Chang thanked Mr. Fleck for his clear explanation and for preparing the notebooks containing the full
text of the US draft of the SOFA. Mr. Chang also stated
he wanted to share the honor he recently had in Washington,
D.C. He had been present when the leaders of the two

governments, in a spirit of cooperation and understanding, had reached agreement on two major problems in the Criminal Jurisdiction and Labor Articles. Mr. Chang expressed the hope that the SOFA negotiators in Seoul could proceed in this same cooperative spirit and complete the negotiations in a short time. He emphasized the need to concentrate the negotiations on major issues, and not to dwell on minor points. He urged both sides to tackle the problem in a spirit of mutual concession and pave the way for early conclusion of the Agreement. Mr. Chang indicated he felt progress was being made toward resolution of the problems in the Claims Article. The Korean negotiators would study the US statement and the new proposals and respond at the next negotiating session next week.

11. Mr. Fleck thanked Mr. Chang for his comments on his recent trip to the United States, and for the part he had played in Washington in helping to reach agreement in principle on several important issues. He stated that the US negotiators fully share the feelings of the Korean negotiators that a SOFA must be concluded as soon as possible. It was specifically for the purpose of expediting conclusion of this Agreement that the US negotiators had tabled the full US draft at this meeting. He expressed the hope that the Agreement could be concluded speedily on the basis of the U.S. draft tabled at this meeting.

Criminal Jurisdiction Article

12. Mr. Fleck stated that the proposals of the Korean negotiators regarding waiver, pretrial custody and duty certificates, presented at the 77th negotiating session, and those regarding trial safeguards, presented at the 70th negotiating session, had been given careful considera-tion. The US side had attempted to be responsive to the

0128

desires of the Korean negotiators to the maximum extent possible. At the same time, this draft is believed to be consistent with essential requirements of the United States. Mr. Fleck said he would comment on the remaining unresolved issues.

13. Agreed Minute Re Paragraph 3(b):

With reference to the proposal of the Korean negotiators to insert the words "at the request of the United States" at the beginning of paragraph 1, the US negotiators had stated at the time it was proposed that this was unacceptable. The Korean negotiators are well aware of the US position. This would completely change the waiver formula as tabled by the US, and would be inconsistent with the remaining paragraphs of the Agreed Minute. The so-called German formula provides for a general waiver at the time the agreement becomes effective. It does not provide for individual requests for waiver in each case. Mr. Fleck stated that the inclusion of the phrase cannot be accepted and that the U.S. negotiators understand that the Korean negotiators were prepared to withdraw this proposal.

14. With reference to the Korean proposal for an additional sentence to be inserted at the end of paragraph 4, the right of final determination by the Government of the Republic of Korea is affirmatively established in the US draft and the US negotiators see no reason for duplicating this language, Mr. Fleck continued. The US negotiators believe that the 21-day time limitation would be an unnecessary restriction. Although they expect that the consultations referred to would normally be concluded within this time, such might not always be the case.

0129

However, even though they do not believe it necessary, they are prepared to generally accede to the desires of the Korean negotiators, by including an understanding in the Joint Agreed Summary. This understanding would read as follows:

"Recall of waiver shall be final and conclusive unless the statement for recall referred to in paragraph 3 of this minute is withdrawn by the Government of the Republic of Korea."

15. The next matter to be considered, Mr. Fleck noted, was Paragraph 6 of the Agreed Minute. This pertains to the place where trials for offenses committed against Korean interests take place. As had been pointed out in the 77th meeting, the previous U.S. agreement to hold these trials in the Republic of Korea, unless mutually agreed otherwise, was directly related to the waiver formula which the U.S. negotiators were proposing at that time. They had now offered the German waiver formula. Paragraph 6 is identical to Article 26 of the German Agreement. These two provisions were designed to operate together. In addition, as had been stated, cases of the types referred to in paragraph 6 are extremely rare. The U.S. negotiators do not expect them to present any problem. However, even though rare, such cases may arise and trial elsewhere may be required. For these reasons, it is deemed necessary to retain paragraph 6.

16. Agreed Minute Re Paragraph 3(a): (Duty Certificates)

Mr. Fleck stated that the US negotiators accepted the modifications pertaining to duty certificates proposed by the ROK negotiators at the 77th negotiating session, with the following modifications:

a. They agreed to inclusion of an understanding in the Agreed Joint Summary stating: "A certificate shall be issued only upon the advice of a Staff Judge Advocate, and the competent authority issuing the duty certificate shall be a General Grade Officer or his designee." The Korean negotiators are well aware, Mr. Fleck continued, that a general officer must, of necessity, delegate many of his functions to his senior subordinates. The US language requires that the responsibility remain at general officer level and only allows delegation of authority to act.

b. They accepted substitution of the word "shall" for the word "may" in the second paragraph of Agreed Minute Re Paragraph 3(a) "shall be made the subject of review." They also accepted the modification of the first understanding proposed by the Korean negotiators.

c. With regard to the US definition of "official duty," the Korean negotiators originally had proposed and the United States had already agreed to, inclusion of this as an understanding in the Joint Agreed Summary. The United States negotiators are still willing to include this definition in the Agreed Joint Summary. However they cannot accept the proposal of the Korean negotiators that it be included in the Agreed Minute, Mr. Fleck said.

17. Paragraph 5: Pretrial Custody

Mr. Fleck stated that the United States negotiators accepted all modifications proposed by the Korean negotiators at the 77th Session relating to pretrial custody. Therefore, the two sides had reached full agreement on paragraph 5.

한·미국 간의 상호방위조약 제4조에 의한 시설과 구역 및 한국에서의 미국군대의 지위에 관한 협정(SOFA) 523
전59권. 1966.7.9 서울에서 서명 : 1967.2.9 발효(조약 232호) (V.52 실무교섭회의 합의의사록, 제69-82차, 1965-66)

18. Trial Safeguards

With reference to the trial safeguards contained in Paragraph 9 and its related Agreed Minutes, Mr. Fleck emphasized that the Korean negotiators are well aware of the importance which the US Government attaches to these guarantees. The acceptance by the Korean negotiators at the 70th Negotiating Session of the principle of enumerating the trial safeguards had been a major step toward resolution of the differences on this important matter. At that session, the Korean negotiators proposed modification of some of the listed safeguards. These proposals had been given careful consideration in a maximum attempt to be receptive to the Korean desires. At the same time, the United States has certain essential needs that must be fulfilled. The United States negotiators would like to discuss each of the Korean proposals in detail.

a. Agreed Minute Re Paragraph 9a: Mr. Fleck said the US negotiators agree that the original second sentence of this Agreed Minute was related to the use of the word "civil" in paragraph 1(b) of the text. They had carefully studied the Korean negotiators' proposal to delete both of these items and substitute an understanding in the Agreed Joint Summary. The U.S. negotiators believed that agreement had been reached on the principle that US personnel should not be subject to the jurisdiction of Korean military tribunals. What the negotiators had been discussing was where this principle should be stated. As indicated in the tabled U.S. draft, the U.S. negotiators are willing to delete the original second sentence of Agreed Minute Re Paragraph 9(a) in return for acceptance by the Korean negotiators of the word "civil" in paragraph 1(b).

0132

b. <u>Agreed Minute Re Paragraph 9(g)</u>: At the 70th Session, the Korean negotiators had expressed disagreement with that portion of the Agreed Minute rendering inadmissible as evidence any statement taken from an accused in the absence of a United States representative. The Korean negotiators had contended that their proposed language for the 3rd unnumbered paragraph of Agreed Minute Re Paragraph 9, pertaining to the inadmissibility of statements obtained by illegal means, should render unnecessary this portion of the Agreed Minute. The negotiators had previously discussed this provision in detail. The US representative has an affirmative duty to be present at these sessions. He will be available at all times and the United States authorities will insure that he fulfills this duty. The U.S. negotiators believe this provision is absolutely necessary to insure that no confession is obtained by coercion or other improper means. The United States Government is firmly committed to the principle embodied in this provision and we cannot agree to its deletion.

c. <u>Agreed Minute re Paragraph 9, subparagraph (a) of the Second Unnumbered Paragraph</u>: Mr. Fleck noted that this provision guarantees the accused the right to appeal a conviction. It is the understanding of the US negotiators that the appellate procedure of the Korean Courts allows the accused to request a review of the evidence used in the trial court. It is also their understanding that the appellate court may examine new evidence or witnesses and make new findings of fact on either its own motion or that of the accused. In order to prevent any possible confusion, they therefore proposed insertion of the following understanding in the Agreed Joint Summary:

0133

"Under the appellate procedure of the Courts of
the Republic of Korea the accused may request a reexamination of the evidence, including new evidence
and witnesses, as a basis for new findings of
fact by the appellate court."

They believe this is entirely consistent with Korean
appellate procedure.

    d. Agreed Minute Re Paragraph 9, subparagraph (d)
of the Second Unnumbered Paragraph and, the 4th Unnumbered
Paragraph: Mr. Fleck recalled that the Korean negotiators
had proposed the deletion of the fourth paragraph and the
adoption of an alternative subparagraph (d). The U.S.
negotiators were aware of the fact that Article 361 of
the Code of Criminal Procedure allows appeals by the
prosecution based upon errors of law. They were also
aware that increasing a sentence on appeal is a part of
Korean law. At the 61st Session, they had pointed out
that this was contrary not only to American judicial
practice, but also to the fundamental understanding of
justice held by the US Government and US personnel. Like
the Korean negotiators, the U.S. negotiators must have an
agreement that is acceptable to our government and people.
An appeal by the prosecution, based upon mistake of fact or
the increase of a sentence on appeal, would be viewed by
the American people as a miscarriage of justice. The US
negotiators deem these limitations essential safeguards
which must be retained. They cannot, therefore, agree
to alteration of subparagraph (d) or the deletion of
unnumbered paragraph (4).

0134

e. Agreed Minute Re Paragraph 9, Subparagraph (j)
of the Second Paragraph: With regard to this provision
prohibiting trial of the accused if physically or mentally
unfit, Mr. Fleck said the U.S. negotiators believe their
position is adequately clear. The Korean negotiators seem
to fear that this will be subject to abuse by the accused
if the final determination as his fitness is not left to
the court. This provision gives firm right to postponement
of trial if the accused is physically or mentally unfit.
The Joint Committee is the proper place to develop mutually
satisfactory procedures for making this determination.
The right of postponement in event of mental or physical
unfitness is a substantive safeguard deemed absolutely
essential by the United States.

f. Agreed Minute Re Paragraph 9, Third Unnumbered
Paragraph: Mr. Fleck recalled that, at the 70th session
the Korean negotiators had proposed a revision of the
paragraph which would omit the term "real evidence".
The United States cannot agree to omission of the term
"real evidence" or of a guarantee that it will not be used
if obtained illegally. The use of evidence obtained by
unreasonable search and seizure or by illegal or improper
means is inadmissable under the US Constitution in all
courts of the United States. The United States cannot
consent to the use of evidence obtained by this manner
against any US citizen tried in a Korean Court under
this agreement. The United States negotiators believe that
the provision in our draft is quite suitable. In response
to the proposals of the Korean negotiators, however, they
were prepared to accept the Korean revision of this
paragraph subject to the modifications indicated in the
tabled draft. The United States negotiators wish it to be
clearly understood that this is an essential requirement 35

and that under no circumstances will the United States agree to the use of illegally obtained evidence.

19. Mr. Fleck recalled that, at various times in previous negotiating sessions, the Korean negotiators had expressed a desire that the word "military" be inserted before the word "authorities" when referring to US military officials throughout the US draft. He said the US side accepts this proposal and has inserted the word "military" throughout the draft of this article, as follows:

1(a); 2(a); 3(a); 4; 5(a); 5(b); 5(c); 6(a); 6(b); 7(a); 8; 11; and in the following Agreed Minutes: No.1 and No. 2 re paragraph 9(b); No.1 re paragraph 3(a); No. 1 and No. 3 re paragraph 6; re paragraph 9; and re paragraph 10(a) and 10(b).

20. In summary, Mr. Fleck noted that the United States had made major concessions throughout the Criminal Jurisdiction Article in an effort to hasten conclusion of this agreement. The U.S. negotiators asked the Korean negotiators to carefully consider these proposals. They awaited Korean acceptance of this draft of the Criminal Jurisdiction Article.
Labor Article

21. Mr. Fleck stated that the US negotiators were tabling a revised Labor Article, which incorporates compromise language in keeping with the recent agreement by the leaders of the two governments in Washington. In this new draft, paragraph 4 has been revised. The previous subparagraphs 4(a), 4(c), and 4(e), have been deleted, as suggested by the ROK authorities. A new subparagraph 4(a) (5) has been included, incorporating the concept of the Korean proposal made at the 79th negotiating session, and providing for a 70-day cooling-off after a labor dispute has been referred

0136

to the Joint Committee. The new subparagraph 4(b) incorporates the substance of the ROK draft of subparagraph 4(b). It gives the Joint Committee the responsibility for determining those categories of essential employees who shall not exercise the right of further collective action in the event a labor dispute is not resolved by the mediation procedures. A new subparagraph 4(c) incorporates the language previously tabled by the Korean negotiators in Paragraph 5. It provides that in a national emergency, application of this article will be limited in accordance with emergency measures taken by the Government of the Republic of Korea. In connection with this new subparagraph, it is the understanding of the U.S. negotiators that it was proposed by the Korean negotiators in order to assist in our joint defense effort in case of national emergency. During such an emergency every resource must be utilized to meet the crisis. Therefore, it is the understanding of the US negotiators that the limitation of the Labor Article would be selective. In other words, those provisions which might hamper US operations during such a national emergency would be suspended. At the same time those provisions which would further our joint defense efforts and would be of assistance would remain in effect. The substance of the previous subparagraph 4(b) of the US draft, which is an essential provision, had been incorporated as a new Agreed Minute No. 5 in this draft.

22. Mr. Fleck stated that this revised draft incorporates the Korean proposal to exclude the Korean Service Corps from coverage of the Labor Article. The KSC personnel

0137

are to be covered by a separate agreement. Therefore, the revised US draft on this subject merely affirms that they are not covered by the Article. The U.S. negotiators agree to delete Agreed Minute No.1, on the basis that a separate agreement for the KSC will be negotiated. This deletion of Agreed Minute No.1 is made with the understanding that, pending conclusion of a separate agreement, KSC personnel will continue to be made available by the ROK Government as at present. In other words, the 1960 US-Korean agreement will remain in effect until it is superceded by a new agreement, separate from the SOFA.

23. In tabling this revised US draft, Mr. Fleck continued, the US negotiators believe they have met the Korean requirements on the key point of difference in the two drafts. In making this concession, they would like to reiterate that the U.S. armed forces are here solely for the defense of Korea. Their Korean employees are vital to the joint US-ROK defense mission. As the U.S. negotiators had explained, the U.S. armed forces are relying more and more on their Korean employees in semi-skilled and skilled occupations. Many of these employees are engaged in work which is essential to the combat readiness of both the US and Korean armed forces. Therefore, the U.S. negotiators were making these important concessions with the understanding the Korean negotiators would accept the remainder of the US draft of the Labor Article, and that in future the Joint Committee, when considering the role of the Korean employees of the US armed forces under subparagraph 4(b), will take into full consideration the importance of the U.S. armed forces Korean employees in the defense of their homeland and the special status of these employees.

0138

24. Mr. Chang thanked Mr. Fleck for his presentation and indicated that the Korean negotiators would respond at the next negotiating session. The Korean negotiators asked questions about the meaning of Para 4 (a) (5) of the Labor Article, especially whether the reference therein should not be to subparagraph (2) rather than to subparagraph (3). Mr. Fleck explained that reference of a dispute to the special committee, provided for in subparagraph (2), was not intended to be compulsory or automatic. Under the provisions of the US draft, if the Joint Committee decides to refer the dispute to the special committee and the special committee having failed to resolve the dispute, then returns the dispute to the Joint Committee, the 70-day period would begin when the special committee returns the dispute to the Joint Committee. However, if the Joint Committee should decide not to refer the dispute to a special committee, the 70-day period would begin from the date the dispute was referred to the Joint Committee by the Office of Labor Affairs. The Korean negotiators expressed the opinion that subparagraph (5) appeared to be faultily drafted, since it does not clearly provide for procedure explained by the US negotiators.

Articles on Duration and Ratification of Agreement.

25. Mr. Fleck tabled the U.S. drafts of articles on duration and ratification of the agreement. He explained that the article on the Duration of the Agreement provides that this agreement shall remain in force while the Mutual Defense Treaty between the US and the ROK remains in force, unless terminated earlier by agreement between the two Governments. This is standard language for such articles in US status-of-forces agreements.

0139

26. In the article on the Ratification of the Agreement, Mr. Fleck explained that paragraph one provides that this agreement shall enter into force four months after the date of a written notification from the Government of the Republic of Korea that it has approved the agreement and has taken the legislative and budgetary action necessary to give effect to its provisions. In specifying "legislative and budgetary action", the U.S. Government also expects that any other necessary implementing action will have been taken by the ROK Government authorities. The US Government would further expect to inform the ROK Government and be informed by the ROK authorities on a continuing basis of progress in the implementation (including exchange of texts of implementing materials) so that consistent and coordinated action by both sides would be assured. Mr. Fleck emphasized that, in the period between the notification of ROKG approval of the agreement and its entry into force, both Governments will have time to make further preparations for orderly and effective implementation of the Agreement. ROK and US authorities can utilize this period to organize the Joint Committee and its Sub-Committees, and to take other measures to insure smooth implementation of the Agreement.

27. The second paragraph of the US draft provides for termination of the Taejon Agreement for US armed forces, subject to the paragraph in the Criminal Jurisdiction Article which provides that the Taejon Agreement will cover offenses which occur before entry into force of the SOFA.

28. Mr. Fleck expressed the belief that the ROK negotiators, after study of these two drafts, would find them acceptable. Mr. Fleck stated that, in addition to the five articles he had discussed thus far in this meeting, there remained

0140

several other articles on which full agreement has not been
formalized. Remaining differences in these articles are
believed to be minor, and Mr. Fleck urged ROK acceptance
of the US drafts of these articles, which previously
had been fully explained. Having thus presented the
over-all US position on remaining issues, Mr. Fleck concluded
that the US negotiators looked forward confidently to
early conclusion of the Agreement. Mr. Chang thanked
Mr. Fleck for his comprehensive presentation of the US
position and indicated the Korean negotiators would respond
on all unresolved issues at the next meeting.

0141

한·미국 간의 상호방위조약 제4조에 의한 시설과 구역 및 한국에서의 미국군대의 지위에 관한 협정(SOFA) 533
전59권. 1966.7.9 서울에서 서명 : 1967.2.9 발효(조약 232호) (V.52 실무교섭회의 합의의사록, 제69-82차, 1965-66)

JOINT SUMMARY RECORD OF THE 81ST SESSION

1. Time and Place: 4:00-7:00 P.M., June 7, 1965 at the
   Foreign Ministry's Conference Room
   (No.1)

2. Attendance:

   ROK Side:

   Mr. Chang, Sang Moon   Director
                                 European and American Affairs
                                 Bureau
                                 Ministry of Foreign Affairs

   Mr. Hur, Hyong Koo   Chief
                                 Prosecutors Section
                                 Ministry of Justice

   Mr. Lee, Nam Ki   Chief
                                 America Section
                                 Ministry of Foreign Affairs

   Mr. Choo, Moon Ki   Chief
                                 Legal Affairs Section
                                 Ministry of Justice

   Mr. Kim, Tai Chung   Chief
                                 Labor Administration Section
                                 Office of Labor Affairs

   Mr. Kim, Young Soo   Chief
                                 Operations Section
                                 Ministry of Finance

   Mr. Lee, Chai Sup   Customs Bureau
                                 Ministry of Finance

   Maj. Lee, Kye Hoon   Military Affairs Section
                                 Ministry of Foreign Affairs

   Mr. Kim, Kee Joe   3rd Secretary
                                 Ministry of Foreign Affairs

   Mr. Lee, Keun Pal   3rd Secretary
   (Interpreter)   Ministry of Foreign Affairs

   Mr. Hwang, Young Jae   3rd Secretary
                                 Ministry of Foreign Affairs

   Mr. Lee, Chung Bin   3rd Secretary
                                 Ministry of Foreign Affairs

   Mr. Park, Won Chul   3rd Secretary
                                 Ministry of Foreign Affairs

   U.S. Side:

   Mr. Benjamin A. Fleck   First Secretary
                                 Aemrican Embassy

0142

Col. Allan G. Pixton	Deputy Chief of Staff 8th U.S. Army
Capt. George Hagerman	Assistant Chief of Staff USN/K
Col. Kenneth C. Crawford	Staff Judge Advocate 8th U.S. Army
Mr. Frank R. LaMacchia	First Secretary American Embassy
Mr. Robert A. Kinney	J-5 8th U.S. Army
Mr. Goodwin Shapiro	Second Secretary American Embassy
Maj. Alton H. Harvey	Staff Judge Advocate's Office 8th U.S. Army
Mr. David Y.C. Lee (Interpreter)	Second Secretary American Embassy
Mr. Ogden C. Reed (Observer)	Civilian Personnel Director 8th U.S. Army
Mr. G.W. Flower (Observer)	8th U.S. Army
Col. Charles M. Thompson (Observer)	Claims Service 8th U.S. Army

1. Mr. Chang opened the meeting by stating that the Korean negotiators wished to articulate their position at this final stage of negotiations. Mr. Chang said that it has been the desire and intent of the Korean negotiators to reach full agreement and to conclude these long-pending negotiations as soon as possible. Taking cognizance of the different opinions between the two sides, they have exerted their utmost effort to accommodate the requirements of the U.S. negotiators as far as possible.

2. As the U.S. negotiators had stated at the 80th meeting, Mr. Chang continued, the leaders of the two governments, at the recent conference in Washington, had

0143

reached agreement in principle on the major outstanding issues of this Agreement. Therefore, it is the belief of the Korean negotiators that both sides should exert their utmost efforts to resolve the remaining differences which have been hindering an early conclusion of the Agreement.

3. Mr. Chang said the Korean negotiators were now prepared to propose their final, comprehensive draft of this Agreement. With appropriate understandings and minor modifications, they accepted the U.S. drafts of the following articles: Non-Appropriated Fund Organizations, Customs, Military Payment Certificates, Security Measures, Foreign Exchange Controls, Duration of the Agreement, Facilities and Areas, and Civil Claims.

4. However, Mr. Chang continued, after having given their most careful consideration to the rest of the articles (Criminal Jurisdiction, Labor, Invited Contractors, and Ratification of the Agreement), they were prepared to accept the U.S. drafts only after incorporating modifications of an important nature. These modifications are essential and imperative to the Government of the Republic of Korea. As had been pointed out by the Korean negotiators at the past discussions, the people and the National Assembly are deeply concerned and critical toward the possible outcome of these negotiations. This concern is clearly indicated in recent criticisms directed at both governments in the columns of the newspapers and voiced by some eminent and responsible citizens. Mr. Chang stated that such embarrassing consequences would be in the interests of neither the host state nor the sending state. Keeping these facts in mind, Mr. Chang said, the Korean negotiators

0144

wished to present their final position on each of the
as-yet unagreed upon articles of the SOFA.

Security Measures Article

5. Mr. Chang recalled that at the 55th meeting
the U.S. negotiators had proposed deletion of the phrase
"of the persons referred to in this paragraph, and their
property" if the Korean negotiators would agree to the
inclusion in the Agreed Joint Summary of the following
understanding:

> "In cooperating with each other under this
> Article, the two governments agree that each will
> take such measures as may be necessary to ensure
> the security and protection of the U.S. armed
> forces, the members thereof, the civilian component,
> the persons who are present in the Republic of Korea
> pursuant to the Article dealing with Invited
> Contractors, their dependents and their property."

Mr. Chang said the Korean negotiators accepted the U.S.
proposal and the U.S. draft of the Article as tabled ~~81 st Meeting~~
at the 80th meeting.

Non-Appropriated Fund Organizations Article

6. Mr. Chang noted that the only remaining issue
in the Non-Appropriated Fund Organizations Article was
the question of who should be granted the use of these
organizations under item (f) of the Agreed Minute proposed
by the U.S. negotiators. To meet the requirements expressed
by the U.S. negotiators, the Korean negotiators were now
prepared to accept the Agreed Minute. However, in
accepting, the Korean negotiators wished to include in
the Agreed Joint Summary the following understanding:

> "It is understood that the present use of
> Non-Appropriated Fund organizations by organizations
> and persons other than those referred to in items
> (a),(b),(c),(d), and (e) shall immediately be
> suspended at the time of the entry into force of
> this Agreement. The extent of organizations and
> persons to be granted the use of such organizations
> under item (f) of this Minute shall be left to

0145

further negotiations between the appropriate
authorities of the two Governments."

7. Mr. Chang noted that agreement on the Non-
Appropriated Funds Organizations Article meant automatic
agreement on Agreed Minute #7 of the Customs Article.
The negotiators had thereby reached full agreement on the
latter article as well.

Foreign Exchange Controls Article

8. Mr. Chang stated that the Korean negotiators
accepted the U.S. draft of the Agreed Minute to the
Foreign Exchange Controls Article, thereby reaching full
agreement on that article.

Military Payment Certificates Article

9. Mr. Chang recalled that at the 55th meeting
both sides agreed to delete their respective drafts of
an Agreed Minute and to include in the Agreed Joint
Summary the following understanding:

"The ROK and U.S. negotiators agree that
nothing in the Status of Forces Agreement in any way
prevents the appropriate authorities of either
the Republic of Korea or the United States from
raising any appropriate matter at any time with
each other. The U.S. negotiators recognize the desire
of the ROK authorities to discuss the disposal of
Military Payment Certificates under custody of the
ROK Government. However, both the ROK and U.S.
negotiators have agreed to remove from the SOFA
text any reference to the question of compensation
for Military Payment Certificates held by unauthorized
persons. This agreement does not prejudice the
position of either party in connection with
discussion of this question through other channels."

10. Mr. Chang noted that the remaining issue to be
solved was whether to include the phrase "to the extent
authorized by United States Law" proposed by the U.S.
negotiators or the phrase "subject to the military law
of the United States" proposed by the Korean negotiators.
The Korean negotiators, he said, accepted the language
of the U.S. draft, thereby reaching complete agreement on

0146

this article. However, the Korean negotiators wished to stress that their acceptance was made in the belief that the U.S. authorities would take every measure necessary to prevent abusive transactions of Military Payment Certificates by the persons authorized to use such certificates.

Facilities and Areas Articles

11. Mr. Chang recalled that discussion of the article relating to facilities and areas (U.S. draft article IV) had been deferred since the 42nd meeting, held on February 14, 1964. He recalled that there had been a difference in the positions of the two sides over the question of compensation to owners of private property. The Korean negotiators were now prepared to withdraw their previous contention with respect to compensation for privately-owned property extremely demolished as a result of use by the U.S. armed forces. The Korean negotiators accepted the three paragraphs and Agreed Minute of the U.S. draft. However, they wished to propose a second Agreed Minute reading as follows:

> "2. All removable facilities, equipment
> and material or portions thereof provided by the
> Republic of Korea under this Agreement and located
> within the areas and facilities referred to in this
> Article shall be returned to the Republic of Korea
> whenever they are no longer needed for the purpose
> of this Agreement."

12. Mr. Chang said the additional Agreed Minute was proposed with the same intent as the Agreed Minute already contained in the U.S. draft. The Korean negotiators consider it logical that all removable properties provided by their government and located in any area or facilities should be returned to the owners whenever the properties are no longer needed by the U.S. armed forces. This additional Agreed Minute should present no difficulty to

0147

the U.S. negotiators. Furthermore, it is also intended to supplement the provisions of Paragraph 2 and 3 of Article II because those provisions are merely related to the return of the facilities and areas, as a whole or in part, which are no longer needed. Those provisions, therefore, do not refer to removable property located within the areas or facilities.

13. Turning to Article V, relating to cost and maintenance, Mr. Chang stated that the Korean negotiators were now prepared to withdraw their draft regarding compensation to owners of private property and to accept the U.S. draft following clarification of the language by the U.S. negotiators. Mr. Chang said the Korean negotiators thought the language of Paragraph 1 was too broad. It spoke of "all expenditures incident to the maintenance of the U.S. armed forces in the Republic of Korea" rather than expenditures incident to the maintenance of facilities and areas. Since this article was intended to deal with facilities and areas only, why should the language not be more restrictive?

14. Mr. Fleck replied that this language was identical with the language of the similar article in the SOFA with Japan. Therefore, the U.S. negotiators did not understand why the Korean negotiators should object to it, inasmuch as the Korean negotiators had frequently expressed the desire to obtain language in other parts of this agreement which would be identical or similar to the language of the SOFA with Japan. Furthermore, since the language was broader, it gave the ROK Government a broader exemption from maintenance costs. The term "maintenance of the U.S. armed forces" included maintenance of the facilities and areas occupied by those forces.

0148

The Korean negotiators, therefore, should have no difficulty in agreeing to this language.

15. Mr. Chang thanked Mr. Fleck for this explanation and said that the Korean negotiators accepted the U.S. draft of the article.

Claims Article

16. Mr. Chang stated that the Korean negotiators, with a view to reaching full agreement, were prepared to accept the revised draft of the Claims Article tabled by the U.S. negotiators at the 80th meeting, subject only to minor modifications.

17. With regard to Paragraph 5(e)(i), the Republic of Korea accepts the standard 25% - 75% distribution ration, as proposed by the U.S.

18. With regard to Paragraph 5(e)(iii), Mr. Chang continued, the Korean negotiators are prepared to withdraw their proposed Agreed Minute if the U.S. negotiators will agree to modify the subparagraph as follows (proposed changes underlined):

> "iii. Every half year, a statement of the sums paid by the Republic of Korea in the course of the half-yearly period in respect of every case regarding which the liability, amount, and proposed distribution on a percentage basis has been approved by both governments shall be sent to the appropriate authorities of the United States, together with a request for reimbursement. Such reimbursement shall be made in won within the shortest possible time. The approval by both governments as referred to in this subparagraph shall not prejudice any decision taken by the arbitrator or adjudication by a competent tribunal of the Republic of Korea as set forth in paragraphs 2(c) and 5(c) respectively."

19. Mr. Chang said the proposed modifications are necessary to clarify the contradictory provisions in the U.S. draft. Paragraph 5(c) of that draft provides that all the payments made by the Korean government, whether made pursuant to a settlement or to an adjudication, shall be binding upon the Parties, whereas Paragraph 5(e)(iii) implies that none of the payments made by the Korean

government, regardless of whether the payment was made
pursuant to a settlement or to an adjudication, shall
be binding unless the U.S. authorities approve the payment
in advance. Therefore, the Korean negotiators propose
the above modifications to Paragraph 5(e)(iii) in order
to avoid possible misunderstanding.

20. With regard to Paragraph 12, Mr. Chang
said the Korean negotiators would accept the U.S. proposal
to delete the final clause and to include an understanding
in the Agreed Joint Summary, with a minor modification.
The Korean negotiators believe that any decision as to
whether claims generated by Korean Service Corps members
should or should not come under the provisions of this
article cannot be made until the status of the KSC
personnel is determined. Therefore, the Korean negotiators
propose deletion of the first sentence of the understanding,
which would then read as follows:

> "The liability for claims generated by KSC
> personnel will be determined by other negotiations
> between the Republic of Korea and the United States."

21. With regard to Paragraph A2 of the Agreed
Minute, Mr. Chang said the Korean negotiators accepted the
principle that the effective date of the claims provisions
in areas other than that of the Seoul Special City shall
be determined by the Joint Committee, as proposed by the
U.S. negotiators at the previous session. However, to meet
the requirements of both sides, the Korean negotiators
proposed the following modified draft of Paragraph A2:

> "The provisions of paragraphs five, six, seven,
> and eight will be extended, at the earliest date
> practicable, to other areas of the Republic of Korea
> as determined by the Joint Committee."

22. As the U.S. negotiators were well aware, Mr.
Chang continued, the Korean Claims Service has recorded

0150

an efficient operation since 1962. The State Compensation
Committee is manned with qualified commissioners and
investigators who have ample experience in legal affairs.
For the equitable settlement of claims, proper laws and
regulations are provided. At the present time, the claims
Service is processing and settling the claims arising out
of various cases of damage caused by members of the
Korean armed forces as well as by government officials,
to the satisfaction of the claimants concerned. This
effectiveness of the Korean Claims Service had been demonstrated
by the Korean negotiators, Mr. Chang stated, in previous
formal and informal negotiating meetings. Therefore,
the Korean negotiators are certain that the Korean Claims
Service is capable of assuming all of the claims
responsibilities from the date the SOFA enters into force.

    23. Mr. Chang recalled that the U.S. negotiators had
agreed to adopt the proposed system in the Seoul Special
City area automatically six months after the entry into
force of this agreement without any decision of the Joint
Committee. This acceptance, in the belief of the Korean
negotiators, was nothing but an admission on the part of
the U.S. negotiators that the Republic of Korea has a working
and efficient claims system, applicable to other parts
of the Republic. Moreover, the authority of the Korean
State Compensation Committee extends to the entire territory
of the Republic of Korea, as does that of the U.S. armed
forces Claims Service. The Korean negotiators cannot
understand the insistence of the United States that the
application of the Korean system be limited to a specific
area.

24. However, to expedite the negotiations and reach full agreement on this article at the earliest possible date, the Korean negotiators were making an important concession regarding this provision, Mr. Chang continued. The Korean negotiators believe that the United States would give due consideration, in the Joint Committee, to the capability of the Korean Claims Service, so that the provisions of paragraphs five, six, seven and eight could be extended to other areas of the Republic of Korea at the earliest date practicable.

Labor Article

25. Turning to the Labor Article, Mr. Chang said that the Korean negotiators, with a view to reaching prompt agreement, were prepared to accept the U.S. draft as a whole, with modifications of the following provisions: Paragraphs 1(b), 3, 4(a), 5(b), and Agreed Minutes #4 and #5. Most of the proposed modifications, he pointed out, were technical in nature rather than substantive and the Korean negotiators believed they would present no difficulty to the U.S. negotiators since they are all valid and reasonable.

26. Paragraph 1 (a) and (b)

Mr. Chang stated that the Korean negotiators were now prepared to agree to inclusion of the invited contractors in the provisions of this article. The Korean negotiators were prepared to accept subparagraph (b) of the U.S. draft if the U.S. negotiators would agree to the addition of the following sentence:

"Such civilian personnel shall be nationals of the Republic of Korea."

By accepting the U.S. draft of subparagraph (b), Mr. Chang stated, the Korean negotiators were acceding to the specific exclusion of KSC personnel and domestics from

0152

the definition of employee. In making this most
significant concession, the Korean negotiators wished to
the Agreed Joint Summary to clearly indicate that
exclusion of KSC personnel from the definition of
employee shall not be construed as a change in the position
taken by the Korean negotiators with regard to the
status of KSC personnel. Moreover, the addition of the
second sentence, proposed by the Korean negotiators, with
regard to the nationality of employees is considered necessary
by the Korean negotiators to minimize the employment
of third-country nationals in Korea.

27. Paragraph 2 and Agreed Minute #2

Mr. Chang said the Korean negotiators were
now prepared to accept the U.S. draft of this paragraph
and Agreed Minute, with the following understanding:

> "The termination of employment on account
> of the U.S. military requirements referred to in
> the second sentence of Agreed Minute #2 shall be
> referred to the Joint Committee, in advance whenever
> possible, for mutual agreement, as provided for
> in Agreed Minute #4. But such termination of
> employment as may be made in accordance with the
> relevant provisions of labor legislation of the
> Republic of Korea will not be subject to mutual
> agreement at the Joint Committee."

28. Paragraph 4(a)

Mr. Chang stated that the Korean negotiators
were prepared to accept the U.S. draft of Paragraph 4(a)
except for subparagraph (5). They proposed that
subparagraph (5) be altered to read "as stipulated in subparagraph (2), above" instead of "subparagraph (3), above."
Although they maintain that the cooling-off period should
comprise 70 days after the dispute is referred for
conciliation, the Korean negotiators now proposed, as
a compromise, to fix the starting date of the cooling-off
period at the second stage of the conciliation process,

0153

regardless of whether the Joint Committee deals with
the dispute itself or refers it to a specially designated
committee. The U.S. draft of this subparagraph does not
clearly accommodate the case when the Joint Committee
takes up the dipute itself without having referred
the matter to the special committee. Therefore, the Korean
negotiators urge that their compromise proposal be
accepted.

29. Paragraph 4(b) and (c)

Mr. Chang said the Korean negotiators accepted
the U.S. draft of Paragraph 4 (b) and (c), relating to
collective action and emergency measures, without any
change of wording.

30. Paragraph 5(b)

Turning to Paragraph 5(b), Mr. Chang said the
Korean negotiators were now prepared to accommodate the
contention expressed by the U.S. negotiators by accepting
the word "shall" instead of "will" and by substituting the
phrase "through mutual consultation" for the phrase "through
mutual agreement". The language in question would then
read as follows:

> "....employees who have acquired skills
> essential to the mission of the United States Armed
> Forces shall, upon request of the United States
> armed forces, be deferred through mutual consultation
> from Republic of Korea military service or other
> compulsory service."...."

The Korean negotiators hoped, Mr. Chang continued, that
through amicable consultation no disagreement would
arise between the appropriate authorities of both sides
in deferring skilled employees essential to the mission
of the U.S. armed forces.

31. Agreed Minute #5

Mr. Chang said the Korean negotiators believe
that the words "interests of the United States" referred

0154

to in the phrase "inimical to the interests of the
United States" in the U.S. draft of Agreed Minute #5
do not imply interests in terms of wages, compensation,
or other forms of payments and protection of workers.
Rather, they imply those interests of a political nature,
such as when the leadership of a union is dominated or
influenced by leftist or communist elements. The Korean
negotiators believe that if such an unlikely situation
should develop, it would undoubtedly be inimical to the
interests of the Republic of Korea. Therefore, they
would like to change the language to read as follows:

> "...inimical to the common interests of the
> United States and the Republic of Korea......"

32. Paragraph 3 and Agreed Minute #4

The Korean negotiators tabled the following
proposed revision of Paragraph 3:

> "3. To the extent not inconsistent with the
> provisions of this Article or the military requirements
> of the U.S. armed forces or except as may otherwise
> be mutually agreed, the conditions of employment,
> compensation, and labor-management relations
> established by the United States armed forces for
> their employees shall conform with provisions of
> labor legislation of the Republic of Korea."

They also tabled the following proposed revision
of Agreed Minute #4:

> "4. When employers cannot conform with provisions
> of labor legislation of the Republic of Korea
> applicable under Paragraph 3 on account of the military
> requirements of the United States armed forces,
> the matter shall be referred, in advance whenever
> possible, to the Joint Committee for mutual agreement."

Mr. Chang noted that in order to meet the U.S. requirements,
the proposed revision of the Agreed Minute retaines the
phrase "whenever possible". However, the Korean negotiators
believe that "under Paragraph 3" is preferable to "under
this Article" because the latter phrase might lead to dual
application of an already agreed-upon deviation which
the Korean negotiators believe to be irrelevant and

0155

unnecessary. With regard to the phrase "whenever possible",
Mr. Chang said the Korean negotiators wished to include
in the Agreed Joint Summary the following understanding:

> "The deviation from Korean labor legislation
> shall be referred to the Joint Committee for mutual
> agreement in advance, except in the case when reaching
> advance agreement by the Joint Committee would
> seriously hamper military operations in an emergency."

Mr. Chang said the Korean negotiators believed this
understanding would present no difficulty to the U.S.
negotiators in view of the statement made by the latter
at the 71st meeting.

Ratification Article

33. Turning to the Ratification Article, Mr. Chang
tabled the following proposed revisions:

> "1. This Agreement shall enter into force
> sixty days after the date of a written notification
> from the Government of the Republic of Korea to the
> Government of the United States that it has approved
> the Agreement in accordance with its legal procedures.

> "2. The Government of the Republic of Korea
> shall undertake to seek from its legislature all
> legislative and budgetary action necessary to give
> effect to its provisions of this Agreement.

> "3......

> "4. Within the scope of this Agreement,
> Paragraph 13 of Article III of the Agreement on
> Economic Coordination between the Republic of Korea
> and the Unified Command of May 24, 1952, shall not
> apply to members of the U.S. armed forces, civilian
> component, invited contractors, or dependents thereof."

34. Mr. Chang said the Korean negotiators wished to
modify the U.S. draft along the lines of other Status of
Forces Agreements by separating the clause regarding
legislative and budgetary action by the legislature, in
view of the fact that the entry into force of the Agreement
is one thing and legislative and budgetary action is
another. Furthermore, the Korean negotiators would like to
point out that Article 5 of the ROK Constitution clearly
stipulates that treaties duly ratified and promulgated in
accordance with the Constitution have the same effective force

0156

as do domestic laws of the Republic of Korea. Therefore, the ROK Government is bound to enforce the Agreement as domestic law, regardless of whether legislative and budgetary actions necessary for the execution of its provisions have been taken.

35. The Korean negotiators, Mr. Chang continued, believe that the four-month interval following ratification and legal procedures, proposed by the U.S. negotiators, was not only too long but also contradictory to the desire expressed by both sides for early conclusion of the Agreement. Moreover, the Korean negotiators cannot find such a long interval in any other Status of Forces Agreement. They believe the Agreement should enter into force upon ratification. However, they were proposing sixty days in order to accommodate the U.S. negotiators. They accepted Paragraph 3 of the U.S. draft and hope that the U.S. negotiators would find it possible to accept their revisions of Paragraph 1 and 2.

36. Mr. Chang said the Korean negotiators were proposing the additional Paragraph 4 in the belief that the Agreement was meant to cover the status of the U.S. armed forces in Korea and would have no relevance to the Unified Command _per se_. Therefore, the privileges, immunities and facilities granted to the U.S armed forces as individuals or agencies of the Unified Command should come under the provisions of the SOFA and no other agreement.

Criminal Jurisdiction Article

37. Taking up the Criminal Jurisdiction Article, Mr. Chang said that the Korean negotiators were prepared to accept verbatim the following provisions of the U.S. draft: Paragraph 1(a), Paragraph 11, Paragraph 12, and the following Agreed Minutes: Preamble #2 Re Paragraph 1(b), Re Paragraph 2,

0157

Re Paragraph 6, all those Re Paragraph 9, except for the
Agreed Minute Re Paragraph 9(g). They withdrew their
proposal for an Agreed Minute Re Paragraph 4 regarding
dual nationals. With modifications, they were prepared to
accept the following provisions of the U.S. draft:
Paragraph 1(b), Paragraph 7(b), and the following Agreed
Minutes: Re Paragraph 3(a), Re Paragraph 3(b), Re Paragraph
9(a), Re Paragraph 10 (a) and 19(b).

38. Paragraph 1(a)

Mr. Chang said that with regard to persons
subject to the jurisdiction of the military authorities
of the United States, it has been the position of the
Korean negotiators that since 1960 dependents have been
excluded from the categories of persons subject to the
military law of the United States and that they should,
therefore, be left out of the discussion of this article.
However, taking into account the oft-repeated concern
of the United States negotiators, the Korean negotiators
were now prepared to accept the U.S. proposal, thereby
clearly spelling out that "members of the United States
armed forces, civilian component, and their dependents"
are covered by the provisions of this article, as proposed
by the U.S. negotiators.

39. Agreed Minute #2 Re Paragraph 1(b)

Mr. Chang recalled that the Korean negotiators
had maintained the position that the U.S. proposal
with respect to offenses committed outside the Republic
of Korea, in the Agreed Minute #2 Re Paragraph 1(b),
had been unacceptable. First, Article 5 of the Korean
Criminal Code clearly stipulates that this law shall
apply to aliens who have committed certain offenses of
a serious nature outside the territory of the Republic
of Korea. Therefore, the provisions of this Agreed

0158

Minute are clearly contradictory to the legal system of
the Republic of Korea. Secondly, since the United States
does not have a similar provisions in its legal system,
offenses committed outside the Republic of Korea or
outside the territory of the United States cannot be
punished under the provisions of the U.S. draft. However,
in view of the fact that the presumption envisaged in
the Agreed Minute is highly hupothetical and occurence of
such offenses would be exceptional and extremely rare,
the Korean negotiators now accepted this Agreed Minute.

40. Agreed Minute Re Paragraph 2

Mr. Chang recalled that the Korean negotiators
had proposed deletion of the Agreed Minute Re Paragraph 2
from the U.S. draft. The exclusive jurisdiction granted
to the Korean authorities includes jurisdiction conferred
on then with respect to offenses, including offenses
relating to the security of the Republic of Korea,
punishable only by the law of the Republic of Korea.
The exclusive jurisdiction involved here would be
exercised mostly over such offenses against the security of
the receiving state as treason, sabotage, espionage, or
violation of any law relating to official secrets or
secrets relating to the national defense of the receiving
state. In other words, Mr. Chang continued, the nature
of such offenses is so serious that any mishandling
thereof might result in grace danger to the very survival
or existence of the government of the receiving state.
Secondly, the U.S. draft calls for waiver of exclusive
jurisdiction of the host country over offenders whom the
U.S. military authorities have no legal right to punish
eqitably as required by the relevant laws of the Republic
of Korea. Thirdly, the Korean negotiators had been unable

한·미국 간의 상호방위조약 제4조에 의한 시설과 구역 및 한국에서의 미국군대의 지위에 관한 협정(SOFA)
전59권. 1966.7.9 서울에서 서명 : 1967.2.9 발효(조약 232호) (V.52 실무교섭회의 합의의사록, 제69-82차, 1965-66) 551

to find any precedents for this language in any other Status of Forces Agreement.

41. However, Mr. Chang said, in the light of the U.S. concern that legal grounds should be provided in the Agreement so that if the Korean authorities do not wish to exercise their exclusive jurisdiction in specific cases they could waive in favor of the United States offenses of a minor nature, for disciplinary action, the Korean negotiators accepted the Agreed Minute with the inclusion of the following understanding in the Agreed Joint Summary:

> "It is understood that the U.S. authorities shall exercise utmost restraint in requesting waivers of exclusive jurisdiction as provided for in the Agreed Minute Re Paragraph 2 of this Article."

42. Trial Safeguards

Mr. Chang said the Korean negotiators were now prepared to accept all of those trial safeguards still at issue which the U.S. negotiators, in subjecting their personnel to Korean jurisdiction, felt to be necessary for guaranteeing a fair trial. Their acceptance included reinsertion of the second sentence in the Agreed Minute Re Paragraph 9(a), and in the Agreed Minute Re Paragraph 9 acceptance of the following the understanding proposed by the U.S. negotiators at the 80th meeting with regard to subparagraph (a) of the second unnumbered paragraph, subparagraphs (d) ands (j) of the second unnumbered paragraph, the third unnumbered paragraph, and the fourth unnumbered paragraph.

43. Agreed Minute Re Paragraph 9(g)

However, Mr. Chang continued, with regard to the Agreed Minute Re Paragraph 9(g), the Korean negotiators had

0160

maintained that that portion of the Agreed Minute which
would render inadmissible as evidence any statement
taken from an accused in the absence of a U.S. representative
should be deleted, on the ground that since a representative
of the U.S. Government, a counsel, an interpreter, and
the accused himself are all given the right to be present
at all of the judicial proceedings, it is entirely within
the discretion of the U.S. Government representative
whether or not to appear in such cases. Furthermore, the
absence of the U.S. Government representative from the
judicial proceedings should not impair the admissibility
of a statement. Mr. Chang recalled also that when the two
sides had been discussing the problem of trial safeguards
pertaining to Agreed Minute Re Paragraph 9(g), the U.S.
negotiators had insisted that a representative of the U.S.
Government should be entitled to be present at all criminal
proceedings, while the Korean negotiators had objected,
on the ground that the presence of the representative in
case of an in camera proceeding, however rare, would
prejudice the provisions of the Korean Constitution
as well as relevant laws of the Republic of Korea with respect
to public trials. Nevertheless, Mr. Chang continued, the
U.S. negotiators, contrary to their previous position,
had recently proposed, in paragraph 6 of the Agreed Minute
Re Paragraph 3(b), language which states that "a Korean
representative shall be entitled to be present at the
trial, except where his presence is incompatible with the
rules of the court of the United States or with the
security requirements of the United States, which are not
at the same time the security requirements of the Republic
of Korea." In the light of previous statements by the U.S.
negotiators that the representative of the U.S. Government

한·미국 간의 상호방위조약 제4조에 의한 시설과 구역 및 한국에서의 미국군대의 지위에 관한 협정(SOFA)
전59권. 1966.7.9 서울에서 서명 : 1967.2.9 발효(조약 232호) (V.52 실무교섭회의 합의의사록, 제69-82차, 1965-66)

has an affirmative duty to be present at the trial
session and will be available at all times, and that the
United States Government will ensure that he fulfills
this duty, the Korean negotiators, while accepting the
U.S. position in principle, in order to be consistent with
the relevant portion of this Article, propose, as a condition
of their acceptance of Paragraph 6 of the Agreed Minute
Re Paragraph 3(b), the addition of the following language
at the end of the Agreed Minute Re Paragraph 9(g):

> ".....except where his presence is incompatible
> with the rules of the court of the Republic of Korea
> or with the security requirements of the Republic
> of Korea, which are not at the same time the security
> requirements of the United States."

Mr. Chang predicted that cases of this type would be
extremely rare and the Korean negotiators do not foresee
any problem. The Republic of Korea and the United States
are both sovereign states and the ties between them are
especially close. Therefore, it is only reasonable that
representatives of each government should have corresponding rights and should not be discriminated against.

44. Paragraph 1(b) and Agreed Minute Re Paragraph 9(a)

Mr. Chang stated that the Korean negotiators
preferred the deletion of the word "civil" from Paragraph
1(b) to deletion of the second sentence of the Agreed Minute
Re Paragraph 9(a). Therefore, they proposed that the
second sentence, which had been deleted from the most
recent U.S. draft, be reinserted and the word "civil"
be deleted. The sentence to be reinserted would read:

> "A member of the United States armed forces,
> or civilian component, or a dependent, shall not be
> tried by a military tribunal of the Republic of Korea."

By accepting the above trial safeguard, Mr. Chang said,
the Korean negotiators had fully met the U.S. concern that
under existing Korean law a member of the U.S. armed forces,
civilian component, or a dependent may be tried by a Korean

0162

military court.

45. Paragraph 7(b)

Mr. Chang stated that the Korean negotiators were prepared to accept Paragraph 7(b) of the U.S. draft, with the addition of the following language at the end of the paragraph:

"In such cases, the authorities of the United States shall furnish relevant information on a routine basis to the authorities of the Republic of Korea, and a representative of the Government of the Republic of Korea shall have the right to have access to a member of the United States armed forces, the civilian component, or a dependent who is serving a sentence imposed by a court of the Republic of Korea in confinement facilities of the United States."

46. Mr. Chang explained that although the Korean negotiators are prepared to accept the unprecedented provisions of Paragraph 7(b) with respect to post-trial custody, they believe it necessary that the U.S. authorities routinely furnish to the Korean authorities such relevant information as the behavior and degree of repentance of those who are in penal servitude. In addition, the Korean authorities should be given the right of access to such persons not only for the purpose of seeing to it that they are carrying out their penal terms to the mutual satisfaction of the authorities of both governments but also in the interest of the persons in confinement. Denial by the U.S. negotiators of the Korean proposal would result in undue deprivation of those persons of such privileges as provisional release (parole) provided for in Article 72 of the Korean Criminal Code and Articles 49 to 52 of the Korean Prison Act.

47. Agreed Minute Re Paragraph 3(a)

Mr. Chang referred to the amended understanding pertaining to the issuance of duty certificates which the U.S. negotiators had proposed at the 80th meeting.

0163

He recalled that, in responding to a question at the 75th meeting, the U.S. negotiators had stated that "since there are only five Staff Judge Advocates assigned to the U.S. armed forces in Korea and since the lowest-ranking one is assigned at the division level, issuance of the duty certificate would take place at the division level or higher and the lowest-ranking competent authority issuing a duty certificate would be a Brigadier General." Taking this explanation in good faith, Mr. Chang continued, the Korean negotiators had proposed the understanding that:

> "A duty certificate shall be issued only upon the advice of a Staff Judge Advocate, and the competent authority issuing the duty certificate shall be a General Grade Officer."

However, contrary to their previous explanation, the U.S. negotiators had proposed the addition of the words "or his designee" at the end of the understanding and had further elaborated their position that a general officer must, of necessity, delegate many acts to his senior subordinates.

48. In view of the decisive role the duty certificate plays in determining whether or not a certain offense is done in the performance of official duty, the Korean negotiators had originally proposed the Staff Judge Advocate as the authority issuing the duty certificate. However, in the hope of concluding discussion of this point, the Korean negotiators had accepted in the text the wording "competent military authorities of the United States forces", coupled with the condition envisaged in the understanding which they had proposed. In the light of the lengthy discussion of the duty certificate question and the basic agreement which had been reached thereon, the Korean negotiators consider that the proposed additional wording will delay complete agreement on this issue.

0164

Therefore, they sincerely hope that the U.S. negotiators will voluntarily withdraw their proposed revision of the understanding.

49. Colonel Crawford stated that he wished to correct the record to show that there are actually six Staff Judge Advocates assigned to the U.S. armed forces in Korea, instead of five as he had previously stated. The sixth is a U.S. Air Force officer assigned to Osan Air Base.

50. Mr. Chang resumed his remarks regarding official duty certificates by stating that the Korean negotiators maintained unchanged their position that the definition of official duty should be incorporated in an Agreed Minute in order to eliminate any possibility of ambiguity regarding the question of what constitutes official duty. The Korean negotiators, Mr. Chang continued, are well aware of the difficulties and concern expressed by the U.S. negotiators in connection with this problem. Nevertheless, they feel very strongly that if the U.S. negotiators would generously accept their proposal, it would greatly help them in obtaining the understanding of the Korean people and members of the National Assembly.

51. Agreed Minute Re Paragraph 3(b)

Mr. Chang stated that with regard to Paragraph 1 of the Agreed Minute Re Paragraph 3(b) the Korean negotiators were now prepared to make one of their most significant concessions by accepting the principle of the one-time, en masse waiver of primary jurisdiction. Accordingly, they were withdrawing their proposal to insert at the beginning of Paragraph 1 the words "At the request of the United States."

52. After taking into account the difficulties expressed by the U.S. negotiators at the 80the meeting with

0165

regard to the 21-day ~~limitation~~ contained in the sentence
proposed by the Korean negotiators for addition to Paragraph
4 of the Agreed Minute, Mr. Chang continued, the Korean
negotiators withdrew their previous proposal and now
proposed instead the following additional sentence:

> "In case the Government of the Republic of Korea,
> in resolving disagreement in accordance with the
> foregoing provisions, determines that it is imperative
> that jurisdiction be exercised by the authorities of
> the Republic of Korea, the recall of waiver shall
> be final and conclusive."

53. As the U.S. negotiators were aware, Mr. Chang
said, the above proposal is patterned after the question
raised by the Korean negotiators at the 78th session
and the affirmative reply given by the U.S. negotiators.
Therefore, the Korean negotiators believe that this
proposal does not deviate from, but is consistent with,
the waiver formula proposed by the U.S. negotiators.
Both sides are in agreement on the principle involved but
differ only over the manner of stating the principle.
Furthermore, the Korean negotiators wished to point out
that just as their acceptance of the principle of a
blanket waiver will fully meet the U.S. requirements,
reciprocal acceptance by the U.S. negotiators of this
proposed additional sentence would be very helpful to the
ROK Government in securing the understanding and
cooperation of the Korean people and the National Assembly.
At the same time, it would dispel any misunderstanding or
unnecessary dispute which might arise in the implementation
of the waiver formula. The Korean negotiators hoped,
therefore, that the U.S. negotiators would give full
consideration to their proposal and accept it.

54. Mr. Chang said that, in view of the explanation
by the U.S. negotiators that cases arising under the
provisions of Paragraph 6 of the Agreed Minute Re 3(b)

0166

would be extremely rare and cannot be expected to present any problems, the Korean negotiators accepted the U.S. draft of that paragraph.

55. Agreed Minute Re Paragraph 10(a) and 10(b)

Mr. Chang said the Korean negotiators wished to propose some modifications of the Agreed Minute Re Paragraph 10(a) and 10(b). According to the U.S. draft, he pointed out, the Korean authorities are not allowed to make any arrest within facilities and areas. The Korean negotiators, he said, are not demanding any unconditional right of arrest; the Korean authorities would seek consent in advance from the U.S. military authorities when such arrest within facilities and areas is necessary. The Korean negotiators would also like to point out that the right of pursuit of a flagrant offender who has committed a serious crime is an established principle of international law. Furthermore, if the arrest of a person who is within facilities and areas is desired by the Korean authorities, his arrest should be carried out by the U.S. authorities on request. The Korean negotiators believe mutual cooperation in these matters, as envisaged in their proposals, is essential. They wished to point out that the U.S. draft is also silent on the question of turning over to the Korean authorities persons arrested within facilities and areas. (In the light of the recent agreement of both sides on the custody provisions of this Article, the Korean negotiators believed the original U.S. position with regard to this Agreed Minute should be modified accordingly.)

56. Mr. Chang said that for the reasons just given, the Korean negotiators wished to propose the following modifications in the Agreed Minute:

0167

a. "....The authorities of the Republic of Korea will normally not exercise the right of arrest, search, seizure, or inspection with respect to any person or property within facilities and areas in use by the military authorities of the United States or with respect to property of the United States wherever situated, except in cases where the competent military authorities of the United States consent to such arrest, search, seizure, or inspection by the Korean authorities search, seizure, or inspection by the Korean authorities of such persons or property or in cases of pursuit of a flagrant offender who has committed a serious crime."

b. "Where arrest or detention, search, seizure, or inspection with respect to persons or property within facilities and areas in use by the United States or with respect to property of the United States in the Republic of Korea is desired by the Korean authorities, the United States military authorities will undertake, upon request, to make such arrest or detention, search, seizure, or inspection....."

c. ".....Any person arrested or detained by the U.S. military authorities within, or in the vicinity of, a facility or area who is not a member of the United States armed forces, civilian component, or a dependent shall immediately be turned over to the authorities of the Republic of Korea."

57. Agreed Minute #1 Re Paragraph 1(b)

Mr. Chang stated that the martial law clause, proposed by the U.S. negotiators in their Agreed Minute #1 Re Paragraph 1(b), would require that during a period of martial law the provisions of the Criminal Jurisdiction Article would be suspended in that part of the Republic of Korea under martial law and that during the period of martial law the military authorities of the United States would exercise exclusive jurisdiction over U.S. personnel with respect to offenses committed in the area under martial law. The Korean negotiators are unable to understand the importance which the U.S. negotiators attach to this provision. In the light of the large concessions already made by the Korean negotiators with regard to other provisions of this Article, and for reasons which they would now state, the Korean negotiators, Mr. Chang declared, are unable to accept this Agreed Minute.

0168

58. First, Mr. Chang said, the Korean negotiators had already made an "unbearable" concession to the U.S. negotiators in accepting the U.S. proposal with regard to requests for waiver of exclusive jurisdiction by the ROK Government over offenses, including offenses against the security of the Republic, which are punishable by its law but not by the law of the United States. They had made this concession in the earnest hope that the U.S. negotiators would accede to the Korean requirements with regard to martial law.

59. In the second place, Mr. Chang continued, the Korean negotiators had given assurances in the past that under no circumstances would members of the U.S. armed forces, the civilian component, or their dependents be subject to trial by military tribunals of the Republic of Korea. To further convince the U.S. negotiators of their sincerity, the Korean negotiators had, at this meeting, indicated their willingness to accept the reinsertion of the second sentence of the Agreed Minute Re Paragraph 9(a) rather than as an understanding in the Agreed Joint Summary as they had proposed at the 70th meeting. Furthermore, they had accepted the principle of waiver of primary jurisdiction. Finally, Mr. Chang said, they had been unable to find any precedents for this provision in any other Status of Forces Agreement. Therefore, the Korean negotiators proposed deletion of this Agreed Minute, which would open the way for full agreement on the Criminal Jurisdiction Article and, eventually, the entire SOFA.

한·미국 간의 상호방위조약 제4조에 의한 시설과 구역 및 한국에서의 미국군대의 지위에 관한 협정(SOFA)
전59권. 1966.7.9 서울에서 서명 : 1967.2.9 발효(조약 232호) (V.52 실무교섭회의 합의의사록, 제69-82차, 1965-66)   561

Invited Contractors Article

60. Taking up the Invited Contractors Article, Mr. Chang recalled that full agreement had been reached on all of its provisions with the exception of Paragraph 8, relating to the question of criminal jurisdiction over contracters, their employees, and the dependents of such persons. The Korean negotiators had taken the position that the Republic of Korea should have the primary right to exercise jurisdiction over such persons while the U.S. negotiators had argued that they should be subject to the provisions of the Criminal Jurisdiction Article.

61. Mr. Chang said the Korean negotiators were unable to accept Paragraph 8 for the following reasons. First, since the status of the persons under discussion was that of special commercial entrants with military contracts, if they were turned over to the military authorities of the United States in accordance with the relevant provisions of the Criminal Jurisdiction Article, the U.S. military authorities would have no legal grounds on which to apprehend and punish them equitably. Secondly, their status cannot be equated to the status of members of the civilian component because the former are civilians engaged in profit-seeking business in connection with a military contract while the latter are employees of the Government of the United States, working for the U.S. armed forces. Consequently the members of the civilian component are under strict punitive regulations of the armed forces. Furthermore, the privileges which the Korean negotiators deem essential for the performance by the contractors of their contracts will be given to them

0170

under the provisions of Paragraph 3 of this Article.
Finally, Mr. Chang said, the Korean negotiators had
been unable to find any precedents for Paragraph 8 in
other Status of Forces Agreements.

62. In view of the considerations which he had just
stated, Mr. Chang continued, acceptance by the ROK
Government of such a discriminatory and unprecedented
proposal would result in added burdens to the Government
and might eventually jeopardize its position with the
people and the National Assembly at the time of ratification
of the Agreement and during its implementation. Therefore,
the Korean negotiators requested the U.S. negotiators
to take into full account the relevant factors and
generously accept the Korean position, thereby strengthening
the position of the ROK Government in its efforts to cope
with possible future difficulties.

63. Mr. Chang said the Korean negotiators wished to
retain in the Agreed Joint Summary the following understandings
which had already been agreed to:

   a. The U.S. armed forces shall no longer bring
   into the Republic of Korea any employees of third-
   country nationality after the entry into force of
   this Agreement.

   b. If the U.S. authorities determine that
   there would be significant advantage for U.S. -ROK
   mutual defense to utilize one or more third-
   country corporations as USFK-invited contractors,
   the authorities of the Government of the Republic
   of Korea shall give sympathetic consideration to a
   U.S. request to extend the benefits of this Agreement
   to such non-U.S. corporations.

64. Mr. Chang stated that the Korean negotiators also
wished to record their understanding that under the provisions
of Paragraph 2 of this Article, designation as invited
contractors of corporations and persons already located
in the Republic of Korea at the time of entry into force
of the Agreement shall be subject to review by the competent

0171

authorities of the Republic of Korea and the United States in the Joint Committee. Further, any future renewal of the designation or any new designation with respect to the corporations and persons referred to in Paragraph 1 of the Article would be the subject of consultation in advance in the Joint Committee.

65. Mr. Fleck thanked Mr. Chang for the very detailed and comprehensive presentation made by the Korean negotiators and stated that the U.S. negotiators would give very careful and serious consideration to the Korean proposals.

0172

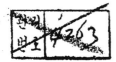

STATUS OF FORCES NEGOTIATIONS: 82d Meeting

SUBJECTS:
1. Facilities and Areas
2. Non-appropriated Fund Organizations
3. Invited Contractors
4. Labor
5. Criminal Jurisdiction
6. Claims
7. Entry into Force of Agreement

PLACE: Ministry of Foreign Affairs

DATE: July 8, 1966

PARTICIPANTS:

Republic of Korea	United States
CHANG Sang-mun	Richard A. Ericson, Jr.
YUN Wun-yong	Col Allan G. Pixton, USA
HO Song-chun	Col Herbert C. Hicks, Jr., USA
YI Nam-ki	Capt George M. Hagerman, USN
KIM Tong-hwi	Col Wilson Freeman, USA
HO Hyong-ku	Richard M. Herndon
Col KIM Won-kil, ROKA	Robert A. Kinney
Lt Col Suh In-suk	Goodwin Shapiro
KIM Ki-cho	Ronald P. Myers
PAK Won-chol	Ogden Reed, Observer
YI Kun-pal (Interpreter)	

2 Inclosures
1. Ltr from Minister of Foreign
   Affairs Tong Won Lee
2. Ltr from Ambassador Brown

0173

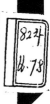

Article IV - Facilities and Areas - Return of Facilities

1. Mr. Ericson noted that, at the 81st session the Korean negotiators proposed a new Agreed Minute, to be added as Agreed Minute No. 2 to the US draft. The US negotiators agree that this new Agreed Minute is the corollary to Agreed Minute No. 1. It is logical that all removable properties located in any area or facilities which are provided by the ROK Government should be returned whenever such properties are no longer needed for the US armed forces.

2. Therefore, Mr. Ericson continued, the US negotiators are happy to accept the new proposed Agreed Minute No. 2, and thereby achieve full agreement on this Article.

Article XIII - Non-appropriated Fund Organizations Article

3. Mr. Ericson noted that, at the 81st meeting, the ROK negotiators accepted the Agreed Minute of Article XIII as proposed by the US negotiators. The US side agrees to the understanding for the Agreed Joint Summary proposed by the ROK negotiators at the 81st meeting relating to this Agreed Minute, and full US-ROK agreement on this Article has now been achieved.

Article XV - Invited Contractors

4. Mr. Ericson stated that, at the 81st negotiating session, the Korean negotiators reiterated their objection to Paragraph 8 of the US draft and requested the acceptance of their Paragraph 8. This matter was subsequently extensively discussed at informal meetings between members of the ROK and US negotiating team. As a result of these

2

0174

discussions, the United States negotiators now accept Paragraph 8, as proposed by the Korean negotiators, with minor modifications as follows:

"8. The authorities of the Republic of Korea shall have the right to exercise jurisdiction over such persons for offenses committed in the Republic of Korea and punishable by the law of the Republic of Korea. In recognition of the role of such persons in the defense of the Republic of Korea, they shall be subject to the provisions of paragraphs 5, 7(b), and 9 and the related Agreed Minutes, of Article XXII. In those cases in which the authorities of the Republic of Korea decide not to exercise jurisdiction they shall notify the military authorities of the United States as soon as possible. Upon such notification the military authorities of the United States shall have the right to exercise such jurisdiction over the persons referred to as is conferred on them by the law of the United States."

5. Mr. Ericson noted that in the first sentence, the word "primary" was deleted. This was necessary to prevent misunderstanding since the term "primary jurisdiction" relates to the exercise of concurrent jurisdiction. Under the present state of U.S. laws, the Korean jurisdiction over contractor employees is exclusive, although it is understood that the effective administration and disciplinary sanctions available to the United States may be appropriate in certain cases.

6. Mr. Ericson stated that the second sentence is a proposed addition to Paragraph 8. It provides that personnel under this article

3

will be subject to the provisions of the Criminal Juristiction Article and its Agreed Minutes relating to custody, confinement and trial safe-guards. This takes nothing away from the right of jurisdiction retained by the Republic of Korea. It merely confers upon these persons the same protections relating to custody, confinement and trial safeguards as are accorded members of the civilian component. Mr. Ericson emphasized that invited contractors have an important role in the defense of the Republic of Korea and are indispensable to the United States military forces. It is deemed essential that they receive the minimal protections offered by the custody, confinement and trial safeguard provisions. The last two sentences of Paragraph 8 are accepted as proposed by the ROK without change. The US negotiators trust that these modifications will be acceptable to the Korean negotiators and that full agreement can now be reached on this Article.

7. Mr. Chang replied that, with regard to the modified proposals tabled by the U.S. negotiators regarding Paragraph 8 of the Invited Contractors Article, the Korean negotiators wish to present the following response. The Korean negotiators are prepared to accept deletion of the word "primary" from the first sentence on the basis of the statement by the US negotiators to the effect that:

> "Under the present state of U.S. law, the Korean
> jurisdiction over contractor employees is exclusive
> although it is understood that the effective
> administration and disciplinary sanctions available

4

0176

to the United States may be appropriate in
certain cases."

8. With respect to the proposed new second sentence which is to be
incorporated into the provisions of Paragraph 8, which provides that in
recognition of the role of such personnel in the defense of the Republic
of Korea, the persons referred to in Paragraph 1 shall be subject to the
provisions of Paragraph 5, 7(b), 9 and its related Agreed Minutes of
Article XXII. Mr. Chang recalled that the U.S. negotiators had in the
past placed their special emphasis on guarantees of fair trial for U.S.
personnel on the grounds that as U.S. citizens they are entitled to such
rights as are guaranteed under the Constitution of the United States.
In the course of negotiations regarding the Invited Contractors Article,
they had further stated that although those third-country employees
who are present on the effective date of this Agreement will be entitled
to enjoy the privileges contained in this Article, there is no
intention to bring in any third-country nationals after the Agreement
goes into force, but if any were brought in, they would have no
privileges under the terms of this Article, thereby indicating their
flexibility toward the extent of privileges to be granted to third-
country employees under this Article.

9. Mr. Chang stated that, in the light of the above position of
the U.S. negotiators, the Korean negotiators believe that application
of such privileges as proposed by the U.S. negotiators in their second
sentence of Paragraph 8 pertaining to the provisions of Paragraphs 5,

5

0177

7(b), 9 and its related Agreed Minutes of the Criminal Jurisdiction Article should naturally be limited to U.S. nationals only. Consequently, it is also the view of the Korean negotiators, Mr. Chang continued, that the privileges to be granted under Agreed Minute No. 2 of this Article to the contractor employees of third-country nationality who are present in the Republic of Korea on the effective date of this Agreement shall, to be consonant with the above observation of Paragraph 8, not include any privilege provided for in the proposed second sentence of Paragraph 8.

10. Mr. Chang pointed out that in this connection, the Korean negotiators, before accepting the U.S. modifications, wish to seek clarification from the U.S. negotiators on their intention as to the following two points:

a. Whether or not third-country employees and those employees who are ordinarily resident in, but are not nationals of the United States, and their dependents will be subject to the provisions of Paragraph 5, 7(b), 9 and its related Agreed Minutes of the Criminal Jurisdiction Article?

b. Whether or not the privileges to be granted to third-country employees under Agreed Minute No. 2 include the privileges in the proposed second sentence of Paragraph 8 relating to the Criminal Jurisdiction Article?

6

0178

11. Mr. Ericson replied that the United States negotiators, in response to the ROK queries in Paragraph 10, agree to the following understanding for the Agreed Joint Summary.

"Unless otherwise agreed in the Joint Committee, the privileges provided for in the second sentence of Paragraph 8 of this Article shall be extended only to United States nationals."

The US negotiators also can assure the Koreans, as indicated in the informal discussions, that such requests for Joint Committee consideration on this point are expected to be rare.

12. Mr. Chang stated that, with these explanations and under-standings in the Joint Summary Record, the Korean negotiators now accept the proposed U.S. modifications regarding Paragraph 8, thereby reaching full agreement on this Article.

Article XVII - Labor

13. Mr. Ericson tabled a revised Labor Article, which he stated was responsive to the proposals made by the ROK negotiators at the 81st session, and at subsequent informal meetings. He expressed the belief that this revised Labor Article fully meets the ROK requirements, and he anticipates full agreement can now be reached on the revised text of the Labor Article.

14. Mr. Ericson stated that the following comments refer to specific changes in the previously tabled United States draft, made in response to the Korean proposals at the 81st session:

7

0173

a. <u>Paragraph 1(b)</u>. The US negotiators accept the ROK proposal for the inclusion of a new sentence in Paragraph 1(b), as follows: "Such employees shall be nationals of the Republic of Korea." This sentence is accepted on the condition of ROK acceptance of two understandings for the Agreed Summary Record, as follows:

> (1) "Local residents, who are third-country nationals and are also local-hire USFK employees and local-hire contractor employees paid in won, on the effective date of the agreement, shall be excluded from the application of this provision."

There are only a few USFK employees in this category, who have been working with USFK in good faith for some years, and the US negotiators feel their exclusion from this provision would not present problems and would only be fair to all concerned.

> (2) The second understanding is as follows:
> "The provisions of Paragraph 1(b) do not preclude the United States armed forces from bringing into Korea, <u>without privileges,</u> third-country contractor employees possessing special skills not available from the Korean labor force."

The US negotiators believe general US-ROK agreement on this point is reflected in previous informal discussions. In adding the new sentence to Paragraph 1(b), it is also necessary to add, in the parenthetical phrase "(other than a member of the civilian component)" the phrase "or a contractor employee under Article XV," to enable invited contractors to hire American personnel. Mr. Ericson pointed

8

0180

out that invited contractor employees are not included as part of the civilian component in the Definitions Article (I). Therefore, this added phrase is made necessary by the ROK-proposed added sentence, and it makes it clear that the word "employee" as used in this Article does not refer to non-Korean employees of invited contractors.

b. <u>Paragraph 2 and Agreed Minutes No. 1, 2, 3</u>. The US negotiators believe the two sides are now in full agreement regarding Paragraph 2 and Agreed Minutes 1, 2, and 3 as previously tabled by the US. Mr. Ericson noted that, during the informal discussions which took place since the 81st meeting, it was mutually agreed that the ROK-proposed understanding relating to Agreed Minute No. 2, reported in Paragraph 27 of the Agreed Summary Record of the 81st meeting, would be withdrawn.

c. <u>Paragraph 3 and Agreed Minute No. 4</u>. Mr. Ericson stated that the US negotiators accept the revisions in Paragraph 3, as tabled by the ROK negotiators at the 81st meeting. With regard to the related Agreed Minute No. 4, subsequent to the 81st meeting the ROK negotiators proposed revision of the text of this Agreed Minute which they had previously tabled. Their new proposal is as follows:

"4. When employers cannot conform with provisions of labor legislation of the Republic of Korea applicable under this Article on account of the military requirements of the United States armed forces, the matter shall be referred, in advance, to the Joint Committee for consideration and appropriate action. In the event mutual agreement cannot be reached in the Joint Committee regarding appropriate action, the issue may be made the subject of review through discussions between appropriate officials of the Government of the Republic of Korea and the diplomatic mission of the United States of America."

9

0181

Mr. Chang noted that the ROK negotiators had revised their previously tabled Agreed Minute No. 4, deleting the words "whenever possible". In proposing this revised language, Mr. Chang stated that the ROK Government is appreciative of the need for the United States armed forces to have the flexibility in an emergency to deviate from ROK labor legislation without referral to the Joint Committee, as presented by the US negotiators at the 71st meeting (Paragraph 15 of the Agreed Joint Summary) and at the 73rd meeting (Paragraph 5 of the Agreed Joint Summary). Therefore, the ROK negotiators proposed the following agreed understanding which will be included in the Agreed Joint Summary, as follows:

> "It is understood that the deviation from Korean labor
> legislation need not be referred to the Joint Committee
> in cases when such referral would seriously hamper mili-
> tary operations in an emergency."

Mr. Ericson stated that the US negotiators were authorized to accept the ROK proposal to delete the phrase "whenever possible" in Agreed Minute 4 on the basis that the ROK-proposed agreed understanding, which the US accepts, clearly indicates that the United States military authorities can deviate from Korean labor legislation without referral to the Joint Committee when such would seriously hamper military operations in an emergency. Mr. Chang stated that whenever the matter is referred to the Joint Committee after the deviation had already been made on account of military requirements in an emergency, it is presumed that the Korean side could raise objection in the Joint Committee to the

10

0182

action taken by the employer and request that appropriate action, i.e.,
corrective action or measures for remedy be taken. It is understood that
such corrective action will be taken as and when the Joint Committee so
directs. In the event that mutual agreement cannot be reached in the
Joint Committee regarding appropriate action, the matter may be discussed
between officials of the Government of the Republic of Korea and the US
diplomatic mission. Mr. Chang indicated that these remarks are not
intended to introduce any new understanding, but rather are intended to
provide guidance to the members of the Joint Committee in their interpretation and implementation of the new agreed Labor Article.

    d. Paragraph 4: The US side concurs in the proposed ROK changes
at the end of Paragraph 4 (a) (5), changing the number in parentheses
from "3" to "2" in the following phrase: "as stipulated in subparagraph
(2), above."

    The US side also accepts the revised Paragraph 4 (b), as proposed
by the ROK side, as follows:

> "Employees or any employee organization shall have the
> right of further collective action in the event a labor
> dispute is not resolved by the foregoing procedures
> except in cases where the Joint Committee determines
> such action seriously hampers military operations of the
> United States armed forces for the Joint defense of the
> Republic of Korea. In the event an agreement cannot be
> reached on this question in the Joint Committee, it may
> be made the subject of review through discussions

11

0183

between appropriate officials of the Government of the Republic of Korea and the diplomatic mission of the United States of America."

In accepting this ROK proposal on this important point, the US side should like it understood and agreed that the Joint Committee will take up as one of its earliest items of business the delineation of those activities the interruption of which would seriously hamper military operations of the United States armed forces for the joint defense of the ROK. In the Joint Committee's consideration of this matter, the Korean Labor Disputes Act of 1953 should be used as a general guide.

e. Paragraph 5: The US side accepts the ROK-proposed added phrase, "through mutual consultation," after the word "deferred."

f. Agreed Minute No. 5: The US negotiators also accept the modifications of Agreed Minute No. 5, as proposed by the ROK negotiators at the 81st meeting, with the addition of the phrase "by the employers" as agreed upon in informal discussions. The full text of Agreed Minute No. 5 is as follows:

> "5. A union or other employee group shall be recognized by the employers unless its objectives are inimical to the common interests of the United States and the Republic of Korea. Membership or non-membership in such groups shall not be a factor in employment or other actions affecting employees."

15. Mr. Ericson states that he felt that the revisions of text of the Labor Article, as tabled by the US side at this meeting, will be fully

12

0184

acceptable to the ROK negotiators. These proposals are presented as a package and the US revisions of its draft in response to ROK proposals are contingent upon ROK acceptance of the rest of the text and understandings.

16. Mr. Chang stated that the Korean negotiators appreciate the general acceptance of the revised draft of the Labor Article, as tabled at 81st session and as revised as a result of informal discussions. The Korean side accepts the modifications effected in Paragraph 1 (b) and Agreed Minutes No. 4 and No. 5, as well as in the agreed understandings, and therefore full agreement has been reached on the Labor Article.

Article XXII - Criminal Jurisdiction

17. Mr. Ericson noted that, at the 81st negotiating session, the Korean negotiators accepted the US draft of the Criminal Jurisdiction Article with certain modifications. The United States negotiators are now pleased to accept the proposals made by the ROK negotiators at that session, subject to Korean acceptance of several minor changes. Specifically, the US side accepts:

a. The Korean proposals relating to Paragraph 7(b), verbatim.

b. The understanding on the Agreed Minute Re Para 2, as follows:

"It is understood that the United States authorities shall exercise utmost restraint in requesting waivers of exclusive jurisdiction as provided for in the Agreed Minute Re Paragraph 2 of this Article."

c. The Understanding on Agreed Minute Re Para 3(a), with deletion of the previously proposed phrase "or his designee," as follows:

13

0185

"A duty certificate shall be issued only upon the advice of
a Staff Judge Advocate, and the competent authority issuing
the duty certificates shall be a General Grade officer."

d. Mr. Ericson stated the US side accepts the Korean proposal to
delete the word "civil" from Paragraph 1(b) and to reinsert the second
sentence of Agreed Minute Re Paragraph 9(a), on the condition ROK negotiators accept the following understanding on Paragraph 1(b) for inclusion
in the Agreed Joint Summary:

"The civil authorities of the Republic of Korea will retain
full control over the arrest, investigation and trial of a
member of the United States armed forces or civilian
component or a dependent."

The US negotiators believe that this statement represents the positions of
both sides and that this is a mutually agreeable understanding.

e. Regarding the definition of official duty, the US side is
prepared to compromise by including the first sentence of the official
duty definition as the second sentence of Agreed Minute No. 1 Re Para 3(a).
The second sentence will be included as an understanding in the Agreed
Joint Summary, as follows:

"With regard to the Agreed Minute Re Paragraph 3(a),
a substantial departure from the acts a person is
required to perform in a particular duty usually will
indicate an act outside of his "official duty."

f. With reference to Agreed Minute Re Para 9(g), the additional
language proposed by the Korean negotiators at the 81st session is

14

0186

unacceptable. It is recognized that similar language contained in subpara (b) of Agreed Minute No. ⑥ Re Para 3(b) of the US draft is likewise objectionable to the Korean negotiators. Therefore, the US side proposes deletion of the following portion of the second sentence of subpara (b):

> "... except where his presence is incompatible with the rules of the court of the United States or with the security requirements of the United States, which are not at the same time the security requirements of the Republic of Korea."

This proposal is conditioned on acceptance by the Korean negotiators of the US draft Agreed Minute Re Para 9(g) as tabled.

g. Regarding Agreed Minute Re Para 10(a) and 10(b), the US negotiators have given careful consideration to the Korean proposal tabled at the 81st session and also the informal discussions held thereafter. The US negotiators are now tabling a modification of this US draft which it is believed will more than fulfill the desires of the Korean negotiators. It should be noted that the language is virtually identical to the similar provisions of the Japanese SOFA.

18. Mr. Ericson emphasized that the US negotiators agree to all of the foregoing ROK proposals made at the 81st meeting, on the condition that the ROK accept the few proposed changes the US side has made. Mr. Ericson stated that he is confident that these changes will be agreeable to the Korean negotiators and that full agreement can be reached on this Article as now tabled.

15

0187

19. Mr. Chang expressed the appreciation of the Korean negotiators to the United States negotiators for the most careful consideration and acceptance of those proposals tabled by the Korean negotiators at the 81st session, i.e.:

    a. The additional proposals relating to Paragraph 7(b).

    b. The understanding on the Agreed Minute Re Paragraph 2.

    c. The understanding on Agreed Minute Re Paragraph 3(a).

20. Mr. Chang stated that the Korean negotiators are now prepared to accept the following proposals tabled by the US negotiators:

    a. The Agreed Minute No. 1 Re Paragraph 1(b), verbatim.

    b. The US proposal regarding the definition of official duty which includes the first sentence of the definition as the second sentence of the Agreed Minute No. 1 Re Paragraph 3(a) and the second sentence of the definition as an understanding in the Agreed Joint Summary.

    c. The US proposals relating to Agreed Minute Re Paragraph 9(g) and subparagraph (b) of Agreed Minute No. 3 of Re Paragraph 3(b) with deletion of the following identical languages therefrom:

> "... except where his presence is incompatible with the rules of the court of the United States or with the security requirements of the United States, which are not at the same time the security requirements of the Republic of Korea."

    d. The modifications of the US draft regarding Agreed Minute Re Paragraph 10(a) and 10(b).

16

0188

21. Mr. Chang stated that, with respect to Paragraph 1(b) of the US draft, the Korean negotiators express their thanks to the U.S. side for deletion of the word "civil" from their draft coupled with reinsertion of the second sentence of Agreed Minute Re Paragraph 9(a). However, the Korean negotiators have noted that the deletion of the word "civil" from their draft is conditioned upon ROK acceptance of the following understanding in the Agreed Joint Summary:

> "The civil authorities of the Republic of Korea will retain full control over the arrest, investigation and trial of a member of the United States armed forces or civilian component or a dependent."

To accommodate the U.S. concern over this problem, the Korean negotiators had in the past reiterated their assurances that the U.S. personnel shall under no circumstances be tried by the military tribunal of the Republic of Korea, and thus have accepted the second sentence of Agreed Minute Re Paragraph 9(a) and Agreed Minute No. 1 of Re Paragraph 1(b) of the U.S. draft regarding martial law. In the light of the trend of the past negotiations on this problem, the Korean negotiators, to expedite and complete the negotiations as soon as practicable, and at the same time to fulfill the requirements of the US negotiators, accept the proposed U.S. understanding with the Korean interpretation of the understanding that the US negotiators are merely reaffirming their basic position that the U.S. personnel referred to in Paragraph 1(b) of this Article shall under no circumstances be arrested, investigated, or tried by the military authorities or military tribunals of the Republic of Korea.

17

0189

22. The US side indicated, in June 1965, acceptance of the addition of the new sentence in Agreed Minute No. 4, Re Paragraph 3(b), as proposed by the ROK side at the 81st meeting. However, in June 1966, when it became clear as a result of informal US-ROK discussions that a new approach to this Agreed Minute was required, if agreement was to be reached, the US side formally proposed a new package approach to the problem. The new package included three interrelated elements, including Agreed Minute Re Paragraph 3(b), an open exchange of letters between the ROK Foreign Minister and the US Ambassador to Korea and new agreed understandings for the Agreed Joint Summary.

a. The text of the new Agreed Minute Re Paragraph 3(b), as modified as a result of informal negotiations, is as follows:

Re Paragraph 3(b)

1. The authorities of the Republic of Korea, recognizing that it is the primary responsibility of the United States military authorities to maintain good order and discipline where persons subject to United States military laws are concerned, will, upon the request of the military authorities of the United States pursuant to Paragraph 3(c), waive their primary right to exercise jurisdiction under Paragraph 3(b) except when they determine that it is of particular importance that jurisdiction be exercised by the authorities of the Republic of Korea.

2. With the consent of the competent authorities of the Republic of Korea, the military authorities of the United States

18

0190

be transferred to the courts or authorities of the Republic of Korea for investigation, trial and decision, particular criminal cases in which jurisdiction rests with the United States.

With the consent of the military authorities of the United States, the competent authorities of the Republic of Korea may transfer to the military authorities of the United States for investigation, trial and decision, particular criminal cases in which jurisdiction rests with the Republic of Korea.

3. (a) Where a member of the United States armed forces or civilian component, or a dependent, is arraigned before a court of the United States, for an offense committed in the Republic of Korea against Korean interests, the trial shall be held within the Republic of Korea

(i) except where the law of the United States requires otherwise, or

(ii) except where, in cases of military exigency or in the interests of justice, the military authorities of the United States intend to hold the trial outside the Republic of Korea. In this event they shall afford the authorities of the Republic of Korea timely opportunity to comment on such intention and shall give due consideration to any comments the latter may make.

(b) Where the trial is held outside of the Republic of Korea the military authorities of the United States shall inform the authorities of the Republic of Korea of the place and date of

19

0191

the trial. A representative of the Republic of Korea shall be entitled to be present at the trial. The authorities of the United States shall inform the authorities of the Republic of Korea of the judgment and the final outcome of the proceedings.

4. In the implementation of the provisions of this Article, and to facilitate the expeditious disposal of offenses, arrangements may be made between the United States military authorities and the competent authorities of the Republic of Korea.

b. The full texts of the unclassified letters to be exchanged between the ROK Foreign Minister and the U.S. Ambassador, which were modified as a result of informal negotiations, are attached as Inclosures 1 and 2.

c. The new agreed understandings to be included in the Agreed Joint Summary, as modified as a result of informal negotiations, are as follows:

"1. It is understood that the term "of particular importance" has reference to those cases in which, after a careful examination of each specific case, the exercise of jurisdiction by the Republic of Korea is deemed essential and the term has reference, in general but not exclusively, to the following types of offenses:

(a) security offenses against the Republic of Korea;

(b) offenses causing the death of a human being,

20

0192

robbery and rape, except where the offenses are directed against a member of the United States armed forces, the civilian component, or a dependent; and

(c) attempts to commit such offenses or participation therein.

"2. In respect of the offenses referred to in the above paragraph, the authorities concerned shall proceed in particularly close cooperation from the beginning of the preliminary investigation in order to provide the mutual assistance envisaged in paragraph 6 of Article XXII."

23. Mr. Chang had indicated the strong desire of the ROK side to delete the second sentence of the first paragraph of the revised Agreed Minute Re Paragraph 3(b), as initially proposed by the US side. This sentence, which had originally been proposed by the ROK side, was as follows:

"In cases where any question concerning such determination as may be made by the authorities of the Republic of Korea in accordance with the foregoing provisions cannot be resolved in discussions between the authorities concerned, the United States diplomatic mission will be afforded an opportunity to confer with the proper authorities of the Republic of Korea."

After informal negotiations, the US agreed to delete this sentence, if the ROK will accept the following agreed understanding on this point:

21

0193

"In cases where, in view of the United States authorities, any question arises concerning the determination that a case is one 'of particular importance,' the United States diplomatic mission reserves the right and expects to be afforded an opportunity to confer with the proper authorities of the Republic of Korea."

Mr. Chang stated that the ROK side agrees to this understanding. Notwithstanding the foregoing understanding, however, Mr. Chang stated that authorities of the Republic of Korea shall not be prevented from exercising their primary jurisdiction under Agreed Minute Re Paragraph 3(b) of Article XXII. Mr. Ericson responded that this is also the US interpretation.

24. Mr. Chang stated that the ROK side accepts the US package proposal for Agreed Minute Re Paragraph 3(b), thereby reaching full US-ROK agreement on this key issue of waiver.

25. Mr. Chang indicated, finally, that there were two other minor changes which the ROK side desired to propose, as follows:

a. The first is a new Agreed Minute Re Paragraph 1(a). Mr. Chang stated that notwithstanding the provision of Paragraph 1(a) of the Article, the U.S. military authorities have no criminal jurisdiction in peacetime over members of the civilian component and dependents. Therefore, the Korean negotiators propose the following new Agreed Minute Re Paragraph 1(a) regarding the extent of U.S. military criminal jurisdiction:

"It is understood that under the present state of

22

0194

United States law, the military authorities of the
United States have no effective criminal jurisdiction
in peacetime over members of the civilian component
or dependents. If the scope of United States military
jurisdiction changes as a result of subsequent legislation, constitutional amendment, or decision by
appropriate authorities of the United States, the
Government of the United States shall inform the
Government of the Republic of Korea through diplomatic channels."

b. The second proposed change relates to Agreed Minute Re
Paragraph 2, which the ROK side desires to revise as follows:

"The Republic of Korea, recognizing the effectiveness in
appropriate cases of the administrative and disciplinary
sanctions which may be imposed by the United States
authorities over members of the United States armed
forces or civilian component, and their dependents, may,
at the request of the military authorities of the United
States, waive its right to exercise jurisdiction under
paragraph 2."

26. Mr. Ericson stated that the US side could accept the change
in Agreed Minute Re Paragraph 2 and a new Agreed Minute Re Paragraph
1(a), if the ROK Government would accept the following agreed understanding:

23

0195

"The Government of the Republic of Korea agrees

that, upon notification under the second sentence

of the Agreed Minute Re Paragraph 1(a), the

military authorities of the United States may

exercise jurisdiction over such persons in

accordance with the terms of the Criminal Juris-

diction Article."

27. Mr. Chang indicated ROK acceptance of this agreed understanding in paragraph 26, above. He stated that, with the acceptance of
this agreed understanding by the Korean negotiators, both sides have now
reached full agreement on the Article dealing with Criminal Jurisdiction,
the heart of the Status of Forces Agreement between the United States
and the Republic of Korea.

Article XXIII - Claims.

28. Mr. Ericson noted that, at the 81st negotiating session, the
Korean negotiators tabled a revised draft of the Claims Article, including modifications of Paragraph 5(e) (iii) and Agreed Minute No. 1
and paragraph 12 relating to the Korean Service Corps. The United
States negotiators are pleased to accept this revised Claims Article,
subject to ROK acceptance of the following revised Agreed Minute No. 1
of the Claims Article:

"1. Unless otherwise provided, the provisions of para-

graphs 5, 6, 7 and 8 of this Article will become effective

six months from the date of entry into force of this

24

0196

Agreement with respect to claims arising from incidents in the Seoul Special City area, and one year from that date with respect to claims arising elsewhere in the Republic of Korea."

29. Mr. Ericson pointed out that this revised Agreed Minute No. 1 provides for a specific timetable for the progressive turnover of United States Claims Service responsibilities to the ROK Government Claims Service. This progressive US transfer of claims responsibilities to the ROK Government, first in the Seoul Special City area six months after the entry into force of the SOFA, and throughout the Republic of Korea six months later, should provide the basis for an orderly transfer of these complex responsibilities. The primary US concern in this matter is to insure prompt and equitable settlement for Korean claimants against the USFK. This proposal should meet the needs of both Governments and assure justice to deserving Korean claimants in the transition period during which the United States transfers the responsibilities for settlement of claims to the Government of the Republic of Korea.

30. Mr. Chang stated that the Korean negotiators accept the US proposal regarding the Claims Article in order to reach full agreement at the present session. Mr. Chang continued that the Korean negotiators also believe, as just stated by the US negotiators, that the primary concern of the Korean negotiators in this matter is to insure prompt and equitable settlements of the claims for damages caused by USFK.

25

0197

Mr. Chang noted that with this fact in mind, the Korean negotiators accept the revised Agreed Minute No. 1, which provides for transfer of the claims responsibilities to the ROK in Seoul Special City area six months after entry into force of the SOFA, and throughout the ROK 12 months after the entry into force of the SOFA, thereby reaching full agreement on this Article.

31. The ROK and US Chief Negotiators agreed the two sides are now in full agreement on the Claims Article, on the basis of the ROK draft tabled at the 81st meeting and the revised Agreed Minute No. 1, as set forth in Paragraph 25. 28 7 the Runway

Article XXIX - Entry into Force of Agreement.

32. Mr. Ericson stated that the United States Government will accept the Ratification Article proposed by the ROK negotiators at the 81st session, subject to minor modifications in which it is understood the ROK side concurs.

33. Mr. Ericson stated that the US side accepts the full text of the ROK proposal made at the 81st session, verbatim, with only the following two modifications:

a. In Paragraph 1, the phrase "three months" is substituted for the phrase "sixty days." There is mutual agreement regarding the need for the longer time interval between ratification and the entry into force of the Agreement. It is proposed that the precise date of entry into force should be mutually acknowledged at the time of the receipt of the ROK Government's written notification that it has

26

0198

approved the Agreement in accordance with its legal procedures (probably the same date three months later).

b. In Paragraph 2, a change is proposed which it is believed will make the sentence read more smoothly without changing its meaning. Substitution of the word "the" for "its" in the last clause of the sentence is proposed. This change makes the last clause read "to give effect to the provisions of this Agreement."

34. In accepting the ROK draft of this Article, with these minor modifications, Mr. Ericson indicated he would like to reiterate the US views concerning implementation of the Agreement, as previously presented at the 80th session. The US negotiators believe both sides are in full agreement on the importance of careful planning and action by their respective governments to insure the maximum possible efficiency and effectiveness in the implementation of the SOFA. In the language of Paragraph 2, the ROK Government will endeavor to take "all legislative and budgetary action necessary to give effect to the provisions of this Agreement." The US negotiators believe such necessary action also includes any other necessary implementing action, such as issuing appropriate administrative regulations. United States authorities in Korea will inform the Government of the Republic of Korea, on a continuing basis, of their progress in implementation of the Agreement. The US side expects that the ROK Government, similarly, will inform appropriate United States officials of its progress in implementation of the SOFA and that copies of pertinent documents and regulations

27

0199

issued by ROK and United States authorities will be exchanged. We
believe both sides are in mutual agreement on the necessity for
consistent and coordinated action, to insure smooth implementation
of the SOFA.

35. Mr. Chang stated that the Korean negotiators appreciate
the concurrence of the U.S. negotiators to the revised Korean draft
of the Ratification Article and accept the two modifications proposed
by the U.S. side in Paragraphs 1 and 2. Both sides, thereby, have also
reached full agreement on this Article. Mr. Chang further stated that,
similarly, the Korean side has no objection to exchange, on a
continuous basis, of copies of pertinent documents and regulations
issued by authorities of both Governments to give effect to the
provisions of the Agreement, as well as any other information on the
progress of the Korean Government in carrying out the Agreement, in
order to insure the maximum possible efficiency and effectiveness in
the implementation of the present Status of Forces Agreement between
the Republic of Korea and the United States.

36. Mr. Chang replied that the ROK negotiators are in full agreement with the US negotiators on this Article, and with this agreement
the US and ROK negotiators have now achieved agreement on all 31
Articles of the US-ROK Status of Forces Agreement. Therefore, formal
negotiations of this Status of Forces Agreement is finally concluded,
after 45 months of negotiations.

37. In concluding the final session of the negotiations, both

28

0200

the Republic of Korea and the United States negotiators exchanged their heartfelt praise for the patience and friendly cooperation rendered by those who have tirelessly participated in one of the most lengthy yet epoch-making negotiations, which resulted in the achievement of a US-ROK Status of Forces Agreement.

29

0201

July 9, 1966

His Excellency
Winthrop G. Brown
Ambassador of the United States of America
Seoul, Korea

Excellency:

Today the Governments of the United States and the Republic
of Korea have formally signed the Agreement between the
United States of America and the Republic of Korea regarding
facilities and areas and the status of United States armed
forces in the Republic of Korea. Article XXII of that
Agreement and its agreed minutes provide for the exercise of
jurisdiction over members of the United States armed forces,
the civilian component, and their dependents in the Republic
of Korea. In this regard, the Government of the Republic of
Korea, conscious of the strong ties of mutual respect and
friendship which bind our two countries, and recognizing the
vital role which United States armed forces play in the
defense of the Republic of Korea, proposes the following
understandings for procedural arrangements pursuant to Paragraph 4 of the Agreed Minute Re Paragraph 3(b):

      That, to facilitate the processing of cases
resulting from the presence of United States armed
forces deployed in the Republic of Korea for mutual
defense purposes, in implementation of the provisions
of the Agreed Minute Re Paragraph 3(b), the Government of the Republic of Korea will not require the
military authorities of the United States to make a
request for a waiver in each particular case, and the
military authorities of the United States shall have
jurisdiction unless the Government of the Republic of
Korea determines in a specific case that it is of
particular importance that jurisdiction be exercised
therein by the authorities of the Republic of Korea;

      That, in the interest of expediting the
administration of justice, any such determination by
the Government of the Republic of Korea shall be

Incl 1

0202

shorter period as may be mutually agreed upon pursuant to Paragraph 4 of the Agreed Minute Re Paragraph 3(b). The military authorities of the United States shall not exercise jurisdiction before the expiration of the fifteen days or other agreed period.

Very sincerely yours,

Winthrop G. Brown
Ambassador

2

0203

July 9, 1966

His Excellency
Tong Won Lee
Minister of Foreign Affairs
 of the Republic of Korea
Seoul, Korea

Dear Mr. Minister:

I have received your letter of this date on the subject of
the agreement signed today between the Republic of Korea
and the United States of America regarding facilities and
areas and the status of United States armed forces in the
Republic of Korea, and confirm the following understandings
contained therein with respect to the exercise of jurisdiction
over members of the United States armed forces, the civilian
component, and their dependents:

    That, to facilitate the processing of cases
resulting from the presence of United States armed
forces deployed in Korea for mutual defense purposes,
in implementation of the provisions of the Agreed
Minute Re Paragraph 3(b), the Government of the
Republic of Korea will not require the military
authorities of the United States to make a request
for a waiver in each particular case, and the military
authorities of the United States shall have jurisdiction
unless the Government of the Republic of Korea
determines in a specific case that it is of particular
importance that jurisdiction be exercised therein by
the authorities of the Republic of Korea;

    That, in the interest of expediting the adminis-
tration of justice, any such determination by the
Government of the Republic of Korea shall be provided
in writing by the Minister of Justice to the appropriate
military authorities of the United States within fifteen
days after the Republic of Korea is notified or is
otherwise apprised of the commission of an offense
falling within its primary jurisdiction, or such

Incl 2

0204

provided in writing by the Minister of Justice to the appropriate military authorities of the United States within fifteen days after the Republic of Korea is notified or is otherwise apprised of the commission of an offense falling within its primary jurisdiction, or such shorter period as may be mutually agreed upon pursuant to Paragraph 4 of the Agreed Minute Re Paragraph 3(b). The military authorities of the United States shall not exercise jurisdiction before the expiration of the fifteen days or other agreed period.

I would be grateful for your confirmation of the above understandings.

Sincerely yours,

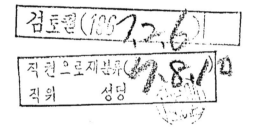

2

외교문서 비밀해제: 주한미군지위협정(SOFA) 21
주한미군지위협정(SOFA) 서명 및 발효 21

초판인쇄 2024년 03월 15일
초판발행 2024년 03월 15일

지은이 한국학술정보(주)
펴낸이 채종준
펴낸곳 한국학술정보(주)
주 소 경기도 파주시 회동길 230(문발동)
전 화 031-908-3181(대표)
팩 스 031-908-3189
홈페이지 http://ebook.kstudy.com
E-mail 출판사업부 publish@kstudy.com
등 록 제일산-115호(2000. 6. 19)

ISBN   979-11-7217-032-5 94340
       979-11-7217-011-0 94340 (set)